Christopher Hill has for decades been acknowledged as a leading—if not the leading—historian of the English Revolution, and his books on the political, intellectual, and social history of the seventeenth century are acknowledged masterpieces. In this important new work, which comes as a third volume closely linked to *The World Turned Upside Down* (1972) and *Milton and the English Revolution* (1978), he explores the ways in which the writings, thought, and personal lives of the great Puritans were affected by the failure of the English Revolution when the monarchy was reestablished in 1660. Radical clergy, intellectuals, and writers responded to the defeat of their proudest hopes in a variety of ways—but there were central themes and bitter disappointments that affected them all. Arguing that the revolutionary beliefs, savage social judgments, and disillusionments that Milton expressed in his writings at the time were shared by many of his contemporaries, Mr. Hill offers a close analysis of the writings of the Levellers and Diggers, of Fox and other important early Quakers. He makes a provocative case that Milton's three great poems—*Paradise Lost, Paradise Regained,* and *Samson Agonistes*—came directly out of his painful reassessment of man and his society, of society's relation to moral order. As always, the clarity, vigor, and urgency of Mr. Hill's historical analysis bring these major issues to life in a dramatic, authoritative, and exciting way.

THE EXPERIENCE OF DEFEAT

THE EXPERIENCE OF DEFEAT

Milton and Some Contemporaries

CHRISTOPHER HILL

Elisabeth Sifton Books
VIKING

ELISABETH SIFTON BOOKS · VIKING
Viking Penguin Inc.,
40 West 23rd Street,
New York, New York 10010, U.S.A.

First American edition
Published in 1984

LIBRARY OF CONGRESS CATALOGING IN PUBLICATION DATA
Hill, Christopher, 1912–
    The experience of defeat.
    "Elisabeth Sifton books."
    Includes bibliographical references and index.
    1. Great Britain—History—Puritan Revolution, 1642–
1660—Influence.   2. England—Intellectual life—17th
century.   3. Religious thought—England.   4. Religious
thought—17th century.   5. Milton, John, 1608–1674—
Political and social views.   I. Title.
DA405.H49   1984   941.06   83-40211
ISBN 0-670-30208-2

Printed in the United States of America by
The Book Press, Brattleboro, Vermont

For Norman O. Brown,
in gratitude for fifty years' friendship, stimulus and provocation

Contents

Preface

In this book I have modernized seventeenth-century spelling and punctuation (except for titles of books and pamphlets); years are given in the new style. I have tried to give references for any statements made, except for biographical facts to be found in the *Dictionary of National Biography*.

In the past I have thanked employers for allowing me leave of absence. Since my retirement my gratitude goes to those who have given me employment—the Open University from 1978 to 1980, where I was a Visiting Professor and member of a team producing a course on seventeenth-century English civilization; the Humanities Research Centre of the Australian National University, Canberra, and Rutgers University, New Jersey, at each of which I was a Visiting Professor for three months of 1981. I am most grateful to colleagues and students at these institutions for useful discussions on (among many other things) some of the ideas in this book—especially to Cicely Havely, Ann Hughes (now at Lancaster University), Arnold Kettle, Anne Laurence, Bob Owens, John Purkis and Kevin Wilson of the Open University. I am still benefiting from a seminar on Milton which I gave at the Folger Library in 1976: Joan Bennett, Georgia Christopher, Joseph Martin, Jean Moss, Jason Rosenblatt, Florence Sandler and Brenda Szittya continue to ply me with ideas, many of which have been incorporated in this book.

I have greatly profited from the generosity of fellow scholars who allowed me to read work in progress, particularly Hugh Barbour, Alan Cole, Jackie DiSalvo, Ian Donaldson, J. R. Jacob, A. M. Johnson, Nicholas Jose, John Laydon, J. F. McGregor, Ruth Perry, Gary Puckrein, Barry Reay, Sheila Reynolds, Paul Salzman, David Taylor and C. M. Williams. I have also benefited from discussing the seventeenth century with W. M. Lamont, Peter Linebaugh, Gill Parker, Lady Radzinowicz, Marcus Rediker, Stella Revard, Judith Richards, Judith Sproxton and John Walter. I hope I have acknowledged in the footnotes where I am conscious of having drawn on their ideas. My thanks go especially to Alan Cole, whose splendid essay on 'The Quakers and Politics, 1652–60' started me thinking on the subject of this book nearly thirty years ago; to J. R. Jacob, whose work I have pillaged shamelessly in Chapter Eight, section 3; and to Bernard Capp (Chapter Three, section 1) and Barry Reay (Chapter Five). Penelope Corfield gave me much needed encouragement at an early stage. Austin Woolrych read the whole typescript and saved me from many howlers as well as generously suggesting useful improvements. But none of them bears any responsibility for what has emerged.

Diana Levinson very kindly read the proofs.

In the past I fear I have always taken Balliol College Library for granted: I should like to make amends by thanking very warmly the successive Librarians—Vincent Quinn and Penny Bullough—and Alan Tadiello for innumerable patient kindnesses over many years. My warmest thanks, not for the first time, go to Bridget for unfailing help, counsel, stimulus and support.

C.H.
March 1983

Abbreviations

The following abbreviations have been used in the footnotes:

CPW	*Complete Prose Works of John Milton*, 8 vols. (Yale UP 1953–82)
CSP Dom	*Calendar of State Papers, Domestic*
DNB	*Dictionary of National Biography*
EHR	*English Historical Review*
Gangraena	Thomas Edwards, *Gangraena* (3 parts, 1646)
HMC	Historical Manuscripts Commission
JFHS	*Journal of the Friends' Historical Society*
MER	C. Hill, *Milton and the English Revolution* (1977)
P. and P.	*Past and Present*
PL	*Paradise Lost*
PR	*Paradise Regained*
SA	*Samson Agonistes*
TRHS	*Transactions of the Royal Historical Society*
UP	University Press
VCH	*Victoria County History*
WTUD	C. Hill, *The World Turned Upside Down* (Penguin edn., 1975)

THE EXPERIENCE OF DEFEAT

Chapter 1

Introduction

In an historian we are not to be critical for every punctilio, not relating to his main design; yet I think 'tis but just to demand that what he doth write be true.

Henry Stubbe, *The Lord Bacons Relation of the Sweating-Sickness Examined* (1671), p. 2

This book derives from two others which I published in the 1970s. In *The World Turned Upside Down* (1972) I tried to present the ferment of radical ideas which welled up in England in the revolutionary 1640s and 1650s. I suggested—almost as an afterthought—that Milton in the 1640s shared much of the Wordsworthian excitement of those days when it was bliss to be alive, but to be young was very heaven. This excitement comes across in *Areopagitica* and *The Tenure of Kings and Magistrates*. In *Milton and the English Revolution* (1977) I tried to work out in more detail Milton's relationship to the radical ideas of the Revolution, and to suggest that for him the defeat of the Revolution which he had believed to be God's Cause, and to which he had given up the best years of his life, was a shattering blow. The three great poems of his last years represent, among many other things, his attempt to come to terms with this defeat: to rethink his whole position in order to be able to 'Assert eternal Providence/And justify the ways of God to men.' Milton started *Paradise Lost* in about 1658, and finished it in 1665. In these years he was alone only in his genius. Many others were querying either the goodness or the omnipotence of a God who had apparently so badly let down his servants. The present book attempts to survey the reactions of other radicals to the experience of defeat.

The World Turned Upside Down was criticized for overstating the significance of the radical ideas which I portrayed. In the excitement of discovering far more and far more coherent ideas than I had anticipated, I may indeed have exaggerated the *numerical* significance of the radicals—though there is much investigation to be done before this can be stated with assurance. I do not think I exaggerated the historical significance of the ideas, both in themselves, and in the reaction which they provoked. They were the ideas of a minority, it is true; but then so were the ideas which dominated English society before 1640 and after 1660, under the protection of the censorship. The extraordinary difference between the novel ideas of the 1640s and 1650s and those which could be printed in the pre- and post-revolutionary periods must lead us to ask where the apparently new ideas came from, and where they went to. Had they been there, below the surface, in some form or other, before 1640? If so, that tells us something important about the society, about the role of the church and the censorship. If not, then we have to explain their sudden appearance and rapid diffusion once the censorship and ecclesiastical controls collapsed. I suggested that upper-class concern about the spread of radical ideas (and especially their apparent revival in 1659–60) made a significant contribution to the swing of opinion which brought the enemies of Charles I to support the restoration of his son in 1660. This suggestion has received some support, but again further investigation is needed.[1]

Some critics disliked *Milton and the English Revolution* because in it I seemed to them to degrade Milton by relating him to the political and intellectual problems of the society in which he lived: they prefer to think of the great poet writing in a timeless vacuum. However inadequate the execution may have been, I am unrepentant about my attempt to associate what Milton wrote with the triumphs and defeat of his Cause. Our understanding of history can illuminate the writing of even the greatest of poets, just as no historian can possibly understand any epoch—least of all a revolutionary epoch—without grasping its impact on the great writers who are its most sensitive recorders. Where would our understanding of the Russian Revolution be without Chekhov and Gorky, without Blok's *The Twelve*, in which Winstanley's 'head Leveller' Jesus Christ leads the advancing revolutionary soldiers? How should we understand the French Revolution without Rousseau, Choderlos de Laclos, Beaumarchais and Stendhal? The Chinese Revolution of our own century has been illuminated by J. D. Spence's study of scholars, novelists and poets, with epigraph from *Areopagitica*.[2]

---

[1] See for example Barry Reay, 'The Quakers, 1659 and the Restoration of the Monarchy', *History*, 63 (1978), pp. 193–213; 'Quaker Opposition to Tithes', *P. and P.*, 86 (1980), pp. 98–120; 'Popular Hostility towards Quakers in Mid-Seventeenth-Century England', *Social History*, 5 (1980), pp. 387–407.

[2] Spence, *The Gate of Heavenly Peace: The Chinese and Their Revolution, 1895–1980* (New York, 1981).

Milton, vanguard intellectual as well as sensitive poet, seems to me essential for our understanding of the English Revolution. He was not only an active and deeply committed participant: he narrowly escaped being executed in 1660 for his participation. Properly understood, *Paradise Lost, Paradise Regained* and *Samson Agonistes* tell us as much about the Revolution as Parliamentary debates and state papers. Since my argument in *Milton and the English Revolution* did not meet with universal acceptance, I hope to strengthen it by considering the similar experiences which some of Milton's contemporaries went through. Milton's presence I hope will be felt throughout this book even when he is not specifically mentioned.

This book deals with ideas. We know something of the practical consequences of defeat. After 1660 nearly one in five of the beneficed ministers lost their livings, without even the meagre compensation which the ejected of the 1640s and 1650s had received. Lay dissenters had to endure nearly thirty years of sporadic but often very damaging persecution.[1] My concern is not so much with the fate of radicals after the restoration, but to study how some individuals coped with the experience of living through a revolution which they initially welcomed, and with the defeat of that revolution—a defeat which for some of them occurred before 1660. Those whom I have selected for discussion had to be taken from the few who left evidence of their reactions: many radicals lapsed into silence. I have tried to show what my chosen characters thought the Revolution had been about, where it had gone wrong, and how they adapted to its defeat. I hope that the cumulative effect of their testimony will be to reinforce the argument of *The World Turned Upside Down*, that there was an intellectually significant and numerically not insignificant congeries of radical ideas; and to demonstrate that Milton was one of many revolutionaries wrestling with common problems.

The experience of defeat meant recognizing the collapse of the system of ideas which had previously sustained action, and attempting to discover new explanations, new perspectives. The first defeat of the more extreme radicals came in and after 1649. Leveller leaders were arrested and imprisoned, Leveller-led mutinies in the Army were suppressed, culminating in the total rout of mutinous regiments at Burford in May 1649. After that the Leveller leaders abandoned hope of winning control of the Army and either subsided into the obscurity from which they had briefly emerged, or took to underground conspiracy,

---

[1] See pp. 294–6 below.

sometimes in conjunction with Royalists. The less numerous Diggers were dispersed in April–May 1650; Ranters were made to recant in 1650–1. Both groupings ceased to exist in any organized form.[1]

Fifth Monarchists appeared strong in the Army in 1653, when they collaborated in the dismissal of the Rump of the Long Parliament and its replacement by Barebone's Parliament. But they too had no effective organization, and were divided in their aims. Very few dogs barked at the disappearance of either the Rump or Barebone's Parliament. Venner's tiny Fifth Monarchist group staged revolts in London in 1657 and 1661. But apart from their readiness to use violence, their programme differed little from those of other radicals. There had been a strong millenarian element among those who sat in judgement on Charles I in 1649: many regicides executed after the restoration still held tenaciously on to the conviction of divine approval which they believed had justified their action.[2] But—significantly—many of those executed by the restored government had been imprisoned under the Protectorate. 1660 was only the confirmation of their defeat. In the 1650s William Erbery, William Sedgwick, Isaac Penington and early Quakers lectured the Army on its duties but had no aspirations to win control over it. Adaptation of their ideas to defeat proceeded throughout the decade: 1660 was a final blow. I suspect the same was true of Milton.[3]

I look at some Independent revolutionaries—Oliver Cromwell and his chaplains, John Owen and Thomas Goodwin, at the republican James Harrington.[4] I have included a group of moderate Puritan ministers, who also found themselves among the defeated after 1660.[5] Quakers adopted the peace principle in January 1661 and organized themselves more rigidly as a sect; the Harringtonians adapted their master's ideas to the constitutional and economic circumstances of the restoration period. Finally I look in more detail at the ideas of other survivors—Samuel Pordage, author of an epic on the Fall of Man well before Milton: he went on to be a Whig exclusionist; Andrew Marvell, who passed from millenarianism to Harringtonianism; Henry Stubbe, who advanced from being a disciple of Henry Vane through Harringtonianism to something like deism.[6]

---

[1] See Chapter Two below.
[2] See Chapter Three below.
[3] Chapter Four below.
[4] Chapter Six below.
[5] Chapter Seven below.
[6] Chapters Five and Eight below.

I hope I have brought together characters interesting in their own right. I have made no great literary discoveries; but Erbery, Sedgwick and Isaac Penington in his early pamphlets are no mean writers of English prose. Samuel Pordage is far from being a distinguished poet. I sympathize with the lines attributed to Rochester:

> Poet, who'er thou art, God damn thee,
> Go hang thyself, and burn thy *Mariamne*.

But the analogies between Pordage's epic and the writings of Milton and Bunyan help to put the latter two into historical context.[1] The total effect should, I hope, be to flesh out our experience of what the restoration meant. For many, perhaps for most, it was a return to normality; for others, not the least sensitive, it was a defeat no less devastating for having been long foreseen.

Other characters tempted me. There are things to say about George Wither and John Bunyan in this context, but I have said most of them already.[2] I have also written about William Dell and John Webster, radical reformers who might otherwise have found a place in Chapter Four,[3] and briefly about the adaptations made by Milton's nephews, John and Edward Phillips.[4] Broghill was intriguing as an ex-royalist who became Cromwell's right-hand man in Scotland. He helped to bring Ireland to accept the restoration, and then was an early writer of heroic drama in rhymed couplets, preceding Dryden. But although Broghill did less well financially under Charles II than under Oliver,[5] nevertheless such great aristocrats can switch easily from one regime to another without the word 'defeat' being applicable. Ashley-Cooper, later Earl of Shaftesbury, is another example; so is the more complex William Howard, later Lord Howard of Escrick, to whom I refer briefly in Chapter Two. Algernon Sidney was an aristocratic republican who (as Milton put it) 'has ever been loyal to our side',[6] and continued the political struggle until his execution in 1683. His *Discourses concerning Government* (published posthumously in 1698) handed on many of the

---

[1] Chapter Eight below.
[2] 'George Wither and John Milton', in *English Renaissance Studies Presented to Dame Helen Gardner*, ed. John Carey (Oxford UP, 1980); 'John Bunyan and the English Revolution', in *The John Bunyan Lectures, 1978*, published by the Bedfordshire Education Services.
[3] See my *Change and Continuity in Seventeenth-Century England* (1974), Chapter 5. Webster, an Army chaplain, was William Erbery's disciple and editor. See pp. 95, 97 below.
[4] *MER*, Appendix 2.
[5] K. M. Lynch, *Roger Boyle, First Earl of Orrery* (Tennessee UP, 1965), p. 127.
[6] *CPW*, IV, p. 677.

political ideas of the English revolutionaries to eighteenth-century Whigs, American and French republicans. He was of greater historical significance than some I have included, but evidence concerning his experience of defeat is meagre. Marchamont Nedham, whose writings also became part of the Whig canon, still remains as difficult to assess as Henry Stubbe was before the work of J. R. Jacob.[1] I did not feel capable of tackling that very complicated man.

Robert Everard seemed an intriguing candidate for inclusion. He was a spokesman for the Agitators in the Putney Debates in 1647 who became an Army officer and sectarian preacher and pamphleteer. His critique of the doctrine of original sin was 'spread far and near, to the deceiving of many poor souls and to the troubling of others', Nathaniel Stephens lamented in 1658.[2] After the restoration Everard was the only former revolutionary who publicly converted to Roman Catholicism. But the pamphlet in which he announced this conversion is most disappointing. It purports to record the conversation of a Catholic layman, and one can well believe that Everard himself did not compose it.[3] Apart from a few expressions of regret for his own role in the civil war, the pamphlet could have been written at any time, anywhere: it is not directed to the specific problems of post-revolutionary England. The unknown speaker throughout assumes what was necessary to be proved, that no certainty is to be found outside the Roman church.

Sir Henry Vane might have been added to my republicans, but I shrank from the impenetrable thickets of his prose. I might have looked at more Quakers: George Bishop and Anthony Pearson both diverge from the accepted image. John Sadler and Henry Denne would have been interesting: so would the great naturalist John Ray, who resigned his fellowship at Trinity College, Cambridge, in 1662 to live on the charity of others and who survived to welcome 'the yoke of slavery ... broken' in 1688.[4] I might have made more of those whom defeat drove into

---

[1] See Chapter Eight, section 3 below.
[2] Nathaniel Stephens, *Vindiciae Fundamenti: Or a three fold defence of the Doctrine of Original Sin* (1658), Sig. A 3; cf. pp. 1, 7–9, 20, 83. Stephens was attacking Everard's *The Creation and Fall of Adam* (1649). Stephens had earlier replied to Everard's *Baby Baptism Routed* (1650) in *A Precept for the baptism of infants ... vindicated ... in special from the cavils of Mr Robert Everard* (1651) and to his *Natures Vindication: or, a check to all those who affirm Nature to be Vile, Wicked, Corrupt and Sinful* (1652). Cf. Alan Betteridge, 'Early Baptists in Leicestershire and Rutland', *Baptist Quarterly*, XXV (1974), pp. 204–11, 354–78.
[3] Everard, *An Epistle To the Several Congregations of the Non-Conformists* (Paris, 1664). The Paris imprint was a blind, 'J.I.' tells us: 'a London printer will witness to your face, if occasion serve', that the book was printed in England (*Rome is no Rule: Or, An Answer to an Epistle Published by a Roman Catholick Who Stiles Himself Captain Robert Everard*, 1664, pp. 4–5).
[4] C. E. Raven, *John Ray* (2nd edn., 1950), pp. 57–8, 251–2, 441, 457, 461.

emigration—Joseph Salmon, Edward Byllynge, John Perrot. I could have added Edward Taylor, church- and school-outed by the restored prelates, who had to go to New England to get a university education. There he wrote nature poetry in the metaphysical mode. He too lived to welcome 1688, having retained an 'aversion to the aristocracy of England, alike in church and state'.[1] He might have been balanced against Thomas Traherne, whom at one time I thought of including. Radical influences on Traherne are important, but the worst defeat he suffered at the restoration was to have to be re-ordained at the age of 24.

I was disappointed not to be able to find any woman who left adequate evidence of her experience of defeat. Women played an important part in the religious sects, so this is a comment on the survival of evidence about women in the seventeenth century. Lucy Hutchinson should have been a candidate, but in her *Memoirs* of her husband she is far too concerned to cover up the Colonel's weaknesses to allow her own views to come through. We get the impression that she was the stronger character of the two, but she would have repudiated such an idea.[2] Margaret Fell was another possibility, but her main contribution was in the sphere of Quaker organization rather than of ideas. Mary Cary and Anna Trapnell both fell silent after defeat. Aphra Behn was not visibly a radical before 1660. Who else?

One problem to be faced in dealing with seventeenth-century England, and particularly with radicals, is the censorship. It was there all the time before 1640, its strictness increasing in the 1630s. In the 1640s it was intermittent and rarely effective: it was gradually restored in the 1650s, though there was still greater freedom for radical voices to be heard than after 1660. I discussed some of the effects of the censorship in *Milton and the English Revolution*:[3] we must never forget its existence, and how exceptional men felt its brief absence to be. 'I must speak plain to you,' Gerrard Winstanley told Oliver Cromwell in 1651, 'lest my spirit tell me another day, "if thou hadst spoke plain, things might have been amended."'[4] Under censorship men restrained themselves from telling the whole truth as they saw it, proceeding by analogy, implication and innuendo. Milton quoted Bacon: 'authorized books are but the

---

[1] *The Poems of Edward Taylor*, ed. D. E. Stanford (Yale UP, 1963), pp. xiii, xvi, 9, 75, 293; K. Keller, *The Example of Edward Taylor* (Massachusetts UP, 1975), p. 25.
[2] L. Hutchinson, *Life of Colonel Hutchinson*, ed. J. Sutherland (Oxford UP, 1973), p. 48.
[3] Esp. pp. 64–6, 93–4, 217–18, 405–9.
[4] G. Winstanley, *The Law of Freedom and other Writings* (Cambridge UP, 1983), p. 277.

language of the times.'[1] From Spenser to Bunyan those with something original to say found it safer to make use of allegory or pastoral; others cited the Bible or the classics to convey unorthodox views without actual commitment.[2] 'Of the maintenance of our Saviour and his Apostles,' wrote Thomas Hobbes, a master of this art, 'we read only that they had a purse (which was carried by Judas Iscariot)'.[3] No one could fault that factual statement; but implications for current disputes about tithes could be drawn from it. Bunyan used the same technique. God's own people, he wrote, 'cannot, with Pontius Pilate, speak Hebrew, Greek and Latin'.[4]

Others equivocated by giving precise but unorthodox sense to biblical terms. Thus when Winstanley declared, 'I do walk in the daily practice of such ordinances of God as Reason and Scriptures do warrant',[5] we have to remember that he believed Reason and Scriptures did *not* warrant prayer, preaching, holy communion, baptism or Sabbath observance. Winstanley tells us that 'all the prophecies, visions and revelations of Scriptures, of prophets and apostles concerning the calling of the Jews, the restoration of Israel and making of that people the inheritors of the whole earth, doth all seat themselves in this work of making the earth a common treasury' which the Diggers advocated.[6] Everybody was against Antichrist; so his name could be extended from Pope to bishops, to the whole hierarchy of the state church, to the King and royalists who defended them; similarly the Norman Yoke could be extended from obsolete laws which Parliament could reform to the whole body of the law itself, and to the Norman gentry and freeholders who opposed the digging on St. George's Hill.

In this book I have considered poets and prophets, pacifists and politicians. I hope it may contain something for those interested in literature, political ideas and religion; but not all specialists will find all of it equally relevant to their particular interests. Just because of this, the book may perhaps be of some use to those interested in a non-specialist way in the seventeenth century. The study of seventeenth-century England is undergoing one of its regular crises. Those who have come to

---

[1] *CPW*, II, pp. 534, 542.
[2] For this use of the classics as a cover, see Loretta Valtz Mannucci, *Ideali e classi nelle poesia di Milton* (Milan, 1976), pp. 178–9.
[3] Hobbes, *Leviathan* (Penguin edn., 1968), p. 564.
[4] Bunyan, *Works*, ed. G. Offor (1860), III, p. 695.
[5] Winstanley, *Truth Lifting up its Head above Scandals* (1648), in *The Works of Gerrard Winstanley*, ed. G. H. Sabine (Cornell UP, 1941), pp. 136–40.
[6] Winstanley, *The True Levellers Standard Advanced* (1649), in *The Law of Freedom*, p. 88.

be called 'revisionists' have attempted to deny that there was an English Revolution. The gentry, in and out of Parliament, we are often (and rightly) told, did not want civil war, did not want revolutionary change. There was no parliamentary opposition: incompetent politicians blundered into an unwanted conflict, after which there was a period of chaos until order and normality were restored in 1660.

Now it is quite clear that the characters studied in this book did not see things like that. They may have been untypical when they spoke of the battle of Christ against Antichrist, of the breakdown of the Gothic balance, or of casting 'the kingdom old/Into another mould', just as Milton no doubt was when he declared that the Revolution had seen 'the most heroic and exemplary achievements since the foundation of the world'.[1] They all thought something important and something of long-term consequence had happened. Harrington looked back to Henry VII's reign, others to Wyclif and the Lollards, to the protestant reformation or to the Waldensians: none spoke of accident, and those who denounced incompetence did not regard it as a primary cause of the civil war.

There had been men and women before 1640 who did want change—sufficiently to brave exile in the Netherlands or New England when they saw no immediate hope of getting it at home. As early as 1629–31 John Winthrop and Thomas Hooker believed that God was abandoning England; Mrs Anne Hutchinson had 'a sure word that England would be destroyed'.[2] Hence the excitement in New England when God seemed to be returning in power to England in the 1640s, and their disappointment later.

The leaders of the emigration were gentry and clergy, but the rank and file came from lower social groups. We have no idea whether they were as typical of their social classes as MPs are assumed to have been of theirs. Tom May, official historian of the Long Parliament, frequently emphasizes that the common people were more ready to defend their liberties and their religion than were lords and gentlemen.[3] The violent hostility towards religious toleration which most MPs showed in the 1640s, 1650s and 1660s suggests that they thought there was a great deal

---

[1] Milton, *Second Defence of the English People* (1654), in *CPW*, IV, p. 549.

[2] *The Antinomian Controversy, 1636–1638*, ed. D. D. Hall (Wesleyan UP, 1968), p. 338; Patrick Collinson, *The Religion of Protestants: The Church in English Society, 1559–1625* (Oxford UP, 1982), p. 283. Professor Collinson gives other examples.

[3] T. May, *The History of the Parliament* (1647), I, pp. 113–19, II, p. 97, III, pp. 30–1, 69, 78–9, and *passim*.

of potential support for the sectaries. But what we do know is that on specific issues—foreign policy, for example—an exile like Thomas Scott in the 1620s was only expressing in stronger language criticisms of the government with which many MPs agreed. This also came to be true in relation to bishops in the 1630s.

We get some sort of idea of how men felt in the early years of the civil war from Francis Woodcock. Writing in 1643 he spoke of 'that common question almost in everyone's mouth, "What will become of us? What do you think of these times?"'[1] Woodcock's explanation was that the Two Witnesses prophesied in Revelation XI had been slain 'five or six years agone'—i.e. in 1637–8—by the Beast who ascends 'out of the bottomless pit, the Antichristian kind of government'—i.e. episcopacy. 'They much mistake themselves that tell us 'tis *jure divino*.'[2] Godly ministers who had testified against Antichrist had been silenced by the Laudians, the pulpit 'shut against them, yea the press also'. After three and a half years they were restored to liberty at the beginning of the Long Parliament, 'the multitude of people congratulating with them for their freedom: this is the cloud wherein they ascend to heaven' (verse 12). Already by 1643 a remarkable change had been wrought. 'Prelacy and ceremonies gone in Scotland, agoing in this country': that fulfilled the prophecy about the tenth part of the city in Revelation XI. The slaughter of the 7,000 signified the prelates, deans and chapters, with all their appurtenances. The civil war was the great earthquake continuing (Rev. XI); and we may 'expect ere long much greater things than I shall dare to speak of'.[3]

The sense that many radicals had (after the event) that 'the saints called a Parliament' in 1640, and that 'it was God raised up the saints to an Army',[4] their feeling that long-term impersonal forces were at work, may express the social truth that control of political events began to slip from the hands of the natural rulers once the Long Parliament met. It must have felt as if some external power was taking over. Many of the Parliamentarian leaders were less scared of sectaries who might be socially subversive than of the government. So they started on the slippery slope which led from Agitators seizing the King in June 1647 to

---

[1] F. Woodcock, *The Two Witnesses* (1643), p. 3; cf. J. Tillinghast, *Generation-Work* (1655), III, pp. 1–2, 15, 30. Woodcock was minister at St Olave's, Southwark, and a member of the Westminster Assembly of Divines. He preached a Fast Sermon in February 1646.

[2] Woodcock, op. cit., pp. 12, 32.

[3] Ibid., pp. 82–90. Cf. the analysis of John Rogers in his conversation with Oliver Cromwell in 1654, ed. E. Rogers, *Some Account of the Life and Opinions of a Fifth-Monarchy Man* (1867), pp. 210–11.

[4] See pp. 86, 32 below.

his execution in January 1649. So far were they in 1640–1 from willing such an outcome that they never even contemplated its possibility. Who else but God could be held responsible?

In the course of the last two generations, the history of theology, law, philosophy, science, literature and art has ceased to be the exclusive preserve of theologians, lawyers, philosophers, scientists, literary and art critics. In consequence our understanding of history has been enriched: it has become the history of society, not of chopped-off segments of society. It still remains to persuade demographers that the statistics on which they rely for the history of population are socially produced and therefore open to criticism from social historians. A last bastion, ironically enough, is administrative history, some of whose practitioners believe that they alone are 'real' historians, and that their preserves are sacrosanct. Their shrill cries reveal however that they know theirs is a losing cause. History, we might say, is against them.

'Revisionists' have concentrated their attention on the central administration and Parliament, or on the gentry who ran the counties. They have less to say about the great movements of ideas which make the age of Shakespeare, Bacon, Hobbes and Milton so exciting; or about the shifts in social forces of which Ralegh, Bacon and Harrington were aware. Fortunately the balance has been redressed over the past decade by Brian Manning's *The English People and the English Revolution*,[1] Derek Hirst's *The Representative of the People?: Voters and Voting in England under the Early Stuarts*, Margot Heinemann's *Puritanism and Theatre: Thomas Middleton and Opposition Drama under the Early Stuarts*, Keith Wrightson's *English Society, 1580–1680*,[2] and P. W. Thomas's 'Two Cultures? Court and Country under Charles I' in *The Origins of the English Civil War* (ed. C. Russell). The best of all the revisionist historians, Conrad Russell and John Morrill, have taken the cue, and a number of younger historians of seventeenth-century English counties have broadened their outlook to study the whole county community, not just 'the county community' in the misleading sense in which seventeenth-century gentlemen used it.

The trap some historians have fallen into here illustrates the dangers of the principle put forward recently by John Morrill and taken up by John

---

[1] See also his articles 'The Nobles, the People and the Constitution', *P. and P.*, 9 (1956); 'The Aristocracy and the Downfall of Charles I', and 'Religion and Politics: the Godly People', both in *Politics, Religion and the Civil War*, ed. Manning (1973).

[2] See also Wrightson and D. Levine, *Poverty and Piety in an English Village: Terling, 1525–1700* (1979).

Bossy, that in discussing seventeenth-century society we must not use terms of analysis which were then unknown.[1] Words like 'class' and 'revolution' were not used then in their modern sense: ergo there cannot have been classes or revolutions. The gentry thought they were the 'county community': ergo we must perpetuate the illusion of a 'one-class society' in which only the gentry mattered. Contemporaries had no word to 'conjoin ... yeomen and urban master-craftsmen';[2] ergo .... But, as we shall see when we come to look at Harrington, they had such a word—they called them 'people', a category from which servants and the poor were excluded.[3] We are much more likely to be confused if we use terms like 'county community' and 'people' in their seventeenth-century sense than if, with proper definition, we use the terms of art devised by later political analysts. The word 'revolution' in fact acquired its modern meaning in the later seventeenth-century because of experience of what happened in the mid-century.[4] The absence of the word does not prove that the thing could not have existed: the thing had to come first for men to find a word for it. How indeed could it have been otherwise? For this reason, when I use the word 'people' in its normal seventeenth-century sense, excluding servants and the poor, I have often put it in inverted commas to remind us that it does not mean what the word means today. On the other hand, when I use 'saints' in the technical seventeenth-century sense, I have not put it into inverted commas, since confusion is not likely to arise.

But if we need not be shackled to the words of the men and women of the seventeenth century, we must take their ideas seriously, even when they strike us as silly. Revolutions are not wholly rational events. We do not now look to the book of Revelation for our analysis of political processes; but the concept of the slaughter and resurrection of the Two Witnesses helped Francis Woodcock to explain what was happening, and to forecast what was likely to happen. Similarly we may find it difficult to take seriously the idea that fear of popery was a significant reason for supporting Parliament in 1642; but it was for Richard Baxter, no fool.[5] When Lady Eleanor Davies in 1633 foretold a violent death for Charles I, Archbishop Laud dismissed her as 'never so mad a lady'. But after 1649 it

---

[1] J. S. Morrill, *Seventeenth-Century Britain, 1603–1714* (Folkestone, 1980), pp. 108–9; J. Bossy, 'Some Elementary Forms of Durkheim', *P. and P.*, 95 (1982), pp. 17–18.
[2] Morrill, loc. cit.
[3] See pp. 194–5 below.
[4] Cf. p. 274 below.
[5] W. M. Lamont, *Richard Baxter and the Millennium: Protestant Imperialism and the English Revolution* (1979), pp. 294, 330–1.

was less easy to laugh her off. Laud had already met his violent death by then.

So this book is a plea for total history, across disciplines. It illustrates not only reactions to the defeat of the English Revolution, but also acceptance of the fact of revolution itself. My emphasis has been on the late 1650s and early 1660s, but I have also tried to show how men looked back to the origins of their Cause in the 1630s and 1640s, if not earlier. 'The war was begun in our streets before the King or Parliament had any armies,' Richard Baxter recalled after the event.[1] Those who fought in village streets were not gentry: one of the purposes for which the latter carried swords was to put down lower-class disorder if it should chance to occur. But when government controls broke down between 1640 and 1642, it was ordinary people whose quarrels were most difficult to restrain. This book will follow Manning, Hirst and Wrightson in suggesting some of the ideas behind popular movements which the gentry were unable to control.

This should help to restore a lost dimension. Those great nineteenth-century historians Guizot and Gardiner had no inhibitions about talking of a revolution in mid-seventeenth-century England: the focus of more recent historians has narrowed. Gardiner had no doubts about the ideological nature of what he called 'the Puritan Revolution', a phrase which he popularized if he did not invent it. In understandable reaction against treating 'religion' as a self-sufficient historical force some Namier-influenced historians have tended to underestimate the importance of ideas in motivating political action. That great historian, R. H. Tawney, had a wider, more all-human perspective: it is a pity that the revisionists in correcting some of his weaknesses have ignored this particular strength. It is high time that we look at what contemporaries thought were the issues at stake, especially contemporaries below the rank of gentry, from whom the civil war began.

I hope, therefore, that this book may play its small part in re-establishing the consensus which the valuable work of the revisionists seemed to have shattered. Their meticulous studies of Parliament, the administration and the gentry in the counties have provided us with a lot of information which Tawney, the last great synthesizer, did not have. Conrad Russell has given us a lead in looking for a new synthesis[2] which I hope will embrace the whole nation, not merely the ruling class, and the

---

[1] R. Baxter, *A Holy Commonwealth* (1659), p. 457.
[2] Russell, 'Introduction' to *The Origins of the English Civil War*, ed. Russell (1973), pp. 8–9.

whole life and thought of the English people, not merely the politics of its upper strata. These, we may agree with Harrington, were largely irrelevant to what was actually happening.

If we are allowed to give the phrase 'God's purposes' only the meaning which it had for seventeenth-century radicals, its use to explain the English Revolution will not advance our understanding. But if we take it as expressing something like 'the historical process' it may offer insights which we have overlooked. We do not have to agree that the Parliamentarian Cause was the Cause of God. But knowing that many good and intelligent people believed this may help us to understand the elation of the fight and the desolation of defeat when they realized that the world was not after all to be turned upside down.

Chapter 2

The First Losers, 1649–1651

1   Levellers

The Levellers have some claim to be regarded as the first organized political party, as opposed to religious groupings pursuing political ends. They came into existence in London in 1645–6 as the radical wing of the Independent coalition. They invented or popularized many modern political techniques—mass demonstrations, collecting signatures to petitions, pamphleteering, leafleting, lobbying MPs. They won support in the Army, especially among its lower ranks. They were always a heterogeneous body, with minimal formal links and organization: no party cards, no membership tests, no local branches. So their views were correspondingly varied. A Leveller wanted a democratic republic in which the House of Commons was superior to the House of Lords (if there was one); he wanted redistribution and extension of the franchise, legal and economic reforms on behalf of men of small property—artisans, yeomen, small merchants—but not communism: though communist views were attributed to the Leveller William Walwyn, and the communist Diggers called themselves True Levellers. Levellers advocated democratization of the gilds and City government of London, decentralization of justice, election of local governors, stability of tenure for copyholders. Some Levellers wanted enclosures to be thrown open. But the strength of the movement lay mainly in London and other towns—and in the Army. Here they took up the problem of pauperism, not exclusively from the point of view of the poor. 'Thousands of men and women', declared *The Large Petition* of March 1647, 'are permitted to live in beggary and wickedness all their life long, and to breed their children to the same idle and vicious course of life, and no effectual means used to reclaim either, or to reduce them to any virtue or industry.'[1] One or two Levellers—Walwyn, Prince—opposed the reconquest of Ireland on the ground that 'the cause of the Irish natives in seeking their just freedoms ... was the very same with our cause here in endeavouring our own rescue and freedom from the power of oppressors.'[2]

The Levellers were democrats who could never have been returned to power by any possible electorate—or only after a long period of freedom to propagate their views, to educate a democratic electorate. As they became aware of this problem, so they tried to find constitutional devices for getting round it. The draft constitution produced in 1647, the Agreement of the People, assumed that the English state had broken down in the civil war and must be refounded. Certain fundamental 'native rights' were safeguarded even from a sovereign Parliament—religious toleration, no tithes, no conscription, indemnity for actions committed in the war, equality before the law. 'As the laws ought to be equal, so they must be good and not evidently destructive to the safety and well-being of the people.' Some at least of these 'good laws' were spelt out in later versions of the Agreement. They included biennial Parliaments, responsibility of ministers to Parliament, franchise reform; only those who contracted in to the new state by accepting the Agreement were to have the vote.[3]

The Levellers had no distinctive religious policy, apart from wanting toleration and abolition of tithes. They drew support from diverse radical religious groups, though after 1649 leading Independents and Baptists repudiated them. Individual Leveller leaders had very heretical views: Richard Overton was a mortalist, Walwyn a sceptical antinomian; Wildman may have been something like a deist.[4] Walwyn's *The Compassionate Samaritane* (1644), with its early plea for toleration, particularly annoyed the Presbyterian clergy. It was attacked in three Fast Sermons in 1644–5.[5] In 1647 John Trapp joined the critics in his *Commentary on the New Testament*.[6]

---

[1] In Haller, *Tracts on Liberty in the Puritan Revolution* (Columbia UP, 1933), III, p. 401. Attributed to Walwyn.

[2] [Anon.], *Walwyns Wiles* (1649), in *The Leveller Tracts, 1647–1653*, ed. W. Haller and G. Davies (Columbia UP, 1944), p. 310. Similar views had been attributed to Walwyn by Edwards in *Gangraena* (1646), II, p. 27.

[3] See *WTUD*, pp. 66, 271–3.

[4] *Puritanism and Liberty* ed. A. S. P. Woodhouse (1938), pp. 107–8, 128, 161; *WTUD*, pp. 165–6. But contrast K. V. Thomas, *Religion and the Decline of Magic* (1971), pp. 236–7 (on Wildman and magic).

[5] Matthew Newcomen, *A Sermon* (1644), p. 38; Lazarus Seaman, *Solomons Choice* (1644), p. 41; A. Burgess, *Publike Affections* (1646), p. 16.

[6] Op. cit. (1958 reprint), p. 515.

Levellers could have put their policies into effect only if they had captured control of the Army. They failed to accomplish this through the Agitators and the Army Council in the summer of 1647; the generals outmanoeuvred and outwitted them. Again in the winter of 1648–9 the generals needed the support of the Levellers until Parliament had been purged and the King executed: a new Agreement of the People was negotiated. But it was never taken seriously by the Army leaders or the Rump. Leveller influence on Army rank and file had been due in great part to their call for arrears of wages and indemnity for actions committed during the civil war. After Pride's Purge in December 1648 these ceased to be problems, and it was revealed that the hold of the political and constitutional ideas of the Levellers was less strong. In March 1649 Cromwell told the Council of State, 'You must break these men or they will break you';[1] by May 1649 both civilian and Army Levellers had been broken.

Once they had lost their base in the Army, the Levellers had to find new political approaches. In 1649 they laid greater emphasis on opposition to enclosure and support for stability of tenure for copyholders. These had long figured in the Leveller programmes, and in suitable areas—in Buckinghamshire, for instance—Levellers encouraged attacks on enclosure in 1647–9.[2] In 1650–1 Lilburne and Wildman were in the Isle of Axholme supporting the commoners' opposition to fen drainage. It does not appear, however, that they did the fenmen much good; their activities certainly did not help to lay the basis for a mass movement.[3] The Levellers suffered a crisis of leadership.

Lilburne was notoriously volatile, and had thriven on his personal popularity in London. He was not at his best in defeat. In October 1649 he offered to emigrate with his adherents to the West Indies if the government would finance them.[4] Lilburne, like Winstanley, recommended taking the Engagement to be true and faithful to the Commonwealth, and in 1650 he was again on good terms with

---

[1] See p. 189 below.
[2] I owe this point to A. M. Johnson, 'Buckinghamshire 1640–60: A Study in County Politics' (unpubl. MA Thesis, University of Wales, 1963), pp. 261–2.
[3] J. Hughes, 'The Drainage Disputes in the Isle of Axholme', *The Lincolnshire Historian*, II (1954), pp. 13–34; C. Holmes, *Seventeenth-Century Lincolnshire* (Lincoln, 1980), pp. 210–11; K. Lindley, *Fenland Riots and the English Revolution* (1982), pp. 194–6, 204–5, 211, 258. Lilburne and Wildman also agitated on behalf of a democratic party in City politics in 1650 (M. Ashley, *John Wildman, Plotter and Postmaster*, 1947, p. 76).
[4] Lilburne, *The Innocent Mans Second Proffer* (1649). Many radicals emigrated to the West Indies after defeat (*WTUD*, pp. 254–5).

Cromwell. But in 1651 he was advising the Presbyterian Christopher Love at his trial for treason against the Commonwealth.[1] In 1652 he was exiled. Next year he returned to face a spectacular trial in which his popularity in London was reaffirmed; but it was his last political appearance. He was illegally detained in prison until his death in 1657.[2] In 1655 he 'troubled and offended' his 'old and familiar friends' by turning Quaker. Typically, Lilburne outdid the Quakers at this date by renouncing 'carnal weapons of any kind whatsoever'.[3]

During his exile Lilburne had been in contact with royalists, though he protested vehemently that he had not plotted for a restoration of monarchy.[4] Wildman, Sexby and Overton had no such scruples. They may have entered into negotiations with exiled royalists only in order to deceive them, to take royalist (or Spanish) money in order to forward their own schemes.[5] But by this date it is doubtful whether they represented any significant organization in England. It appears that Overton and Wildman at least were double agents, taking money from Thurloe as well as from royalists.[6] What political alternative was there for such men if they wished to continue political activity and not—like Walwyn, Winstanley and Coppe—withdraw into passivity?

The ex-Agitator Edmund Sexby, after being cashiered from the Army in 1651,[7] was for a short time the Commonwealth's agent with French rebels in Bordeaux, where he had the Agreement of the People translated into French.[8] After the establishment of the Protectorate, Sexby advocated Cromwell's assassination in *Killing No Murder*, and plotted

[1] G. D. Owen, 'The Conspiracy of Christopher Love', *Trans. Hon. Soc. of Cymmrodorion* (1964), p. 97.

[2] C. J. Rolle was inclined to allow him a *habeas corpus* (W. Style, *Narrationes Modernae, or Modern Reports Begun in the now Upper Bench at Westminster* (1658), pp. 397–8).

[3] *The Resurrection of John Lilburne, now a Prisoner in Dover-Castle* (1656), pp. 1–5, 9–13, 21.

[4] P. Gregg, *Freeborn John: a Biography of John Lilburne* (1961), Chapter 27; H. N. Brailsford, *The Levellers and the English Revolution* (1961), p. 623; D. Underdown, *Royalist Conspiracy in England, 1649–60* (Yale UP, 1960), pp. 24–5.

[5] *A Collection of Original Letters and Papers Concerning the Affairs of England*, ed. T. Carte (1739), II, p. 103; cf. HMC *Portland MSS*, I pp. 591, 601; *Thurloe State Papers*, ed. T. Birch (1742), IV, pp. 161, 698, 743; cf. ibid., V, pp. 37, 100, and Underdown, op. cit., pp. 192–4, 198.

[6] Brailsford, op. cit., p. 624; Underdown, op. cit., pp. 123–4, 135, 172; Ashley, op. cit., Chapters 7–10; Marie Gimelfarb-Brack, *Liberté, Egalité, Fraternité, Justice: la vie et l'œuvre de Richard Overton, Niveleur* (Berne, 1979), pp. 287–304. Ashley argues that Wildman's intention throughout was to work for an English republic.

[7] G. E. Aylmer, *The State's Servants* (1973), p. 135.

[8] *Clarke Papers*, ed. C. H. Firth, III (1899), p. 189; P. A. Knachel, *England and the Fronde: the Impact of the English Civil War and Revolution on France* (Cornell UP, 1967), pp. 161–3, 197–214, 269.

with another ex-Leveller, Miles Sindercombe, to kill the Protector, 'it being certain,' Sindercombe was reported as saying, 'that the great ones of the King would never agree who should succeed, but would fall together by the ears about it, and then in that disorder the people would rise and so things might be brought to a commonwealth again'.[1] It is a hope with which many terrorists since have consoled themselves. Sexby died in gaol in 1657.

Walwyn took up medicine in the last thirty years of his life, defending the practice of professional secrecy from which he profited.[2] Wildman combined conspiracy with making money by land speculation.[3] One reason for his agreeing to act as a spy for Thurloe in 1656 may have been to recover extensive estates in Lancashire which had been sequestrated after his arrest for conspiracy in 1655.[4] Wildman spent the rest of his long life plotting against every regime from Cromwell to William III. In 1659 he was a member of Harrington's Rota Club. He had meanwhile established contacts with the Duke of Buckingham which lasted until well after the restoration: Pepys called Wildman 'a great creature of the Duke of Buckingham' in December 1667.[5] Wildman was involved in numerous plots against Charles II and James II, as well as in William of Orange's invasion in 1688.[6] In 1689 he advocated giving power to the people: failing that, he accepted a knighthood in 1692.[7]

So, lacking leadership, Leveller activity dwindled in the 1650s. There were rumours of Levellers in Cheshire in 1652,[8] of an 'insurrection' in Bedfordshire in 1653.[9] Lilburne's trial in the latter year produced an outburst of support in London, including demonstrations and over

---

[1] *Thurloe State Papers*, V, p. 775; *Mercurius Politicus*, No. 348, 5–17 February 1657, pp. 7587–92, 7604–8. Sindercombe had been one of the mutineers of 1649. He was a mortalist and believed in universal redemption.

[2] See my *Change and Continuity in Seventeenth-Century England* (1975), pp. 173–7.

[3] Ashley, op. cit., pp. 103, 237, 253–4; A. Fletcher, *A County Community in Peace and War: Sussex, 1600–1660* (1975), pp. 332–3 (Wildman rack-renting); cf. Lucy Hutchinson, *Memoirs of the Life of Colonel Hutchinson* (Oxford UP, 1973), p. 198; *Seventeenth-Century Economic Documents*, ed. J. Thirsk and J. Cooper (Oxford UP, 1972), pp. 282–3.

[4] *Thurloe State Papers*, IV, pp. 179, 215, 333, 340; V. p. 241.

[5] Ashley, op. cit., pp. 103, 184, 207, 217; *State Papers Collected by Edward Earl of Clarendon*, III (1786), pp. 219–20; Pepys, *Diary*, 6 December 1667. Pepys called Wildman 'the Fifth Monarchy Man', which is hardly accurate. On 12 December 1667 and 4 November 1668 he called him a Commonwealthsman.

[6] See Sir Robert Southwell's Diary, in *Diaries of the Popish Plot*, ed. D. C. Greene (New York, 1977), pp. 57, 60–1, 68, 99; cf. *Portland MSS*, II, p. 49.

[7] Ashley, op. cit., pp. 277, 299.

[8] J. S. Morrill, *Cheshire, 1630–1660* (Oxford UP, 1974), p. 275.

[9] T. Gataker, *His Vindication of the Annotations by him published* (1653), p. 12.

twenty pamphlets.[1] By now many former Leveller supporters seem to have come to think that Charles Stuart might be preferable to the Army.[2] There was indeed some logic in this. The Army dominated the state, and once the Leveller bid to capture control over the Army had failed, a weak monarchy balancing diverse interests might be less burdensome than the very expensive military rule.[3]

In the 1650s Levellers were attacked as subversives who would overthrow law and property. They were often deliberately confused with the Diggers or True Levellers. Cromwell denounced Levellers as 'a despicable and contemptible generation of men', who despised magistracy; their principles tended 'to make the tenant as liberal a fortune as the landlord'.[4] The idea that Levellers were 'bad men', 'robbers', was echoed by preachers and government propagandists, by James Harrington and later by Samuel Butler.[5]

When open propaganda was possible once more, in 1659, the surviving Levellers tried to refurbish their image by stressing their devotion to legality and property, their hostility to arbitrary rule. This made them virtually indistinguishable from Harringtonian republicans, with whom Wildman was associated in 1659–60, perhaps earlier, certainly later.[6] Most of the Leveller pamphlets published in these years were low-key and defensive, like *The Leveller: Or, the Principles and Maxims Concerning Government and Religion, which are asserted by those commonly called, Levellers*, possibly by Wildman.[7] It was directed mainly against military rule, stressing the Levellers' concern with legality, their defence of 'our liberties and properties'. Magna Carta was no longer the 'beggarly thing' that Overton had seen in it. Two-chamber

---

[1] Woolrych, *Commonwealth to Protectorate* (Oxford UP, 1982), pp. 130, 250.

[2] [Anon.], *The Levellers (Falsly so called) Vindicated* (1649), in *Freedom in Arms: A Selection of Leveller Writings*, ed. A. L. Morton (1975), pp. 314, 316. This pamphlet was signed by six troopers of regiments involved in the mutiny which ended at Burford in May 1649.

[3] See e.g. Carte, op. cit., I, pp. 332–3; II, p. 69; cf. *Clarendon State Papers*, III, pp. 272–3. 'Their intention is a free Parliament', which would recall the King to rule as 'administrator and not master of laws'; cf. pp. 315, 431.

[4] W. C. Abbott, *Writings and Speeches of Oliver Cromwell* (Harvard UP, 1937–47), III, pp. 435–6; cf. IV, p. 267. See p. 187 below.

[5] E.g. *Mercurius Politicus*, No. 354, 19–26 March, 1657, pp. 7674–5; cf. 9–16 October, 1656, p. 7315; W. Hughes, *Magistracy Gods Ministry* (1652), To the Reader (assize sermon preached at Abingdon); ed. G. F. Nuttall, *Early Quaker Letters from the Swarthmore MSS. to 1660* (1952, duplicated), p. 150; *The Political Works of James Harrington*, ed. J. G. A. Pocock (Cambridge UP, 1977), p. 292; Samuel Butler, *Prose Observations*, ed. H. de Quehen (Oxford UP, 1979), p. 74; cf. pp. 226, 283.

[6] Ashley, op. cit., pp. 133, 218.

[7] Ibid., pp. 128, 136; Woolrych, 'Last Quests for Settlement, 1659–1660', in *The Interregnum: the Quest for Settlement, 1656–1660*, ed. G. E. Avlmer (1972), p. 193.

government was advocated, though on Harringtonian rather than traditional lines. Toleration and equality before the law were demanded, but there is nothing about the franchise or about economic or legal reform.[1] Other tracts revived bits of the former Leveller programme, but 'none of them restated that programme in anything like its entirety.'[2]

We get a glimpse of Leveller reunion with middle-of-the-road republicans in a letter of 1656 to Charles II, signed by William Howard and eight others, offering him their services. The signatories, Howard told the King in a separate note, were Levellers, neither 'of great families or great estates'. This letter seems to represent an analysis and a programme on which the signatories had agreed to unite. They start from the experience of defeat. 'It is our lot ... to be embarked in a ship-wrecked commonwealth', thanks to 'the dark and mysterious effects of Providence'. These events 'command an (unwilling) silence upon our (sometimes mutinous and over-enquiring) hearts, resolving all into the good-will and pleasure of that all-disposing One whose wisdom is unsearchable and whose ways are past finding out'. There is no point in presumptuously kicking 'against the irresistible decrees of heaven'.[3] (Eternal Providence must be asserted, even if God's ways are not clearly justifiable.)

How has this state of affairs arisen? Under Charles I, great though his private virtues were, 'the whole commonwealth was faint, the whole nation sick.... There were many errors, many defects, many irregularities, many illegal and eccentrical proceedings, ... blots and stains upon the otherwise good government of the late King.' Charles had had to be rescued from 'evil councillors ... who did every day thrust him into actions prejudicial to himself and destructive to the common good and safety of the people'.[4] In 1642 'we went out in the simplicity of our souls', the letter claims, motivated by 'the sure, safe, sound and unerring maxims of law, justice, reason and righteousness'. If they were deceived, it was by 'that grand imposter, that loathesome hypocrite, that detestable traitor [etc.] ... who now calls himself our Protector'.[5]

---

[1] *The Leveller* is reprinted in *Harleian Miscellany* IV (1744–6), pp. 515–21. Cf. *A Plea for the Peoples Good Old Cause* (October 1659) and *A Plea for the Peoples Fundamental Liberties and Parliaments* (1660—written autumn 1659).

[2] Woolrych, 'Last Quests', pp. 193–4, lists many of these pamphlets. He notes their lack of interest in the franchise.

[3] Edward, Earl of Clarendon, *The History of the Rebellion and Civil Wars in England*, ed. W. D. Macray (Oxford UP, 1888), VI, pp. 67–8.

[4] Ibid., pp. 69, 75–6.

[5] Ibid., p. 70. One recalls later revolutionaries who were deceived by Stalin, solely guilty of everything that had gone wrong.

After much discussion, the writers had decided that a restoration of Charles II would be best for the 'common good, public safety, the honour, peace, welfare and prosperity of these nations'. Yet, 'lest we should seem to be altogether negligent of that first good though since dishonoured Cause, which God has so eminently owned us in', they offered conditions, whose acceptance by the King would win their support for his restoration.[1] These conditions were far indeed from the Leveller programme: restoration of both Houses of Parliament as they existed before Pride's Purge; confirmation of all concessions made by Charles I in the Isle of Wight Treaty of 1648; acceptance of legislation (or the repeal of existing legislation) by Parliament 'for the better securing of the just and natural rights and liberties of the people, for the obviating and preventing all dangerous and destructive excesses of government for the future'. There was to be religious toleration, tithes were to be replaced by some other means of financing the national ministry; there was to be an act of oblivion.[2]

In a covering note, and later in a personal interview with Charles II, Howard suggested that some of the demands in this letter might be modified. He also asked for £2,000 to be going on with—a sum which the King was in no position to provide even if he had been willing.[3] This was not untypical of Howard, who came of a 'great family' himself even if not of 'great estate'. Son of a peer who had taken the Parliamentarian side in the civil war, Howard was an unstable personality—'a great preacher' among the Anabaptists and 'of special trust amongst the Levellers'. He was a friend of Wildman's and 'very intimate with Sindercombe', the man who tried to assassinate Cromwell in 1657.[4] After the restoration Howard plotted with the Dutch against Charles II, was frequently imprisoned and ended as a double agent, helping to get Lord Russell and Algernon Sidney convicted after the Rye House Plot.[5]

There continued to be Levellers and rumours of Levellers after 1660— in Worcestershire in 1670,[6] at various places in the 1720s and 1730s.[7]

---

[1] Ibid., pp. 71–3.
[2] Ibid., pp. 73–4.
[3] Ibid., pp. 75–8.
[4] Ibid., pp. 66–7; *Thurloe State Papers*, V, p. 395; Underdown, op. cit., pp. 193–4, 198.
[5] K. H. D. Haley, *William of Orange and the English Opposition, 1672–4* (Oxford UP, 1953), pp. 28, 35–7, 70–1, 78–83, 116, 174, 194, 201–2; Haley, *The First Earl of Shaftesbury* (Oxford UP, 1968), pp. 314, 714–20.
[6] *VCH, Worcestershire*, IV, p. 192.
[7] Nicholas Tindal's *Continuation of Rapin's History of England* (1744–5), IV, p. 682 (enthusiastic Levellers who pulled down enclosures and sought equality in 1724); E. P. Thompson, *Whigs and Hunters* (1975), p. 256 (Ledbury, 1735); Thompson, 'The Moral

Levellers were discussed in the House of Commons in 1673;[1] in 1708 the French prophets were believed to be reviving 'Levelling principles'.[2]

Lilburne in 1649 looked to posterity which, 'we doubt not, shall reap the benefit of our labours, whatever shall become of us'.[3] His cause was lost when he wrote those words. But one Leveller left a more enduring message. Richard Rumbold was one of the guards at the scaffold when Charles I was executed. In February 1649—the month when Lilburne was looking to posterity—Rumbold petitioned for the re-establishment of the Council of Agitators. After the restoration he was the owner of Rye House, and seems to have played a leading part in the Rye House Plot of 1683, after which he fled to Holland. In 1685 he joined Argyll's invasion of Scotland, was captured and executed. On the scaffold he uttered words which long survived him: 'None comes into the world with a saddle upon his back, neither any booted and spurred to ride him.'[4] Defoe used part of this phrase, without acknowledgement, in 1705; and it was often repeated.[5] It was probably a well-known Leveller phrase when Rumbold used it; it gained its apotheosis when Jefferson quoted it in 1826.[6]

2 True Levellers

The True Levellers or Diggers established a colony in April 1649 to cultivate in common the waste land of St George's Hill, Surrey, and later of the nearby Cobham Heath. They claimed that commons and waste land belonged to the people, not to lords of manors. The poor had borne the burden of fighting, taxation and free quarter in the civil war: they had a right to share in the freedom which Parliament had promised to

Economy of the English Crowd in the 18th Century', *P. and P.*, 50 (1971), p. 126 (Newcastle in 1740); cf. P. J. Corfield, *The Impact of the English Towns* (Oxford UP, 1982), p. 65; and my 'From Lollards to Levellers', in *Rebels and their Causes: Essays in Honour of A. L. Morton*, ed. M. Cornforth (1978), pp. 65–6.

1 J. Stoughton, *History of Religion in England* (1881), III, p. 411.
2 M. C. Jacob, *The Newtonians and the English Revolution, 1689–1720* (Cornell UP, 1976), pp. 262, 268.
3 *Englands New Chains Discovered*, in Haller and Davies, op. cit., p. 166.
4 *State Trials* (1811), pp. 873–81; James Wellwood, *Memoirs of the Most Material Transactions in England for the Last Hundred Years* (1700), p. 173. Wellwood claimed to have been present when Rumbold uttered these words.
5 Daniel Defoe, *The Consolidator*, printed with *The History of the Plague in London in 1665* (1840), p. 216. Partridge echoed it in 1708 (B. S. Capp, *Astrology and the Popular Press: English Almanacs, 1500–1800*, 1979, p. 229).
6 D. M. Wolfe, *The Image of Man in America* (Dallas, 1957), p. 19.

establish. 'By the law of righteousness', wrote Gerrard Winstanley, 'the poorest man hath as true a title and just right to the land as the richest man.'[1] Cultivation of commons and wastes would solve England's food problems and abolish poverty and begging.

Within a year, at least ten Digger colonies had been started in central and southern England, with more anticipated.[2] But they were all small affairs, harassed by local landowners and parsons; when the government withdrew Army protection they were swiftly broken up. By April 1650 all was over. After defeat, Winstanley in *The Law of Freedom in a Platform* (1652) worked out a programme for the introduction of a communist society by state action, example having failed. Winstanley's ideas are too rich to be briefly summarized. I must refer to what I have written elsewhere,[3] and here simply list aspects of his thought which are relevant for our purposes.

Winstanley used Scripture language, but gave his own sense to the biblical stories. The Crucifixion, the Resurrection and the Ascension may or may not have been historical events ('it matters not much'):[4] they are more important as metaphors for psychological transformations within men and women. The Christ who lived at Jerusalem is less significant for us than the Christ within. The establishment of private property had been the Fall of Man: its abolition, together with that of wage labour, would allow a return to the innocence of Adam and Eve in the Garden of Eden. Winstanley's God is not to be found above the skies after we are dead, but within each one of us, here on earth. There is no heaven or hell after death, no personal immortality. Heaven, hell, Satan, are all within us. The universe—as Milton thought too—had been created out of the substance of God.[5] The Second Coming of Jesus Christ is the rising of Reason within sons and daughters, and Reason means awareness of the need for co-operation. Winstanley used the word Reason in preference to God. As Christ rises, so all men and women will come to see the necessity of co-operation. There is no other Second Coming.[6] Ultimately all mankind, without exception, will be saved—i.e. brought into the haven of peace and rest on earth—not by the descent of a Saviour from the clouds but by the rising of communal consciousness within

---

[1] Winstanley, *The Law of Freedom and Other Writings*, p. 131.
[2] K. V. Thomas, 'Another Digger Broadside', *P. and P.*, 42 (1969), pp. 57–61.
[3] *WTUD*, esp. Chapters 7 and 8; Introduction to Winstanley, *The Law of Freedom: The Religion of Gerrard Winstanley* (*P. and P.* Supplement, 5, 1978).
[4] *The Law of Freedom*, p. 232.
[5] *The Religion of Gerrard Winstanley*, pp. 3, 8, 17–18, 31, 47; cf. p. 230 below.
[6] Ibid., pp. 29–37.

them. All men shall become Sons of God united by the Christ within.[1] Universalism was of course highly unorthodox when Winstanley began to preach it in 1648:[2] in his final version it was hardly Christian at all.

Winstanley saw the clergy as his main adversaries because they made a handsome living out of persuading the poor to accept their poverty on earth and look for their reward in heaven after death. The Diggers expected their heaven on earth. In Winstanley's ideal commonwealth there would be no state church; preaching for hire (i.e. an endowed ministry) would be as illegal as buying and selling, or lawyers taking fees. Winstanley rejected all church ordinances—prayer, preaching, baptism, holy communion, Sabbath observance. What mattered was 'the anointing' by the spirit of God. Winstanley believed that 'all the inward bondages of the mind' are 'occasioned by the outward bondage that one sort of people lay upon another', and will disappear in an equal society.[3]

Winstanley had accepted that England was a nation chosen as a model to the world. *The Law of Freedom* is analogous to *Paradise Lost* in that it attempts to explain how this hope had been frustrated.[4] Large excerpts from the pamphlet appeared in February 1652 in Daniel Border's newspaper *The Faithful Scout*, even before *The Law of Freedom* was published. Professor Woolrych points out that Border may have been taking his material at second hand, since three contemporary tracts also printed matter from *The Law of Freedom*.[5]

Winstanley's last pamphlet thus attracted some contemporary attention. But by 1652 Winstanley himself was exhausted and bitterly disillusioned. The dedication of *The Law of Freedom* to Oliver Cromwell may have been more than a device for winning publicity: like the Quakers later, Winstanley may still have had hopes of the Army. God, he said, had honoured Cromwell 'with the highest honour of any man since Moses's time'; Cromwell had not yet revealed himself as the lost leader of radical mythology. The Parliament which had proclaimed the Commonwealth might be persuaded to remove some of the burdens which afflicted the people. 'You have power in your hand', he told Cromwell, 'to act for common freedom if you will: I have no power.'[6]

---

[1] Ibid., pp. 5–6, 10; see p. 306 below.
[2] But cf. pp. 84, 88–9 below—Erbery.
[3] Ibid., pp. 5–6, 8, 28–9, 33, 48. For the anointing see pp. 304–9 below.
[4] I owe this point to Sheila Reynolds, 'Gerrard Winstanley: his Search for Peace' (unpubl. MA thesis, McGill University, 1976), pp. 54, 61.
[5] Woolrych, *Commonwealth to Protectorate*, p. 39.
[6] Winstanley, *The Law of Freedom*, pp. 275, 278–85.

But by the time he had reached the end of his pamphlet Winstanley seems to have realized that his hopes were vain.

> O power where art thou, that must mend things amiss?
> Come change the heart of man, and make him truth to kiss.
> O death where art thou? Wilt thou not tidings send?
> I fear thee not, thou art my loving friend.[1]

Winstanley did not in fact die for another twenty-four years, but so far as we know he abandoned political activity and writing. In 1654 he visited Edward Burrough and told him that the Quakers were 'sent to perfect that work which fell in their hands'.[2] Or so Burrough said: Winstanley may not have spoken quite so strongly. Twenty-two years later he was buried as a Quaker, but there is no evidence in between that he played any active role in the Society of Friends. On the contrary: he held various parish offices at Cobham between 1659 and 1668, and in 1671 and 1672 he was one of two chief constables of Elmbridge Hundred. This would suggest that he conformed to the state church during those years.[3]

His influence may have been greater in the seventeenth century than used to be thought. Contemporaries indeed noted similarities between the ideas of Winstanley and the early Quakers which were obscured by developments of Quaker theology after 1660.[4] More than one later seventeenth-century author regarded Winstanley as the originator of the Quakers.[5] A more direct influence can be seen on the pamphlets of William Covell of Enfield, where in 1650 there had been a Digger colony. In 1649 and again in 1659 there were riots against the enclosure of Enfield Chase, from which purchasers expected to make comfortable profits. It was sold tithe-free, and improvements suggested by the surveyors would have increased the value by nearly 150 per cent—for example by evicting

---

[1] Ibid., p. 389.

[2] *The Religion of Gerrard Winstanley*, p. 51.

[3] J. Alsop, 'Gerrard Winstanley's Later Life', *P. and P.*, 82 (1979), pp. 73–81; cf. R. T. Vann, 'The Later Life of Gerrard Winstanley', *Journal of the History of Ideas*, XXVI (1965), pp. 133–6; D. C. Taylor, *Gerrard Winstanley in Elmsbridge* (1982), pp. 4–5; Barry Reay, 'Early Quaker Activity and Reactions to it, 1652–1664' (unpubl. Oxford D.Phil. thesis, 1979), p. 5.

[4] See for example F. H. Higginson, *A Brief Relation of the preaching of the Northern Quakers* (1653), p. 26; Francis Harris, *Some Queries* (1655), p. 23. I owe both these references to the kindness of Dr Barry Reay.

[5] Thomas Comber, *Christianity no Enthusiasm* (1678), pp. 90–2, 181; Thomas Tenison, *An Argument for Union* (1683), p. 8. I owe this last reference too to Dr Reay. ∙

thirty-four squatters who had built cottages without leave.[1] The former Agitator, Cornet George Joyce, now Colonel Joyce, was one intending purchaser.[2]

Covell spoke of having had eight years' service with the Army,[3] and was careful to describe himself as a 'gentleman' (as Winstanley was), and to deny being 'a Leveller who would destroy property'. Nevertheless, he proposed a return to the 'good ancient laws and customs which were before the Norman Yoke'. He wanted to abolish an endowed clergy: 'if any will have parish ministers, let them that will have them pay them.' Tithes, together with delinquents' estates and the lands of Inns of Court, Chancery and universities should be confiscated and used to pay public debts. All commons and waste lands should be settled on the poor for ever. 'The patents and grants by the kings to lords of manors may be well searched into, for they are encroachments upon the people.' Co-operative communities were to be established, which differed from those of the Diggers in that they were to be financed by some rich men. Within these communities there was to be no buying and selling. The rich were to be taxed in proportion to their estates to maintain the impotent and aged poor and to provide work for all the unemployed. A remarkable concluding provision was that all other laws were to be null for ever.[4] The whole pamphlet might have been written by Winstanley in his 'possibilist' mood of 1652. Covell believed that every man was king, priest and governor in, to and over himself. The people had a *right* to choose their own officers.[5] Covell's last publication was *The True Copy of a Letter* sent to Charles II in 1660, in which he addressed the King as 'thou'. (Enfield was to become a Quaker stronghold.) As late as 1666 there were rumours of a Fifth Monarchist conspiracy based on Epping

---

[1] S. J. Madge, 'Rural Middlesex under the Commonwealth', *Transactions of the London and Middlesex Archaeological Societies*, N.S., IV, pp. 432–43; cf. [Anon.], *A Relation of the Cruelties and Barbarous Murthers ... committed* [at] *... Enfield* (1659).

[2] For Joyce see *Harleian Miscellany*, VIII (1744–6), pp. 293–6 and Woolrych, *Commonwealth to Protectorate*, p. 259. Joyce was cashiered in September 1653, allegedly for saying that he wished the pistol pointed at Cromwell on Triploe Heath in 1647 had gone off. Joyce on the contrary claimed that the charge of treason resulted from a dispute over land purchase between himself and Richard Cromwell.

[3] A Captain Covell was cashiered in October 1650 in Scotland (eight years after enlisting in 1642?) for allegedly saying 'sin was no sin' and denying the humanity of Christ (C. H. Firth and G. Davies, *Regimental History of Cromwell's Army* (Oxford UP, 1940), I, pp. 69–70). But this Covell's Christian name is given as Christopher.

[4] Covell, *A Declaration unto the Parliament* (1659), pp. 8, 17–22.

[5] W. Covell, *A Proclamation to all, of all sorts, high and low* (n.d., ?1654), single sheet. See also J. M. Patrick, 'William Covell and the Troubles at Enfield in 1659: A Sequel of the Digger Movement', *University of Toronto Quarterly*, XIV (1944).

Forest and Enfield Chase.[1] Echoes of Winstanley, as well as of *Areopagitica*, may also be heard in two pamphlets which Peter Cornelius Plockhoy published in 1659, not least in their fierce anti-clericalism: Great Antichrist (Bishop and King) had been succeeded by little Antichrists (priests). At least one Digger appears to have become a Harringtonian.[2]

It used to be thought that after the seventeenth century Winstanley was unknown until he was rediscovered at the end of the nineteenth century. But Benjamin Furley (1636–1714), Quaker friend of Algernon Sidney and Locke, owned Winstanley's writings.[3] In the mid-eighteenth century the radical Whig Thomas Hollis (who was interested in the mortalism of Richard Overton) gave a copy of *The Law of Freedom* to Henry Fielding.[4] In the 1790s ministers in the parish of Llangyfelach near Swansea were reading and discussing Winstanley's works.[5] A. F. Villemain's *Histoire de Cromwell d'après les mémoires du temps et les recueils parliamentaires* (1819) devoted a paragraph to the Diggers.[6] Now that historians have started to look out for it, more evidence will almost certainly be forthcoming.[7]

3   From Ranters to Muggletonians

Ranters began to be identified as a group of like-minded individuals after the crushing of the Levellers, though they never had any organization. There are many links between Levellers and Ranters. Laurence Clarkson wrote a Leveller pamphlet in 1647, in which he demanded the restoration

---

[1] Rogers, *Life and Opinions of a Fifth-Monarchy Man*, pp. 328–9.

[2] P. Cornelius Plockhoy, *The Way to the Peace and Settlement of these Nations* (March 1659) and *A Way propounded to make the poor in these and other Nations happy* (May 1659), esp. p. 21. For *Areopagitica* see O. Lutaud, *Les Deux Revolutions d'Angleterre: documents politiques, sociaux, religieux* (Paris, 1978), p. 439. For the Harringtonians see pp.201–6 below.

[3] M. C. Jacob, *The Radical Enlightenment: Pantheists, Freemasons and Republicans* (1981), p. 161.

[4] C. Robbins, 'Library of Liberty', *Harvard Library Bulletin*, 5 (1951), p. 17, quoted by J. R. Jacob, *Henry Stubbe: Radical Protestantism and the Early Enlightenment in England* (1983), p. 161.

[5] Philip Jenkins, *A Social and Political History of the Glamorgan Gentry, c. 1650–1720* (unpubl. Cambridge Ph.D. thesis, 1978), p. 298. I am grateful to Dr Jenkins for permission to quote from this thesis, and to M. C. Jacob for drawing my attention to it.

[6] O. Lutaud, op. cit., p. 161.

[7] Professor Linebaugh pointed out that an 18th-century song, 'Property must be, Save the Queen, save the Queen' appears to be written to the tune of the Diggers' song ('All the Atlantic Mountains Shook': paper delivered at a conference on Radicalism in England and America in the Seventeenth and Eighteenth Centuries, Philadelphia, 14 November 1981).

of the long-lost liberties of the freeborn subjects of England.[1] Abiezer
Coppe and George Foster called God 'that mighty Leveller'. The blood
of Levellers whom the Army Grandees had shot cried for vengeance,
though Coppe disavowed both 'sword-levelling' and 'digging-
levelling'.[2] The Leveller newspaper *The Moderate* described Richard
Coppin's *Divine Teachings* as 'an excellent book'.[3] Coppin and his
followers in Rochester in 1655 were called 'church and state Levellers'.[4]

I shall again be brief on the Ranters, isolating doctrines which seem
relevant for our purposes.[5] Coppe was a young man in a fury at the
hypocrisy and humbug of the self-styled godly. He taught that God's
service was 'perfect freedom and pure libertinism'. Sin and transgression
were finished. God would 'overturn, overturn, overturn'. 'The neck of
horrid pride' must be chopped off, so that 'parity, equality, community'
could be established.[6] The Lord comes 'as a thief in the night' to take the
money of the rich and give it to the poor. 'Have all things common, or
else the plague of God will rot and consume all that you have.'[7] 'All our
bondage and death' comes in by 'appropriating things to ourselves and
for ourselves'. The death and resurrection of Christ at Jerusalem 'is
nothing to the dying of the Lord in us, and the resurrection of the day-
star in our hearts'.[8]

In the same year 1649 Coppe wrote a Preface to *John the Divines
Divinity, or the Confession of the Generall Assembly or Church of the
Firstborn in Heaven*, ostensibly by 'I. F.', but on grounds both of style
and content almost certainly by Coppe himself. 'I. F.' declared that there
was now no need of ordinances such as preaching, baptism, holy
communion, church fellowship, etc. Scripture is not the Word of God.
Only the spirit of God 'and his working in us is our Scripture and rule of
life'. The incarnation, death, resurrection and ascension of Christ and the
last judgement are but a shadow of what takes place within us. The saints

---

[1] L. Clarkson, *A Generall Charge or Impeachment of High Treason, in the name of Justice
   Equity, against the Communality of England* (1647). For Clarkson see also Morton, *The
   World of the Ranters*, pp. 115–42.
[2] Coppe, *A Fiery Flying Roll* (1649), Part I, pp. 1–5, 11; G. Foster, *The Pouring Forth of the
   Seventh and Last Viall* (1650), Sig. A 3, p. 12; *The Sounding of the Last Trumpet* (1650), p. 50.
[3] Morton, op. cit., p. 98. Mr Morton emphasizes the move from Leveller to Ranter in 1649.
[4] Walter Rosewell, *The Serpents Subtilty Discovered* (1656), p. 16.
[5] Those interested are referred to A. L. Morton's *The World of the Ranters*, J. F. McGregor's
   'Ranterism and the Development of Early Quakerism', *Journal of Religious History*, 9 (1977),
   pp. 349–63, and my *WTUD*.
[6] *A Fiery Flying Roll*, I, pp. 1–5.
[7] Ibid., II, pp. 2, 4.
[8] Coppe, *Some Sweet Sips, of some Spirituall Wine* (1649), Sig. A 4v.

are gloriously filled with God: they and Christ make up but one body. There is no other heaven and hell than God's gracious or wrathful presence. Sin is a non-entity, a defect only.[1]

In 1650 Parliament condemned Coppe's two *Fiery Flying Rolls* to be publicly burned, and Coppe claimed that the two Blasphemy Acts of that year were 'put out because of me'. Coppe was imprisoned until he recanted. His first recantation was not good enough,[2] but *Coppes Return to the wayes of Truth* (1651) was to outward appearance more satisfactory: Marchamont Nedham helped him to find appropriate phrases.[3] Coppe clearly had many mental reservations. He never even knew anyone who affirmed that man was God (one of the accusations laid against him). Nevertheless 'the Sons of God ... partake of his nature', and 'all the fullness of the godhead' dwells bodily in them.[4] Coppe rather superfluously insisted on the strictness of his life, and emphasized that *all* have sinned: so of course he rejected the error attributed to him, 'that to act sin is the highest way to perfection'.[5] What Coppe had advocated was no doubt acting 'so-called sins'. Coppe declared against 'that community which is sinful, or destructive to soul or body, or the well-being of a commonwealth' (who wouldn't?), but he remained in favour of an 'apostolical, saint-like community', which provides bread for the hungry, clothes the naked, breaks every yoke and lets the oppressed go free.[6]

Even more revealing is Coppe's annexed letter to John Dury, who had called on him to renounce his sins as publicly and plainly as possible. Coppe appeared to agree: 'I will throw stones (as fast as I can drive) at ... all sorts of adultery.' 'Heart-adultery and eye-adultery' are sins, 'whereof those are greatly guilty that cry out of adultery and uncleanness in others'.[7] Drunkenness and murder are sins: 'so is pride, covetousness, hypocrisy, oppression, tyranny, cruelty, unmercifulness, despising the poor and needy, ... whether men imagine it to be so or no'. Then— coming a little nearer to Dury—'the laying of nets, traps and snares for

---

[1] Op. cit., pp 14–17, 29–34, 39, 47, 50–1.
[2] *A Remonstrance of the Sincere and Zealous Protestation of Abiezer Coppe against the Blasphemous and Execrable Opinions Recited in the Act of August 10, 1650* (1651), p. 1. Note that Coppe condemns only opinions *attributed* to him.
[3] Op. cit., pp. 27–8.
[4] Ibid., pp. 7, 24–5.
[5] Ibid., Sig. B 2, pp. 3–6, 23; cf. *A Fiery Flying Roll*, Part II, pp. 10–13.
[6] Ibid., pp. 13–15; cf. Fox, *Newes Coming up out of the North* (1654), p. 12: the rich grind the faces of the poor and feast while they starve.
[7] *Coppes Return*, pp. 17–20; cf. pp. 8–10.

the feet of our neighbours is a sin, whether men imagine it to be so or no.'
Failure to relieve the poor and oppressed, failure to break every yoke, are
also sins.[1] A few years later Laurence Clarkson made a more explicit
attack on 'the moderate, hypocritical saint-like devil', who 'is of all devils
most to be suspected': the devil who came to tempt Christ was well-read
in Scripture.[2]

So Coppe went down to defeat with colours flying. He was a master of
words, and by irony and innuendo he could outwit his clumsy
opponents. But the operative sentence in *Coppes Return* was his
undertaking 'both by life and doctrine' henceforth to 'decry whatsoever
hath occasioned outcries against me'.[3] Whatever his verbal triumphs, he
was effectively silenced. The main thrust of *A Fiery Flying Roll* had been
against the hypocrisy of the well-fed godly. 'His religion is vain, that
seeth his brother in want, &c.'[4] He was defeated before he started. 'The
rich will rule in this world,' Richard Baxter concluded.[5] Coppe was
silenced by Parliament, but he and the Ranters generally were silenced
even more effectively by those whom Parliament represented. 'The well-
favoured harlot shrugs at this...'[6]

Coppe was still moving in Ranter circles in 1655, but after the
restoration he changed his name to Higham and lived an apparently
blameless life as a physician and occasional preacher until his death in
1672. His last words were in *A Character of a True Christian*, published
posthumously over his own name:

> Through Christ he all things doth scan
>   He's wholly the Lord's free man....
> Evil and good the Lord doth bless....
> When self is swept away and gone
>   He says and lives, God's will be done.[7]

Coppe got most of his theology from Richard Coppin, for whose
Divine Teachings he wrote a Preface in 1649. Coppin lacks Coppe's
experimental vigour of expression, but his theology is more coherent.
God is in everyone. Heaven and hell exist only in men's consciences.[8]

---

[1] Ibid., p. 21.
[2] L. Clarkson, *Look about you* (1659), pp. 109–16; cf. pp. 22, 29–30.
[3] *Coppes Return*, Sig. B 2.
[4] *A Fiery Flying Roll*, II, p. 23 (should be p. 21).
[5] See p. 217 below.
[6] *A Fiery Flying Roll*, II, p. 22. In 1651–2 the Ranter John Robins and his disciples also recanted.
[7] Op. cit. (1680), single sheet.
[8] *Divine Teachings: In three parts* (1653), p. 75. First published 1649.

'God who is love cannot be angry with the persons of any men as they are made by him.'[1] God is both teacher and learner.[2] 'To deny that there is a full end of sin for all men … in the Lord Christ' is 'damnable heresy', the doctrine of devils.[3] Coppin had an agreeable sense of humour, as well as strong political convictions. 'I will delight myself', he wrote, 'with the worst of men as well as with the best (even a prelate or a cavalier).'[4] Antichrist's kingdom is 'a kingdom of gain, hire and self-interest'.[5] 'Through the birth of Christ' men will 'return to a more excellent state' than the Paradise from which Adam was cast.[6] Coppin suffered many imprisonments, but never appears to have recanted, though resigning himself to increasing persecution.[7]

Joseph Salmon in *A rout, a rout* (1649) told the Army Grandees that God acted first through Parliament, then through the Army. The generals were 'the rod of God'. But because of their self-interest 'the Lord our spiritual Samson … will … shake you all to pieces and in you the whole edifice of this swordly power shall be annihilated.'[8] Two years later he had a dizzying sense of politics as a conflict of particular interests 'travailling together in pain and groaning under enmity; labouring to bring forth some one thing, some another, and all bring forth nothing but wind and confusion'. Victory had turned to dust and ashes: 'I have lived to see an end to all perfection.' Salmon retreated into silence,[9] and emigrated to Barbados.

Laurence Clarkson was a mortalist, who believed that heaven was in this world only. The Fall, the Second Coming, the Last Judgement, all took place within the individual conscience. He believed that all comes by Nature, that the world is eternal and that God is in all things.[10] Sin was an invention of the ruling class. He learnt from William Sedgwick and Erbery that there had been no true church since the apostasy, after the death of the Apostles: preaching and prayer are to cease. 'The perfect liberty of the Sons of God' exempted them from the moral law; and

---

[1] *Divine Teachings: The Exaltation of All things in Christ* (3rd part, 1649), p. 21.
[2] *A History of the Glorious Mystery of Divine Teachings* (1649), pp. 11–13.
[3] *Mans Righteousness Examined* (1652), pp. 9–10, 18.
[4] *Crux Christi* (1657), p. 52.
[5] *Truths Testimony* (1655), p. 15.
[6] *A Man-Child Born* (1654), p. 1.
[7] *Crux Christi*, pp. 57, 62–3.
[8] Salmon, op. cit., pp. 4–5.
[9] Salmon, *Heights in Depths and Depths in Heights* (1651), Preface and pp. 7, 28.
[10] Clarkson, *A Single Eye* (1650), Sig. A lv, pp. 13, 15–16; *Look about you*, p. 30; *The Lost sheep Found* (1660), pp. 28, 32–3, 60–1.

Clarkson drew the full libertine conclusions, in theory and practice.[1]

Clarkson was on discussing terms with his fellow Lancastrian Winstanley, whom he accused of 'self-love and vain-glory'.[2] In 1650 Clarkson was arrested and sentenced to banishment—a sentence not carried out, perhaps because he gave some assurances for the future. He turned to astrology and magic, from which he made money as he had previously done by preaching. He was accepting defeat, and came near to losing any conviction at all as he travelled in the wilderness.[3] But in 1658 (or possibly earlier) he met John Reeve—also a former Ranter—and was convinced that Reeve was the last commissioned prophet of the Lord.[4] Reeve died in 1658, and Clarkson tried to oust Lodowick Muggleton from his position as heir to Reeve's authority. In *Look about you* and *The Lost sheep Found* Clarkson did not even mention Muggleton, and claimed that Reeve had prophesied that Clarkson would be 'a glorious instrument ... the like should never come after me'; Clarkson claimed to be 'a fellow-labourer' with Reeve, 'beyond all now living'—i.e. beyond Muggleton.[5] Clarkson referred to 'our last commission', meaning his and Reeve's.[6] He claimed—like Reeve before him and Muggleton after him—to speak and write infallibly, with direct divine revelation.[7] Clarkson declared himself 'the true and beloved bishop of the Lord, ... the true and only bishop now living'.[8] Muggleton counter-attacked fiercely and at once, excommunicating Clarkson. More effectively, perhaps, he cut off his salary. Clarkson eventually submitted, and suffered the ultimate defeat of being forbidden to write any more. He died in 1667, in prison for debt.[9] Muggleton was left to rewrite the history of the movement, claiming equality for himself with Reeve and ignoring Clarkson.[10]

---

[1] *A Single Eye*, pp. 7–11; *The Lost sheep Found*, pp. 19, 25–7, 48.

[2] *The Lost sheep Found*, p. 27.

[3] Ibid., pp. 10, 19, 24–5, 32–3, 38.

[4] Clarkson, *Look About You*, Sig. B. For Reeve and Muggleton, see C. Hill, B. Reay and W. M. Lamont, *The World of the Muggletonians* (1983). This includes an essay by Reay on Clarkson.

[5] *The Lost sheep Found*, pp. 38, 43, 48, 62–3.

[6] Ibid., pp. 42–6, 50, 52–3, 56, 59

[7] *Look about you*, pp. 77–81; *The Quakers Downfall* (1659), p. 1, as quoted by John Harwood, *The Lying Prophet Discovered and Reproved* (1659), p. 1; *The Lost sheep Found*, pp. 34–8, 43–4, 48–56.

[8] Ibid., pp. 59–60, 48; cf. Harwood, op. cit., Sig. A 2.

[9] Muggleton, *The Acts of the Witnesses of the Spirit* (1764), Chapter 6. First published 1699.

[10] Cf. pp. 167–9 below. In *The World of the Muggletonians* I compared Muggleton's manipulation of the memory of John Reeve to Stalin in relation to Lenin. I missed the point that Muggleton had first outmanoeuvred and crushed the ultra-leftist Clarkson—and then took over many of his ideas, as Stalin did Trotsky's.

In some respects Clarkson's views were closer to Reeve's than Muggleton's were. In 1656 Reeve had expected the millennium to arrive within a few months. He took an optimistic view of the millenarian potentialities of Oliver Cromwell, reminiscent of Marvell's.[1] In 1656 Reeve dedicated his *Divine Looking-Glass* to the Protector. He expected God to 'make use of Oliver Cromwell to be an instrument of general good'; he might become the 'faithful defender and deliverer of all suffering people'.[2] Clarkson echoed this in 1659: 'had it not been for the late Lord Protector, whose soul was merciful to tender consciences, oh ... what a bloody persecuting day had been in England.'[3] When Muggleton republished *A Divine Looking-Glass* in 1661, he prudently omitted Reeve's dedication, and revised the text in other ways. He introduced a doctrine which he admitted was not Reeve's—the doctrine that God takes no notice of men and women on earth, does not heed their prayers. Ironically, Muggleton seems to have taken this idea over from Clarkson, who taught it a decade before Muggleton did.[4] Clarkson claimed it was 'the highest pitch of revelation' that God does not hear even 'us his last commission'.[5] Even prayer is ineffective. The advantage of the doctrine, which Muggleton no doubt observed, was that it allows no court of appeal from the authority of the prophet: Muggleton, as the survivor of the Two Witnesses, could alone interpret the Scriptures, once Clarkson had been disposed of.[6] The doctrine leads on to a religion which is totally this-worldly. Given faith in the prophet, conduct alone matters, unaffected by hope of reward or fear of punishment.

What are we to make of Clarkson's Muggletonianism? (Reevonianism would be a more appropriate word.) In *The Lost sheep Found* he cheerfully admitted that he lied, cheated and made money whilst preaching all the other doctrines through which he passed. What Reeve's commission gave was *authority*. Truth can be established only by a commission, conveyed by direct divine revelation.[7] Reason, admirable enough in its own way, could deal only with the things of this world—

---

[1] Lamont, in *The World of the Muggletonians*, pp. 125–6. For Marvell see pp. 244–9 below.
[2] Op. cit., Dedication.
[3] *Look about you*, pp. 31–2.
[4] Clarkson, *A Single Eye*; cf. the Ranter Jacob Bauthumley, *The Light and Dark Sides of God*, also published in 1650.
[5] *The Lost sheep Found*, pp. 56, 59–62; Muggleton, *Epistle to Believers* (?1671), p. 7.
[6] *The Quakers Downfall*, p. 41, quoted by Harwood, op. cit., p. 13; *The Lost sheep Found*, p. 36; Muggleton, *A True Interpretation of the Eleventh Chapter of the Revelation* (1751–3), Chapter lxxxiii; first published 1662.
[7] *The Lost sheep Found*, p. 46.

arts and sciences, the economic and political sides of life. Even here it did not do a very good job: 'Reason hath erected magistrates, judges and lawyers to reconcile Reason divided against itself, or else condemn it to be executed by the hangman.' Faced with the problems of the defeated Revolution, Reason 'cries and desires that God would send fire from heaven and blast the proceeding of its enemies'. But, Clarkson told his public, 'your hands are full of blood, your lips have spoken lies, nor have you done justice or equity when the power was in your hands.' How fortunate for them that God takes no notice of them or their prayers! 'Our Lord will not preserve you nor destroy you, but Reason subtlety must deliver you, as it hath delivered your enemies into your hands before now. If ye will not believe me, believe the fruits of your own prayers, and much good may they do you.' 'Where Reason is lord, its operations are never satisfied' but always shifting, 'as these late transactions will confirm'.[1]

Problems that Reason could not solve, faith might; and the demands of faith in John Reeve's commission were minimal. The Muggletonians too had a minimum of organization, of worship, of discipline, of enforcement of norms of conduct.[2] Clarkson had never perhaps had very strong emotional religious responses: he had always been cynical and realistic, and now he was defeated and world-weary. He was the type of libertine to whom Pascal's wager was intended to appeal. If a man as intelligent and devout as Pascal thought that a sensible way of settling the ultimate problem, why not Clarkson? I would take him to be naturally more of a gambling man than Pascal; and perhaps with a stronger sense of humour.[3]

The conclusion which Clarkson drew from his theology was that 'we the last commissioners' and the commission's followers 'shall not plot or conspire against no power then reigning, but submit to you however you deal with us'. The world 'is your inheritance by birthright, and not the saints' at all'.[4] So perhaps it was the pacifism which Reeve so vigorously proclaimed, whilst insisting on the sinfulness of all rulers, that attracted Clarkson, in the years when Fifth Monarchists were expecting God to send fire from heaven and Quakers were rejoining the Army and offering their services to the last forlorn governments of Reason. After 1660 the

---

[1] Ibid., p. 54–9.
[2] *The World of the Muggletonians*, pp. 34–42; cf. pp. 165, 290–2 below.
[3] *The World of the Muggletonians*, esp. pp. 176–8.
[4] Clarkson, *The Lost sheep Found*, p. 59.

Quakers would follow Reeve's example, abandoning the hope of seeing God's kingdom on earth as well as in heaven.[1]

Since the Ranters never formed an organized movement, the survival of their ideas is difficult to document with certainty. Clarkson was not the only Ranter to become a Muggletonian. Even more Ranters (as well as Levellers and Diggers) became Quakers; I shall give evidence of this later. Others conformed to the state church, with whatever private reservations.[2] I have tried elsewhere to give examples of Ranter ideas which recurred among later religious and political radicals.[3] Similar ideas passed into the English libertine tradition, which embraced poets like Rochester, playwrights like Aphra Behn. The Ranters, as well as Winstanley and Wildman, may have contributed something to deism.

---

[1] See pp. 149–50, 160–3 below.
[2] *The World of the Muggletonians*, p. 47; *WTUD*, p. 257.
[3] Cf. my 'From Lollards to Levellers', and M. C. Jacob, *The Radical Enlightenment*, p. 98.

Chapter 3

The Second Losers, 1653–1660

1 Fifth Monarchists: Preachers and Plebeians

I

Historians are agreed these days, thanks mainly to the work of B. S. Capp, that Fifth Monarchism as a movement belongs to the 1650s. Before then there had been plenty of millenarianism among the Parliamentarians, of course: the Scottish Presbyterian Robert Baillie wrote disapprovingly in September 1645 'the most of the chief divines here, not only Independents but others such as Twisse, Marshall, Palmer and many more, are express Chiliasts.'[1] Stephen Marshall indeed said that the issue in the civil war was 'Should Christ or Antichrist rule?'[2] —a question echoed by Vavasor Powell in December 1653, though his alternatives were Christ or Oliver Cromwell.[3] Even so unradical a character as William Prynne declared that the Earl of Essex was 'General of the Lord of Hosts' to set up Christ's kingdom.[4] Edmund Calamy too thought Parliament's Cause was God's,[5] a truth passed on to the troops in *The Souldiers Pocket Bible* of 1643, with the addition that 'the Lord hath ever been accustomed to give the victory to a few.'[6] Henry Wilkinson in the same year told the House of Commons that the 'general talk throughout the household among the domestics' was 'that Christ their king is coming to take possession of his throne. They do not only

---

[1] Baillie, *Letters and Journals* (1775), II, p. 156.
[2] Capp, *The Fifth Monarchy Men*, p. 39. I have drawn on Capp's excellent book throughout this chapter.
[3] S. R. Gardiner, *The History of the Commonwealth and Protectorate* (1903), III, p. 5. See mv *Puritanism and Revolution* (Panther edn., 1968), pp. 133–4, 313–15.
[4] W. Prynne, *The Popish Royall Favourite* (1643), Sig. 2.
[5] Quoted in Capp, op. cit., p. 39.
[6] Op. cit., p. 10.

whisper it and tell it in the ear, but they speak it publicly.'[1] It was
expected that domestics would hold strange views, but unusual that they
proclaimed them publicly.

Capp found millenarianism in 70 per cent of the works published by
Puritan divines (Presbyterian or Independent) between 1640 and 1653.[2]
Lady Ranelagh in the 1640s was expecting the millennium soon, no less
than her brother Robert Boyle and her friends John Dury, Henry
Oldenburg and John Milton.[3] Some date in the 1650s had indeed solid
scholarly support.[4]

So there was a general millenarianism in the 1640s, but no Fifth
Monarchist organization. This, I think, is what Robert Purnell must
have meant when he said in 1649 that there are 'but few ... millenaries'.[5]
There may indeed have been some lower-class groups which associated
millenarianism with claims that the wicked had no right to property, and
with demands that the ungodly should be put to death.[6] Millenarianism
as preached by Thomas Goodwin and many others in the 1640s had been
a great stimulus to radical politics.[7] 'What do you know', rank-and-file
Parliamentarian soldiers were asking, 'but that we are the men that must
help' to pull down the Whore of Babylon in England? 'The people, the
multitude' should pull her down, and should define who and where the
Whore of Babylon was.[8] Capp refers to a lower-class millenarian
movement as in existence by 1649, and dates the emergence of organized
Fifth Monarchism to the end of 1651.[9]

The word 'millenarian' was used loosely, to cover a variety of opinions
about the exact form which Christ's rule during the millennium would
take. Some believed that Christ would rule in person for a thousand
years. But most Fifth Monarchists would have agreed with William
Aspinwall that Christ 'delegates his authority to the saints', who 'shall be
his vice-gerents'.[10] Indeed the object of political action was to establish

---

[1] Henry Wilkinson, *Babylons Ruine, Jerusalems Rising* (1643), p. 21.
[2] Capp, op. cit., p. 38; see ibid., pp. 46–9 for a list of writers.
[3] J. R. Jacob, 'Boyle's Circle in the Protectorate: Revelation, Politics and the Millennium', *Journal of the History of Ideas*, 38 (1977), pp. 133–6.
[4] See my *Antichrist in Seventeenth-Century England* (1971), Chapter 1.
[5] R. Purnell, *Good Tydings for Sinners, Great Joy for Saints* (1649), p. 64.
[6] Capp, op. cit., p. 43. The allegations come from a hostile anonymous pamphlet, *A Short History of the Anabaptists* (1642).
[7] See pp. 180–1 below.
[8] E. Symmonds, *Scripture Vindicated* (Oxford, 1644), Preface, quoted in my *Antichrist in Seventeenth-Century England*, pp. 79–80.
[9] Capp, op. cit., pp. 56–8, 88–9.
[10] W. Aspinwall, *A Brief Description of the Fifth Monarchy* (1653), pp. 4, 9–10.

this rule: it would hardly have made sense to attempt a coup to put Jesus Christ on the throne in any but a metaphorical sense. When Moses Wall in May 1659 reminded Milton that it was soldiers who 'watched our Saviour's sepulchre to keep him from rising', his meaning was clearly that the Army was preventing the rule of the saints in England.[1]

But 'the rule of the saints' is a more complex idea than appears at first sight. Sixteenth-century Familists expected to assist in judging the world.[2] Many who were not Fifth Monarchists believed this in the mid-seventeenth century. Thomas Collier, for instance, in a sermon preached at Putney on 29 September 1647, said that Christ would rule the world 'in and by his saints'. This rule would involve legal and social changes—law reform, abolition of tithes and free quarter, etc.[3] Robert Purnell in 1651 thought that the Lord would rule the world in and by his saints.[4] Milton expected that 'God would come/To judge them with his saints': Fox, Erbery, Sedgwick, Penington and John Sadler shared this belief.[5] Milton and John Cook as well as Hugh Peter, Mary Cary, William Aspinwall and John Canne argued that the court which sentenced Charles foreshadowed the Day of Judgement, when the saints should judge the world.[6]

The rule of the saints, moreover, can mean more than one thing. Before 1653 Fifth Monarchists seem mostly to have hoped that magistrates would become godly, or would respond to godly influences: the idea that the saints themselves should take over the government gained strength during and after Barebone's Parliament.[7] As John Tillinghast (1604–55) put it, if the work of overturning 'is to be performed by the saints ... then ... there must be civil and military

---

[1] D. Masson, *Life of Milton* (1859–80), V, p. 602.
[2] Jean Dietz Moss, '"Godded with God": Hendrik Niclaes and His Family of Love', *Transactions of the American Philosophical Soc.*, 71, part 3 (1981), p. 32.
[3] In Woodhouse, *Puritanism and Liberty*, pp. 394–5. I am grateful to Gill Parker for drawing my attention to this passage.
[4] Purnell, *No Power But of God* (1651), pp. 209–10, 227.
[5] PL, XI. 705; this corresponds to *De Doctrina Christiana* (*CPW*, VI. p. 621; cf. *CPW*; VIII, p. 291 and *PL*, X.62). See also pp. 88–9, 107–8, 126, 159, 309 below, and Sadler, *Olbia: The New Island lately discovered* (1660), p. 15.
[6] *MER*, p. 282, and references there cited; E. Ludlow, *A Voyce from the Watchtower*, ed. B. Worden (Camden Fourth Series, 1978), p. 235; Mary Cary, *The Little Horns Doom and Downfall* (1651), pp. 35–6; Aspinwall, *An Explication and Application of the Seventeenth Chapter of Daniel* (1653), pp. 32, 36; Capp, op. cit., pp. 51–2.
[7] I owe this point to John Laydon, 'The Kingdom of Christ and the Powers of the Earth: the Political Uses of Apocalyptic and Millenarian Ideas in England, 1648–53' (unpubl. Ph.D. thesis, University of Cambridge, 1976); cf. J. Rogers, *A Christian Concertation with Mr. Prin, Mr. Baxter, Mr. Harrington, For the True Cause of the Commonwealth* (1659), pp. 76–82.

power in the hands of the saints ... before the day of Christ's appearance'.[1]

The events of 1649 were a great stimulus to millenarian thinking, following as they did on pre-existing expectations of the Second Coming in the 1650s. What more natural than that King Charles should be succeeded by King Jesus? 'The power and spirit of our Cause', Christopher Feake wrote in 1659, 'was great and high after the King's death, more than at any time before.' The Good Old Cause, which had become a 'pitiful, dull, dry, lean, barren, ill-favoured thing', was transformed by the King's execution into 'the most lovely, lively, growing, sparkling prosperous Cause in all the earth'.[2] Feake had preached against the Long Parliament earlier, but now he 'owned the Commonwealth'.[3]

The Declaration of Musselburgh on 1 August 1650 expressed this elation. Significantly, it was issued in the name of under-officers and soldiers, though Cromwell commended it.[4] John Canne thought after Dunbar that 'the Parliament of England's Cause ... hath been proved ... to be the Cause of God.'[5] It was in this euphoric spirit that Vavasor Powell (1617–70) and the Welsh Propagators of the Gospel went to work.[6]

Yet after the crowning mercy of Worcester, when no obstacles to the realization of God's kingdom were to be seen but no progress was made, confidence in the regime began to decline. Failure to extend the Propagators' commission after April 1653 finally destroyed Fifth Monarchist confidence in the Rump.[7] It was in reaction to this lost hope that the first stirrings of a Fifth Monarchist *movement* are to be seen. The first conscious Fifth Monarchist group, Feake tells us, came into existence at the end of 1651 in meetings at All Hallows the Great to draw up a platform. Among other things the group pressed for war against the Netherlands. But within a year, such were the pressures of the times, there had been 'a very sensible decay of spirit'.[8] As faith in the Rump

---

[1] *Mr Tillinghasts Eight Last Sermons* (1655), pp. 60–8. Tillinghast's earlier *Generation–Work* (1653) and *Knowledge of the Times* (1654) had been less specific on the need for military action.

[2] Feake, *A Beam of Light Shining in the Midst of Much Darkness and Confusion* (1659), pp. 30, 35–6. Feake (*c.* 1612–after 1682) was lecturer at St Anne's, Blackfriars, London.

[3] Feake, Preface to *Mr Tillinghasts Eight Last Sermons*, Sig. a 2.

[4] Printed in part in Woodhouse, op. cit., pp. 474–8; Abbott, op. cit., II, p. 302.

[5] Canne, *Emmanuel, or God With Us* (1650), p. 44. Canne (*c.* 1590–1667) was chaplain to Robert Overton at Hull.

[6] See my *Change and Continuity in Seventeenth-Century England*, pp. 34–8.

[7] Capp, op. cit., pp. 57–8.

[8] Feake, *A Beam of Light*, pp. 42, 44; cf. Capp, op. cit., p. 58.

declined, initially men looked to the Army, to Harrison and Cromwell. The dissolution of April 1653 was greeted enthusiastically. John Rogers spoke of Cromwell as 'the people's victorious champion', 'the great deliverer of his people ... out of the house of Egypt', a second Moses. Rogers gave Cromwell unsolicited advice about the selection and functions of what was to be Barebone's Parliament.[1]

But despite the efforts of Harrison and Vavasor Powell in Wales, there seem to have been only some dozen committed Fifth Monarchists in Barebone's Parliament. They soon found themselves outnumbered and outmanoeuvred. From August 1653 Harrison and Carew, both later to be executed as regicides, effectively withdrew from its activities. By November Feake and others were denouncing Cromwell.[2] Feake later saw the dissolution of this assembly as the end of all his hopes.[3]

The dissolution marked indeed a parting of the ways. Even the Army's Musselburgh Declaration was now repudiated.[4] No Fifth Monarchist could be enthusiastic about the Protectorate. But they were divided among themselves on how to react, knowing that support for their cause was falling away from the mid-1650s. The clearest evidence for this was the failure to respond to the government's imprisonment of Carew, Harrison, Rogers, Feake, Simpson and Spittlehouse. The apparently irreversible trend which had led Baptist and Independent congregations to stop supporting the Levellers in 1649 worked to the disadvantage of the Fifth Monarchists after the dissolution of Barebone's. If success justified, failure condemned: stability was what 'responsible' men wanted now. Fifth Monarchism was always something of an instant solution: that was both its initial attraction and its long-term weakness. In 1654 leading General Baptists and Independents denounced the Fifth Monarchists, followed by the Particular Baptists. Only the preachers associated with All Hallows remained in fiercely vocal opposition.[5]

The stark repudiation of the Protectorate which the Fifth Monarchists demanded split the movement, as it split John Simpson's congregation at All Hallows. The majority even there accepted the Protectorate; Simpson himself was with the minority until he changed his mind after a spell in

---

[1] Rogers, *A Few Proposals Relating to Civil Government* (1653), p. 5; Rogers, *Life and Opinions of a Fifth-Monarchy Man*, pp. 110–11, 128; cf. A. Woolrych, *Commonwealth to Protectorate*, p. 351. Rogers (?1627–70) was Lecturer at St. Thomas Apostle's, London.
[2] Capp, op. cit., pp. 68–73; cf. Woolrych, op. cit., Chapter 7.
[3] Feake, *A Beam of Light*, pp. 50–1.
[4] Capp, op. cit., p. 121.
[5] Ibid., pp. 75, 100–2; cf. p. 230.

prison.[1] Propertied supporters of the cause tended to draw back from forlorn-hope insurrections. Vavasor Powell, who had bought crown lands,[2] was fiercely critical of the Protectorate but would have no truck with underground conspiracy. William Aspinwall too rejected plots against any earthly magistrate, advocating obedience to the powers that be.[3] After 1657 he gives no sign of political activity, though he lived until 1662 or later.[4] Feake criticized Henry Jessey for combining verbal abuse of the Protector with *de facto* collaboration.[5] John Rogers denounced the Army as apostate, and was in jail from 1654 to 1657 and again in 1658; his long interview with Cromwell in 1655 reveals much of both men's attitudes.[6] But Rogers was opposed to premature revolt, and refused his backing for Venner's rising in 1657. The initiative thus fell to the radical rank and file of London artisans, who had less to lose. Their desperate courage in 1657 and 1661 was as remarkable as their failure to win support outside their own ranks.

The treachery of the generals in 1653–4, as Fifth Monarchists saw it, disrupted the Cause. 'Oh ye tyrants,' Feake cried in 1655, 'who shall be your Lord Protector in the day when Jehovah's fury shall be poured out like fire?'[7] Rogers professed to be astonished that the Lord could thus reject those whom he had 'owned in the field at Naseby, Dunbar, Worcester'.[8] Spittlehouse attributed it to the temptation of 'vast treasures got by the sweat of other men's brows'. Powell told 'the swordmen in general' that 'their parks and new houses and gallant wives had choked them up'.[9] As some junior officers joined in the scramble to enrich themselves,[10] and as other ranks were purged, the Army ceased to be an organization inspiring confidence.

The rot infected the godly themselves. In 1655 Tillinghast's Norfolk church noted that believers were too concerned with 'profits,

---

[1] Ibid., pp. 276–8.
[2] Powell, *The Bird in the Cage Singing* (2nd edn., 1662), Sig. B 2v.
[3] W. A., *Legislative Power is Christs Peculiar Prerogative* (1656), quoted by L. F. Brown, *Baptists and Fifth Monarchy Men* (New York, 1911), p. 104.
[4] Capp, op. cit., pp. 240–1, and Chapter 5 *passim*.
[5] B. R. White, 'Henry Jessey: A Pastor in Politics', *Baptist Quarterly*, XXV (1973), pp. 103–5. Jessey (1601–63) was Lecturer at All Hallows and closely associated with Fifth Monarchists though not one himself.
[6] E. Rogers, op. cit., pp. 190–217, 299, 301; Capp, op cit., p. 261.
[7] Preface to *Mr Tillinghasts Eight Last Sermons*, Sig. A 2v–3. Feake spoke of 'the new monarchical tyrants, who are but of yesterday'.
[8] Rogers, *Jegar-Sahadvtha: An Oyled Pillar: Set up for Posterity* (1657), Introduction, p. 43.
[9] Spittlehouse, *The first Addresses to His Excellencie the Lord General (1653)*, p. 4; A. Griffith, *Strena Vavasorensis* (1654), pp. 18–19; cf. *CSP Dom., 1653–4*, p. 306.
[10] Cf. Feake, *A Beam of Light*, pp. 44–6.

preferments and encouragements you shall have in the world', and so were anxious 'to please and serve men rather than Christ'. They had become 'fearful and unbelieving'.[1] Rogers looked back nostalgically to 'the spirit and faith and courage of the good old Puritans' of the 1640s. Writing from prison, he referred to 'the present apostasy of spirit, principles and persons, not only among mercenary professors' but also affecting 'the little remnant, whose coldness, cowardice and carelessness is (almost) incredible'.[2] 'I find no faith, no truth or constancy in men'; 'doubtful friends' even cut his writings before publishing them.[3]

Feake too admitted that support for Fifth Monarchists was flagging. He spoke of 'that glorious Cause (which was once the joy of the saints generally throughout the nation, although now it be almost forgotten by the most'. There was, he said, 'great diversity of opinions and apprehensions ... among the assertors of Christ's kingdom'. Feake praised the recently deceased Tillinghast for coming up to London 'to speak his mind freely to the Great Man ... to the stopping of the mouths of all court-flatterers (who are one of the worst sort of creeping vermin in the world)'. Tillinghast 'mightily convinced many ... that the kingdom of Christ is not only a spiritual kingdom, but an outward visible kingdom', which 'shall very shortly begin to break in pieces and consume all these kingdoms'. Feake was himself in prison as he wrote, 'suffering for the Good Old Cause', and addressing himself to 'the Lord's little remnant ... waiting for the breaking forth of the next dispensation'.[4]

Tillinghast too was aware of disunity, treachery and back-sliding among the godly: 'apostasy of such as shall be eminent; a great sleep among professors'.[5] 'Saints of all ages and generations' had the duty 'to pray and believe'. But in the present age it was their task to 'pluck down all, that Jesus Christ when he comes may have his enemies his footstool'. 'Ploughshares are to be beaten into swords.'[6] But Tillinghast was very unspecific about how these bold words were to be translated into deeds. 'It is a special duty of the saints ... to declare for God ... though others count it rashness, hastiness and over-forwardness.' But spirits, he admitted, are much sunk since two or three years ago, when we expected

---

[1] Tillinghast, *Generation-Work*, Part III (1655), Sig. B 4–4v.
[2] Rogers, *Jegar-Sahadvtha*, Introduction, p. 3; cf. pp. 37–8.
[3] *A Necessary Word to the Ingenious Reader*, Sig. x₂–x₃, at the end of *Jegar-Sahadvtha* (separate pagination).
[4] Feake, *A Beam of Light*, Sig. A 4–4v, A 7–7v, 8v, a 4v–6v.
[5] Ibid., pp. 45–58, 89, 97–8.
[6] Ibid., pp. 60–1, 68.

to go on to Rome and to pull down tithes at home. 'Never until this day'—since the beginning of the Revolution—'have God's people prayed as destitute ones: we had a Parliament, an Army, a General that went along with us till of late.'[1] Tillinghast was convinced that 'the flood of God's wrath upon the idolatrous antichristian world' would come in 1656. 'All the people of God at this day', he had written in 1654, 'look for their redemption to be at hand.' Any attempt to put 'those glorious days' into the distant future (as critics of Fifth Monarchists were doing) was 'an unfortunate opinion'.[2] Tillinghast died in 1655.

By 1659 the movement had lost its élan. Although Feake insisted that Christ's Cause would 'appear again ... ere it be long', his interim advice to 'the real fifth-kingdom men' was to 'become a peculiar people (or, as it were, a nation in the midst of the nation) waiting for the word of command from their Leader [i.e. God] to execute the vengeance written against Babylon'. 'The Cause', he rather optimistically protested, 'will be amiable in the eyes of all the nations in due time.'[3] But not now. Perhaps Fuller was right: 'Fifth Monarchy Men's expressions are more offensive than their intentions, their mouths worse than their minds.'[4]

But Fuller was writing in 1660. One can understand the alarm which governments felt in the 1650s. Cromwell made this clear in his speech to his first Parliament in September 1654 and in his interview with John Rogers six months later.[5] Plots in the Army involving Fifth Monarchist officers were of course more disturbing than sermons of voluble preachers. But it seems unlikely that there was any serious danger to the regime from leaders whose rank and file seemed to be ebbing away.

One problem in dealing with Fifth Monarchists is indeed to distinguish between the ideologists and the rank and file. The former were preachers—Aspinwall, Feake, Powell, Rogers, Spittlehouse, Tillinghast—or Army officers like Harrison and Overton. The latter seem to have been mainly London artisans, journeymen and apprentices, with a special interest in the clothing industry.[6] This last fact helps to explain some otherwise odd aspects of Fifth Monarchism—fierce

---

[1] Ibid., pp. 89, 93, 223–4.
[2] Tillinghast, *Knowledge of the Times: Or The resolution of the Question, how long it shall be unto the end of the Wonders* (1654), pp. 41–97, 306, 325.
[3] Feake, *A Beam of Light*, pp. 57–8.
[4] T. Fuller, *Mixt Contemplations in Better Times* (1660), reprinted in *Good Thoughts in Bad Times* (1830), p. 272.
[5] Abbott, *Writings and Speeches of Oliver Cromwell*, III, pp. 436–8; E. Rogers, op. cit., pp. 190–217.
[6] Capp, op. cit., Chapter 4 *passim*, pp. 76, 231.

hostility to the protestant Dutch, for instance, and some of the economic features of Venner's programmes.[1]

A possible explanation for the collapse of the movement in the late 1650s is that it had lost support among the lower classes of London. John Pell had perceptively written in 1655 that 'men variously impoverished by the long troubles, full of discontents and tired by long expectation of amendment, must needs have great propensions to hearken to those that proclaim times of refreshing—a golden age—at hand.'[2] But diminishing returns rapidly set in with the consolidation of the Protectorate and the passing of the millenarian dates of 1655 and 1656. The preachers went on attempting to screw their followers up to fever pitch: believers in an approaching change in which Christ would either descend from heaven or rise in men and women had to be always on the *qui vive*, always strained to the utmost. Too great psychological demands were made on Fifth Monarchy's adherents to be maintained for long in the face of repeated disappointments.[3] Venner's small contingent showed in 1657 what a tremendous lift Fifth Monarchy beliefs could give to the morale of ordinary people; but that his supporters were so few—and lacked the backing of any of the preachers—shows that such convictions were now restricted to a small group. As Capp demonstrates, 'the hostility of property-owning millenarians to the social doctrines of the saints does explain why most avoided the movement'. It also explains why Cromwell stressed that Fifth Monarchists 'tell us that liberty and property are not the badges of the kingdom of Christ'. There were few gentlemen Fifth Monarchists except Army officers, and even they repudiated the social programme of the radicals.[4]

The real weakness of the movement was shown in 1659, when their chance seemed at last to have come. But by then they had split into fragments. From an early stage some Fifth Monarchist leaders seem to have realized that they needed the support of republicans if they were to overthrow the Protectorate. In 1655 Vavasor Powell's petition, *A Word for God*, had accused the government of betraying the Good Old Cause in the dual sense of 'the advancement of Christ's kingdom' and the privileges of Parliament. During the elections of 1656 *Englands Remembrancer* also linked the two senses of the Good Old Cause.[5] John

---

[1] See pp. 62, 65 below.
[2] *The Protectorate of Oliver Cromwell*, ed. R. Vaughan (1839), I, p. 156.
[3] The point was made by Tillinghast's church: see his *Generation-Work*, Part III, Sig. B 5; cf. p. 296 below.
[4] Capp, op. cit., p. 93; Abbott, op. cit., III, p. 438.   [5] Capp, op. cit., pp. 110, 114.

Rogers seems to have formed some sort of understanding with Vane while they were both in prison: Rogers's pamphlets of 1659 praise the restored Rump as well as 'the faithful officers of the Army'. In his controversy with Harrington Rogers agreed that both desired a commonwealth, adding that we can live 'with more freedom' if there are no lords. He opposed monarchy and cried up the Good Old Cause.[1] In 1659 Feake's *A Beam of Light* was subtitled *The True Good Old Cause stated and pleaded*. In this he called for unity among God's people and for fulfilment of 'all those just and good promises, engagements and declarations', presumably of the Army. He included even 'those brethren of the classical way who are of a modest sober spirit' in his appeal.[2]

In September 1659 some Fifth Monarchists co-operated with Sir Henry Vane in opposing a declaration against a single person, lest Jesus Christ should be excluded.[3] But Rogers—who realized that a restoration was imminent—was diverted by controversies with Harrington and Baxter: and there was no solution to the perpetual problem of what the relation was to be between the ruling saints and the remainder of the people.[4]

There was never an agreed Fifth Monarchist programme. But certain items recur, most of them shared by other radical groups. Fifth Monarchists gave a religious basis to Leveller theories of equality (though of course theirs was equality among believers only). 'A nation is more beholding to the meanest kitchen maid in it that hath in her a spirit of prayer, than to a thousand of her profane swaggering gentry.'[5] The latter came in for a bad time, from Feake's alleged assertion in 1646 that there was in aristocracy 'an enmity against Christ' to *A Door of Hope*'s denunciation of the 'old bloody, popish, wicked gentry of the nation'.[6] In between Rogers had attacked 'corrupt and naughty nobles'.[7]

---

[1] *Mr. Pryns Good Old Cause stated and Stunted ten years ago* (1659), pp. 10, 17–20; *Mr. Harringtons Parallel unparallel'd* (1659), pp. 3–4, 10–11; cf. *A Christian Concertation*, Sig. B 2v, pp. 18–24, 41–3, 46, 65–6, 90–1, 124, and Capp, op. cit., pp. 121, 139. Rogers and Henry Stubbe quote one another with approval (E. Rogers, op. cit., p. 321).

[2] *A Beam of Light*, Sig. A 3v, pp. 1–34, 50–1.

[3] Carte, ed., *A Collection of Original Letters and Papers*, II, pp. 203, 216; cf. F. P. G. Guizot, *History of Richard Cromwell and the Restoration of the Stuarts*, trans. A. R. Scoble (1850), I, pp. 474–98.

[4] Rogers, *A Christian Concertation*, pp. 46, 91–8 and *passim*; Feake, *A Beam of Light*, p. 51. See pp. 288–90 below.

[5] [Anon.], *The Failing and Perishing of Good Men* (1663), a funeral sermon for John Simpson.

[6] *Gangraena*, III, p. 148; *A Door of Hope* (1661), p. 8.

[7] Rogers, *Ohel* (1653), pp. 11, 22–3; cf. E. Rogers, op. cit., pp. 169, 171; Capp, 'Extreme Millenarianism', in *Puritans, the Millennium and the Future of Israel: Puritan Eschatology, 1600–1660*, ed. P. Toon (1970), p. 73.

Tillinghast thought that 'the present work of God is to bring down lofty men.'[1] In the millennium, Feake predicted, there would be 'no difference betwixt high and low, the greatest and the poorest beggar'.[2] John Spittlehouse appears to be unusual in saying 'we abominate any wicked action under the notion of levelling, etc.'; but the words are perhaps deliberately ambiguous; he was arguing that economic pressures resulting from the Revolution had led to social transformations of many kinds.[3] Feake, Venner and other Fifth Monarchists, in the traditional manner also adopted by the Quakers, 'thou'd' and refused hat honour to social superiors.[4]

Aspinwall, Powell and Spittlehouse proposed to abolish customs and excise, Venner to remove all taxes. Spittlehouse condemned the Norman law; he, Rogers and Peter Chamberlen called for judges to be elected.[5] Like Winstanley, Rogers spoke of 'the Norman yoke of corrupt lawyers', and linked 'the Babylonian and Norman yokes'.[6] He warned Cromwell against protecting 'the carnal, national antichristian clergy'.[7] The failure of Fifth Monarchists to criticize usury, their demand that thieves and debtors should be set to work in order to make restitution, suggests, in Capp's words, a 'programme attractive to the small producers, sharing the aspirations of mercantilist society.... Humanitarianism coincided with the better protection of property.' Artisans would also no doubt sympathize with the proposal to confiscate the lands of the ungodly.[8]

Fifth Monarchists repeated the general radical hostility to tithes. Law and church must go down before the millennium can come, said *A True State of the Case of the Commonwealth* in 1654. They were the 'outworks of Babylon', a phrase which recalls Edmund Waller in 1641 saying that he looked on episcopacy 'as a counterscarp or outwork' protecting property.[9] Rogers told Cromwell that tithes were antichristian, and that Oliver himself had earlier promised to pull them down.[10] John Canne declared that Christ would not descend until tithes

---

[1] *Mr Tillinghasts Eight Last Sermons*, p. 219.

[2] Capp, *Fifth Monarchy Men*, p. 143.

[3] Spittlehouse, *An Answer to one part of the Lord Protectors Speech* (1654), p. 1. Spittlehouse had served in the Army from at least 1643 till the Battle of Worcester in 1651.

[4] E. Rogers, op. cit., p. 317; Capp, op. cit., pp. 143–4.

[5] Capp, op. cit., pp. 150, 160.

[6] Rogers, *Sagrir, or Dooms-day drawing nigh* (1654), Sig. A 4; E. Rogers, op. cit., pp. 53–4, 76, 82–4.

[7] Rogers, *To His Highness the Lord General Cromwell* (1653), single sheet.

[8] Capp. op. cit., pp. 164–6, 231.

[9] Ibid., p. 70; *Old Parliamentary History* (1763), IX, pp. 388–9.

[10] E. Rogers, op. cit., p. 213; cf. p. 317.

were removed.[1] Rogers also attacked advowsons and the whole system of lay patronage.[2] In 1674 he was associated with Milton as a 'Billingsgate author'.[3]

Fifth Monarchy rhetoric stressed the international aspects of the English Revolution, which to all states not free should climacteric be. England was 'a theatre', Spittlehouse said, 'to act a precedent of what [God] intends to do to all the nations'.[4] Many proclaimed the impending downfall of monarchy all over Europe, though this was not an exclusively Fifth Monarchist idea. Rogers told Cromwell to consider peace with the Dutch only if they would unite with England 'against Antichrist, Rome, prelates'.[5] The venom of Fifth Monarchists against the protestant Dutch republic is difficult to explain except in terms of the economic interests of London artisans and workers in the clothing and leather industries. The ostensible reason given for hostility to the Netherlands—that they had given financial support to Charles I during the civil war[6]—seems an inadequate reason for singling out the Dutch: Catholic powers and Denmark had done the same. Dutch economic competition seems a better explanation. In 1659 Feake, anxious perhaps to win the support of the Army leaders, instanced 'the work of justice in Ireland, ... prospering under the standard of the interest of Christ' and the Dutch war as evidences of divine favour.[7] His pamphlet helps to explain how millenarianism could be transmuted into an ideology of nationalist commercial expansion, whose target was no longer Rome but more economically interesting areas like the West Indies.[8]

II

In 1657, and again in 1661, there were small risings in London of plebeian radical Fifth Monarchists, led by Thomas Venner. They were revolts of desperation, with no positive backing from Fifth-Monarchist preachers or from Fifth Monarchists in the Army. Each of these revolts produced a manifesto which is interesting for our purposes because it gets down to

---

[1] Capp, op. cit., p. 177.
[2] E. Rogers, op. cit., p. 54.
[3] Ibid., p. 322.
[4] Spittlehouse, *The first Addresses to ... the Lord General* (1653), p. 5.
[5] E. Rogers, op. cit., pp. 54, 84–6; Capp, op. cit., pp. 53, 151–5; my *Puritanism and Revolution*, pp. 133–4.
[6] Feake, *A Beam of Light*, pp. 42–4; cf. Capp, op. cit., p. 148, and Chapter 4, *passim*.
[7] *A Beam of Light*, pp. 30, 50–1.
[8] See Chapter Six, section 4, and Chapter Eight, section 2, below.

specific and detailed proposals in a way that the preachers never do. *A Standard Set Up* (1657) was signed by W. Medley, Scribe; but both this and *A Door of Hope* (1661) were probably written by Medley's father-in-law Thomas Venner, a wine-cooper who had been in New England from 1638 to 1651.[1] Like so many returned New Englanders Venner came back to a country of which he had high hopes. His followers in 1657 were described as 'mean fellows of no note', 'inconsiderable and indeed despicable' in quality as in numbers.[2]

In content *A Standard Set Up* is strikingly similar to other radical manifestos. Behind the rhetoric about the coming reign of King Jesus are an analysis and a programme which consciously try to unite the radicals ('laying aside all particular opinions and matters of difference, as we have done ours').[3] The title-page claims to show how 'saints and men as men' will benefit from 'the deliverance of the true church out of Babylon and all confusion' and the setting up of 'the most righteous and free commonwealth state'. It will lead to 'the restitution of all things'.

Before the Revolution, the tract begins, 'the Lord's own people in these three nations were in a very low condition', persecuted by prelates, tyrannized over by the King 'in their estates and liberties, robbed and spoiled of their common rights and privileges, and their representatives deprived of their law-making power and subjected to the negative voice of a single person'. 'A perfect yoke of bondage was upon the bodies and consciences of men'. Then 'the Lord by his wise providence raised up an instrument to work deliverance and salvation from the hands of their common enemy.... About the midst of the war ... the Lord winnowed the forces of this nation' and put them 'into the hands of men of other principles than those engaged at first.... He raised up a poor contemptible company', and this Army issued the Declaration of June 1647: 'we were no mere mercenary army....'[4]

Power was 'given into the hands of this professing, victorious, overcoming Army', which never lost a battle after it was new-modelled. Their work 'was generally owned and acknowledged as the Cause of God', and in its Declaration of 1650 in Scotland this Army proclaimed Jesus Christ to be their King.[5] In July 1653 the Lord 'gave the military

---

[1] Capp, op. cit., p. 267. William Aspinwall was also a returned New Englander.

[2] *Thurloe State Papers*, VI, pp. 184–5.

[3] *A Standard Set Up* (1657), pp. 11, 25.

[4] Ibid., p. 1. Professor Woolrych points out to me that these sentences are adapted from Cromwell's speech to Barebone's Parliament on 2 July 1653 (Abbott, op. cit., III, p. 53).

[5] *A Standard Set Up*, pp. 2–3, quoting the Army's *Remonstrance* of 16 November 1648. See pp. 105–6 below.

and so the civil power ... into the hands of saints.' But Oliver Cromwell 'apostatized from his professions and avowed principles' and usurped the power which should have been Christ's and the saints'. His rule 'doth exceed ... the rage, oppression and treason of the late King'.[1] Such high treason against God justified revolt to restore the rights of the saints and of the people.[2]

The programme which *A Standard Set Up* then put forward was remarkably secular. A 'representative of the whole body of the saints', a better Barebone's Parliament, was to be created, to exercise sovereignty for one year. At the end of the year 'the Lord's freemen', the saints, would elect another annual sovereign assembly, and so from year to year. As under the triennial Act of 1641, 'the people' would act from below if they were not called upon from above.[3] First place in the manifesto was given to the administration of justice, which on the Leveller model was to be decentralized. There were to be monthly town courts and quarterly county courts, with appeals upward, ultimately to the representative assembly. Judges of these courts would be appointed (presumably by the saints) but were to have assistants 'chosen by the freemen'. Every man should plead his own cause, without an attorney. Complete equality before the law was to be established, and men as men (i.e. not only the saints) should enjoy their estates, liberties and privileges. So 'the poor, the needy, the afflicted' would be 'revived by the constant administration of justice'.[4]

Religious intolerance would be ended; so would arbitrary imprisonment, conscription for the armed forces, the excise, and any assessments or taxes upon the people, 'but by their common consent and according to our law'.[5] 'All oppressions and grievances in the tenure of lands, copyhold and customary, heriots, fines, amercements, perquisites and profits of courts, customs, services etc.' would be 'abrogated and clean removed'. So would tithes, though impropriators would receive compensation.[6] 'The baits they lay to catch men with', Thurloe observed, 'are taking away taxes, customs, excise and tithes.'[7]

As a result of the reforms listed in *A Standard Set Up*, its authors

---

[1] *A Standard Set Up*, pp. 4, 6–7.
[2] Ibid., p. 9.
[3] Ibid., pp. 16–19.
[4] Ibid., pp. 17–19, 15.
[5] Ibid., pp. 19–20. It is not quite clear how this consent was to be expressed.
[6] Ibid., pp. 20–1.
[7] *Thurloe State Papers*, VI, p. 185.

hoped, the consequences of the Fall of Man 'shall be in a great measure done away', so that all saints 'may be delivered into the glorious liberties of the Sons of God'.[1] The pamphlet called 'upon all the Lord's people' and 'everyone that professeth the name of God that are yet in Babylon' to sink their differences and join the rebels so that 'the righteous judgements and vengeance of the Lord may be executed . . . by the hands of the saints unto whom God hath given the honour, . . . that the glad tidings of the Everlasting Gospel . . . may be borne . . . to every kindred, tongue and people and nation'.[2]

A Standard Set Up was clear about the privileges of the saints, less so about the relationship between 'the Lord's freemen' and 'the people'. Venner had had experience of life in New England, which was ruled by those who regarded themselves as visible saints.[3] *A Door of Hope* in 1661, appealing to all who 'own at least the negative part of our Cause', referred to 'our birthrights' and tried to bridge the gap between godly and people by a hope that all would become saints in the millennium. It also insisted, disarmingly, that 'whatsoever can be named of a common or public good we mean by the kingdom of Christ.'[4] *A Door of Hope*, like the Levellers, like Hugh Peter, like Harrington, attacked primogeniture, which increased inequalities among men.[5] Thieves should not be executed but set to work till they had compensated their victims: the law of debt should be reformed. *A Door of Hope* also promised to democratize the government of towns and gilds, to conserve timber and to impose a complete ban on the export of unwrought leather, of fuller's earth (used by clothiers) and other industrial raw materials.[6] All this made fairly clear the constituency to which appeal was being made. It was not a totally other-worldly appeal.

A Standard Set Up had talked in very general terms of extending Christ's power 'to the ends of the earth'.[7] The authors of *A Door of Hope* were alarmed by the predominance of the 'old accursed popish party' at the court of Charles II, no less an 'enemy, a rebel and a traitor to Christ' than Oliver Cromwell. They called for an aggressive anti-Catholic foreign policy. 'When the Lord shall have driven forth our enemies here

---

[1] *A Standard Set Up*, pp. 21, 24.
[2] Ibid., pp. 11–12, 25–6. For the Everlasting Gospel see p. 303 below.
[3] Capp, op. cit., p. 139.
[4] *A Door of Hope*, pp. 7, 11.
[5] See p. 200 below. Cf. H. Peter, *Good Work for a Good Magistrate* (1651), p. 31; D. Veall, *The Popular Movement for Law Reform, 1640–1660* (Oxford UP, 1970), pp. 217–19.
[6] *A Door of Hope*, pp. 5, 10; cf. Capp., op. cit., Chapters 4 and 6.
[7] *A Standard Set Up*, pp. 14–15.

in these nations', they would 'go on to France, Spain, Germany and Rome'.[1] We shall encounter many of these themes in writings of Quakers in the 1650s.[2] They perhaps loomed larger in the minds of Fifth Monarchists as prospects at home grew blacker. Feake in 1659 seems to have hoped by this sort of appeal to win the support of Army leaders.[3]

Venner's revolt of 1661 took several days to suppress, despite the small numbers involved. A contemporary letter describes how none of the captives 'will confess anything concerning their complices, crying they will not betray the servants of the Lord Jesus to the kings of the earth'.[4] Wither, who like Ludlow was not unsympathetic towards the rebels, seized the occasion to warn the government that if so small a body of dedicated men could terrorize London, what might not 'the desperation of so many hundred thousands ... amount unto?' What 'if the whole body of God's elect in these nations ... should engage all together as one man in his Cause'?[5] But God's elect had never been united even in the 1650s; and now they were hopelessly divided and demoralized. Fifth Monarchism as a revolutionary creed was dead.

III

After the restoration Fifth Monarchists were the victims of especially severe repression. Their movement—if there ever was anything as organized as that—was decimated in 1660–1. They were silenced by the censorship, and their ranks were penetrated by spies.[6] Some Fifth Monarchists participated in the Northern Plot of 1663;[7] otherwise they were politically inactive after Venner's second defeat in 1661. Vavasor Powell still believed the Fifth Monarchy was imminent, but meanwhile he urged passive acceptance of the restoration and opposed plots. 'It is a great piece of prudence in evil times to be silent,' he said. This did not prevent him spending most of the 1660s in jail. In *A Word in Season* he, like Milton, attempted to justify God's ways to men. Necessary punishment had been imposed for sins of omission and commission: 'how miserably did most men forsake their principles.' But God will

---

[1] *A Door of Hope*, pp. 3–4, 6–7; cf. Capp, op. cit., pp. 151–4.
[2] See esp. Edward Byllynge's *A Mite of Affection*, quoted on p. 137 below.
[3] See p. 62 above.
[4] *Extracts from State Papers Relating to Friends*, ed. N. Penney (1913), p. 125.
[5] Wither, *Fides-Anglicana* (1661), pp. 21–5, in *Miscellaneous Works*, V.
[6] Capp, op. cit., pp. 197, 205.
[7] Ibid., p. 210.

ultimately work all for the best. Meanwhile his servants should not emigrate, and should not desire deliverance before the time appointed. The poor and humble, Powell believed, would stand up to persecution best.[1] He published a pamphlet making conventional religious objections to bishops, put *The Lamentations of Jeremiah* into metre, and occupied himself with a biblical concordance. He died in 1670 'in the assured faith and hope of the resurrection of that Cause that he had so done and suffered for'.[2] Jessey, more active than some with louder mouths, almost certainly had a hand in the publication of *Annus Mirabilis*, a collection of portents and prodigies showing God's disapproval of the restoration and still holding out hope. 'Certainly there is some great thing at the birth.... We know not in what hour our Lord will come.'[3] Dryden's poem with the same title argued that the portents showed divine approval.[4] Jessey was imprisoned for a year, and died shortly after his release, allegedly encouraging a Fifth-Monarchist revolt on his deathbed.[5] Powell and Jessey happen to be the only leaders about whose views after 1660 anything can be ascertained. But what was there for any of them to say?

One reason, though no doubt not the chief one, for the rapid disappearance of Fifth Monarchism as an organized political movement was the fact that many of its leaders died or were silenced. John Rogers (born *c*.1627) was the only leading Fifth Monarchist who could be regarded as a young man. (We must remember this when we see Cromwell treating him as a naughty boy in 1655.) Carew, Feake, Harrison, Jessey, Tillinghast, were all over 30 when civil war broke out in 1642; the date of birth of Aspinwall, Simpson and Spittlehouse is unknown. Even Vavasor Powell was ten years older than Rogers. Tillinghast died in 1655, John Pendarves in 1656, Spittlehouse in 1659.[6] Harrison and Carew were executed in 1660. John Simpson, who had renounced violence after a period in jail from 1654 to 1656, died in 1662. Aspinwall disappears after 1662. Jessey died in 1663. Robert Overton was in prison 1654–9, 1660–1 and 1663–8, when he died. John Rogers, in jail 1654–7 and 1658, fled to the Netherlands in 1660. When he returned it

---

[1] *A Word in Season*, pp. 1–54, 85–6, in *The Bird in the Cage*; cf. T. Richards, *Religious Developments in Wales (1654–1662)* (1923), pp. 239–40.
[2] [Anon.], *The Life and Death of Mr Vavasor Powell* (1671), Sig. A 4v.
[3] Ibid., Sig. A, p. 54.
[4] See Michael McKeon, *Politics and Poetry in Restoration England: The Case of Dryden's 'Annus Mirabilis'* (Harvard UP, 1975), *passim*.
[5] White, 'Henry Jessey', pp. 109–10.
[6] The whole of this paragraph draws on Capp's Appendix I.

was with a medical degree, and he practised physic henceforth—
peacefully, so far as we know.[1] John Canne was in the Netherlands by
1664, and died there three years later. Feake, who seemed all along the
most determined of the Fifth Monarchists, was in and out of prison as an
itinerant preacher after the restoration;[2] but in 1664 he gave a bond to be
of good behaviour, and appears to have been in no further political
trouble. He died in or after 1682. William Medley had been imprisoned
for two years after the revolt of 1657; he took no part in the rising of
1661, after which Venner was executed. In the 1670s, however, Medley
was one of the most active Dutch agents in London, in contact with
William Howard.[3]

It is a sad story of effective political repression against a movement
which had almost certainly lost all its vitality by 1660. We shall see later
how a similar mortality among early Quaker leaders—on average much
younger than the Fifth Monarchist leaders—facilitated George Fox's
control over the Society of Friends.[4] But there was no longer a society of
Fifth Monarchists for anyone to control.

Millenarianism did not die with the Fifth Monarchist movement. What
died was any idea of human political action to establish the rule of the
saints. Indeed the very idea of an earthly rule of the saints was
discredited. Milton continued to believe in it, but he put no dates to its
coming. Richard Baxter followed Foxe in assigning it to the past,
inaugurated by Constantine.[5] Men like John Evelyn, Bishop Lloyd, not
to mention Sir Isaac Newton, continued to discuss a possible future
millennium, as an academic not a political issue.[6] The ideas of the radicals
could hardly have been more conspicuously reversed.

---

[1] Cf. Stubbe, p. 265 below.
[2] E. Rogers, op. cit., p. 328.
[3] Haley, *William of Orange and the English Opposition*, pp. 54–6, 174, and *passim*. For Howard see pp. 35–6 above.
[4] See p. 166 below. For the youthfulness of many of the leading figures in the Revolution, see *WTUD*, pp. 188–90, 366.
[5] Lamont, *Baxter*, p. 305 and *passim*.
[6] C. Webster, *From Paracelsus to Newton: Magic and the Making of Modern Science* (Cambridge UP, 1982), p. 68.

2 Regicides

I

Those—regicides and others—who were victims of exemplary punishment after 1660 had to face defeat in its harshest form. The regicides as a group were socially inferior to those who had dominated politics before 1640. Although initial nominations for the court which tried Charles I included many from leading landed families, 'the men of solidly established rank and status ... drew back.'[1] Of the fifty-nine men who signed the death warrant in 1649, forty-three were MPs.[2] Of these forty-three, twenty-six had been elected as 'Recruiters', to replace members who had died or had defected to the royalists. The rest were mostly Army officers or others who had come into prominence by services to the Parliamentarian Cause during the civil war. Many recruiters similarly owed their election to service either in the Army or on local committees: most were either younger sons, or came from families not normally represented in Parliament. Their relative social obscurity is illustrated by the fact that *DNB* frequently gives no date for the birth of those regicides whom it includes.

Six signatories of the death warrant were executed in 1660—John Carew, Gregory Clement, Thomas Harrison, John Jones, Thomas Scott, Adrian Scroope, together with Colonels Axtell and Hacker, John Cook and Hugh Peter. Two years later George Downing lured three regicides home from the Netherlands—John Barkstead, Miles Corbet and John Okey—and they too were executed.

Among those executed, only John Carew, son of Sir Richard Carew of Antony, Cornwall, came of a major landed family. Miles Corbet—elected for Great Yarmouth in 1640—was a younger son. Thomas Harrison, recruiter, was the son of a grazier and butcher who had been four times mayor of Newcastle-under-Lyme; the son had been a solicitor's clerk. Thomas Scott, another recruiter, was variously described as son of a London brewer or of a Yorkshire country

[1] D. Underdown, *Pride's Purge: Politics in the Puritan Revolution* (Oxford UP, 1971), pp. 187–9. This conclusion is not seriously modified by Blair Worden's criticisms in *The Rump Parliament, 1648–1653* (Cambridge UP, 1974), p. 55.

[2] A. W. McIntosh, 'The Numbers of the English Regicides', *History*, 220 (1982), pp. 195–216, argues that we should count sixty-nine rather than fifty-nine regicides. Of the additional ten, seven were MPs, three of them recruiters. The argument is not affected whichever figure we take.

gentleman; in any case his origins were relatively obscure. Gregory Clement, recruiter, was a Spanish merchant of Plymouth and London; Okey was a London ship chandler. Colonel Barkstead was the son of a London goldsmith; Colonel Axtell, of gentle family, had been apprenticed to a grocer; Adrian Scroope came of a younger branch of his family; John Cook, like the court's President, John Bradshaw, was a lawyer.

Our best evidence for the public image of the regicides comes from the speeches they made at their trial and execution; but these must be used with caution. They were published by sympathizers, naturally, but there is no reason to suppose the text has been tampered with. Yet the regicides were not free to say exactly what they liked. They were interrupted, harassed and silenced if they attempted to defend the legality or justice of the King's trial. At the scene of execution they were continually reminded of their imminent death and urged to concentrate on the condition of their souls.[1] So we have to read carefully and to distinguish indications of their political beliefs from their natural concern with establishing their personal integrity. The last words of Thomas Scott's speech were that God had engaged him 'in a Cause not to be repented of . . .'. The sheriff then interrupted him, and turned him to his prayers.[2] ('We did not assassinate, or do it in a corner,' Scott had told Parliament a year earlier. 'We did it in the face of God and of all men.')[3]

Some assertions of principle made on the scaffold were recorded only later by shocked hearers. Thus Robert South, who had formerly written panegyrics on Oliver Cromwell, tells us that he himself heard Colonel Axtell say that 'he with many more' was so convinced in the early 1640s by the sermons of Brooks, Calamy and other preachers that he 'verily believed they should have been accused of God for ever if they had not acted their part' in 'that execrable war'.[4]

Almost all the regicides expressed strong millenarian convictions. It may be that men were better able to steel themselves to commit so unprecedented an act as regicide by the belief that the kingdom of God was at hand; and this conviction may have helped them to face the

---

[1] For interruptions by the sheriff at the place of execution see [Anon.], *A Complete Collection of the Lives and Speeches of those persons lately executed* (1660), pp. 9 (Harrison), 20 (Carew), 32–4 (Cook), 87 (should be 95) (Axtell).

[2] *A Complete Collection*, pp. 59, 63–6.

[3] *Parliamentary Diary of Thomas Burton*, ed. J. T. Rutt (1828), III, pp. 109–10.

[4] Quoted by Irène Simon, *Three Restoration Divines: Barrow, South, Tillotson* (Bibliothèque de la Faculté de Philosophie et Lettres de l'Université de Liège, Fascicule CLXXXI, 1967–76), II, p. 65.

gruesome death of a traitor. Perhaps this was especially true for those of middling rank; the leading secular republicans came from established aristocratic families—Martin, Harrington, Neville, Sidney. For most of the regicides the millenarian hope was only postponed by the restoration: they did not abandon it. Many indeed had regarded the Protectorate as a defeat for God's Cause, so they were not facing a new problem in 1660. Carew and Harrison had been imprisoned in the 1650s; death was only a more extreme form of testimony to their beliefs. Harrison remained confident of the righteousness of his Cause. 'The finger of God', he declared, 'hath been amongst us of late years in the deliverance of his people from their oppressors, and in bringing to judgement those that were guilty of the precious blood of the dear servants of the Lord.' Even Parliament's enemies had been 'forced to confess that God was with us'.[1]

Justification by success should logically mean condemnation by defeat, but Harrison had no such doubts. Like Carew, he believed that he had become a Son of God.[2] God 'will never leave those that truly trust in him': 'I believe ere it be long the Lord will make it known from heaven, that there was more of God ... than men are now aware of' in the events of the Revolution.[3] 'Be not discouraged by reason of the cloud that now is upon you; for the Son will shine and God will give a testimony unto what he hath been a-doing in a short time.'[4] Carew echoed Milton and Stubbe: this Cause was 'the most noble and glorious Cause that has been agitated for God and Christ since the Apostles' times, ... being for our liberties as men and as Christians for removing all yokes and oppressions'.[5] Like Harrison, he declared that 'the Lord had justified [the Cause] in the field once already in this nation (but that is now accounted as a thing of nought) but he will again do it with a witness.... That judgement ... was at hand.'[6] Carew, like Vane, professed to be as sure of the resurrection of the Cause as of his own body.[7] The rage of this last Beast was the greater 'because his time was short'.[8] Okey said that

---

[1] *A Complete Collection*, p. 7. Harrison thought the Agreement of the People of January 1649 'put power into the hands of the men of the world, when God doth wrest it out of their hands' (*Clarke Papers*, II, p. 185). Even the Rump had been a poor second best compared with the rule of the saints.

[2] *A Complete Collection*, pp. 9, 17.

[3] Ibid., p. 9.

[4] Ibid., p. 10.

[5] Ibid., pp. 40–1. Note that the apostasy may date 'from the Apostles' time', and that its termination has *political* as well as religious consequences. Cf. pp. 319–20 below.

[6] Ibid., p. 12.

[7] Ibid., p. 13.

[8] Ludlow, *A Voyce from the Watchtower*, p. 227.

'it is a most just and glorious Cause', which 'will certainly arise'.[1]

The regicides were lucky in the time of their death: they did not have to face—as Milton, Ludlow, Stubbe and so many others had to face—the gradual recognition that defeat of the Good Old Cause was not soon to be reversed. Carew thought the execution of the regicides 'will make many hundreds more persuaded of the truth of the Cause', as well as being 'of much advantage to the Cause in foreign nations'.[2] ''Tis the duty of the Lord's people to wait patiently, and he that shall come will come, and will not tarry.' 'This blessed Cause', so far from being lost, would 'reach to the end of the earth'.[3] 'Our Cause is invincible,' John Cook thought. The opposing interest 'will not last long ... for they must receive their judgement at the bar of Christ, and we shall judge our judges'. 'Glorious times' are 'to be expected on earth'.[4] Colonel Axtell similarly believed that 'I shall do them more hurt in my death than I could do in my life.'[5] Considerations of this sort no doubt explain the deliberate refusal of Harrison, Carew and Jones to escape when they had the opportunity.[6]

Death was far more public in the seventeenth century than it is today, and the art of dying was carefully studied. Even if you died in your bed, the manner in which you died might testify to the state of your soul. If you died as martyr for a cause, you must die heroically: any weakness would reflect on the Cause itself. The courageous and serene bearing of Carew and Harrison was particularly noted. 'If I had ten thousand deaths,' Harrison declared, 'I could freely and cheerfully lay them down all to witness to this matter.'[7] Later, Sir Henry Vane (not a regicide) died 'in the certain faith and foresight that this Cause shall have its resurrection in my death'.[8] God's people were 'in a wilderness condition, crushed and subdued'; but Vane knew that God would avenge them, speedily, and hoped that his death might help.[9] He had long looked for the thousand-year rule of the saints.[10] In the year of his death Vane wrote

---

[1] H. G. Tibbutt, Colonel John Okey, 1606–1662 (Bedfordshire Historical Record Soc. Publications, XXXV, 1954), pp. 146, 150, 160.
[2] A Complete Collection, pp. 13–14.
[3] Ibid., pp. 14–15; cf. p. 22.
[4] Ibid., pp. 48, 45.
[5] Ibid., p. 82 (should be p. 90); cf. p. 84 (should be p. 92).
[6] Ibid., pp. 9, 11.
[7] Ibid., p. 8. Cf. Dr Judith Richards on the death of Charles I, cited on p. 244 below.
[8] [Anon.], The Tryal of Sir Henry Vane, Knight (1662), pp. 79–80; cf. pp. 120–1.
[9] Vane, An Epistle General to the Mystical Body of Christ on Earth, the Church Universal in Babylon (1662), pp. 2–3.
[10] Vane, The Retired Mans Meditations (1655), Chapter 26.

that the time was 'at the very door for God to take the business into his own hands ... forasmuch as the earthly [instruments] ... have proved ineffectual'.[1] Vane was thought to be 'a timorous man', the unfriendly Baxter commented; but 'the manner of his death procured him more applause than all the actions of his life.' Burnet agreed that the government lost more than it gained by Vane's death.[2]

Gregory Clement, it was observed, was silent and despondent after his condemnation, and 'spoke little at the place of execution'. 'Yet (so far as could be judged by some discerning persons that was near him)', he 'departed this life in peace'.[3] There had been reason to worry about him, for he was not a model Puritan. He had been expelled from the Rump after being found in bed with his maidservant. His signature was deleted from the death warrant as unworthy, but this did not save him in 1660. 'God hath not given me the gift of utterance,' Colonel Hacker declared at Tyburn; so he read out a paper insisting that his conscience was clear, and then asked Colonel Axtell to 'be both their mouths in praying'—which he was, at some considerable length.[4] Colonel Jones was anxious in his speech upon the ladder to explain that he had failed to defend himself at his trial only because he wanted 'to make the work as short as I could', knowing full well what the verdict would be however hard he pleaded.[5] Hugh Peter was concerned about the possibility 'that he should not go through his sufferings with courage and comfort'. He was 'unwilling to die' because he was 'somewhat unprepared'. But in fact he died courageously.[6] For similar reasons Ludlow (like Milton) discussed very seriously 'as well ... the example as precept of Christ' and other biblical models of seeking 'to save our lives to promote God's Cause ... when they can secure themselves without the use of sinful means'.[7] Ludlow in fact showed great courage in remaining for a long time in London, and appearing in the House of Commons until he was expelled.

The editor of Johnston of Wariston's speech at his execution in 1663 made clear its political importance:

---

[1] Vane, *An Epistle General*, pp. 2–3, 53.
[2] *Reliquiae Baxterianae*, p. 76; G. Burnet, *History of my own Time*, ed. O. Airy (Oxford UP 1897), I, p. 286.
[3] *A Complete Collection*, p. 73 (should be p. 81).
[4] Ibid., pp. 86 (=94), 90–6 (=98–104).
[5] Ibid., p. 71 (=79).
[6] Ibid., pp. 59, 62–3; cf. Ludlow, *Watchtower*, pp. 235, 239–40.
[7] Ludlow, op. cit., pp. 126, 305; *MER*, p. 238.

> The Lord hath a very great care of what his ... dying witnesses say.... Hence is it that some faithful dying martyrs have adventured to say much more, and been more peremptory in their encouraging the Lord's people on the scaffold than in their written discourses ere they were led from prison. He changes their premeditations when they come to the scaffold, and giveth them what is in his mind in that hour.

God 'reveals secrets to dying witnesses'.[1] The author instanced the last words of Wariston's fellow-victim, James Guthrie: '"Howbeit our cloud may be long or dark, yet I am persuaded that the Lord shall once more shine with the glorious light of the gospel upon these lands".... At that moment the rain which had previously been falling suddenly ceased and the sun broke through.'[2]

The point was made, less approvingly, by William Sedgwick, who was arguing that public executions were counter-productive:

> If the person judged stands clear in his own conscience, upon any account, and acquits himself in the face of death (when all men ordinarily yield) such have a kind of conquest and do seem to overcome the sentence, which must needs have an effect upon the people. For people do naturally mind a dying man.... In them that can die comfortably and confidently, there is a great appearance of righteous worth.[3]

What was expected of traitors in their last speeches was confession of their guilt and expressions of repentance. Why else should they be allowed to speak? The regicides upset this convention as the Marian martyrs had done, with even more devastating effects, over a century earlier.

Nor was this only the attitude of anti-government propagandists. A Parisian correspondent wrote to Henry Oldenburg at the end of October 1660: 'Everybody here admires the constancy and resolution of those men that were lately executed in England for having judged the late King.'[4] Confirmation came from Roger L'Estrange, Charles II's censor: 'Scarce any one regicide or traitor has been brought to public justice

---

[1] [Anon.], *My Lord Waristounes Speech at his Death* (1663), pp. 14, 18.
[2] Ibid., pp. 15, 19–20.
[3] W. Sedgwick, *Inquisition for the Blood of our late Sovereign* (1660), pp. 262–3.
[4] *The Correspondence of Henry Oldenburg*, ed. A. R. and M. B. Hall (Wisconsin UP, 1965–), I, p. 402.

since your Majesty's blessed return wnom either the pulpit hath not canonized for a saint or the press recommended to be a patriot and martyr.' The effect was to suggest 'that there is no justice to be found either in your cause or in your courts'.[1] L'Estrange quoted a sermon preached by Thomas Watson on the day of the execution of Miles Corbet and John Barkstead. 'The church of God appears in his Cause, and loseth blood in his quarrel. . . . Is not God upon the threshold of his temple, ready to fly? Are not the shadows of the evening stretched out? And may we not fear the sun-setting of the gospel?' But the preacher found consolation in the thought that 'the Lord may let his church be a while under hatches, to punish her security and to awaken her out of her slumbering fits; yet surely the storm will not continue long.'[2]

Cook is the most interesting regicide for our purposes, because the most articulate. He was that rare bird, a committed radical lawyer. He was counsel for Lilburne in 1646 when the latter's Star Chamber sentence of 1638 was reversed. Three years later Cook acted as counsel again for the imprisoned Lilburne, trying to get him a *habeas corpus*.[3] In August 1647 Cook had published *Redintegratio Amoris: or a Union of Hearts*, in which he echoed the Levellers and anticipated Milton in declaring that 'by nature all men are born alike free'. 'Every father', he added, 'is a king in his own family.' In this pamphlet he declared that the Army 'have been the Joshuas that have led God's people into the spiritual Canaan'. They were bound 'by the law of God to deliver God's people and this whole kingdom from oppressions both in souls and bodies'.[4] It was rather early to say such things. In the same year his *What the Independents Would Have* proclaimed Cook's sympathy with the 'comfortable' opinions of the antinomians and with the millenarians. 'Who would not be glad to see Jesus Christ?'[5] *A Vindication of the Law* in 1648 advocated significant reform in the interests of guaranteeing 'cheap property'.[6] *Unum Necessarium: Or the Poore Mans Case* of 1648 was a compassionate and

[1] R. L'Estrange, *Considerations and Proposals in Order to the Regulation of the Press* (1663), Sig. A 3.
[2] Thomas Watson, *A Word of Comfort* (1662), quoted by L'Estrange, op. cit., p. 16. Even such a relatively conservative clergyman as Henry Newcome read the speeches of the regicides (*The Diary of the Rev. Henry Newcome, 30 September 1661 to 29 September 1663*, ed. T. Heywood, Chetham Soc., 18, 1849, pp. 81, 123). For Newcome see pp. 210–11 below.
[3] Style, *Reports* (1658), p. 96.
[4] Op. cit., pp. 3, 66.
[5] Op. cit., p. 8.
[6] E. MacLysaght, *Irish Life in the Seventeenth Century* (Cork UP, 1950), pp. 417–46; cf. Cook, *Monarchy no Creature of Gods making* (1652), Sig. C 4, pp. 26–8.

forceful plea for social reform, including cheap or free medical treatment for the poor.[1] As solicitor for the Commonwealth at the King's trial Cook prepared a powerful indictment which Charles's refusal to plead prevented him from delivering: but he published it subsequently. Charles was condemned, he said, by 'the unanimous consent of all rational men in the world, written on every man's heart with the pen of a diamond in capital letters', an appeal to the law of nature which Milton was to echo.[2] Cook also anticipated Milton, Erbery, Ludlow and many others in claiming that the court which sentenced Charles 'was a resemblance and representation of the great day of judgement, when the saints shall punish kings of the earth upon the earth'.[3] Cook insisted that the King's execution was a revenge for the blood of Barrow, Greenwood, Coppinger, Burton, Prynne, Bastwick and other martyrs.[4] As Chief Justice of Munster in the 1650s Cook introduced significant reforms, reducing fees and decentralizing justice, doing his best to help poor litigants. He won the praise of Oliver Cromwell for setting 'a good precedent even to England' by ensuring that property was 'preserved at an easy and cheap rate'.[5]

John Jones, recruiter MP, was more class-conscious than most of the Army leaders, hoping to see 'all men of estates' banished from Ireland, and 'the Irish ploughman and the labourer admitted to the same immunities with the English.'[6] In Scotland he thought it was 'the interest of the Commonwealth of England to break the interest of the great men … and to settle the interests of the common people upon a different foot from the interests of their lords and masters'.[7] Thomas Scott believed that 'God governs the world, as he governs his church, by plain things and low things.… God submits all his administrations to the people.'[8] Both Scott and Jones tried to face realistically the problem of the relationship between the ruling minority and the people. Scott spoke in November 1650 of 'our new people, scarce yet proselytized'.[9] Jones a

---

[1] Op. cit., pp. 61–5.
[2] King Charls his Case (1649), p. 22; cf. Milton, CPW, IV, pp. 466–7.
[3] King Charls his Case, p. 40.
[4] Cf. Redintegratio Amoris p. 43; Monarchy no Creature of Gods making, Sig. b.
[5] E. Ludlow, Memoirs, ed. C. H. Firth (Oxford UP, 1894), I, pp. 246–7; cf. Monarchy no Creature of Gods making, Preface. Hugh Peter was in favour of local courts and law reform (Good Work for a Good Magistrate (1651) pp. 27–57, 115–17).
[6] A. H. Dodd, Studies in Stuart Wales (UP of Wales, 1952), p. 106.
[7] J. Mayer, 'Inedited Letters of Cromwell, Colonel Jones, Bradshaw and Other Regicides', Trans. Hist. Soc. of Lancashire and Cheshire, n.s., I, p. 192.
[8] Burton, Parliamentary Diary, II, pp. 389, 391.
[9] J. Nickolls. Original Letters and Papers of State (1743), p. 28.

year later was asking how one could 'persuade a people sensible of their present burdens, and not of the reasons and necessity of them, to choose those persons that laid the burdens (or their adherents) to be the next representative? ... Let the Commonwealth have some time to take root in the interests of men.'[1] 'We ... would have enfranchised the people,' Cook declared, 'if the nation had not been more delighted in servitude than in freedom.'[2]

II

Edmund Ludlow (?1617–92), one of the few genuine republicans in the Long Parliament, was absurdly young: at the age of 33 he was ruling Ireland. In 1660 he escaped to the Continent. Like other regicides whom we have considered, Ludlow held a millenarian view of the English Revolution and of the righteousness of the Good Old Cause. Like Cook and Milton, he believed that the High Court of Justice which tried Charles I resembled 'the judging of the world at the last day by the saints'.[3] But Ludlow reminded Harrison that 'the generality of the people that had engaged with us ... acted upon no higher principle than those of civil liberty' and to be governed by their own consent. Therefore 'it could not be just' to establish the rule of the saints.[4]

After 1660 Ludlow had to accept that 'this great change was brought about by the immediate hand of God.'[5] Like Milton, he held that God's people 'were full ripe for chastisement, in that they had not wisdom nor will to improve those opportunities he had put into their hands'.[6] 'The nation in general seemed not to be fitted for the glorious work which he seemed to be doing for them by the means of some of his poor people.' Divisions among God's servants were to blame, but Ludlow was confident that 'when in the furnace they are melted into one lump, they shall come forth as refined gold. But it's the Lord's pleasure they should take this turn in the wilderness, and that man may not have whereof to boast.'[7] 'It will be but a very little while before the indignation of the

---

[1] Mayer, op. cit., pp. 190–1; cf. Woolrych, *Commonwealth to Protectorate*, p. 261, quoting John Hall, *Sedition Scourg'd* (1653), pp. 3, 8. See p. 289 below.

[2] *A Complete Collection*, p. 49.

[3] *Watchtower*, p. 235.

[4] *Memoirs*, II, pp. 7–8. It is of course possible that this passage has been edited by Toland. But it fits pretty well with *Watchtower*, pp. 307–11.

[5] *Watchtower*, p. 119; cf. p. 123.

[6] Ibid., p. 248; cf. p. 287.

[7] Ibid., p. 149; cf. pp. 200, 213, 289, 298.

Lord shall cease, and his anger in the destruction of his enemies.'[1]

Ludlow had a great deal of sympathy with 'these good men' who revolted with Venner in 1661, 'being persuaded in their consciences that they had a call from the Lord thereto'. But God's people must 'be careful we make not haste in the procuring of what is in its own nature lawful (yea, most desirable)'.[2] It is the lesson which the Son of God taught in *Paradise Regained*.

In 1654 Ludlow had been attacked as an Anabaptist, a Leveller. In 1659 he was working with the republicans James Harrington and Henry Neville.[3] After the restoration Samuel Parker called him the head of a conspiracy which included Milton and Marvell.[4] Ludlow's most eloquent statement of his considered political position begins 'the Lord hath appeared in our days to do great things.... He raised up the poor, foolish, unexperienced and weak ones of the earth to confound the rich, the wise and the mighty thereof.' But divisions among God's servants frustrated divine purposes. They must learn through suffering to be 'fitted for the doing of his will, ... that by making haste we may not strengthen the hand of the enemy, nor by standing still neglect the opportunity he puts into our hands'. Hence Ludlow's metaphor of the watchtower, from which 'we may see so plainly, that when the Lord's time is come we may be up and doing, and the Lord may appear to be with us and to own us'.[5] It might be the moral of *Samson Agonistes*.

3   Sir Archibald Johnston of Wariston (?1610–63)

Wariston descended from a rich Edinburgh merchant family which had married well.[6] His first wife came of an eminent legal family. When he contemplated marrying again, after her early death, the choice lay between the daughters of three titled families. So he was extremely well-connected. He is of unique interest among those executed at the restoration because he kept a diary in which he lays bare his hopes and

---

[1] Ibid., p. 127; cf. p. 303.
[2] Ibid., p. 279; cf. pp. 240, 309.
[3] *Memoirs*, I, pp. 545–8; *State Papers Collected by Edward, Earl of Clarendon* (Oxford UP, 1786), III, p. 484; cf. p. 200 below.
[4] *Bishop Parkers History of His Own Time* (1728), pp. 7, 216, 224.
[5] *Watchtower*, pp. 309–10. Christopher Feake spoke of his prison as his watchtower in 1655 (Preface to *Mr. Tillinghasts Eight Last Sermons*, Sig. a 7v).
[6] W. Morison, *Johnston of Wariston* (Edinburgh, n.d., ?1901), pp. 14–17.

ambitions, his weaknesses and anxieties. The *Diary* reveals that he was intensely introverted. The death of his first wife prostrated him and led to scores of pages of lachrymose discussions with the Lord about the reasons for this punishment. Finally he decided that God's 'appearing wrath in my wife's death was a real love to me; ... for thereby I saw God bringing me in within the compass of the promises both of this life and of the life to come'.[1] Wariston was assured of the infallibility of his salvation 'in God's own time'.[2] 'The Lord never granted me an heart to cry but he had an ear to hear.'[3]

Accepting the covenant theology, Wariston soon came to take quite a cannily tough line with Christ. 'Show then thy satisfaction applied to me before the Father, and tell him he cannot take twice payment for one debt.... Thy credit is now engaged, let me know that thy Father denieth thee nothing.'[4] 'Remember, O Lord, thy promises whereon thou forceth thy servant to trust.'[5]

By now Wariston had found the opportunity to render valuable services 'in this great work of God in this land, which he is likely to make go from nation to nation till the Man of Sin be consumed with the breath of his mouth'.[6] He was one of the principal draftsmen of the National Covenant, and later of the Solemn League and Covenant.[7] Moderator and Clerk of the General Assembly, he sat in the Council of War and accompanied the army which invaded England in 1639. He held 'the honourablest, the happiest (albeit the heaviest) charge ever committed to creature'.[8] But God helped him, even with detailed drafting problems.[9] This enabled Wariston, on a later occasion, 'to crave an account' from God, who had overridden Wariston's own wishes and dictated his words.[10] When in 1654 he 'by prayer acquainted the Lord' with the 'necessitous and dangerous and odious' state of his affairs, he 'begged his thinking on it and looking to it': 'Oh Lord, look to my subsistence.' But Wariston was not only the recipient of God's bounty; he was also able 'to warn our Lord Jesus Christ' in April 1654 'that an enemy of his', namely

---

[1] Johnston of Wariston, *Diary* (Scottish History Soc., 1911–40), I, p. 99.
[2] Ibid., p. 101; cf. pp. 104, 287.
[3] Ibid., I, pp. 278–9.
[4] Ibid., I, pp. 222–3. For Wariston's bargains with God see also ibid., II, p. 70.
[5] Ibid., I, p. 380.
[6] Ibid., I, pp. 365, 398–9. Scotland was Israel, the chosen nation (ibid., I, p. 301).
[7] Ibid., II, p. 72.
[8] Ibid., I, pp. 280, 282, 292; cf. pp. 307, 321–3, 328–9, 347, 355, 364, 388.
[9] Ibid., I, pp. 303, 318–19, 333–4, 408; II, pp. 173, 177, 238.
[10] Ibid., II, pp. 79–80; cf. pp. 241–2.

Monck, was coming to take command in Scotland; Jesus Christ should take the necessary action.[1]

Wariston's 'happiness in the being called and guided in this work of God, ... I thought it did far exceed the very happiness of being glorified in heaven.'[2] 'I will glorify myself in thy life and calling', God told him.[3] Wariston sensibly seized the opportunity to remind God that 'I have found my estate and house perishing while the Lord bends my mind solely upon the building of his house.' 'The Lord remembered me to remember him back again', and 'insinuated to my mind that he was visibly and outwardly even to bless and prosper me in this world and to fatten my portion'.[4] But six months later Wariston had to expostulate with the Almighty again, that it was 'a great strait ... to have my estate to melt away when I expected with submission upon his promise for the increase of it'. The Lord conveniently 'forced me to ... be earnest' with him, 'in demanding the reality of those former motions of that kind'.[5]

God took full responsibility for the Scottish cause and 'made us follow his direction contrary to our former resolutions', confounding and contradicting 'all our ways and thoughts', but always to the benefit of the Scottish Kirk.[6] As early as the Scottish defeat of 1650 Wariston realized that each of the choices now available was unsatisfactory. The Scots army was right to oppose 'the errors and unjust invasion of the English', but that prevented them 'from seeing the evil of their way by conjunction with the malignant party'. On the other hand, the Kirk's alliance with malignants prevented the English from seeing 'the sin of their unjust invasion and oppression', not to mention their ungodly tolerance.[7] In 1651 Wariston was unpopular for his opposition to Charles II: he was called 'the inbringer of the sectaries'.[8] He was accused of 'taking silver for places'.[9] Worst of all, the English occupation led to the loss of his well-paid employments.[10] By 1652 his financial state was no better than it had been fifteen years earlier, despite the opportunities and rewards

---

[1] Ibid., II, pp. 287–8, 237.
[2] Ibid., I, pp. 297–8.
[3] Ibid., I, p. 301; cf. II, pp. 125–7.
[4] Ibid., I, pp. 355–8.
[5] Ibid., I, pp. 407, 357–8.
[6] Ibid., I, p. 332.
[7] Ibid., II, p. 58.
[8] Ibid., II, p. 70.
[9] Ibid., II, p. 164.
[10] Ibid., II, p. xlviii; cf. pp. 148, 194–5, 197, 200.

which had come his way in between.[1] In May 1654 he even had doubts of his salvation, 'at least for a quarter of an hour'.[2]

Wariston was assiduously wooed by the Protector.[3] In July 1657 he was reappointed Lord Clerk Register in Scotland, and joined the Protector's government in England. He became a member of Cromwell's Other House and held office in every government till the restoration. Wariston was acutely described by Broghill as a 'Fifth Monarchy Presbyterian'—theologically of the right, temperamentally of the left.[4] After Cromwell's death Wariston depicted his dilemma very clearly: the Presbyterians 'seem more to favour ordinances, but, withal, the malignants also', whom he abhorred; the Commonwealthsmen favoured more godly men, but they relied on the support of Quakers, Anabaptists and Fifth Monarchists, whom he equally abhorred because they wanted to abolish tithes.[5] 'Never was there a pack of men seen more deserted of God and emptied of wit, sense, reason, common honesty and moral trustiness nor the General Council of their officers.'[6] Earlier he had decided that Oliver Cromwell without the malignants was a lesser evil than Charles Stuart with them.[7] Now the case was less obvious. Vane and Salway actually preferred the 1649 Agreement of the People to the Covenant![8] Wariston listened sympathetically to Sir Arthur Haslerig outlining a constitution which sounds very similar to that despairingly offered by Milton in the *Ready and Easy Way*.[9]

After 1660 Wariston was therefore highly vulnerable. He had 'complied too much with the Usurper'[10] and had taken a leading part in succeeding governments of the Commonwealth. He had also long been in the black books of royalists. As early as 1639 he had argued against Charles I to his face, though twice receiving a royal command to be silent.[11] In 1646 he enraged the King again by arguing for his acceptance of the Covenant,[12] and he was equally unlucky in his relations with Charles

---

[1] Ibid., II, pp. 186–7, 282.
[2] Ibid., II, p. 244.
[3] Ibid., II, pp. 282, 220.
[4] Ibid., III, p. 28. Compare Mordaunt's description of Fleetwood as a 'Presbyterian Anabaptist' (*Clarendon State Papers*, III, p. 484).
[5] *Diary*, III, pp. 129–31, 133, 139–40.
[6] Ibid., III, p. 162.
[7] Ibid., III, pp. 91, 63.
[8] Ibid., III, p. 151.
[9] Ibid., III, p. 125.
[10] [Anon.], *The Last Discourse of the Right Honourable the Lord Waristoune* (1664), p. 6.
[11] *Diary of Sir Archibald Johnston Lord Wariston*, ed. G. M. Paul, Scottish History Soc., XXVI (Edinburgh, 1896), pp. 85–7.
[12] *Diary*, I, p. 106. He was still, however, in favour of monarchy (ibid., II, pp. 293, 298).

II in 1650–1. Wariston fled from the country at the restoration, and was condemned as a traitor *in absentia* in May 1661.[1] After a period in the Netherlands and Hamburg, he made the mistake of travelling to France to meet his wife, and was seized and extradited. He was hanged in Edinburgh in July 1663, within sight of the house which he had occupied in the days of his grandeur. He totally lost his memory and faculties in prison, allegedly because of ill-treatment. He forgot everything he was told, forgot even whether he had a wife and children or 'whether Genesis or Revelation did begin the Bible'. Yet he recovered miraculously on the scaffold, and was able to read his speech, thus giving a sore 'dash and stroke to the prelatical interest'. He saw a parallel between himself and Samson, whose strength was 'much wasted' when 'he was brought forth that they might have a day of sport of him'.[2]

So far from being ashamed that God had used him 'in the glorious and blessed work of reformation in Scotland', Wariston 'accounted it his glory'.[3] He expressed penitence only for his self-seeking. He disavowed (truthfully) any share in the King's trial, and prayed for Charles II that he might have 'good and faithful counsellors', as well as for God's 'cause, covenant, work and people' and that the Lord would 'accomplish his good work'.[4] In a last attempt to bargain with God, Wariston reminded the Lord of all the suits (about employment for his family among other things) 'which he hath at any time by his spirit moved and assisted me to make and put up according to his will'. These he left 'before the throne'.[5] His family mostly married well; but at least three of his five daughters remained politically active covenanters, and suffered for it.[6]

'Neither have I in following the Lord's work, his good work, been altogether free of self-seeking, to the grief of my own conscience.' So Wariston said on the scaffold in July 1663.[7] On the evidence of his own *Diary*, he was guilty of 'ambition and avarice', 'self-honour and profit',[8] such as Milton and many others denounced in the leading figures of the 1650s. Wariston was well aware of his weaknesses in this respect. By August 1657 he recognized that he was 'the infamy of the people', a

---

[1] Ibid., III, pp. 146–8.
[2] [Anon.] *My Lord Waristones Speech at his Death* (n.d., ?1663), pp. 11–12.
[3] *The Last Discourse*, p. 6.
[4] Ibid., p. 8.
[5] Ibid., pp. 8–9.
[6] Morison, op. cit., pp. 151–2.
[7] *The Last Discourse*, p. 5. An alternative version of the speech added that his self-seeking 'hath several ways vented to the offence both of God and man' (*My Lord Waristounes Speech*, p. 2).
[8] *Diary*, III, pp. 23–4, 39–40, 42–3, 48, 57, 69, 80, 107, 117–18, 164–6, 180. See pp. 281–2 below.

'reproach and proverb amongst our nation'.[1] 'All my destructions and dangers', he wrote, 'has ever been ... from myself.'[2] He had his own technique of rationalization, so as both to be aware of his sinfulness and to get what he wanted. This was to cast lots, thus leaving the responsibility to God. He spoke of it as God's ordinance.[3] When a decision had to be made, Wariston cast lots not once but many times. It was rather like Parliamentary procedure: first lots were cast on whether to cast lots, then on the question to be put, and then the questions were varied until a satisfactory answer came up.[4] If you cast lots a sufficient number of times, varying the questions when the right answer is not forthcoming, the odds are that in the end you will get the answer you want—whether consciously or subconsciously. Wariston's procedure may not always have been as simple as that, for he wanted to be an honest and godly man; but he usually ended with the desired decision. Sometimes of course he may have been in a state of genuine uncertainty. At best this was a formal piety, shirking the responsibility of moral choice over which Milton, Ludlow, Hutchinson and others agonized. At worst it was a way of deceiving God and himself.

No one could criticize Wariston more severely than he did himself:

> Whereas I thought I was following the call of God's Providence ... the truth is that I followed the call of Providence when it agreed with my humour and pleased my idol and seemed to tend to honour and advantage; but if that same Providence had called me to quit my better places and take me to meaner places or none at all, I had not so hastily and contentedly followed it. ... And now the Lord punishes my ambition.[5]

---

[1] Ibid., III, pp. 97, 181, 183.
[2] Ibid., III, pp. 165, 172–3.
[3] Ibid., III, pp. 125, 299. George Wither suggested electing Parliament by lot (*Salt upon Salt*, 1659, p. 43, in *Miscellaneous Works*, IV; *Furor Poeticus*, 1660, pp. 18–19, in *Miscellaneous Works*, V). Cf. Arise Evans, who wanted a King elected by lot (*A Rule from Heaven*, 1659, pp. 45–57). Fifth Monarchists attached importance to decision by lot (Capp, op. cit., p. 140).
[4] *Diary*, II, pp. 64–5, 70, 73, 75, 83, 125–6, 157, 201–2, 269, 295–7, 299; III, pp. xxxii, xlviii–ix, 45–52, 74–5, 89, 110–11, 132, 169.
[5] Ibid., III, p. 167; cf. p. 57. Samuel Butler describes 'an Hypocritical Nonconformist' who 'does not pray, but prosecute, As if he went to law, his suit' (*Genuine Remains*, ed. G. Gilfillan, Edinburgh, 1854, II, p. 185).

Chapter 4

Seekers

1 William Erbery (1604–54) in the Wilderness

William Erbery, the son of a Glamorganshire gentleman, was born four years before Milton. He graduated from Brasenose College, Oxford, in 1623. As vicar of St Mary's, Cardiff, he became the centre of a Puritan group. He got into trouble for refusing to read the Declaration of Sports, was several times cited before the High Commission, and finally was forced to resign his living and leave the diocese. From 1640 onwards he was in London, preaching against episcopacy and ceremonies. When civil war broke out he supported Parliament and was, he tells us, the first minister in Wales to be plundered by royalists.[1] He became chaplain to Skippon's London regiment—a post apparently obtained for him by Christopher Love, the Presbyterian minister who was to be executed in 1651 but who owed his conversion to Erbery whilst in Cardiff. In the Army, Thomas Edwards said, Erbery 'did broach many antinomian doctrines and other dangerous errors'. In 1645 he was in Ely, Edwards's 'island of errors and sectaries',[2] from which he conducted preaching tours. In July 1645 he was alleged to have preached general redemption: the guilt of Adam's sin should be attributed to no man.

> Within a while God would raise up apostolical men who should be extraordinary to preach the gospel; and after that shall be the fall of Rome. He spake against gathering churches, the Anabaptists' rebaptizing, and said men ought to wait for the coming of the spirit, as the Apostles did....As in the wilderness they had honey and manna but not circumcision and the passover, so now we may have many sweet things,

---

[1] *The Testimony of William Erbery* (1658), pp. 152, 313.
[2] *Gangraena*, I, pp. 77–8. For Ely see *WTUD*, p. 47.

conference and prayer, but not a ministry and sacraments. And then, after the fall of Rome, there shall be new heavens and new earth; there shall be new Jerusalem, and then the church shall be one.

Meanwhile the saints 'were all taught of God', and had no need of 'a man in black clothes' to teach them.[1]

That very fair summary of Erbery's Seeker views in *Gangraena* confirms the accuracy of the reports which Edwards printed, despite his hostile slant. The only doubtful point is the reference to the fall of Rome. Erbery was a protestant internationalist, but I suspect he may have spoken on this occasion of 'the fall of Antichrist', thinking of something nearer home than Rome. Virtually all the other statements attributed to him can be confirmed from Erbery's own writings.

We get a glimpse of Erbery, in Oxford in the winter of 1646–7. His preaching of radical views, and his opposition to the mainly Presbyterian Visitors of the university, made him very popular with rank and file soldiers.[2] The visiting ministers engaged in a series of public discussions with Erbery 'to prove that private men have no authority to preach' (Erbery had renounced 'the title though not the pay and salary of a minister', they observed). Whereupon 'the multitude of the soldiers in a violent manner' called upon the ministers 'to prove our calling'.[3]

Erbery's internationalism derives from his view of the English Revolution. Here he saw the direct intervention of God in human affairs, but he also analysed the events of the 1630s and 1640s in the sociological terms familiar to most of his contemporaries whatever their outlook—Clarendon, Baxter, Hobbes, Harrington, Winstanley and almost everybody who discussed the matter at all. What had 'spilt the King was his setting up the state of his court and courtiers, preferring none but the rich, his friends and favourites, a company of fools and flatterers, though the oppressed peeled nation were ready to perish'.[4] So there was general opposition. But when God came forth against the King and his courtiers, he worked through the saints.

Erbery had a clear idea of who the saints were. They had advanced beyond the teaching of traditional Puritans like Perkins, Preston and

---

[1] *Gangraena*, I, p. 78, II, pp. 89–90. For the wilderness see pp. 301–3 below.
[2] [F. Cheynell], *An Account Given to the Parliament By the Ministers sent by them to Oxford* (1646[–7]), p. 13; cf. *Gangraena*, III, p. 250.
[3] Cheynell, op. cit., pp. 18–22
[4] *Testimony*, p. 209.

Sibbes (though those three had pointed towards the doctrine of free grace); they had advanced beyond even Thomas and John Goodwin, Tobias Crisp and William Dell. William Sedgwick, Peter Sterry and Joshua Sprigge were the nearest to Zion, but even they had not yet come into it.[1] Before 1640 such men had been 'the weakest party for force, and fewest for numbers, two or three in a parish, persecuted by King, Lords and all the Commons, by church and commonwealth'. 'The saints of all men would not stir' till God roused them. But in 1640 ''twas not the King that called a Parliament but the saints called a Parliament to oppose an oppressing King; so 'twas not the Parliament raised an army against him, but we raised an army against an oppressing Parliament.' 'It was God raised up the saints to an army', and 'every high thing is fallen before them', even Parliament itself when it was guilty of 'strangling (by delays) the petitions of the fatherless and widows, of the poor oppressed ones'. 'The saints have seen more of God in these days than they would believe or hope for.'[2]

In 1646–7 Erbery seems to have expected Christ to rise in the saints in the near future—a view which Gerrard Winstanley was to adopt. Erbery believed that the Army was the organization of the saints for carrying out God's purposes. ''Twas not to set up an army, or arm of flesh, but to set himself up in the saints' that God had brought about 'all these wars ... and raised this Army ... I speak not now of our Army of soldiers, but of the Army of saints.'[3] 'When a corrupt Parliament oppressed the people', it was 'the spirit or power of God in his people, in City and country' (and in the Army too) 'who raised up an Army first to purge, then to dissolve them', just as Parliament had subdued the King. 'And the people had a hand in each, both Parliament and Army being the people's servants, as 'twas commonly voted.'[4] The Army had a double right to intervene in the winter of 1648–9, first 'the call of the kingdom, petitioning by several counties, and the common cry of all the oppressed in the land'; but it had also acted 'in the immediate power of God ... for all the saints, yea for all men also'. 'They are as well the Army of God as public persons, and not for a particular interest.'[5]

The Army was at its best when it acted, Erbery declared. 'But as for all

---

[1] Ibid., pp. 67–9.
[2] Ibid., pp. 26–35, 209.
[3] Ibid., pp. 26, 28–9. For Winstanley, see pp. 38–9 above.
[4] *Testimony*, pp. 206, 210. Was there a note of irony in ''twas commonly voted'?
[5] Ibid., p. 25. Milton's Samson similarly described himself as a 'public person'; it is one of many hints linking Samson with the New Model and its Engagement of 5 June 1647. See *MER* p. 436.

their public speakings, their Declarations, Protestations, Remonstrances, 'tis not worth a rush.'[1] What mattered was not overthrowing the power of King or Parliament but 'the destroying of those oppressive principles both in powers and persons, and in courts and laws'. Parliament had ignored innumerable petitions against unjust laws, against tithes. The people are not 'any ways unsettled about government, but they are unsettled about those oppressions that lie upon them'. 'Whilst we were in a way of putting down of authority we had the power of God going along with us'—'not to take away magistracy but to take away ... the oppressions of men.'[2] Like Winstanley, Erbery was aware that 'kingly power' might survive the King.[3]

Initially Erbery had great hopes of the Army-dominated Commonwealth. Under the unpurged Parliament there had been much speechifying and printing of speeches. 'But now the Commonwealth comes on, there is more of action done every day.' 'God hath so visibly appeared' in 'the present powers ... that men cannot choose but be convinced that there is yet more good to be done by them, and for us, in God's due time'.[4] 'The Lord God is coming forth in judgement to turn the earth upside down.'[5] But the honeymoon did not last. Soon Erbery decided that King and Parliament had been 'the two powers who kept the people of the Lord and the people of the land from their expected and promised freedom. For the Keepers of the Liberties of England were Keepers indeed, and of our liberties from us.'[6]

Erbery's strong interest in social reform comes out clearly in a letter which he wrote to Oliver Cromwell in July 1652. He called on the Lord General to 'break in pieces the oppressor, to ease the oppressed of their bondage, to release prisoners of their bonds and to relieve poor families with bread', and also to reduce lawyers' fees. 'Clergymen and common lawyers are the chiefest oppressors', said Erbery in words with which Winstanley would have agreed; prisoners and the poor 'are the chief among the oppressed'. Confiscated lands should be used to provide stocks for the poor. Like Milton in his sonnet to Cromwell of the same year, Erbery exclaimed 'great things hath God done by you in war, and good things men expect from you in peace.' Both expected the Lord General to abolish tithes and a state church.[7]

---

[1] *Testimony*, p. 73.
[2] Woodhouse, *Puritanism and Liberty*, pp. 171–4. For Sedgwick see p. 105 below.
[3] *Testimony*, pp. 206–7. For Winstanley see pp. 39–40 above.
[4] Ibid., pp. 73, 91.   [5] Ibid., pp. 336, 42.   [6] Ibid., p. 205.
[7] Nickolls, ed., *Original Letters and Papers of State Addressed to Oliver Cromwell*, pp. 88–9.

Elsewhere Erbery advocated steeper taxation of 'rich citizens, racking landlords ... and mighty moneyed men', to form 'a treasury for the poor'. God's 'great design' was to undo 'the mighty ones of the earth', so that 'the outward and inward man may have deliverance at last'.[1] Erbery called especially for liberation of the poor from 'the unreasonable gain of the gospel-priests', who 'take up the fifth or fourth of men's lands and labours'.[2]

Erbery's teaching included what Cheynell called the 'damnable doctrine'[3] that the fullness of the Godhead 'shall be manifested in the flesh of the saints, as in the flesh of the Son'. Indeed Christ is already here: only Antichrist denies Christ to be come in our flesh.[4] For Erbery, as for Winstanley and the Ranters, the resurrection meant the appearance of Christ in men and women.[5] 'Christians carnally conceive Christ to come in the clouds.' But in fact 'the appearing of Christ is the appearing of that great God and Saviour in the saints.... God comes when he appears in glory in us.'[6] And 'in us'—again as for Winstanley—includes women: 'all the sons and daughters of men ... may see themselves in God with Christ.'[7] 'The Son and the saints make one perfect man.' 'He that seeth himself with the Son in God, and God in him as in the Son, he shall do greater works than the Son did in the days of his flesh.'[8] Through Christ 'we can do all things, even sit in the throne of God with him, judge angels and men, yea rule the nations with a rod of iron.'[9]

'If the saints saw ... in themselves the fullness of God anointing their flesh, this would free them from great bondage to men, means and ministers. This is Babylon's destruction.'[10] Christ 'is still suffering till he shall rise in us'.[11] Then 'the embondaged saints in spiritual Babylon shall attain to the first resurrection and redemption from Antichrist's captivity.'[12] They 'shall judge the world ... not only in heavenly and spiritual things, but in the civil state also.... We wait for a new heaven

---

[1] *Testimony*, pp. 75, 59; cf. p. 124.
[2] Ibid., p. 53.
[3] Cheynell, op. cit., p. 30.
[4] *Testimony*, pp. 5, 8, 11–15.
[5] Ibid., pp. 246–7; see pp. 38–9, 43–4 above.
[6] Ibid., p. 40
[7] Ibid., p. 203. Cf. *The Religion of Gerrard Winstanley*, pp. 24–30.
[8] *Testimony*, pp. 8–9. Cf. *MER*, pp. 296–305, for Winstanley and Milton on Sonship
[9] *Testimony*, pp. 11, 15, 23, 203.
[10] Ibid., pp. 11–12, 16–17.
[11] *Nor Truth nor Error* (1646), p. 4. The words recall Pascal.
[12] *Testimony*, p. 33; cf. pp. 245–8.

and a new earth.... Not only the saints in common but the state is to act in Christ.'[1]

So the process is not yet completed. 'When God is manifested in the saints', they 'shall judge the world, that is first destroy but afterwards save and govern the world.... God comes reigning and riding on an ass, that is revealing himself in majesty and glory in the basest of men.'[2] (When James Nayler rode into Bristol on an ass in 1656, two years after Erbery's death, with Erbery's daughter strewing palms in his path and crying, 'Holy, holy, holy', one wonders whether either of them recalled that passage.) 'God in the saints shall appear as the saviour of all men; ... the saving of a particular person of a King or Parliament is but a false Christ ... in respect of the salvation of the kingdom and people.'[3] Universal redemption, Erbery thought, was 'nearest the Gospel'.[4]

Inevitably the saints are involved in politics, since God achieves his political effects through them. After the end of the civil war, 'the saints should have gone on': but they drew back. Nevertheless, 'the day of God has begun, though the saints have been and are still in confusion.' The saints 'shall no more act for themselves, but for the world also, to see how liberty may be settled in the whole earth'. 'God appearing in the saints shall punish the Kings of the earth upon the earth.'[5]

Erbery accepted the Joachite doctrine of three dispensations—of the Law, of Gospel Order, of the spirit in the latter days. Yet his view of history inclined him to pessimism, just as Milton's did. Erbery believed that apostasy had prevailed in the churches since the time of the Apostles or soon after.[6] The apostasy was confirmed by Constantine's granting political authority to the church, an antichristian authority which national churches still retained.[7] Erbery had no use at all for national churches; they were cause and consequence of the apostasy. He disliked the revised Agreement of the People which was under discussion in January 1649 mainly because it 'set up a state religion'.[8] Consequently Erbery, like Milton, did not regard the Reformation as a particularly significant turning point. Saints would be 'bewildernessed' until the third dispensation, the age of the spirit in the latter days.[9]

---

[1] Ibid., pp. 207–8.
[2] Ibid., pp. 15, 23–4; cf. p. 207.
[3] Ibid., p. 26.
[4] Ibid., pp. 59–92.
[5] Ibid., pp. 25, 30–5, 40–1, 59.
[6] Ibid., Sig. (a); cf. p. 65. Both passages are by John Webster, the editor.
[7] *Testimony*, p. 268. See pp. 297–301 below.
[8] Woodhouse, op. cit., p. 170.   [9] *Testimony*, pp. 217–52.

For Erbery popery was the first of the four Beasts in Revelation, prelacy the second, presbytery the third; the last was now with us. Prelacy reigned some seventy years, presbytery but three and a half ('the time of the Beast'): 'Independency is down in a month', 'baptized pastors in one day fly away.'[1] He denied that either the state church or the Independent and Baptist congregations were true churches. He totally rejected their doctrine, their discipline, their ceremonies and ordinances, their tithes, their preaching, their Sabbatarianism, their assurance of salvation: all were antichristian. 'Every saint is yet running about, changing their ways and gadding abroad after one of these three—money, means and self,' he wrote in 1647. Erbery renounced his orders, and declared: 'in my own sense I did not preach at all: preaching is for edification, and mine was for destruction.[2]

Erbery had a Miltonic contempt for the hireling clergy of the state church. 'How many men', he asked, 'are made poor by making a few ministers rich?' ... 'Godly ministers' were 'never more greedy of gain'.[3] He admitted that his own 'desire to be rich' had made him at first accept a public stipend from tithes. But in 1652 he renounced his salary of £100 a year as itinerant preacher under the Committee for the Propagation of the Gospel in Wales.[4] 'I do not envy your greatness, God knows,' he told the established clergy, 'but pity your goodness that is besieged with greatness and worldly glory.'[5]

Are men 'fit to be ministers of the Gospel, who think the gospel to be that which is written in the Four Evangelists' and the Epistles, which are 'but an historical relation' and 'particular letters' of special concern only to those who received them? 'Christ never preached the Gospel till after he was dead.' The letter is not the Gospel 'which the Apostles preached to the world'. 'The Gospel is a mystery.' Christ indeed was only 'a legal teacher', a 'minister of the circumcision', preaching only to the Jewish church, not to the world in general.[6]

What, Erbery asked, 'is become of those preachers that had their

---

[1] Ibid., pp. 60, 148, 336.
[2] *Nor Truth nor Error* (1646), p. 3; *Testimony*, pp. 73, 274–6, 281, 284–305, 309–12, 316, 325–7, 337; cf. Cheynell, op. cit., pp. 24–5, 30. Erbery's disciple Webster published in 1653 *The Saints Guide: or Christ the Rule and Ruler of Saints*, in which he rejected any established ministry. Mrs Attaway, Edwards tells us, likewise disclaimed taking upon herself to preach, for 'she could not be convinced that any in the world this day living has any commission to preach.' It did not stop her holding forth (*Gangraena*, I, pp. 87–8).
[3] *Testimony*, pp. 91, 197.
[4] Ibid., pp. 50–3.
[5] Ibid., p. 87.
[6] Ibid., pp. 221, 224.

orders from the bishops, and so from the Pope? There is not one to be found in the North and in Wales, they are gone to fat parsonages from whence malignants have been thrown out.' It was the saints 'who shall build these old waste places, not men in holy orders ... and not those who call themselves ministers, but those whom the people shall call ministers'.[1] Erbery soon lost his enthusiasm for the Propagators of the Gospel, and accused saints in Wales of picking and choosing their members, of giving preference to the rich.[2] Meanwhile Erbery insisted on complete religious toleration: 'to make a man an offender for a word ... this is the spirit of Antichrist.' In an interesting association of ideas he attacked those who would 'have no liberty of conscience nor liberty of trade'.[3]

Edwards had accused Erbery of denying the divinity of Christ and declaring that the texts used to establish his divinity 'were not in the Greek but put in by some who were against the Arians'.[4] When Cheynell repeated the accusation of Socinianism, Erbery protested that he had never read any Socinian writings.[5] His biographer John Webster admitted that 'the Trinity was not perfectly owned by him', and that Erbery (like Milton) rejected a 'trinity of persons',[6] since he could not find the phrase in the Bible. Erbery emphasized the humanity of Jesus, 'the weakness of Christ in his sufferings', the 'sense of sin which took on him.'[7] Erbery was alleged to have said, 'It is no such great matter to know that Christ suffered at Jerusalem, but to know that we suffer as the Son, that our sufferings are the sufferings of God, there is the mystery. I dare not say any more, for the time is not yet come to speak the truth.' It was, the Rev. Francis Cheynell reasonably observed in 1647, 'high time to call Mr Erbery to an account'.[8] This was indeed the sort of story whose circulation helped to give Erbery his reputation as an equivocator.[9]

It was not Christ's death that merited our salvation, Erbery urged: 'merit properly pre-supposeth not love. So satisfaction supposeth wrath to be pacified.' But there is nothing in Scripture about that. 'God is not to be reconciled to man but man to God.' What saves us is 'the life of Christ

---

[1] Cheynell, op. cit., pp. 13, 34.
[2] *Testimony*, pp. 147–61.
[3] Cheynell, op. cit., pp. 35–6. 'To make a man an offender for a word' echoes Winstanley.
[4] *Gangraena*, II, pp. 89–90.
[5] Cheynell, op. cit., pp. 38, 45–6; cf. *MER*, p. 293.
[6] *Testimony*, pp. 264, 278–9.
[7] Ibid., pp. 319–22.
[8] Cheynell, op. cit., p. 38; cf. pp. 47, 50–2.
[9] C. Fowler, *Daemonium Meredianum* (1655), pp. 29, 132.

in God *revealed to us by the spirit*.[1] Erbery spoke against 'the certainty and sufficiency of the Scriptures', since the text was so unreliable.[2] This line of argument was to be carried further by Walwyn, Winstanley, the Ranters, Clement Writer, Samuel Fisher and many more, just as Erbery's incipient Arianism was developed by Milton and Henry Stubbe.[3]

Erbery's pessimistic view of history tempered his optimism about the rule of the saints in the English Revolution. 'You and I,' he told the pastors of Wales, 'with all the saints this day are still in Babylon, both gathered churches and scattered saints.'[4] 'We are dry bones, very dry, not only dead but long dead, for many hundreds of years the churches have been so, ever since the Apostasy.'[5] 'There's no building of temples in Babylon.'[6] Antichrist appears most visibly in particular churches, just because they aspire to greater purity.[7]

Erbery described himself as 'bewildernessed as a wayfaring man, seeing no way of man on earth or beaten path to lead him'.[8] He hoped that the English Revolution marked the beginning of 'the coming of the spirit' and that the new Jerusalem would come on earth in 'these last days wherein the mystery of iniquity hath been most manifest'.[9] But he was not surprised that 'so many miserable creatures are in the Army, and that such base fellows, fools and knaves, join with their designs, that men in debt and discontented, yea bitter spirits, comply with the saints in setting up God and his glory in them'.[10] We are still in Babylon.

Erbery's unhappiness grew as the Commonwealth failed to usher in God's kingdom, and indeed retained a state church. In 1650–1 his disillusionment seems to have taken the form of a flirtation with the Ranters. In 1646 he had been described as the champion of the Seekers;[11] he made a Seeker of Laurence Clarkson, the future Ranter.[12] Erbery was often himself accused of having 'a ranting spirit'. His denials were half-hearted.[13] He was, he admitted, attracted by 'the holiness and

---

[1] *Testimony*, pp. 319–22: my italics. Cf. ibid., p. 73.
[2] *Gangraena*, I, p. 78.
[3] See *WTUD*, Chapter 11.
[4] *Testimony*, p. 218; cf. p. 315.
[5] Ibid., p. 231; cf. pp. 260, 277.
[6] Ibid., p. 237; cf. p. 100.
[7] Ibid., pp. 270–7.
[8] Ibid., pp. 18, 100; cf. pp. 337–8.
[9] Ibid., p. 38.
[10] Ibid., p. 80.
[11] [Anon.], *A Publike Conference Betwixt the Six Presbyterian Ministers and Some Independent Commanders Held at Oxford on Thursday November 12 1646*, p. 3.
[12] See p. 46 above.
[13] *Testimony*, pp. 47, 259.

righteousness in truth flowing from the power of God in us, which by the world hath been nicknamed with Puritanism, and in some now Ranting'. Erbery himself said things about the hypocrisy of the self-styled saints which recall Coppe and Clarkson. He argued that they were *worse* than the Ranters, lusting hypocritically after 'the wisdom, power, glory and honour of the world'.[1] Christ died for sinners as well as for saints. 'The people of God turn wicked men, that wicked men may turn to be the people of God.'[2]

Webster defended Erbery, slightly uneasily, from the charge of being 'a loose person or a Ranter'. It was easier to show that he was not loose than that he was not a Ranter. His doctrines 'concerning the restitution of all things, the liberty of the creation and saints' oneness in Christ with God' looked Ranterish.[3] Webster admitted to Erbery's 'lightness and vanity of spirit in some phrases and expressions'.[4] More accurate perhaps was the reference of an anonymous biographer to 'that innocency that appeared in M. Erbery which is rarely found in any'.[5] Erbery was said to share Hamlet's view that 'there's nothing either good or bad but thinking makes it so'; therefore the only rule was to follow one's own conscience wherever it led.[6] Given Erbery's delight in paradox, his desire to shock the respectable, and a certain coarse roughness of which he could be capable, it is easy to understand his reputation as a crypto-Ranter. In 1652 he was accused of blasphemy.[7]

In England, Erbery said, 'the wickedness of the people of God will first appear ... to all the world.' For having been 'set in power, ... every man may see the shame' if they 'prove oppressors, as former powers have been'. It was inevitable that 'seeming saints' should be corrupted by power. They were far superior to their predecessors in civil government.[8] The traditional rulers, however, were 'gentlemen born ... but when so much money comes into the hands of poor saints, oh how they hold it and hug it, and hunger after it, as dogs do for dry bones!'.[9] But 'if the people of God in power had the spirit of Jesus in them, they

---

[1] Ibid., pp. 124, 312–16, 331; cf. pp. 43–5 above.
[2] Ibid., pp. 176, 319.
[3] Ibid., pp. 258–60, 215.
[4] Ibid., p. 264.
[5] [Anon.], *A Small Mite In Memory of the late deceased ... Mr. William Erbery* (1654), Sig. A 4.
[6] Fowler, op. cit., p. 31.
[7] *The Mad Mans Plea*, pp. 1–4, 7–8; cf. *Testimony*, pp. 195–8, 275–6, for rude and crude jocularity.
[8] Ibid., pp. 167–79.
[9] Ibid., p. 87; cf. p. 90.

would find a thousand ways to ease the people, though they should part
with half of their pay.' 'In saints by calling shall the Apostasy and falling
away be first revealed to the full; there shall Antichrist be found at last, as
[Judas] in the disciples of Christ appeared first.'[1] 'The people of God are
in present power (as 'twas never before).' Yet 'the present government is
judged with so much dissembling and breach of vows.' 'I could name
godly men in the old and new-modelled Army, fallen from their first
love; ... their tears are all dried up, as withered grass and as the flower of
the field, which fades in a month.'[2]

Whilst Barebone's Parliament was sitting Erbery still hoped that 'this
land (though the house of bondage) shall one day break forth into
singing, and smile at those empty forms of religion.'[3] But it soon became
clear that England was to remain in Babylon, that Christ was not going to
rise in the saints. 'It may be other generations may see the glory talked to
be in the last times, but ... we have no hopes to enjoy it, or in this life to
be raised out of our graves.'[4] So Erbery concluded that 'the people of
God should not meddle with state matters.' When he did come to reign
Christ would put down all forms of state power—monarchy,
aristocracy, democracy.[5] The saints are beginning to reign with God,
already, but should manifest their rule not by resisting, not even by
speaking in public, but by privately reproving and rebuking the
authorities.[6] 'All powers are of God, however men come by it.'[7]

In consequence Erbery rejected Fifth Monarchist revolt: 'To shake off
the yoke before the season came was to rebel against the Lord.'[8] 'You say
that the worst of men speak well of the present government; and is it not
well? And a fair way for peace and love?'[9] 'From all God's tumbling the
earth upside down ... nothing but confusion hath appeared. What
certainty then can be expected in such changes? What order in confusion?
Yea, what truth, when God is making man a lie?'[10] 'Is not the state of
Holland and Commonwealth of Venice as much for Antichrist as the
King of France or Spain?' Erbery asked.[11] The implication that the change

---

[1] Ibid., pp. 167–73, 178–9.
[2] Ibid., pp. 175–6, 191.
[3] The Mad Mans Plea, pp. 6–7.
[4] Testimony, Sig. (a), p. 232.
[5] Ibid., pp. 184–5.
[6] Ibid., pp. 212, 214. This is a modification of Erbery's earlier practice: see pp. 86–9 above.
[7] Ibid., pp. 210–11.
[8] Ibid., pp. 109–10; cf. pp. 232, 247–8; cf. Woolrych, Commonwealth to Protectorate, p. 350.
[9] Testimony, p. 186.
[10] Ibid., p. 191.
[11] Ibid., p. 186.

from monarchy to republic in England had not produced essential improvements seems clear.

Erbery therefore, like Sedgwick, like Reeve, like Milton, accepted the rule of Oliver Cromwell. 'From the midst of saints one is risen above us.' Erbery still believed that England was the first nation 'that shall be saved from all their oppressors and oppressions'. But this would be limited to secular matters. Under Cromwell's rule, 'the ecclesiastical state is not set up with the civil power ... as formerly, and as 'tis in New England this day.'[1] For this reason, Erbery, who had earlier praised Cromwell's tolerance,[2] seems even to have been prepared to accept a Cromwellian monarchy. 'So may an honest Christian prince be as happy and honourable in a guard of redcoats as with the most gorgeous attendance ... of nobles.' It would impress 'the nations all about, to behold a man ... saving the nation under him all that needless expense ... and setting up his throne in the hearts of his people.'[3]

So ready was Erbery to acquiesce in the Protectorate that Webster felt it necessary to defend him against the charge of abandoning his ideals and complying with the Chaldeans. He insisted that Erbery was 'rather a presser forward than an apostate'.[4] 'In this darkness', Webster concluded, Erbery 'had rather sit down and wait in silence'.[5] 'I am a man in Babylon,' Erbery himself admitted, 'with all the gathered churches and scattered saints.'[6] But whatever his spiritual disappointments, in civil affairs he claimed, 'I have been ever entire to the interest of this Commonwealth.'[7]

Erbery's praise of silence anticipates the Quakers.[8] He had predicted that it would be the saints, not the established clergy, who would convert the dark corners of the land.[9] He saw confirmation of this prophecy when the Quaker 'whirlwind' came from the North, and Baptist churches multiplied in Wales and in the western parts of England and in Ireland.[10] Though he appears not to have associated himself with any sect, his daughter Dorcas became a Quaker, and he himself was accused of

---

[1] Ibid., pp. 209–11.
[2] Ibid., p. 149; cf. p. 85.
[3] Ibid., pp. 209–10.
[4] Ibid., Sig. (b), pp. 260, 265.
[5] Ibid., pp. 263–4.
[6] Ibid., p. 315.
[7] Ibid., p. 338.
[8] *Nor Truth nor Error*, p. 2.
[9] Cheynell, op. cit., pp. 13, 34. See pp. 90–1 above.
[10] *Testimony*, pp. 57, 91, 126, 135–7, 140

being 'a forerunner and preparer of the way for the Quakers'.[1] Dorcas claimed to have been raised from the dead by James Nayler; she accompanied Nayler on his entry into Bristol in 1656.[2]

Erbery's political evolution is comparable to Milton's. Both thought a state church and its clergy, supported by tithes, the main enemy of religion. Both consequently were critical of the universities which trained the clergy.[3] Both were staunch advocates of religious toleration. Erbery would have extended it to Jews and Turks; but to papists only 'when they give assurance to the state of their peaceful subjection'.[4] Both appear to have ended up members of no church at all,[5] though both were sympathetic to the Quakers.[6] Both rejected Foxe's praise of Constantine's union of church and state which had been repeated by episcopalians and Presbyterians.[7] Both expected the English Revolution to mark the beginning of the establishment of God's kingdom all over Europe.[8] Both in the 1640s shared some of the views of the Levellers, though neither went all the way with them. When in 1652 Erbery was had up before the Committee for Plundered Ministers he claimed 'all the liberties of a freeborn Englishman'.[9] Both put their faith in the Army and Oliver Cromwell, and both supported the Protectorate, though both warned England's rulers of the dangers of degeneration. Like Milton, Erbery rejected Fifth Monarchist revolt.[10]

The names of Erbery and Milton had been linked as heretics by the ministers of Sion College in December 1644.[11] They shared many heresies—unorthodoxy on the Trinity, a belief that God was in the saints, that the saints would rule and judge the earth, that believers could become Sons of God on earth.[12] Both held that hell was an internal rather

---

[1] Ralph Farmer, *Sathan Inthron'd in his Chair of Pestilence* (1657), p. 17.

[2] J. Nayler, *A Collection of Sundry Books*, I, p. liv; G. F. Nuttall, *James Nayler: a Fresh Approach* (1954), p. 14. There was also a London Quaker called Mary Erbery (*An Abstract of the Sufferings of the People Call'd Quakers*, I (1733), p. 165). Cf. K. L. Carroll, 'Martha Simmonds, a Quaker Enigma', *JFHS*, 53 (1972), p. 45.

[3] *Testimony*, pp. 86, 193.

[4] Ibid., pp. 333–4. Milton similarly thought toleration for papists was a political, not a religious question (*MER*, p. 157).

[5] *Testimony*, pp. 292–3, 306–7, 312.

[6] Ibid., pp. 126, 135–6, 140.

[7] *MER*, p. 84; cf. p. 68 above.

[8] *MER*, p. 283.

[9] *Testimony*, p. 310. For Milton, see *MER*, Chapter 8.

[10] *Testimony*, pp. 149, 175–6; cf. *MER*, pp. 193–7; *PL*, v. 367–8, and *PR*, iii. 181–202.

[11] *CPW*, II, p. 800–7.

[12] *Testimony*, pp. 9, 40, 95; *The Mad Mans Plea*, pp. 8–10; Cheynell, *Truth Triumphing*, p. 5; *An Account Given*, p. 30; *WTUD*, p. 192; *MER*, pp. 299–300.

than (or as well as) an external state, and both allegorized the Scriptures.[1] Both were influenced by Boehme. Both regarded hypocrisy—especially in the saints—as the worst of vices; both held that strength came through weakness.[2] Erbery's reference to 'Nimrod, that kingly power' which 'has been from the beginning' helps us to grasp how immediately comprehensible Milton's reference to Nimrod in *Paradise Lost* would be to at least some of his readers: it was like a code.[3]

Erbery died in 1654. John Webster, his disciple and editor, lived on till 1682. In 1654 he published a pungent criticism of the universities, with proposals for radical reform. As he had anticipated, he was denounced as a Leveller in consequence. In 1658 he was arrested and his papers were seized. After that, like Walwyn and Coppe, Rogers and Stubbe, he practised medicine and 'lived a solitary and sedentary life', publishing only *Metallographia: Or an History of Metals* (1661) and *The Displaying of Supposed Witchcraft* (1677). The latter courageously defended witches against the persecution encouraged by Sir Thomas Browne and Joseph Glanvill, FRS. But Webster had adapted to the restoration sufficiently to dedicate the former work to Prince Rupert and the latter to the JPs of the West Riding of Yorkshire, who had known his 'follies and frailities'. Behaviour appropriate to Babylon, Erbery might have thought.[4]

2 William Sedgwick (?1610–?69): Rethinking in Public

I

William Sedgwick was roughly a contemporary of Milton's. Son of a Bedfordshire gentleman, he entered Pembroke College, Oxford, in 1625. From 1635 to 1644 he was rector of Farnham, Essex, though from 1641 or 1642 he lived in London. In 1642 he preached once officially to the House of Commons, and once at St Margaret's, Westminster, 'before sundry of the House of Commons'. On the latter occasion he spoke

---

[1] *Testimony*, p. 40–1; *The Mad Mans Plea*, p. 1; *WTUD*, p. 177; *MER*, p. 309.
[2] *WTUD*, pp. 192, 215, 390, 392; *MER*, p. 330.
[3] *Testimony*, p. 207. Nimrod in this role is discussed by T. R. Preston, 'Biblical Criticism, literature and the 18th-century Reader', in *Books and Their Readers in 18th-Century England*, ed. I. Rivers (Leicester UP, 1982), pp. 109–10. The marginal notes to the Geneva Bible, the Dutch annotations to the Bible, and characters so varied as Thomas Müntzer, John Rogers, Christopher Feake and Edward Benlowes all use Nimrod as a symbol of tyranny and oppression. 'Kingly power', which survived the monarchy, was one of Winstanley's key concepts (*The Law of Freedom*, pp. 113–15, 165–6, 196–204, and *passim*).
[4] For John Webster see C. Webster, *From Paracelsus to Newton*, pp. 71, 96–7.

strongly in favour of ecclesiastical discipline, which 'we have not yet had leave to talk of'. He recognized the objection that 'episcopal government suits best with a monarchy, and that which men would ground upon the Word is dangerous to monarchies.' Was ever prince, he retorted, 'molested in his government by the disciplinaries?' The arguments against discipline were 'political', its opponents were 'but weak in divine things'. 'Set up this wall of discipline and it will keep out Antichristian errors.'[1] Sedgwick's concern with discipline at this date recalls Milton; but Sedgwick, like Milton, was no Presbyterian.

In *Zions Deliverance and her Friends Duty*, a fast sermon preached before the House of Commons on 29 June 1642, just before the outbreak of civil war, Sedgwick uttered a stirring call against defeatism, to action. There are 'hopeful signs' that 'the day of the church's redemption draws nigh'.[2] In *Scripture a Perfect Rule for Church-Government* he had explained 'variety of opinions' and divisions by 'the darkness that we have been kept in [by the bishops]. When we have more light and may see each other's faces and thoughts, we doubt not but we shall convert quickly'.[3] In another Miltonic passage in *Zions Deliverance* Sedgwick argued that it was not the spreading of the light of preaching that caused divisions: 'the present distractions and mistakes are because it is but half day, the mist is not quite dispelled.... Let light scatter, and it will pull down the kingdom of darkness.'[4] 'God seldom doth great things without great commotions.'[5]

Prelacy, Sedgwick suggested in *Zions Deliverance*, was 'the throne of the Beast'.[6] His words were strong. 'If you find anything that may exalt his [God's] majesty ... though it lie under mountains of kingdoms, you shall thresh them to dust: though it be buried under nations and empires, customs, antiquities, he will drive the nations asunder, scatter the everlasting hills. Nothing shall stand in his way.'[7] Above all we must be active in prayer. 'The Lord is at the call of his people's prayers.... Let us resolve to lay hold on God, to wrestle with him, and not to let him go till he hath given us the blessing.'[8] Sedgwick insisted that God must be

---

[1] Sedgwick, *Scripture a Perfect Rule for Church-Government* (1643), pp. 23, 35–6. Mary Queen of Scots presumably felt 'molested in her government by the disciplinaries'. So did James VI.

[2] Op. cit., Sig. A 2, p. 52.

[3] Op. cit., pp. 22, 37. Milton similarly denounced the bishops who first 'put out the people's eyes' and then blamed them for being unable to see (*CPW*, I, pp. 932–3).

[4] *Zions Deliverance*, pp. 50–1.

[5] Ibid., p. 10.   [6] Ibid., p. 26.   [7] Ibid., p. 39.

[8] Ibid., pp. 28–9; cf. Cromwell's letter to the Speaker on the fall of Bristol in 1645 (Abbott, *Writings and Speeches of Oliver Cromwell*, I, p. 377). It was against this activist attitude that Clarkson's doctrine that God takes no notice was protesting. See pp. 48–9 above.

called to account. 'Where is thy promise in which thou causedst me to
trust?' he asked, in words reminiscent of Wariston. 'God himself hath
warranted and allowed boldness in prayer, nay impudence.'[1] The only
note of caution Sedgwick strikes is prophetic: MPs must not seek
themselves: self-interest will lead to divisions. 'You and Cause and
kingdom and all will down and perish if self-ends bias you.'[2]

When war broke out, Sedgwick became chaplain to Sir William
Constable's regiment. Sir William had a long opposition record. He had
been involved in Essex's revolt as long ago as 1601; he refused to
contribute to the forced loan in 1627 and lived to be a regicide. From 1644
to 1649 Sedgwick was a preacher at Ely Cathedral and chaplain to the
garrison.[3] His preaching made him famous as the 'apostle to the Isle of
Ely'. In 1645 Erbery and Sedgwick convinced Laurence Clarkson that
since the death of the last Apostles there had been no true baptism.[4]

In 1647, on the strength of the words of an Ely prophetess, Sedgwick
made the mistake of predicting that Christ would come to judgement
within a fortnight.[5] The name 'Doomsday Sedgwick' stuck. In 1647
Sedgwick was associated with the Levellers, and enthusiastic about the
Army's intervention in politics. He was the more upset by the failure to
preserve Army unity after the Putney Debates of October–November
1647. For this failure he blamed the generals: they were capable only of
fighting.

In 1648 Sedgwick published *Some Flashes of Lightnings of the Sonne of
Man*, a collection of sermons. 'This is the time', he announced, 'of the
Lord's reign and of England's rejoicing.... The kingdom of God must
be established in this earth.... The kingdom of God is within you, in
every one of you ... It is breaking forth in every man. God is lifting
himself up in the saints.'[6] 'The Lord counts himself not to have a
kingdom till we have it with him.'[7] 'The fullness of God, ... all the
power, all the excellency of God', is 'with us and in us'. He will shine
forth 'in those that are the lowest of the people.... They had thought

---

[1] Ibid., p. 33; *Zions Deliverance*, p. 41; cf. p. 46, and Wariston, pp. 79–80, 82 above. In *The
Spirituall Madman* (1648), Sedgwick spoke of 'the power that saints have in Christ to
command God in prayer' (p. 5).

[2] *Zions Deliverance*, pp. 36–8.

[3] I owe this information to Anne Laurence, 'Parliamentarian Army Chaplains, 1642–1651'
(unpubl. D. Phil. thesis, University of Oxford, 1982).

[4] Clarkson, *The Lost sheep Found*, p. 19.

[5] *Clarke Papers*, ed. C. H. Firth, I (Camden Soc., 1891), p. 4.

[6] *Some Flashes of Lightnings*, pp. 5, 11, 15, 42–4; cf. *Mr William Sedgwicks Letter to His
Excellency Thomas Lord Fairfax* (1649), Sig. A 2v.

[7] *Some Flashes*, p. 9; cf. pp. 87–8.

they had some knowledge and acquaintance of God, but now they see they know nothing', that 'they are in a wilderness, in a desolate, barren estate.'[1]

'Christ is weakness as well as strength, darkness as well as light, evil as well as good.... If ye cannot see him in wicked men as well as good men, in his death as well as his resurrection, ... ye do not see him at all.'[2] The paradoxes become more and more extreme. 'The disciples of God shall not enjoy Christ till they have rejected him.... Christ will say, ... I will save none but those that shall kill me.'[3] 'We think that Assemblies and Parliaments and Synods and Councils of great men should give glory to God. No, none at all; they give glory to themselves and to the God of this world. The root and foundation of the glory of God is lost and undone man.'[4] 'Kings, nobles, great ones, ... are but his [Christ's] stewards. .. Satan and wicked men have reigned long, but they shall reign no longer.'[5]

In the same year Sedgwick published *The Leaves of the Tree of Life, for the Healing of the Nations*. 'Do you not know that the saints shall judge the world?' he asked on the title-page. Describing England as the chosen nation, Sedgwick attempted to mediate between royalists and Parliamentarians. He accepted that the two sides in the civil war had divided along class lines. Nobility and gentry, 'whose honour is predominate over their reason and religion', supported the King. The Parliamentarians were men 'of a lower state, men of industry and labour, that love freedom and to be something themselves', 'exercising their own reasons in religion, ... men whose consciences are their own'.[6]

But by 1648 MPs had degenerated. They were men of corrupt and loose lives, wielding arbitrary power, who 'have grossly disowned the people of England' and had become the 'scorn and contempt of the meanest people'.[7] So both sides were guilty,[8] as were the clergy. The Army too had degenerated since 1647, not living up to its early promise.[9] It was now interested in sordid things like arrears of pay: 'Money and a

---

[1] Ibid., pp. 56, 66, 90, 96, 110, 274. For the wilderness, cf. pp. 301–2 below.
[2] Ibid., p. 86.
[3] Ibid., pp. 112–15. For Ranter paradoxes see pp. 43, 49 above.
[4] Ibid., pp. 259, 261–2. Cf. Erbery, pp. 88–90 above.
[5] Ibid., pp. 274–6; cf. p. 279.
[6] *The Leaves*, pp. 2–3, 9. Part of this pamphlet was published as *The Spirituall Madman* (1648).
[7] Ibid., pp. 20, 24, 28.
[8] Ibid., Chapters 3 and 4, esp. pp. 29–31.
[9] Ibid., Chapters 8 and 9.

Saviour cannot subsist together.'[1] With Sedgwick's reaction we may compare Henry Pinnell's in December 1647. The 'Army, which was once so beautiful and lovely in mine eye, is now become most black and ugly, God having made me ashamed of my fleshly confidence therein'.[2] Sedgwick declared that Leveller criticisms of the Army Grandees were justified; 'God is in these Levellers certainly, casting his mountains into the depths of the seas.' 'The eternal love is the Leveller.'[3] 'The Son of God ... with violence wrests from his Father favours for himself and his people.'[4]

But self-love and self-preservation influenced the Levellers too. The hostility of King and Parliament, Cavaliers and Roundheads, draws 'long furrows upon the back of Christ'.[5] With naive optimism Sedgwick called on all to return to God, who henceforth would reign in and by Charles I. The King had been levelled to his people by his sufferings and humiliations, and, 'we have now a King in whom we can confide.' 'A new King and a new Parliament' will find themselves in perfect union.[6] The clergy will learn tolerance. The Army's swords must be employed 'in service against strangers': 'we shall find enemies abroad.'[7]

Like Erbery, Sedgwick seems to have had hopes of the Ranters. They 'shall swear ... the spirit filling every oath with truth.... You shall eat and drink merrily ... and in it be filled with the Spirit of the Lord.'[8] 'We see the Lord' in London, 'in thy grossest filth', in the City's class conflicts. 'In thy engrossing the riches of the kingdom into thee, thou art a shadow of Christ, who treasures up wealth and riches of glory in the City of God for us.'[9]

In this euphoric mood Sedgwick was profoundly shocked by the Army Remonstrance of 16 November 1648, presented to the House of Commons four days later.[10] The General Council of Officers, failing to share Sedgwick's conviction that suffering must have purified the King,

---

[1] *The Spirituall Madman*, pp. 1–3; cf. *Letter to ... Fairfax*, Sig. A 2v–3.
[2] H. Pinnell, *A Word of Prophecy concerning The Parliament, Generall and the Army* (1648), pp. 2–10; cf. pp. 17, 74.
[3] *The Leaves*, Chapter 10 and p. 101. Winstanley called Christ 'the Head Leveller' (*The Law of Freedom*, pp. 204, 223, 242).
[4] *The Spirituall Madman*, p. 5.
[5] *The Leaves*, pp. 63–8.
[6] *The Leaves*, pp. 71–4, 102; *The Spirituall Madman*, p. 11.
[7] *The Leaves*, Chapter 19; *The Spirituall Madman*, pp. 3–4
[8] *The Leaves*, pp. 117–18.
[9] *The Spirituall Madman*, p. 5.
[10] *A Remonstrance of His Excellency Thomas Lord Fairfax ... and of the Generall Counsell Held at St. Albans the 16 of November, 1648*. Drafted by Ireton.

declared against any treaty with him, since he could not be trusted. They called for 'exemplary justice' upon 'the principal author and some prime instruments of our late wars', and for a dissolution of Parliament followed by regular Parliaments elected on a redistributed franchise. The Remonstrance insisted, with a threat of military intervention, that the Commons should abandon all other business to concentrate on these matters. When nothing happened, the Army marched on London on 2 December and Pride's Purge followed on the 6th.

Sedgwick reacted immediately to this sudden violent intervention. The Army was driving 'furiously over the neck of King and Parliament', and was missing a great chance to reunite the country.[1] He was especially incensed by what he saw as the generals' attempt to have it both ways. If they claimed to be the people of God, acting on 'an extraordinary call', then it was their duty to 'trample upon all authorities that stand up against that justice of God that acts you'. But then it was sheer hypocrisy to talk of their 'tender regard to the privileges and freedom of Parliament'. 'The privilege of Parliament is a poor, corrupted thing to that extraordinary providence of God that goes with you.... These spider-webs of privilege and freedom of Parliament' were 'gone and lost long ago'. What had the people of God to do with arguments drawn from contract, moral justice, or from 'that law of nature which teaches men to save themselves'?[2] The generals were no better than the royalists and the MPs.[3]

If the Army was not acting for God, Sedgwick argued, then in human terms there was something to be said for allowing Parliament to treat with the King. Men wanted peace, established religion, freedom of trade, under the King, 'according to their honest and known laws'. The Army's continued existence was ruining the people by taxes and free quarter.[4] It was humbug for the generals to claim that they wanted the rule of the people: 'not one of an hundred will own what you set down as the public interest. ... Should you not rather propose that all power and dominion and reign should be given to the Lord?'[5] 'You are indeed saints by intention,' Sedgwick admitted, but 'you are not dead to the world.' The generals acted 'by the strength of man', and were motivated by 'pride, self-love, contention for the world'. 'Till you lay down this fleshly war

---

[1] *Justice upon the Armie Remonstrance* (1649), Sig. A2.
[2] Ibid., pp. 49, 43, 36.
[3] Ibid., pp. 1–4, 16–21, 36, 43, 49–52.
[4] Ibid., pp. 16, 21.
[5] Ibid., pp. 8–10.

with others, and begin that spiritual war with Antichrist, malignants, etc., in your own hearts, you will never have peace.'[1] It was their own sense of guilt that made them 'seek for satisfaction for blood'.[2] The cause they now proclaimed was very different from what had been fought for: they had opposed the rule of the people when the Levellers called for it.[3] But Sedgwick too had a personal grievance against the Army, and was perhaps himself motivated by *amour propre*. 'God hath declared, you know, rich mercy for the King and his party in my book called *The leaves of the tree of Life*.'[4] The prophet had been scorned, after he had 'deeply engaged himself concerning ... the safe return of the King and his posterity to their glory and greatness': the words are from an anonymous pamphlet attacking Sedgwick.[5]

Indeed Sedgwick did become a little maudlin about Charles. 'I confess his sufferings make me a royalist, that never cared for him.'[6] His 'government (though full of weakness) was far better than those that succeeded him'.[7] 'You thrive and increase in wealth, honour, live better now than ever, are lords where you come', whilst the King is in misery: of course it is difficult for him to yield.[8] The analysis of the Army leaders is acute: that of the King bore no relation to reality whatsoever.

Sedgwick pushed his analysis back. 'When we began the war there was this in our minds, that the King and his party were wicked men, and not ... fit for their places and power they had; and that we were saints, godly.' Place and power 'did properly belong to us.... Though we complain of the King's obstinacy, really we have been always glad of it, because it led to his destruction and consequently to our advantage.'[9] 'There's no kind of men can be such complete new knaves as a Jesuit, a Pharisee, an old well-studied professor of religion.'[10] The Army had taken to the sword, and had been corrupted by the sword. 'Destruction you practise, 'tis your work; ... you cannot see beyond it.'[11]

Sedgwick's pamphlet shocked many of his former associates. Thomas

---

[1] Ibid., pp. 1, 12–14, 47.
[2] Ibid., p. 17.
[3] Ibid., p. 22.
[4] Ibid., p. 18.
[5] Eleutherius Philodemius, *The Armies Vindication in reply to Mr. William Sedgwick* (1649), pp. 1–2; cf. T. Collier, *A Vindication of the Army-Remonstrance* (1649), Sig. 4.
[6] Sedgwick, *Justice*, p. 31.
[7] Ibid., p. 41.
[8] Ibid., pp. 45, 20.
[9] Ibid., p. 23.
[10] Ibid., p. 37.
[11] Ibid., Sig. A 3; cf. pp. 12, 21, 51–2.

Collier accused him of opposing the work of the great Jehovah in the nation. Should the Army have sat down in silence and left all to God?[1] The charge of instability seemed to be justified when within a matter of months Sedgwick reversed his position. He published *A Second View of the Army Remonstrance, Or Justice done to the Armie*. Even in his earlier pamphlet he had assured Fairfax and the Council of Officers: 'Your eternal state is sure, 'tis your present wanderings that are here condemned.'[2] The *Remonstrance*, Sedgwick blandly said in his second pamphlet, 'was a mixed thing of good and evil'. 'The Lord was in it, but hid under so much filth that we could not discern him.' In dedicating *A Second View* to Fairfax and his Council of War Sedgwick told them: 'having cast you into the fire and taken away your dross, we shall hold you forth with a beautiful stamp of the majesty of God upon you.'[3]

Sedgwick seems to have been overwhelmed by the sheer magnitude of the events of December 1648 and January 1649, in which he could not but see the hand of God. He admired the audacity and confidence of the men responsible for them. He was struck by God's use of 'the basest, mean and common sort of men' to 'set the bottom upon the top'.[4] He now comprehended God's purposes better, and therefore the justification for the Army's action. In 1642 Parliament had appealed to the people to judge between it and the King, and erected another power, the Army. By so doing it transferred power from itself to the people in the Army. Parliament had failed to go 'downright to the root of the matter'. It fussed about privilege and prerogative, but failed to provide 'a proper remedy for the huge bulk of wickedness that hath gotten into this kingdom'. It had effectively abdicated when it 'made the Army the Lord's protector of themselves and of the right and interest of England'.[5]

The Army's miscarriage and weakness 'cannot obliterate' the good that is in them. 'An army is a singular ordinance of God appointed for special purposes', as all history shows.[6] Moreover, 'this Army is truly the people of the kingdom, ... men of the common and ordinary rank of people, most of them of trades and husbandry (with a small mixture of gentry) which are the body and strength of the kingdom, in which the common interest most lies.' They are the people 'not in a gross heap or a dull heavy

---

[1] Collier, op. cit., Sig. A 2, pp. 5, 18, 23; cf. Eleutherius Philodemius, op. cit., pp. 1–2.
[2] *Justice*, Sig. A 2–2v.
[3] *A Second View*, Sig. A 2, p. 1.
[4] Ibid., p. 4.
[5] Ibid., pp. 5–7, 9–10.
[6] Ibid., pp. 12–15.

body but in a selected choice way'. The interest of the people now lies in the Army as completely as ever it did in King or Parliament; and this fact will be 'a guide to lead the Army into the ways of common good'.[1] (Rather as the King's sufferings led him to repent!) The Army is our only guarantee of security, for England has 'become a wilderness, the pale of civil power being broke down and men let loose to furious and beastly lusts'. But God 'is upon motion, marching us out of Egyptian darkness and bondage into a Canaan of rest and happiness'.[2]

The Army must see its role in this grand perspective. 'Only this can justify you: honest intentions and good meanings are rotten rags, and too narrow to cover your nakedness.... The Lord Jehovah is your covering.' Marvell had a similar sense of God's inscrutable purposes in the 'Horatian Ode': Cromwell was 'the force of angry heaven's flame'. 'The Lord is with you,' Sedgwick assured the Army, 'in perfect union and communion.... Is there infirmity in you? 'Tis in him as 'tis in you, a clog, a burden, an enemy hated.... The kingdom is so with you, the Lord's people, as it shall never be taken from you.... Spread your arms to receive the whole nation.'[3]

Yet the people are perplexed and in darkness. If the Army puts on 'the goodness, power and wisdom of God ... all people will flow unto it for help'. The 'presence of God will burn up all those low and base spirits that are amongst you, covetousness, pride, self-love'.[4] Above all, Sedgwick insisted, the Army must proclaim its divine role uncompromisingly. It is 'superior to King, Parliament and all'. So far the Army has 'darkly and by twilight' stolen this position by its actions. 'Your halting in this point is very dishonourable and unsatisfactory'—the humbug of claiming to be the servants of Parliament when in fact you are its masters, of patching and bodging, purging some MPs and leaving 'others that are unfit to govern'. You must 'shake yourselves from the dust of formal relations to other powers that are ground to powder by the justice of God, [who] hath sought you out ... when you were in a wilderness and not knowing whither to go.... You are not forsaken, nor left to your own ways, wills or counsel, but taken into the nearest union with the power, wisdom and glory of God.'[5]

The Declaration of Musselburgh, published during the invasion of

---

[1] Ibid., pp. 6, 11, 13; cf. p. 289 below.
[2] Ibid. p. 15.
[3] Ibid., pp. 15–18. For Marvell see pp. 243–5 below.
[4] Ibid., pp. 19–20.
[5] Ibid., pp. 22–3, 34–5.

Scotland on 1 August 1650, seemed to be living up to Sedgwick's demands. 'We are not soldiers of fortune; we are not merely the servants of men; we have ... proclaimed Jesus Christ, the King of saints, to be our king.' But it is perhaps ominous for the future that this declaration was by 'the under-officers and soldiers'; Cromwell commended it as 'plain, simple' and 'spiritual', but did not associate himself with it directly.[1]

Sedgwick's contemporaries were right to accuse him of contradicting himself. Therein lies the great interest of his two tracts. Sedgwick was unique in that he did his rethinking in public. But the rethinking was being done by a great many others, by Marvell in the 'Horatian Ode,' by Ascham, Dury, Nedham and other participants in the Engagement controversy. The enormity of the events of the winter of 1648–9 took some time to appreciate. But it was a great historical turning point, at least for those who had hitherto supported Parliament. Sedgwick's two pamphlets show a volatile mind attempting to adjust to the extraordinary events 'in these last times'.[2]

Sedgwick gave up his preachership at Ely on 29 September 1649,[3] and withdrew from active politics in the early 1650s. We can only guess at his reactions to Cromwell's expulsion of the Rump in April 1653, to Barebone's Parliament and the Protectorate. When he took up the pen again in 1656 he described himself as both offended at and an offence to those in power; he was free from all parties in the nation, no courtier, though he admitted that in the past he had been too gentle to those in authority. He appeared to confirm this by a qualified defence of the Protectorate. However corrupt the present government, it was better than our 'royalist enemies'.[4] 'The blessed Cause', however, is 'now altogether laid aside and lost'. The heavy burden of taxation is continued 'under pretence of necessity'. Cromwell's Western Design was expensive, and it was a failure.[5] His ecclesiastical policy was even worse: parishes and tithes, both popish innovations, were still kept up; the trying and ejecting of ministers was Antichristian too.[6]

---

[1] Woodhouse, *Puritanism and Liberty*, pp. 474, 478; Capp, *Fifth Monarchy Men*, pp. 54, 123. See also pp. 54–5 above.
[2] *A Second View*, p. 2. I return to this point in Chapter Ten below.
[3] *Calamy Revised*, ed. A. G. Mathews (Oxford UP, 1934), p. 432.
[4] W. S., *Animadversions upon A Letter and Paper first sent to His Highness by certain Gentlemen and others in Wales* (1656), Sig. A 2–A 2v, p. 101. The Letter was *A Word for God* from the churches in Wales.
[5] *Animadversions*, pp. 5–7. But later in the same pamphlet Sedgwick defended war against Spain (ibid., p. 90).
[6] Ibid., pp. 7–8; but contrast p. 72 concerning parishes.

Sedgwick's character sketch of Cromwell is interesting: 'Besides the dirt that malice cast upon him, and the pollution contracted from the nature of his work, which hath been destroying work ... there is personal weakness, rash passions, sudden engaging for and as sudden turning from things ... large promises to oblige parties and persons, and too short performance to give satisfaction.'[1] The Lord General should never have become Lord Protector. The Army was the 'sole and proper interest of the godly party'. Cromwell's 'way is in the wilderness, and 'tis crooked'. But 'hath not our course been so from the beginning?'[2]

The political causes of the civil war—the King's prerogative against the privileges of Parliament, disagreements about taxation and the militia—were 'but the outside of the quarrel' in which the King had the better legal case. The real cause, however, was that 'the honest or religious party were by a work of God upon them changed in their minds, and were born into another spirit by the Word of God.' Both the Protector's government and its critics were departing from this spirit.[3] The royalists had 'grown out of an old stock and root of worldly greatness ... unmovably fixed in a state of outward pomp'. The present governors 'sprang from a low and mean condition'.[4]

There was a general apostasy, not only in high places. 'We are escaped from an outward Egypt', but are still spiritually in Sodom. Only the decimation tax gave some assurance that Oliver was not looking back to Egypt.[5] We must not make an idol of Parliament: it represents the interest of the world, not of the saints. And 'We cannot in reason expect a free Parliament at this time, because the people are not fit to have a free choice of members.' 'The greater part of the nation are either malignant and opposing reform, or lately offended at it, or neutral and sottishly mindless of anything but their profit.' Honest men are divided, many fearing 'that the Anabaptist will get the upper hand and pull down both magistracy and ministry'.[6]

The saints have confused spiritual and secular matters, the kingdom of Christ with the privileges of Parliament. 'Honest men ... by spiritual birth as Christians' have 'a peculiar privilege and right of power or government'.[7] But though 'this Army and people had an absolute

---

[1] Ibid., pp. 19–26.
[2] Ibid., pp. 21–2, 39.
[3] Ibid., pp. 52–3.
[4] Ibid., pp. 56–8.
[5] Ibid., pp. 61, 64–6.
[6] Ibid., pp. 67–8.
[7] Ibid., pp. 71–2.

freedom ... to do what they would', they used it to rebuild 'what God had destroyed'.[1] They have abandoned their commission from God and have become 'an interest'.[2] The world is not yet ready for the rule of the saints, and they do not seem fit to rule. At least the present government gives peace and security to property and 'in religious relations'.[3]

Meanwhile ''tis not saint-like to complain of taxes', or to resist them. That is for 'the malignants and the poor neuter' who 'pay for our liberty'.[4] Oliver's foreign policy is achieving what 'honest people' have long wanted.[5] We must take what consolation we can, and recognize that 'a new war amongst ourselves would open a way for the common enemy to destroy both parties. ... We are indeed weary of war.'[6] Clearly much of the early optimism has gone.

I do not think Professor Pocock is quite correct to speak of Sedgwick's 'central and permanent position' as the employment of antinomian scepticism of all claims to authority in order to justify submission to whatever authority exists.[7] There was a stage at which he thought the Army *rightly* held power. But his behaviour from 1656 onwards seems to suggest that by then he had—in reaction to defeat—come round to the position which Pocock describes.

Sedgwick had contacts with more extreme radicals—Abiezer Coppe, John Reeve, James Nayler. He visited the last-named in Bridewell in 1656. There is more than a hint in Coppe's *Fiery Flying Roll* that Sedgwick was well off and might be more generous.[8] Sedgwick also helped Reeve financially, who assured him: 'we have not looked upon you as one of the tithe-mongering ministers of the nation.'[9] But Sedgwick failed to satisfy Reeve that he had 'an unquestionable assurance ... that the Most High hath anointed him' to preach. Sedgwick's replies to Reeve reveal a rather agreeably modest and tolerant scepticism and self-criticism. In 1649 he had virtually quoted *Areopagitica:* 'Truth, which is one in itself and amongst the darkness of men, is divided, cut in

---

[1] Ibid., pp. 74–6.
[2] Ibid., pp. 77–8.
[3] Ibid., pp. 82–3.
[4] Ibid., p. 87.
[5] Ibid., p. 90.
[6] Ibid., pp. 101–3.
[7] J. G. A. Pocock, 'Authority and Property: the Question of Liberal Origins', in *After the Reformation: Essays in Honor of J. H. Hexter*, ed. B. C. Malament (Manchester UP, 1980), p. 334.
[8] Coppe, *A Fiery Flying Roll*, Part II, p. 15.
[9] Reeve, *Sacred Remains*, pp. 13, 19–24, in *Works* of Reeve and Muggleton (1832), III; cf. *The World of the Muggletonians*, p. 36.

pieces and lies scattered about here and there.'[1] 'When I did speak formerly,' he told Reeve, 'I was as fully satisfied as you are now satisfied in your ministry; neither do I wholly condemn my former speaking, but have seen an evil spirit which got into it, and it was not the least evil of that spirit that I did undertake to judge all others.... I fear and tremble every time I preach.'[2] Written just after his *Animadversions upon a Letter*, this throws interesting light on the rethinking that Sedgwick was undertaking at that time.

II

After the restoration Sedgwick astonished his friends by publishing *Inquisition for the Blood of our late Soveraign* (1660) and *Animadversions Upon a Book Entituled Inquisition for the Blood of our late Soveraign* (1661). In these Sedgwick undertook a Miltonic task. *Inquisition* is a sort of allegorical prose poem, in which the fate of the English Revolution is set against biblical history; *Animadversions* is a prose analysis dealing almost solely with English events. Both Milton and Sedgwick had to face defeat, triumphant gloating by God's enemies, but worst of all, an inner uncertainty: either the Cause had been totally misconstrued, or the leaders had let it down; it could not now be rebuilt. The sneers of enemies were as nothing compared with the doubts of former friends. Had it all been a terrible mistake? To answer this question Sedgwick, like Milton, went back to the Fall of Man.

Before the Fall, Sedgwick tells us, there was no political subordination, no King or Lord but God, 'which is the principle of the Levellers and of ... the liberty of the people'. But then some men were tempted, as Adam and Eve had been, to aspire to be gods—i.e. princes—themselves, to know good and evil; and they came to think themselves fit to govern others. 'In this snare of the devil hath this whole [Parliamentarian] party been taken ... conceiving they were able by their religion and knowledge to rule over the church and state.' We can now see how pitifully mistaken they were.[3]

Cain slew Abel, 'because his own works were evil and his brother's righteous'. ('The bishops and clergy ... became barren of gifts, and still

---

[1] Sedgwick, *Justice*, p. 14.
[2] Reeve, *Sacred Remains*, pp. 5–6.
[3] *Inquisition*, pp. 12–14.

are so.')[1] 'The strictest reformed saints' were no less guilty of Cain's sin than bishops. 'The most ignorant and weak were Abel.' The saints, 'strong and high in gifts', were 'the children of pride and rebellion'.[2] 'The church casting them out for their pride and hatred of her and her ordinances, they have wandered, like Cain, from one religion to another, as vagabonds.'[3]

Sedgwick made a running application of Genesis: '*There were giants in those days*: ... 'tis force exalting itself beyond all bounds of law and goodness: a monstrous greatness, raised out of apostate religion or lawless power, might without right, like Major-Generals which oppress the poor people.' '*The Sons of God came unto the daughters of men*: here godly men went into the houses, places, titles and powers of the world.' 'Religion and preferment, preaching and Parliament-men, praying and lordliness' mingled together. They 'made famous prayers and sermons but *devoured*'.[4] 'They were raised from the dust ... because they had a work to do, and were fitted for it, blessed in it: to subdue and conquer the earth.' But 'aspiring to be gods and princes, to reform the church or to form new churches and commonwealths, for which they had no anointing or gifts', no authority from heaven, no rightful and legal authority on earth, they came to grief. The old world became 'universally and irrecoverably corrupt'.[5] Hence the Flood.

Noah's three sons correspond to the three estates: Shem the nobility, Japhet the freemen or gentlemen, Ham ('which signifies black') servants and peasants. These three are 'the original and fundamental matter of a commonwealth, from a root of divine wisdom'. In the old world before the Flood, men might talk of levelling and common freedom. But now such ideas are 'ignorant, absurd and unrighteous'. 'The firm foundations of the earth, upon which the whole frame of nature and all human society stand' is Shem, Japhet and Ham. 'This chain of reason leads us directly to his Majesty's late restoration.'[6]

Charles 'rises from the root of Noah ... with the full consent and desire of the people into absoluteness without requiring conditions'.[7] His recall by Parliament had been a sort of atonement and reconciliation. He would therefore be very ill-advised to flout his people by resorting to the

---

[1] Ibid., p. 34.
[2] Ibid., pp. 23–7
[3] Ibid., p. 35.
[4] Ibid., pp. 41–2.
[5] Ibid., pp. 48, 30–2.
[6] Ibid., pp. 58–63.
[7] Ibid., pp. 149–50.

methods of continental absolutist rule.[1] The original overthrow of monarchy had been 'for sin' and was 'just from the Lord'. The restoration was 'a miracle', owing nothing to 'righteousness in the [royalist] party', for they remained unreformed. But even regicide had been 'the act not of a person but of a people or body'. On grounds of justice and prudence alike the regicides should not be judged and condemned in a human court. 'Outward punishments confirm and spread spirits and principles, if they have any appearance of reason or religion in them.'[2]

Sedgwick's main object throughout the tract was to induce a sense of sin and humility in his former comrades, to convince them of their arrogance and self-righteousness.[3] From being 'a scattered, despised and contemptible people' they had acquired 'houses, greatness and dignity in the nation. But at best thou wert but dust, a confused heap of thoughts tumbled together'; 'and therefore to dust thou must go'. Their divisions had made them 'crumble into faction and confusion', till at last they were 'turned out of your honours, power, riches and possessions, into the same ground out of which you were taken, your families and trades.... No more saints, no more anointed with the spirit of God, but ... like other men, earthly men: as proud, covetous, selfish, weak and corrupt as others.'[4] Why could they not admit 'that they have believed a lie, and advanced that to be the absolute perfect Law of God to all men which proves not to be so?' They 'did judge the church and the ministry to be Antichristian, and the nation and magistracy Babylonish, and themselves the only church'. When they failed to convince, they tried to achieve their ends by violence, by persecution. But 'he that condemns, hates and cries out "Antichrist", he is Antichrist.'[5]

If he really expected to convince the saints, Sedgwick was soon disillusioned. The anonymous *Inquisition for the Blood of our late Soveraign*, he admitted, gave 'great offence', especially to Independents and sectaries. In 1661 Sedgwick tried to explain 'the obscurity of the former book which made it so liable to mistakes'. His worst misfortune, he thought, was his isolation and diffidence, which had caused him to delay publication. 'The book came too late'—though 'twelve years since

---

[1] Ibid., pp. 109, 73.
[2] Ibid., pp. 2, 69, 93–112, 120–1, 143–6.
[3] Ibid., p. 16. Contrast Milton, who thought that men had sinned against the Cause, never that the Cause itself was sinful.
[4] Ibid., pp. 15–16.
[5] Ibid., pp. 24, 101.

I writ and published the same things.' By the time it appeared, 'all parties were so enraged and distracted' that they could not pay proper attention to its arguments.[1] But his ideas had been changing very rapidly. 'There is a continual spring and growth of light in my mind, which makes me distaste this day what I wrote two or three days since.'[2] But if he condemned others, he had 'first suffered that judgement myself' in his own spirit. 'I have gone as far in the way of separation from the Church of England as most men.' Yet 'my mind is now and hath long been enlarged to own and embrace the Church of England'—a decision he took 'when episcopacy was at lowest' and to which he had stuck ever since.[3] The anger that *Inquisition* had aroused was part of 'a foolish and desperate opposing the present Providence and power'. 'You think I am turned courtier; the court thinks I am still a fanatic.' To pluck up 'these principles that lie deep and secret is I know terrible'. From his own experience Sedgwick was aware that 'it seems to threaten the rooting out of religion and godliness itself.'[4]

He reverted to his biblical analogies. 'We were called out at first, not by officers from God, but by part of that we call Egypt or the world, by the Parliament.... We drove Pharaoh and the Egyptians out of Egypt, and kept Egypt for ourselves.' So far from leading Israel into Canaan, we have ourselves become trapped in Egyptian darkness.[5] 'Doth it need to be said, This is Babel?'[6]

Before the civil war 'the church and kingdom of England stood in a dark, fleshly and corrupt state', and its governors 'had sinned against God'. Therefore God 'called you forth for the executing of his judgements upon them.'[7] But the historical role of the Parliamentarians was 'only to destroy, subdue and punish the church and kingdom.... For this work they were anointed and sanctified.' So were 'Cyrus and his Medes, Isaiah XIII. 3.'[8] But being good at fighting and killing was no qualification for rebuilding after the work of destruction. They had no 'rule to act by' and yet rushed in 'without a rule, ... drunk with the wine of your own gifts and success'. Action *per se* was inadequate: what was lacking, in modern parlance, was a set of coherent principles.[9]

---

[1] *Inquisition*, p. 34; *Animadversions Upon a Book Entituled Inquisition for the Blood of our late Soveraign* (1661), Sig. A 4v–5, pp. 4, 10, 13–16, 22, 30; cf. pp. 138, 171. 'Twelve years since' must refer to one or both of his pamphlets upon the Army Remonstrance.
[2] *Animadversions*, p. 31.
[3] Ibid., p. 291.
[4] Ibid., pp. 51–2.   [5] Ibid., pp. 53–9, 88–90, 100.
[6] Ibid., pp. 110–11.   [7] Ibid., p. 131.   [8] Ibid., p. 60.   [9] Ibid., pp. 102–8.

'An army is a harsh, cruel, worldly, brutal, self-seeking power. While it stood it was a burden to all but those that received pay in it or by it.' Its supporters were corrupted 'into gross covetousness, ambition and self-seeking, ... lies and delusions'. 'They dressed up the carcasses of King, Lords and Commons in a Protector, an Other House and Commons: and had more stability than in any of their inventions beside.' But then 'from corruption they fell into divisions, jealousies, persecuting others and one another.' 'The ancient government of the nation was suppressed by force; if it had been by light and reason, that light that removed one would have showed us a better.'[1]

The use of violence had distorted the Cause from the start. The Parliamentarians had learnt lordliness from the Cavaliers: now 'they ride upon you as you rode upon them.'[2] 'Why should there be such unwillingness to bury' the Cause? 'It hath had its time, done its work, fulfilled its ministry.' 'While you thought to reform the world, you were defeated by it.' Now God 'hath laid you aside, as unworthy of, and false to, the work of reformation which you professed'.[3]

Sedgwick was impressed by the fact that 'the whole magistracy and ministry of the nation, the King, nobles and gentry, with many thousands of oppressed people' had risen up 'against you in all the power and strength of the nation'.[4] You 'are but a small part of the nation, it may be a tenth', even if 'a more active, vigilant, more spirited part'. You can never hold power except by force.[5] 'You are but men and may err', even though 'you be much better than others.'[6] The ease with which the traditional rulers resumed their dominant positions seemed like a natural process; and any such process must be at least approved by God. Since the royalists were manifestly morally inferior, at least to what the Parliamentarians had been in their prime, God could only have intended their victory as a punishment for sin.[7] 'They who refuse to bear the cross must become crucifiers of others.' Those who will not endure persecution will persecute. '*He became poor that he might make others rich*: you have made others poor that you may be rich.'[8] 'Now you have

---

[1] Ibid., pp. 60–5, 121, 138.
[2] Ibid., pp. 81–2; cf. p. 157.
[3] Ibid., pp. 63–71; cf. p. 175, and p. 126 below.
[4] Ibid., p. 74; cf. pp. 110, 113, 273.
[5] Ibid., p. 195.
[6] Ibid., p. 87.
[7] This point was echoed by Penington and Quakers; see pp. 110–11 above, pp. 126, 137, 152–3 below.
[8] *Animadversions*, pp. 95–6.

lost both your Cause and your religion, retaining only the form or carcasses of both.'[1] We should 'go back and repent of all these years' work', insofar as 'it was our work, and therein justify both the righteousness of God in his works and our honesty and innocence in serving of him'.[2]

The fact that there had been 'a spiritual Antichrist' within the supporters of the Cause 'from the beginning of your work' should lead you to 'consider the possibility that there is something of Christ in your adversaries'.[3] 'Their religion is corrupt ... clothed with outward pomp and worldly honours'; it was 'given by blind superstitious people'. Yours is 'corrupted with the worst kind of corruption, malice and hypocrisy'; it was 'taken by force of arms'. If 'their religion is not according to Scripture, nor is any form of religion now in the nation'. 'We have multiplied notions and opinions, but have decayed both in innocency and love.' 'Zeal for God and his Cause' is now the devil's main fort. 'You may therefore seek a kingdom for yourselves', but not for God.[4] God 'is already upon the throne, judging you.... You can give him no kingdom; you may acknowledge the kingdom he hath.'[5]

So Sedgwick tried to preach tolerance and humility to both sides. Both must abandon their principles, or rather their prejudiced opinions.[6] 'There can be no peace but in that love which can bear with that which to him doth not appear to be God's mind.'[7] 'God hath brought me down, and made me taste death again and again, because he will not endure me to stand or to minister before his throne, till I can bear and forgive all the folly and sin of those to whom I minister.'[8] We have asked for liberty only for ourselves,[9] but 'the first step into freedom is out of ourselves.' 'Good intentions will not avail in a man's own soul, much less in a nation.' 'Would you think to beat this freedom into the nation by force?'[10]

His remedy for England was liberty of conscience for all, including papists. 'Outward punishments ... cannot heal the understanding, but they may and do harden the heart', as well as being bad for those who

---

[1] Ibid., p. 141.
[2] Ibid., pp. 246–7.
[3] Ibid., pp. 150–1.
[4] Ibid., pp. 156, 160–1, 163, 167.
[5] Ibid., pp. 171–2.
[6] Ibid., pp. 75–6.
[7] Ibid., p. 166.
[8] Ibid., pp. 172–5.
[9] Ibid., pp. 189–90, 192.
[10] Ibid., pp. 193–4, 196.

inflict them.[1] Much harm has been done by the 'absurd opinions' and 'loose practices' which liberty of conscience brought forth. Nevertheless, religious toleration is 'a thing of national and rational equity', it is less dangerous to the government than repression, and Charles II has promised it.[2] The execution of the regicides, contrary to Sedgwick's advice, had only 'revived a zeal, confidence and boasting of their cause'.[3]

Sedgwick, like Fox after 1661, came to reject all political action. 'Many are wholly taken off from war by the great experience we have had of the beastly deceits, the horrible cruelty and corruption that hath attended it.' They would rather suffer than seek deliverance by war.[4] Revolt would be both 'irrational and unsafe'—an argument which Commonwealth propagandists had used against royalists in the early 1650s.[5] 'The great Providence' of Charles II's restoration 'hath eaten up all your lesser Providences' and 'directs you to agree with his majesty'.[6]

But Sedgwick realized that it took two to end a quarrel, and he pointed out that England was now a very different place from what it had been fifty or a hundred years before. The minds of men have been raised 'to a greater height of reason, religion and resolution'. Ordinary remedies will not cure new and extraordinary diseases.[7] The government must recognize that there are 'two opposite parties in the nation', both 'firmly rooted in the earth and in heaven'.[8]

Sedgwick was not unreasonably denounced as a renegade for writing these books, not least because he published the first anonymously. But the idea that he was an irresponsible weathercock—which is also suggested by his tracts on the *Army Remonstrance*—a self-seeking turncoat or a consistent antinomian are all inadequate explanations, I think. Clearly Sedgwick had a volatile, unstable temperament; and as a successful topical preacher he felt it his duty to pronounce on public affairs without prudentially considering the possible consequences. Antichrist's servants were prudent in a worldly sense, not God's. Access to print in the 1640s and 1650s was novel and exciting. But certain consistencies can be pointed out.

First, Sedgwick had a deep sense of the significance of the English

---

[1] Ibid., pp. 200–1, 205–8, 252, 265.
[2] Ibid., pp. 215–16, 265.
[3] Ibid., p. 257.
[4] Ibid., pp. 225, 248–9.
[5] Ibid., pp. 273–4.
[6] Ibid., p. 293.
[7] Ibid., p. 261.
[8] Ibid., pp. 276–7, 281–2, 285–6.

Revolution. He never doubted that its achievements were a demonstration of the power of Providence. For this reason he had supported Parliament in the civil war, for this reason he changed his mind about the Army in 1649; and he retained this sense in the very different circumstances of 1660–1. God gives power to whom he pleases and may achieve his ends through wicked persons employing abominable means. Christians should acknowledge the work of God's hand, even though clouded with the darkness of the human means.[1] Secondly, Sedgwick gradually came to appreciate the strength of the traditional social order and the traditional constitution. His first reaction to the *Army Remonstrance* was that the generals had light-heartedly challenged this and so were riding for a fall. He changed his mind when he was intoxicated by the success of the republic. But the events of the later 1650s revived his awareness of the power of inertia in the old constitution and social order. Sedgwick did not abandon his belief in the divine and historical significance of the Revolution, but he realized that the impetus, the divine afflatus, which had seemed to revive in 1648–9, had not survived the light of common day. Sedgwick was not rejecting the achievements of the 1640s when he called on the godly party to repent of *all* their actions; he still believed that God had used the wicked to achieve his purposes then, as he was using the wicked restored royalists in the 1660s. In this ultimately Calvinist attitude Sedgwick parted company with Milton and is far closer in outlook to the French Huguenot poet D'Aubigné.[2]

Many factors caused this shift of emphasis in the 1650s. Milton, Erbery and others thought that first the Rumpers and then the generals had betrayed their ideals through avarice and ambition.[3] Sedgwick differed from most radicals in that he did not—with Milton—hold that the men had been unworthy of the Cause; he was led to ask whether the fault had not been endemic in the Cause from the start, as a modern communist might ask whether Stalinism was Stalin's fault or whether its roots lay in Lenin's Bolshevism. Sedgwick concluded that the Cause—though good in its consequences—had been managed by sinful men all along.

In the 1650s the writings especially of Marchamont Nedham, but also of most of the participants in the Engagement controversy, including Hobbes, had publicized the view that governments exist only to give

---

[1] *Animadversions upon a Letter* (1656), p. 81.
[2] Judith Sproxton, 'D'Aubigné, Milton and the Scourge of Sin', *Journal of European Studies*, XI (1981).
[3] See pp. 281–2 below.

security, that it is otiose to ask whether a given government is legitimate
or illegitimate. If it adequately performs this task of protection, that is all
that subjects have any right to ask.[1] Sedgwick's providential view of
history prepared him to accept sweeping changes; but he was not, I
think, a cynic like Nedham (if Nedham was). More important was his
sense of sin: all rulers are wicked, but so long as they hold power they are
approved by God: therefore we must accept them. It was an old
combination of ideas, but it acquired new and more immediate force in
the post-revolutionary era. It contributed to the pacifism and withdrawal
from politics of Muggletonians, Quakers and others.

What remains impressive is Sedgwick's power and passion, his deep (if
incompletely successful) desire not to deceive himself, and his total
inability to assess critically whatever strong emotion seized him at the
moment—his confidence in God and the Parliamentarian Cause in the
1640s, the sudden revelation in December 1648 that the Army was not
composed only of saints, and the swift return of confidence in them a few
months later, an overwhelming sense of the power of traditional society
and the traditional constitution in 1660. Intellectually I think Sedgwick
always believed monarchy to be the best form of government. We are apt
to smile when Ireton or Cromwell say that if they were convinced that
the Lord had rejected monarchy, then they would reject it too;[2] but I
think that is exactly what happened to Sedgwick in the second half of
1649. He allowed his awe at God's providential actings to overcome his
traditional convictions and prejudices. Perhaps Cromwell, Ireton and
many others were having the same experience at the same period?

What adds pungency to Sedgwick's accusations against the saints,
though he rarely admits it, is that he is in effect attacking himself among
the 'saints'. *He* had been intoxicated by the Army's victory in the civil
war, and again by its intervention in politics in 1648–9. He is therefore
expiating for himself as well as attacking others when he reminds them of
their human frailty. Again we may ask whether Milton had similar
feelings about his own even more committed role as official propagandist
for the Commonwealth. And we may admire the many shrewd insights
into the behaviour of others which Sedgwick's self-criticism gave him.

---

[1] I have benefited from discussing this point with Judith Richards.
[2] Woodhouse, *Puritanism and Liberty*, pp. 8–9, 17, 23, 49–50, 103–7, and *passim*; cf. John
Morrill, 'King Oliver', in *Cromwelliana* (1981–2), pp. 20–5.

3   Isaac Penington (1616–79): From Ranter to Quaker

Isaac Penington's father was sheriff of London in 1638, and MP for the
City in the Short and Long Parliaments. His influence in the capital
proved invaluable to Pym and his party. Isaac Penington senior became
Lord Mayor in 1642, an election which the King refused to recognize. He
was a friend of Milton and of John Goodwin, whose church he attended.
He was one of the judges at Charles I's trial, but refused to sign the death
warrant. In 1660 he surrendered on the indemnity, but was tried and
convicted as a regicide. He died in prison in December 1660.

Isaac Penington the younger was dissatisfied with his father's Calvinist
Independency, and after a long period of doubt and heart-searching
ultimately became a Quaker, in 1657 or 1658. A pretty stiff exchange of
letters with his father ensued, in which the son was brutally frank in his
criticisms.[1] After the restoration the younger Isaac suffered many
periods of imprisonment, some of them instigated by his neighbour the
Earl of Bridgwater (the elder brother in Milton's *Comus*), who resented
Penington's failure to remove his hat in his presence.[2] Penington's
stepdaughter married William Penn, another son of a prominent Puritan
revolutionary who reacted against his father's religion. It would be
interesting to consider Quakerism as a revolt of teenage boys against their
parents (not apparently of girls).[3]

The younger Penington's most interesting works were written
between 1648 and 1656, when his ideas seem to have had much in
common with those of William Erbery. In 1650 he declared 'never was I
perfectly at enmity with anything but folly'. It was not just sin that he
disliked but the *foolishness* of sin. But now he had been 'so tossed and
tumbled, melted and new-moulded' that he began 'to prefer folly at my
heart above wisdom'. 'In this state of folly I find a new state of things
springing up in me.'[4] God 'hath often preferred folly to bring wisdom
down'. He 'may be about the same work again, in a way as uncouth,
strange, unexpected, yea impossible to the present wise men as those

---

[1] Maria Webb, *The Penns and Peningtons of the Seventeenth Century* (1867), pp. 76–82, 87.
[2] Isaac Penington, *Works* (3rd edn., 1784), I, pp. xlviii–ix.
[3] Cf. the rejection of Edward Burrough by his family (p. 143 below), and Thomas Ellwood's
monumental rows with his father.
[4] Penington, *Light or Darkness* (1650), Sig. A 2–A 2v. See *WTUD*, Chapter 13, for folly; and
pp. 93–4 above for Erbery.

ways he formerly picked out still were to the wisest in their generations'.[1]

Penington was both terrified and attracted by the arbitrary omnipotence of God.

> He that bringeth both the perfect and the wicked upon the stage may turn either of them off from the stage when he will. There is no more to hinder him from destroying the perfect than there is to hinder him from destroying the wicked.... God is Lord of all, and has the dispose of all, and ... has the power of life and death in his own hands.... Perfect and wicked are both of the same lump, only differently clothed to act their several parts, which when they have done, their clothes must be taken off, and they turned back into the lump again. There is nothing durable but *the eternal state of things*. Now therefore hath God treasured up destructions for all dispensations, because it is suitable for all dispensations. It is as fit for the King to be stripped of his gorgeous apparel when the play is done, as the beggar of his rags.[2]

Isaac Penington's title, *Light or Darkness*, and his emphasis on being a fool for Christ, recalls the Ranters as well as Erbery. Lodowick Muggleton later referred to this as a period when Penington 'was upon the ranting principle'.[3] And indeed Penington had to explain his use of the phrase 'pure sporting with sin'.

> To the creature [he explained], in the present state of the creature, under the present law of the creature, according to the judgement of the eye of the creature, everything is unlovely; and he that sees them not to be so, falls short of perfection of the creaturely eye. But come deeper, beyond this state, beneath this Law; look with a true eye, and then you shall find all this unloveliness pass away, and an excellency appear, that the creature could never so much as imagine or dream of. And now come back with this eye into the present state of all things, and behold them through the true glass, and you shall see them all new here also, and as far differing from what you did or could take them to be in your creaturely apprehension.[4]

---

[1] *Light or Darkness*, Sig. A 4; cf. Penington, *A Warning of Love from the Bowels of Life* (1660), p. 8.

[2] *Light or Darkness*, pp. 7–9.

[3] L. Muggleton, *A Looking-Glasse for George Fox* (1668), p. 56. See also p. 121 below.

[4] *Light or Darkness*, p. 3; cf. H. Barbour and A. Roberts, *Early Quaker Writings* (Grand Rapids, 1973), p. 605.

The phrases anticipate Traherne's vision. Penington criticized the Ranters because, although they saw the unity of darkness and light properly enough, they missed the distinction within the unity, and they dangerously ignored the possibility that they might be mistaken.[1]

> The world is now very dark and barren; and if a little light should break forth, it would mightily refresh it. But alas: man would be lifted up above himself and distempered by it at present, and afterwards he would die again and become more miserable. But the perfect man could both enjoy it more truly and more fully, more substantially at present; and also not be in such danger afterward, because it would not be his life, but his life would rather be lord over it: and so his chief happiness not depending upon it, his chief happiness would not pass away with it. Miserable is that man who is only differenced from the rest of the world by a present dispensation: but happy is he whose difference lieth in the root of his own nature, which changeth not in the midst of vanities of all conditions or dispensations.[2]

God was manifestly on trial for Penington at this date, as he was to be for Milton and many others after 1660.[3]

> Satan hath made such a noise, there have been such multitudes of his loud voices and languages, that thy low still voice might easily be drowned. No doubt, O Lord, but thou wilt be able to justify thyself in all these things; but in the mean time what shall become of these poor souls? Shall they always wander and please themselves in this little moment (which is their only time) with strange invented vanities?[4]

As well as Erbery, Isaac Penington's spiritual agonies recall those of Anthony Pearson, another gentleman who ultimately found his way (for a time) towards Quakerism, and wrote the classic denunciation of tithes. In May 1653 Pearson described himself as being 'like a poor shattered vessel tossed to and fro without a pilot or rudder'. He became a Quaker after Nayler and Fox had so confounded him that 'all my knowledge and wisdom became folly.'[5] Pearson too thought that 'some that are joined to

---

[1] Penington, *Divine Essays* (1654), pp. 15–23.
[2] Ibid., p. 126.
[3] See pp. 307–9 below.
[4] *Divine Essays*, p. 128.
[5] Quoted by W.C. Braithwaite, *The Beginnings of Quakerism* (1912), pp. 112–13.

the Ranters are pretty people', but they were associated with too many 'rude, savage apprentices and young people'.[1]

Like William Sedgwick,[2] Penington got involved in correspondence with John Reeve. The date is uncertain, but it was probably in the mid-1650s, when Muggleton regarded Penington as still a Ranter.[3] Penington not only queried Reeve's divine commission, he also compared him to John Robins, on whom Reeve had pronounced sentence of damnation in 1652. Penington told Reeve that he would have prayed for him if he had not been afraid of giving offence; but offence was taken anyway.[4]

Isaac Penington's upbringing as a strict Calvinist left its mark: he worried desperately for many years about election and reprobation.[5] He was 'broken and dashed to pieces' in religion; 'everything is darkness, death, emptiness, vanity, a lie.'[6] He left 'the congregational way', though 'in great love'; and joined no other 'way or people' until he became a Quaker.[7] Although perhaps more desperate than most in his spiritual anguish, Penington was not untypical of many Seekers, some of whom were to become Ranters, some Quakers, some to lapse into apathy.

For Penington it was a period of dissatisfaction, both with a state church and with all available alternatives. Penington rejected the church set up by kings and Parliaments—'built by force, settled by force, her ministers maintained by force'. It suppressed 'the progress of the reforming spirit' and substituted 'a formal spirit ... which ran backwards towards popery'.[8] The protestant spirit of the Lord 'calleth to follow him further and further from all the things of popery'. But many even of those who rejected popery 'have erred from the simplicity'.[9] 'The good old Puritan principle (wherein once was true life in its manner)' was dead and buried under formal devotion.[10]

It was in his Ranterish, or Erberian, mood of 1650 that Penington cried:

---

[1] A. E. Wallis, 'Anthony Pearson (1626–1666)', *JFHS*, 51 (1963), p. 15.

[2] See pp. 108–9 above.

[3] See p. 119 above, note 3.

[4] John Reeve, *Sacred Remains*, pp. 36–45, in *The Works of John Reeve and Lodowicke Muggleton* (1832), III. Muggleton was later to pronounce sentence of damnation on Penington, along with many other Quakers (*The World of the Muggletonians*, p. 96).

[5] *A Brief Account of my Soul's travel Towards the Holy Land*, in *Works*, III, pp. 98–100.

[6] Penington, *A Voyce out of the thick Darkness* (1650), pp. 19–20.

[7] *Works*, IV, pp. 295–6.

[8] *A Question* (1659), in *Works*, I, p. 337.

[9] Penington, *An Answer to that Common Objection against the Quakers, that They Condemn All but Themselves* (1660), pp. 4, 7; *A Question*, Works, I, pp. 337–40.

[10] Penington, *The Axe Laid to the Root* (1659), Sig. A 3–A 4.

Woe be to thee, O holy man! O righteous man! O strict exact
man! It is against thee that true righteousness and true holiness
hath the greatest quarrel, because thou standest most in its
way.... The High Court of Justice is chiefly erected in
reference to thee, to examine and find thee out. And woe unto
thee, for thou shalt not stand in judgement, whatever thou
thinkest of thyself.[1]

Where are the convocations, the synods, the assemblies of divines?
Penington asked in 1658. They have gone, because they are of the earth.
And he added:

it is easier for publicans, harlots, drunkards, swearers, all sorts
of sinners, to own truth and enter into life, than for these. For it
is easier to empty them of their profaneness than it is to empty
these of their settled conceited religion and devotion.[2]

Penington shared Erbery's view that 'there hath been a great apostasy
from the spirit of Christ', which 'began in the Apostles' days and ripened
apace afterwards'.[3] Throughout history there had been a pattern of
apostasy. The Jews in Egypt rejected Moses; later they rejected Samuel
and Elijah, stoned Stephen. 'Jerusalem was all along the persecutor of the
prophets.... The Church of Rome hath slain the Witnesses against her,
and the Protestants have slain the Witnesses against them.'[4] The fight,
recorded in Revelation, between the Dragon and his angels and Michael
and his angels, concerned the early church: the Dragon won, and erected
his false church. The true church fled into the Wilderness for her safety
and preservation.[5] Penington's gloomy view of history—'there is no new
thing under the sun'—recalls *Paradise Lost*, Books XI and XII.

---

[1] Penington, *Several Inward Openings*, in *Light or Darkness*, p. 21.
[2] Penington, *The way of Life and Death Made manifest* (1658), p. 68; cf. pp. 93–4 above.
[3] Ibid., p. 1; cf. pp. 10, 29–53, and *The Scattered Sheep Sought After* (1659), title-page. Cf. also
Works, II, p. 371, III, pp. 135, 146–50, IV, pp. 69–72, 102. See pp. 297–301 below.
[4] Penington, *The Jew Outward: Being a Glance at the Professors of this Age* (1659), Sig. A 2–2v;
cf. *Some Considerations Concerning the State of Things, Works*, I, pp. 453–7.
[5] Penington, *The Consideration of a Point Concerning the Book of Common Prayer* (1660),
pp. 21–2. Did any such idea lurk behind the war in heaven in *Paradise Lost*? Pareus and Mede
had related the war in heaven to the early history of the church, but Mede put the Dragon's
defeat in the fourth century AD. (Stella Revard, *The War in Heaven: Paradise Lost and the
Tradition of Satan's Rebellion* (Cornell UP, 1980), p. 10.)

> When God redeems his people out of Babylon [wrote
> Penington], he brings them not immediately unto Sion ... but
> into the Wilderness where the church lies unbuilt.... There is
> a long travel [travail?] from Babylon to Sion.[1]

Babylon, Penington had written in 1650,

> was built—and is daily built—in imitation of Sion, painted just
> like Sion. The intention of its building was to eat out Sion, to
> suppress Sion, to withdraw from the truth by a false image and
> to keep her inhabitants in peace and satisfaction under a belief
> and hope that it is the true Sion, and therefore it must needs be
> made like Sion.

Antichrist sits in the temple. 'Whatever is not of the spirit of God in
religion and worship is of the spirit of Antichrist.'[2] But 'alas, alas,
Babylon hath prevailed.'[3] 'The reforms since the apostasy ... have been
still building too fast.... They have not waited their time of preparation
in the Wilderness.'[4] Erbery knew of that Wilderness: so did Edward
Burrough.[5] For Penington, as perhaps for Milton, the history of
mankind since the apostasy had been one of inconclusive struggle: the
outcome depends on decisive divine intervention, in God's own time.[6]

Episcopacy had tried to 'quench the spirit that stirred in the protestants
against popery'. After bishops, presbytery 'stunk presently'.
Independency and Anabaptism had 'more simple and honest things
stirring them, ... seeking and waiting; but death overcame them also,
making a form of it.... Thus have their carcasses fallen in the
Wilderness.' Neither Rome, England, Scotland nor the several gathered
churches were 'the church in the Wilderness'.[7] All sects are mistaken, but
there has always been 'a simplicity of heart' in some members of the
English church even in 'the time of darkness';[8] and 'now the apostacy

---

[1] Penington, *Some Considerations Concerning the State of Things, Works,* I, p. 452.
[2] Penington, *Babylon the Great Described* (1650), pp. 8, 40.
[3] *The Scattered Sheep Sought After,* p. 2.
[4] *Some Considerations,* in *Works,* I, p. 453.
[5] See pp. 89–90, 92 above for Erbery; Burrough, *The Memorable Works of a Son of Thunder and Consolation* (1672), p. 85. See also pp. 301–3 below.
[6] I owe this point to Jackie DiSalvo, 'War of Titans: Blake's Confrontation with Milton' (unpubl. Ph.D. thesis, University of Madison, 1977), pp. 508–9.
[7] *The Axe Laid to the Root,* Sig. A 3, pp. 19–20; cf. *A Warning of Love from the Bowels of Life,* p. 6.
[8] *The way of Life,* pp. 33–4, 79, 85.

draws towards an end'. As the kingdom of darkness 'daily falls', so 'the kingdoms of this world shall become the kingdoms of the Lord and his Christ, and ye shall reign upon earth where sin and Antichrist have long reigned and kept him down.'[1]

'Exceeding great hath been the apostasy of this age.' 'The light that was showing at the beginning of the troubles of these nations was very precious.... God heard the cry and arose to deliver, and did begin to break the yoke, both outwardly in the nation and inwardly in people's spirits.' But the Tempter divided Israel with forms and notions, 'and so the captivity returns'.[2]

Penington's appeal came to be directed increasingly to 'the simple-hearted'. The forbidden fruit in the Garden of Eden had been 'knowledge without life'. If men would be satisfied 'only to get knowledge and wisdom from what they can comprehend', then all would 'have power to believe'.[3] But most men remain 'fully satisfied with the Egyptian knowledge and wisdom'. To be truly wise they must 'become a fool in the flesh'.[4] Penington shared Milton's distrust of excessive intellectual curiosity. 'Keep to the sense, keep to the feeling, beware of the understanding, beware of the imagining, conceiving mind.'[5] Even Scripture is inadequate as a code of conduct.[6]

In 1650 Penington attacked the smug cruelty which underlay conventional belief in hell: 'He that can be content to please himself in escaping hell, where others must scorch in unutterable torment, is he righteous? Oh how my soul loathes all that which men call righteousness! I see as much need of a proportionable fire to burn it up as to burn up wickedness.'[7]

Penington had no doubt that England was the chosen nation. Even in the dark days of the apostasy, he wrote in 1650, 'there hath been a simplicity and sincerity of heart stirring in some people towards God in all ages.... In this nation the simplicity hath more stirred than in other nations.' The English nation had been especially favoured by being redeemed from popery; and then God refused to allow presbyterianism to be imposed on them. 'Israel is his first-born, whom he will not have

---

[1] Ibid., pp. 100, 53.
[2] *The Scattered Sheep Sought After*, Preface and pp. 4–5.
[3] Ibid., pp. 2, 17–22.
[4] *A Warning of Love*, pp. 1–8.
[5] *The way of Life*, p. 70; cf. *MER*, pp. 398–402.
[6] *The way of Life*, pp. 12–13; cf. *MER*, Chapter 19.
[7] *A Letter impleading a Conversion*, bound with *Light or Darkness*.

any longer kept in bondage.' He 'rebuketh kings and Parliaments, Armies and Councils, for their sake'.[1]

Isaac Penington related his spiritual crisis of the early 1650s to the events of the English Revolution; and he had a clear view of what that Revolution had and had not achieved. 'At the beginning of the troubles in these nations,' he wrote in 1650, 'there was a lively stirring in me, and a hope that God was bringing forth somewhat; I likewise felt the same stirring in many others, at which my heart was rejoiced.'[2] This stirring of life 'was very precious because it did unite to God and it did unite to one another'. 'There was a taste of [God] and fellowship with him, and sweet hopes and refreshments to the soul. But I found it soon begin to flag within, which forced me to retire and separate from that where I found the life and power dying and decaying.'[3] So began the period in which he was 'broken and dashed to pieces' in his religion.

Looking back in 1658 Penington recalled 'the grievous shakings and rendings that have been in this nation, which ... made every heart ache and every mind astonished'. Before 1640 'this nation was settled in religion and outward peace, in such a way as was pleasing to most.' But there were those who 'had been long groaning under oppression', whose cries the Lord heard. 'And he arose up in his fury and jealousy, and rent the heavens and rent the earth', creating a period of confusion which affected 'magistracy, ministry, the common people, the people of God (both such as were accounted so and such as were indeed so): ... They did all reel and totter like a drunken man.'[4]

In the early 1650s Penington was equally concerned with civil and religious liberty. In 1651 he published *The Fundamental Right, Safety and Liberties of the People*, calling for 'universal freedom' and 'universal speedy and unpartial justice'. The 'right liberty and safety of the people consists', he said in words that recall the Levellers, 'in the choice of their government' and 'in enjoying the power of altering their government'. It was the duty of Parliaments 'to strike at the very root and foundation of oppression in any kind', but 'this present Parliament is not unquestionably free'. 'Be not weary of the pursuit after liberty,' he urged his readers.[5] Some thought, he had said in 1650, 'a King would help all,

---

[1] *Babylon the Great*, p. 53; *Some Considerations Proposed to the Distracted Nation of England* (1659), *Works*, I, p. 327.
[2] *Babylon the Great*, Sig. A 3.
[3] Ibid., p. 38; *The Scattered Sheep*, pp. 4–5.
[4] *The way of Life*, Sig. A 2; *The Axe Laid to the Root*, Sig. A 3–4; *The Scattered Sheep*, p. 5.
[5] Op. cit., Sig. B–B 4v, pp. 1–9, 26; cf. *A Voyce out of the Thick Darkness* (1650), Preface.

some a Parliament, and some hoping for good from the Army: but every
eye sees' now that the nation's case is desperate.[1] By 1653 Penington was
becoming aware that 'so soon as a man is exalted, he forgets the Lord;
... all his good thoughts die and perish.' He still thought it 'a great
truth' that the saints shall govern the world,[2] but he became increasingly
critical of the degeneracy of the Army after seizing power. 'Men were
countenanced and advanced not according to their fidelity to the Good
Old Cause, but according to their compliance with this new selfish
interest.'[3]

'Mighty was the appearance of God inwardly in his people's spirits,' he
recalled in 1659, 'mighty was the appearance of God outwardly in the
nation, many great hopes there was of a thorough reformation. But how
suddenly was the spirit of the Lord forgotten!'[4] Nevertheless, 'the Lord
hath been just and good ... and can, in his own good time, recover the
ground which he hath seemed to lose.'[5]

The Lord did not recover his lost ground, but Penington never
abandoned his conviction of the righteousness of the original Cause. In
1660 he still insisted to King and Parliament that 'the Lord did overturn
the former powers', and did 'raise up other powers out of the dust, ...
even from among them of low degree.'[6] It would therefore be wrong,
Penington insisted with remarkable courage, 'to call any to account for
what they have done against you. There was an extraordinary hand of
God in these things.... For their iniquity the Lord hath laid them aside,
and raised you up again, giving you another day of trial.'[7] Penington
indeed demanded of the Cavaliers whether their sufferings during the
interregnum had not been justified by their previous sins. The
Parliamentary Cause had been just 'in its first rise'; and though the Lord
had allowed it to fall, he could turn things about again.[8] The rulers and
teachers of the land would be well advised to surrender to God 'his due,

---

[1] *Babylon the Great*, p. 56.
[2] Penington, *A Considerable Question about Government* (1653), pp. 6–8.
[3] Penington, *To the Parliament, the Army and All the Wel-affected in the Nation* (1659),
pp. 1–2.
[4] *The Scattered Sheep*, Preface.
[5] Penington, *Some Considerations Proposed to the City of London and the Nation of England*
(1659), *Works*, I, pp. 321–2.
[6] *Three Queries Propounded to the King and Parliament* (1666), *Works*, II, p. 378.
[7] *Some Queries concerning the Work of God in the World* (1660), *Works*, II, p. 103; cf.
Sedgwick, p. 181 below.
[8] *Some few Queries and Considerations Propounded to the Cavaliers* (1660?), *passim*. This
pamphlet was not printed in Penington's *Works*.

before he appear in his strength to force it from them'.[1] Persecution, Penington thought, is a mark of the apostate church.[2]

As early as 1650 Penington had become aware of '*de facto*' arguments for obedience, and he was cautious about 'over-violent' resisting. 'If thou labourest for freedom with all thy might, and a greater power appears, what wilt thou then gain by the contest?' It may be that 'present oppression' is 'determined by him who hath power to dispose of all things'. Men should 'groan, pant after and in a just way pursue the attainment of perfect freedom'. They should lose no opportunity to prosecute the cause of liberty, 'yet not in such a violent and irrational manner as to make your noble parts far worse slaves to brutish passions within to avoid a more inferior slavery of the outward and more ignoble part'.[3]

This was a waiting rather than a pacifist position, as Professor Cole justly pointed out;[4] it is analogous to one which I believe Milton came to occupy after the restoration.[5] Penington retained hopes of the Army long after his conversion to Quakerism. After its coup of October 1659 he suggested that 'in this late revolution there may be more of God than man is aware of.' He appealed to the Army to make it clear that they sought God's cause and the good of his people: so that 'every ... sort of men might feel their oppressions broken and their just rights and liberties recovered.' This would 'draw the hearts of all the honest-hearted people to you as one man; and those which have been scattered would be again united'. 'The Cause hath long lain a-bleeding, yet there is at length a true reviving of it.'[6] But by December 1659 he was warning the Army against another betrayal, praying that God would 'keep you close to the stirrings and honest movings for public good that have sprung up in the days of your adversity'.[7] 'Here is the patience and faith of the saints,' Penington wrote, 'to wait under the yoke, under the daily cross ... till all the bonds of captivity be broke through by the life.'[8] Patient suffering: but also hope. Even after the restoration Penington declared that it was

[1] *The Consideration of a Point Concerning the Book of Common Prayer* (1660), p. 25.
[2] *The way of Life*, p. 43.
[3] *A Voyce out of the Thick Darkness*, Preface; cf. *PL* xii. 83–101.
[4] W. A. Cole, 'The Quakers and Politics, 1652–1660', unpublished Cambridge University Thirlwall Prize Essay, 1954, p. 30.
[5] See *MER*, Chapter 28.
[6] *Some Considerations Proposed to the City of London and the Nation, Works*, II, pp. 332–3.
[7] *To the Army* (1659), single sheet.
[8] Penington, *The New-Covenant of the Gospel* (1660), p. 41.

honourable to use the sword in defence of one's country.[1]

Isaac Penington's approach to Quakerism had been difficult, William Penn tells us, because 'the Lord's way of appearance' disappointed his expectation. 'He was not without doubts and jealousies concerning it,' Ellwood confirms. Penington was 'the most educated of any that had closed with this way', and the Quakers' 'manner seemed contemptible to him' until he heard George Fox.[2] John Reeve spoke of Penington's 'ponderous aspect', and Muggleton was to make fun of 'Squire Penington'.[3]

Penington is most interesting, and writes better, in his period of doubt and despair. After his conversion the vigour and vitality of his writing falls away. This is perhaps more than a personal matter. The loose, lax style of most Quakers (and of Wither), relying on inspiration from the spirit of God, marks a great falling off from the taut prose of Overton, Walwyn, Winstanley, Coppe. Quaker writings become almost a stream of consciousness, pouring out endlessly and uncritically, one thing leading to another, most things leading to the wickedness of hireling priests. Since they felt it their duty to answer every attack or criticism, there is continual repetition: often different Quaker pamphleteers use identical words and phrases.

Penington's Quaker editors omitted from his collected works everything that he wrote before he joined them, including even the *Divine Essays* of 1654 as well as the 'Seeker' pamphlets of 1650 and the libertarian tracts of 1651–3. Some at least of his pamphlets of 1659–60 were also left out, perhaps because they were too political for later Quaker tastes.[4] This excluded material reveals a mind of great sensitivity and openness, whose prose style—like Erbery's and Sedgwick's—still reflects some of the provocative liveliness which characterizes that of Levellers, Winstanley and Ranters. The early Fox's writing had something of the same fresh sharpness. Its disappearance is not the least of the losses in later Quakerism.

Penington was closer personally to Milton than anyone studied in this book, with the exception of Marvell. So perhaps the analogies which I have suggested between their ideas are worth pondering.[5]

---

[1] *Works*, II, p. 183.
[2] *Works*, I, pp. vii–viii, xxxviii, lii.
[3] Reeve, *Sacred Remains*, p. 36; Muggleton, *The Acts of the Witnesses of the Spirit*, p. 78.
[4] See p. 126 above for an example; see also pp. 167–9 below.
[5] Cf. A. W. Brink, 'William Riley Parker's *Milton* and Friends', *JFHS*, 52 (1968–71), pp. 183–91.

Chapter 5

Quakers, 1651–1661

1 Quakers and the Good Old Cause

'Defeat' may seem an inappropriate word to use about the Quakers. They survived—the only sect originating from the interregnum that still exists, since the last Muggletonian died in 1979[1]—and they have made a unique contribution to British and world civilization. But the contribution they made was not what the founders of the 1650s would have anticipated: a great change came over the Society of Friends, slow but unmistakable. There were perhaps two defeats. The first was the trial, condemnation and savage punishment of James Nayler for riding into Bristol on a donkey in 1656 in imitation of Christ's entry into Jerusalem. This led to much rethinking about the role of symbolic actions, and about the nature of the inner light. Eighty years ago the Rev. Alexander Gordon argued that 'the emotional mysticism of Nayler's devotees was ... anterior to Quakerism proper.'[2] This is not the way I should put it, but Quakerism certainly changed after and because of Nayler's fall. Second was the collapse of the Army in 1659–60, and the restoration of monarchy, House of Lords, bishops.

The number of Quakers who had been in the Army and Navy, until they were forced out, is legion.[3] Bishop,[4] Byllynge, Edward Pyott,

---

[1] *The World of the Muggletonians*, p. 1.
[2] *DNB*, 'Nayler'.
[3] See, for instance, *Extracts from State Papers relating to Friends*, pp. 27, 47, 116–17, 268, 273–4, 285, 310, 437, 445, 490; Braithwaite, *Beginnings*, p. 170, 186, 214, 232, 350, 364, 383, 386, 394, 399, 402, 456, 519–22; Braithwaite, *The Second Period of Quakerism* (1919), pp. 18, 422; Cole, 'The Quakers and Politics', pp. 17–20, 37–53, 64–6, 128–30, 134, 152, 176, 191; 'The Quakers and the English Revolution', *P. and P.*, 10 (1956), pp. 39–40, 46; *First Publishers of Truth*, ed. N. Penney (1907), p. 324; Maria Webb, *The Penns and Peningtons of the Seventeenth Century*, p. 249; M. R. Brailsford, *A Quaker from Cromwell's Army* (1927), pp. 19–21; K. L. Carroll, 'Quakerism and the Cromwellian Army in Ireland', *JFHS*, 54 (1978), pp. 148–9; Carroll, *John Perrot, early Quaker Schismatic, JFHS*, Supplement No. 33 (1970), p. 77; *WTUD*, p. 246.
[4] Captain Bishop attended the Putney Debates in 1647 (Woodhouse, op. cit., pp. 81, 107, 438–9)

Richard Hubberthorne, were all officers in the New Model; Nayler a quartermaster, Ames, George Fox the Younger, Deusbury, John Whitehead, Johm Camm, John Stubbs and William Edmundson were all soldiers.[1] As long as the Army existed, Quakers continued to hope that it might once again become an instrument for achieving God's purposes on earth. Howgil in 1660 revived the idea that the revenue from confiscated estates of royalists could be used to maintain 'an army in the nation for many years'.[2] The threat of preserving an army by such means intensified the hostility of the natural rulers to Army and Quakers alike. The major rethinking which led to the peace principle, first clearly enunciated in January 1661, and to withdrawal from political action, came after Quakers had ceased to believe in the imminence of Christ's kingdom: the collapse of the Army and the reassertion of the power of the natural rulers seem to have been decisive in ending the utopian millenarian hopes to which Quakers and Fifth Monarchists clung on longer than other groups in English politics.[3]

In this chapter I shall stress Quaker social and political rather than religious ideas, partly because I want to show how important such ideas were for them, partly to emphasize the links between them and other radicals. It is perhaps as misleading to speak of 'the Quakers' before 1661 as it is to speak of 'the Levellers'—more so indeed, since 'Quakers' were far more widely scattered across England and even less homogeneous. In the euphoric early 1650s George Fox found congregations everywhere in the North, apparently waiting for his message. But these congregations had their own traditions—Familist, Grindletonian, Seeker. There must have been many early 'Quakerisms'. Before 1661 there were premature pacifists: after 1661 many clung belatedly to bellicosity. The regional history of first-generation Quakerism remains to be written.[4] 'Quakers' were lumped together by their enemies, who in early days used the word as if it were identical with 'Ranters', later as if identical with 'Anabaptists'. Critics tended naturally to exaggerate the political and social deviations of men and women who reminded them of Levellers and

---

[1] Reay, 'Early Quaker Activity', pp. 57–64; Craig W. Horle, 'John Camm: Profile of a Quaker Minister during the Interregnum', *Quaker History*, 70 (1981), p. 70; W. Edmundson, *A Journal of the Life* (1715), p. 2.

[2] Howgil, *One Warning More* (1660), p. 9. The suggestion had been made by Robert Purnell in 1649, and doubtless by many others (Purnell, *Good Tydings for Sinners, Great Joy for Saints*, pp. 74–5).

[3] Cf. Capp, *Fifth Monarchy Men*, p. 118.

[4] See Horle, 'John Camm', *Quaker History*, 71 (1982), pp. 10–12.

Diggers. The hysteria of MPs in the Parliament of 1656[1] shows that they believed, rightly or wrongly, that there was still a real threat of social subversion; and this fear revived in 1659–60.

A balanced picture of early Quakerism would pay far more attention to their internal divisions, to their opposition to tithes and to their millenarianism (though suppressions by later Quakers make this difficult to recapture). It would also give greater prominence to more traditionally acknowledged aspects of Quaker thinking like the inner light, the pacifism which developed after 1660 and the sense of the meeting. What most of us regard as characteristic features of 'Quakerism'—refusal of 'hat honour', insistence on 'thou' rather than 'you', opposition to oaths (and tithes too, for that matter) are in fact traditional features of English radical movements, going back to the Lollards, through sixteenth-century Familists and Anabaptists.[2]

Enemies of the Quakers, from Francis Higginson and Ralph Farmer onwards, accused them of being 'downright Levellers', steeped in the 'learning of Winstanley and Collier'.[3] George Wither too, who was favourable to the Quakers, said 'they are our Levellers new-named'.[4] It is difficult to be sure about connections of this sort in a fluid society, but certainly many former Levellers became Quakers. In addition to Lilburne we may count George Fox the Younger, ex-soldier as well as ex-Leveller.[5] Down to 1660 at least Edward Byllynge is hard to distinguish from a Leveller.[6] Richard Hubberthorne thought God had owned Lilburne 'in opposing many of the unjust powers of the nation'.[7]

---

[1] One MP described Quakers as 'all Levellers, against magistracy and property' (Burton, *Parliamentary Diary*, I, pp. 169; cf. pp. 24–5, 49, 128).

[2] *WTUD*, Chapters 9 and 10; *MER*, Chapters 6–8. Venner's rebels in 1657 refused to remove their hats, and 'thou'd' (Capp, *Fifth Monarchy Men*, p. 143).

[3] F. Higginson, *A Brief Relation of the Irreligion of the Northern Quakers* (1653), p. 16. Ironically enough, Thomas Collier also denounced the Quakers as Levellers (*A Looking-Glasse for the Quakers*, 1657, p. 12). R. Farmer, *The Great Mysteries of Godliness and Ungodliness* (1655), esp. dedication; *Thurloe State Papers*, VI, pp. 167–8; G. F. Nuttall, 'Overcoming the World: the Early Quaker Programme', *Studies in Church History*, X (Oxford, 1973), pp. 155–6; A. Cole, 'The Quakers and the English Revolution', p. 39; Reay, 'Popular Hostility towards Quakers in Mid-Seventeenth-Century England', *Social History*, 5 (1980), pp. 388–9.

[4] Wither, *Vaticinia Poetica* (1666), p. 10, in *Miscellaneous Works*, IV; *Parallelogrammaton* (1662), (Spenser Soc., 1882), p. 44. See *WTUD*, pp. 239–41, 246, for many examples. Samuel Butler similarly lumped Levellers and Quakers together (*Prose Observations*, p. 17).

[5] Cf. *Early Quaker Writings* ed. H. Barbour and A. Roberts (Grand Rapids, 1973), pp. 357, 388.

[6] See p. 187 below.

[7] Hubberthorne, *The Horne of the Hee-goat Broken* (1655), in *Collected Writings* (1663), p. 83, quoted in E. Brockbank, *Richard Hubberthorne* (1929), p. 100.

In 1659 Quakers used Leveller techniques of petitioning Parliament, including women's petitions.[1]

Early Quakers had some things in common with Fifth Monarchists. Both expected Christ's kingdom on earth in the near future, and both shared many views of the radicals of the 1640s.[2] Governments in the 1650s feared Fifth Monarchists much more than they feared Quakers. JPs, on the other hand, hated Quakers and seem to have taken little account of Fifth Monarchists. The reason is probably that Fifth Monarchists were based on London preachers and artisans, and on the Army. They could stir up unrest in the capital. Quakers were rural, with no base in the Army. They testified against local magistrates and parsons: Fifth Monarchists testified against betrayal by the government and by Army leaders. After 1660, however, despite the Quaker proclamation of the peace principle, governments became more hostile to and suspicious of them, in this perhaps reflecting the greater influence of the gentry on government as well as the virtual extinction of Fifth Monarchism.[3]

In the 1650s Quakers made no secret of their political radicalism. Hubberthorne thought the civil war had been a defensive war, 'for our rights and liberties' against the King's negative voice and control of the militia. 'We freely brought in our moneys, plate, horses, arms and other habiliments of armies,' Hubberthorne added; but the leaders of Parliament and Army had not settled us in these 'external rights and liberties'.[4] Howgil agreed that 'many precious men ventured their lives and lost their blood and consumed their estates' to win liberty 'as men and as Christians'.[5] The Quakers 'are they that stood by the authority [of Parliament] in time of greatest danger, in time of the bishops, when persecution was greatest ... and also in all the late wars in the three nations; there are few of them but have joined with them and cried up reformation'.[6] This seems to have been a general assumption.

---

[1] Cole, 'The Quakers and the English Revolution', pp. 124–6.
[2] For links between Fifth Monarchists and Quakers, see Capp, op. cit., p. 111.
[3] Cf. Reay, 'The Authorities and Early Restoration Quakerism', *Journal of Ecclesiastical History*, 34 (1983), pp. 69–84.
[4] Hubberthorne, *The Good Old Cause Briefly Demonstrated* (1659), quoted by Brockbank, *Hubberthorne*, pp. 43, 154–8; cf. W. Deusbury, *A True Prophesie of the Mighty Day of the Lord* (1654), pp. 3–4; *The Discovery of the great enmity of the Serpent against the Seed of the Woman* (1655), pp. 16–29.
[5] Howgil, *One Warning more unto England* (1660), pp. 6–7, 10, 14–15; cf. George Fox the Younger, *A Noble Salutation unto thee ... Charles Stuart* (1660), pp. 7, 10; Cole, 'The Quakers and Politics, 1652–1660', pp. 25, 41, 91, 224; Reay, 'The Quakers, 1659 and the Restoration of the Monarchy', *History*, 208 (1978), p. 191 and *passim*.
[6] Howgil, *The Popish Inquisition Newly Erected in New-England* (1659), p. 65.

Some Quakers regarded the execution of Charles I as a righteous judgement of God.[1] George Bishop thought it was 'for the preservation of the public interest'.[2] He also looked back with approval to the Agitators, Pride's Purge and the conquest of Ireland. His views had not changed much since in the Putney Debates he had attacked 'the Man of Blood' whom God 'hath manifestly declared against'.[3] But as early as 1651 Bishop thought 'we have too few honest hearts among us.... A tender heart would weep for the day of visitation that is coming,' he told Cromwell.[4] 'It would never be well,' he was alleged to have said, until some of the Presbyterian clergy had been executed.[5] (Bishop's own intelligence activities had contributed to the condemnation of Christopher Love in 1651.) Bishop and Anthony Pearson were on the fringes of Wildman's Plot in 1654.[6] Bishop and Howgil defended the Army's second expulsion of the Rump in October 1659.[7] Men should not be 'wedded and glued to names', Howgil declared in Cromwellian fashion.[8] 'Was it only a form of government ... that ye pursued after? Or was it not ... freedom itself ?'[9] George Fox the Younger thought that 'many thousands of men in England have been wronged of their birthright', and advocated extension of the franchise, since otherwise 'the rich covetous oppressing men' would make all laws.[10]

The original Parliamentary Cause, Bishop told Cromwell in 1656, had been 'the highest on which men were ever engaged in the field', words that echo Milton. He was rebuking Cromwell for betraying this Cause. 'Did thy sword (till of late) ever return empty from the blood of the slain and the spoil of the mighty?' he asked.[11] An anonymous Quaker pamphlet of 1655, in the style of Abiezer Coppe, told 'great men and rich men of the earth' to 'weep and howl, for your misery is coming; ... the day of

---

[1] Cole, 'The Quakers and Politics', p. 59, and references there cited.
[2] Bishop, *Mene Tekel* (1659), pp. 37, 45.
[3] Ibid., pp. 3–4, 26, 30, 34–40.
[4] Nickolls, *Original Letters and Papers of State*, p. 50.
[5] Farmer, *The Impostor Dethron'd* (1658), p. 43. Farmer is of course not the most reliable authority for Bishop's words.
[6] Gardiner, *Commonwealth and Protectorate*, III, pp. 228–9.
[7] Bishop, *The Warnings of the Lord* (1660), p. 35; Howgil, *An Information, and also Advice to the Armies* (1659), pp. 6–7. Cf. Isaac Penington, *Some Considerations proposed to the City of London and the Nation* (1659), single sheet; Burrough, *A Message to the Present Rulers of England* (1659), p. 11 (rightly 9).
[8] Howgil, op. cit., p. 10.
[9] Howgil, *Works* (1676), pp. 335–8.
[10] Fox, *A Few Plain Words* (1659), pp. 2–5; cf. Cole, 'The Quakers and Politics', pp. 159–63.
[11] Bishop, *The Warnings of the Lord to the Men of this Generation* (1660), pp. 1–7, 13. For Milton see p. 23 above.

the Lord is appearing'.[1] An ex-Quaker later recalled that in the 1650s he had been attracted by the Quaker doctrine that 'men should not lord it over one another by reason of their great estates'.[2] Anthony Pearson argued, in words which recall Winstanley, that tithes should have been cut off with the King's head. The abolition of the Court of Wards had 'granted many great men such freedom for nothing as they could neither in right claim nor in reason expect; ... and surely they will not deny the poorer sort of people their own and dear-bought increase'.[3] Byllynge, Pearson, Samuel Fisher and others in 1658 rejected 'all unequal, imperfect and changeable laws of men'; in litigation 'to the poor the remedy is frequently worse than the disease'.[4] Again we remember Winstanley. Richard Hubberthorne was against 'slavish tenures of land held at the will of the lord' as well as irregular Parliamentary elections and impressment for foreign wars.[5] Dr Reay has argued that much early Quaker support derived from their anti-tithe policy, which incorporated traditional attitudes.[6]

George Bishop continued to play an active part in Bristol's politics after his conversion to Quakerism in 1654 or 1655.[7] There had been some national Quaker political activity in 1656—electioneering, undertaking public office, etc. In 1659 Edward Burrough, Edward Byllynge, George Bishop and other leading Quakers were negotiating seriously with leaders of the Rump and of the Army for co-operation. Quakers who had been dismissed from the Army and Navy, they suggested, might return; and Quakers might accept posts as militia commissioners and JPs.[8] Denis Hollister was a militia commissioner in Bristol; Pearson—also a militia

---

[1] [Anon.], *To all that would Know the Way to the Kingdom* (1655), p. 9. For Quaker social policy see Braithwaite, *Second Period*, pp. 555–60; *WTUD*, pp. 240–8.

[2] Nathaniel Smith, *The Quakers Spiritual Court Proclaimed* (n.d.—after 1668), p. 2; cf. Howgil, *A Woe to Magistrates* (1654).

[3] Pearson, *The Great Case of Tithes* (1732), pp. 55–6, 60–2. First published in 1657, this book had reached its third edition by 1659.

[4] *State Papers relating to Friends*, pp. 39–44.

[5] Hubberthorne, *The Good Old Cause Briefly Demonstrated* (1659), pp. 10 ff. For Quakers and law and social reform, see Cole, 'The Quakers and Politics', pp. 110–13.

[6] Reay, 'Quaker Opposition to Tithes, 1652–1660', *P. and P.*, 86 (1980), *passim*.

[7] The best source for Bishop's career is Cole, 'The Quakers and Politics', pp. 270–7; Hugh Barbour, *The Quakers in Puritan England* (Yale UP, 1964), p. 192.

[8] Braithwaite, *Beginnings*, pp. 313, 460; *Second Period*, pp. 18, 90, 112, 122–3; Barbour, *Quakers in Puritan England*, pp. 199–202; cf. Barbour and Roberts, *Early Quaker Writings*, p. 387; Fox, *Journal* (8th edn., 1902), I, pp. 226–7; ed. N. Penney, *The Short Journal and Itinerary Journals of George Fox* (Cambridge UP, 1925), p. 294; Reay, 'The Quakers, 1659 and the Restoration of the Monarchy', *History*, 208 (1978); *State Papers relating to Friends*, pp. 6–7, 10, 13, 105–16; Isabel Ross, *Margaret Fell: Mother of Quakerism* (1949), pp. 160, 181. Cf. pp. 283–5 below.

commissioner—raised the country round Kendal to oppose Booth's rebellion.[1] 'At this point,' Professor Cole comments, 'some of the Quaker leaders moved closer towards active approval of armed resistance to unjust authority than at any other time since the rise of the movement.'[2] George Fox the Younger argued against the clamour for a 'free Parliament' that it would mean the return to power of the natural rulers.[3] He was ready to support the Army 'if ever the Lord God should make use of you again'.[4] In June 1659 Byllynge declared himself to be 'an owner of the sword in its place', and protested against the expulsion of Quakers from the Army.[5] He briefly re-enlisted himself. The Quaker William Woodcock, possibly the father of Milton's second wife, was invited in the same month to serve in the militia along with other Quakers.[6] Isaac Penington gave cautious approval to the Army's coup of October 1659: he continued to think the sword might be used to defend one's country.[7]

'Many Quakers are made justices,' complained a Gloucestershire MP in April 1659. 'There is one in my county that could lead out three or four hundred with him at any time.'[8] In August Wariston 'saw the Anabaptists and Fifth Monarchy Men all winning upon this occasion to arms and regiments'. He feared 'the design and endeavour of some party to put the Anabaptists and the Quakers into arms' and so to take away tithes.[9] Six months later it was reported from Cheshire that 'a Quaker hath a troop of horse yet in arms'. At the same time there were complaints from Dublin of Anabaptists, Quakers and suchlike on the commission of the peace.[10] In March there were rumours in London that 'Quakers and Independents and Anabaptists' threatened to plunder gentlemen's houses and to disarm the gentry.[11] (The labels 'Quaker' and 'Anabaptist' are of

[1] Woolrych, *Commonwealth to Protectorate*, p. 189; Barbour, *Quakers in Puritan England*, p. 202, correcting Braithwaite, *Beginnings*, p. 114; Cole, 'The Quakers and Politics', pp. 134–6, 138; cf. Reay, 'Early Quaker Activity', p. 126. Hollister had been a JP since 1653.

[2] Cole, 'The Quakers and the English Revolution', pp. 159–63.

[3] Fox the Younger, *A Few Plain Words* (1659), pp. 3–5.

[4] Fox the Younger, *This is for You who are called the Comon-wealths-Men both in the Army and Parliament to read* (1659), p. 3.

[5] Byllynge, *A Word of Reproof, and Advice to my late Fellow-Souldiers and Officers* (1659), pp. 46–7 and *passim*.

[6] A. W. Brink, '*Paradise Lost* and James Nayler's Fall', *JFHS*, 53 (1973), p. 101.

[7] See p. 128 above.

[8] Burton, *Parliamentary Diary*, IV, p. 337.

[9] Wariston, *Diary*, III, pp. 131, 133; cf. pp. 139, 157. For fear of Anabaptists and Quakers arming see *Calendar of Clarendon State Papers*, ed. F. J. Routledge, IV (Oxford UP, 1932) pp. 220, 228, 235–6, 330, 381, 405, 440 and *passim*.

[10] HMC, *Leyborne-Popham* (1899), pp. 157, 141.

[11] *Diurnal of Thomas Rugge*, ed. W. L. Sachse (Camden Soc., 3rd Ser., XCI, 1961), p. 53.

course used loosely in this context, with no precise theological significance but a good deal of social horror.) As late as April 1660 Quakers were said to have joined Lambert's revolt, after having 'sold their whole estates to raise money for the present design'.[1] There had been general alarm in 1659 and early 1660 that arms were being given to Quakers and Anabaptists. Some Friends, we know, did join in military action.[2] Arise Evans in 1661 snorted that 'the Quakers give out forsooth that they will not rebel nor fight, when indeed the last year and all along the war the Army was full of them.'[3]

Professor Cole described Quakerism as 'a movement of protest against the suppression of "the Good Old Cause"'.[4] The phrase was frequently on Quaker lips in 1659—Burrough,[5] Bishop,[6] Byllynge (law is 'the badge of the Conqueror'),[7] Isaac Penington,[8] Hubberthorne,[9] John Collins ('the Good Old Cause, the Cause of my [the Lord's] people'),[10] George Fox[11] and George Fox the Younger.[12] Both Burrough and Bishop called for a 'statement of the Good Old Cause' in clear and plain principles and positions.[13]

In October 1659 Byllynge addressed *A Mite of Affection, manifested in 31 Proposals* 'to all sober and freeborn people of this Common-wealth'. It came at an interesting time: after the millenarian optimism which had hitherto made it seem superfluous for Quakers to draft constitutions and yet before the withdrawal from politics which succeeded the débâcle of the restoration. Byllynge proposed the nomination of an assembly by the different religious sects, which would arrange and supervise elections on

---

[1] *Clarendon State Papers*, III, p. 730.

[2] Braithwaite, *Beginnings*, p. 460; Reay, 'Early Quaker Activity', p. 129; *idem*, 'Popular Hostility', p. 388 and *passim*; Cole, 'The Quakers and Politics', p. 169; HMC, *Leyborne-Popham*, p. 161; cf. *First Publishers of Truth*, p. 324.

[3] Evans, *To the Most High and Mighty Prince Charles the II* (1660[-1]), p. 64, quoted by Reay, 'Popular Hostility', p. 391; cf. 'The Quakers, 1659 and the Restoration of the Monarchy', pp. 194–6.

[4] Cole, 'The Quakers and the English Revolution', p. 4.

[5] Burrough, *Good Counsel and Advice Rejected by Disobedient Men* (1659), p. 65; *To the Whole English Army* (1660), single sheet; *Satans Design Defeated* (1660), p. 17.

[6] Bishop, *The Warnings of the Lord* pp. 18–20; *Mene Tekel*, title-page.

[7] Byllynge, *A Word of Reproof* (1659), p. 20; cf. E. B., *A Declaration of present sufferings* (1659), pp. 27–8.

[8] Penington, *To the Parliament, the Army, and all the Wel-affected in the Nation who have been faithful to the Good Old Cause* (1659).

[9] Hubberthorne, *The Good Old Cause Briefly Demonstrated* (1659).

[10] Collins, *A Message from the Spirit of the Lord to the People called Anabaptists* (1660), p. 3.

[11] Fox, *To Those that have been formerly in Authority* (1659), p. 2.

[12] George Fox the Younger, *A Noble Salutation*, p. 10.

[13] Burrough, *To the Whole English Army*; Bishop, *The Warnings of the Lord*, pp. 18–24.

a new, more equal franchise. There were to be annual Parliaments, unchangeable fundamental laws; all state officers were to be elected and accountable. Byllynge called for a whole series of economic and legal reforms, reminiscent of Leveller programmes.

Byllynge had hoped that the Quakers would endorse his pamphlet officially, which suggests that he expected them to approve a near-Leveller platform. It was not so endorsed, but whether this was because of objections to some of Byllynge's proposals or because it was thought unwise to commit the Society to a specific political programme at that very difficult moment is unclear.[1] Byllynge himself knew how desperate the situation was: 'the night cometh shortly,' his title-page declared, 'wherein no man can work.' When the night came, George Fox the Younger for one was far from apologetic about the Good Old Cause in his *Salutation* to Charles II: 'there was an eminent hand of God in breaking ... down' Charles I's supporters. 'The iniquity in them provoked the holy God to anger.... Those that took part with thy father,' he informed Charles II, 'were generally (according to outward appearance) accounted the wisest, richest, noblest and stoutest men ... and they did glory in their wisdom, riches, nobility, stoutness and strength.' God 'did then appear in contemptible instruments (as to outward appearance), as in tradesmen, ploughmen, servants and the like'. Though they

> did act several things against you beyond the commission they had from God, yet he did permit them. And in several of them ... there was once a tender, honest, good principle, in the day when they were low ... and they were truly sensible of many oppressions which were in the nation, both in matters of religion and in the laws and customs of the land.... But alas, covetousness, self-seeking and lusts sprang up in most of them....

The restoration of Charles thus had happened 'because they unto whom God gave such power over you were not faithful unto God', and not because of any rightful claims to the kingdom Charles might have. He should therefore take heed of seeking revenge.[2]

---

[1] J. L. Nickalls, 'The Problem of Edward Byllynge', in *The Children of Light*, ed. H. H. Brinton (New York, 1938), pp. 120–3. See also H. N. Brailsford, *The Levellers and the English Revolution* (1961), pp. 639–41, whose comments are interesting.
[2] Fox, *A Noble Salutation*, pp. 2–9, 20.

2 James Nayler (1617–60): The 'Head Quaker'

Nayler was born in the West Riding of Yorkshire, of yeoman stock. He joined the Parliamentarian Army in 1642 and served for eight or nine years until he was invalided out after taking part in the Battle of Dunbar.[1] He denied the charge that he had been 'at Burford among the Levellers'.[2] In 1657 Major-General Lambert testified to Nayler's usefulness as quartermaster. In 1651 God called Nayler when he was at the plough and, 'having neither taken leave of wife or children',[3] he set off like Bunyan's Pilgrim on an itinerant career. Hereupon he was excommunicated by the congregational church near Wakefield to which he had hitherto belonged. There were later scandalous stories that he was expelled on grounds of adultery. Apparently he did not live with his wife for many years after joining the Army in 1642; we may have here a case of *de facto* divorce by removal.

Nayler was eight or nine years Fox's senior, and much more experienced. He was regarded by many as 'the head Quaker in England',[4] 'the most important of all Quakers', 'the chief of the Quakers', 'a most eminent ringleader and head of that faction', 'the grand Quaker of England'. Baxter later called him 'their chief leader', Ralph Farmer Fox's 'old chief companion'.[5] Henry More said, 'at least equal with Fox'.[6] Lilburne in prison in 1656, announcing his conversion to Quakerism, referred in the first place to writings by Nayler ('that strong and tall man in Christ') and by William Deusbury, and also to James Parnell, Richard Hubberthorne and Luke Howard: his one passing reference to Fox was derogatory.[7] MPs in 1656 almost certainly thought they were dealing with the leading Quaker. 'Cut off this fellow and you will destroy the sect,' they were told: 'he writes all their books.'[8] Nayler's *Spiritual*

---

[1] J. L. Nickalls, 'The Problem of Edward Byllynge', p. 116.
[2] G. F. and J. N., *Sauls Errand to Damascus* (1654), p. 30; cf. R. Farmer, *Sathan Inthron'd in his Chair of Pestilence* (1657), p. 21.
[3] *Sauls Errand*, p. 30; J. N., *To the Life of God in All* (1659), p. 1.
[4] [Collier], *A Looking-Glasse for the Quakers*, p. 17.
[5] E. Pagitt, *Heresiography* (5th edn., 1654), pp. 135–6 (rightly 137–8); E. Fogelklou, *James Nayler: The Rebel Saint, 1618–1660* (1931), p. 189; cf. pp. 126–7; *Reliquiae Baxterianae*, pp. 98, 77; [Christopher Wade], *Quakery Slain irrecoverably* (1657), attacked over twenty Quakers by name, of whom Nayler was first; Farmer, *Sathan Inthron'd*, p. 8.
[6] M. Nicolson, *Conway Letters* (1930), p. 418.
[7] *A Resurrection of John Lilburne Now in Prison in Dover-Castle* (1656), pp. 5, 9, 21.
[8] Burton, *Parliamentary Diary*, I, p. 98; cf. *A Collection of Sundry Books .... written by James Nayler* (1716), I, p. xii: 'All the severities [against Nayler] appeared to be designed to bring odium and reproach upon us as a people.' I try to analyse the reason for Parliament's especial severity in *WTUD*, Chapter 10.

Wickedness was the first Quaker book to be published, in 1653. He wrote at least thirteen pamphlets between 1655 and 1656, nearly all of them answers to attacks on Quakers.

Nayler's sense of social justice was as strong as that of any of the early Quakers. 'The wants of all the poor in the nation cry out against you,' he told England's rulers in 1654; 'you have exceeded all that ever went before you.... Covetous and cruel oppressors, ... you grind the face of the poor.... And when you have got great estates, you say God hath given you them; you are set up above them who are made poor by you.'[1] Nayler denounced the hireling priest 'that works not at all, ... taking by violence what's other men's labours'.[2] The law, he declared, 'as it is now used, is scarce serviceable for any other end but for the envious man who hath much money to revenge himself of his poor neighbours'.[3] (Oliver Cromwell said something similar.) 'Saith Antichrist, thou must live by the wits that God hath given thee, and this is no covetousness but a provident care.... If thou stand to wait upon God and do not help thyself by thy wits, both thou and thine may be poor enough.'[4] This echoes Coppe.[5] 'Carnal professors', wrote Nayler, were 'most afraid of freedom, lest any of you should believe in the Son who leads to it.'[6]

Quakers 'generally did adventure lives and estates with those who are in present government', Nayler wrote in 1658, 'purchasing their freedom as men with great loss'.[7] In February 1653 Nayler seems to have sympathized with the Army against the Rump.[8] In March he and Fox could hope that God would 'never suffer that monster persecution again to enter within the gates of England's Whitehall'.[9] But by August he was warning the saints (of Barebone's Parliament?) that if they exalted themselves over the poor and set up their own laws, God would overturn them.[10] Like Fox and Burrough, Nayler came to believe that God's Cause had been betrayed.

---

[1] G. F. and J. N., *Several Papers*, pp. 21–2; cf. Nayler, *Wisdom from Beneath* (1653).
[2] Nayler, *A Public Discovery, Of the Open Blindnes of Babels Builders* (1656), p. 17.
[3] Nayler, *A Few Words occasioned by a Paper lately printed, Stiled, A Discourse concerning the Quakers* (n.d.), p. 23; cf. *A Call to Magistrates, Ministers, Lawyers and People to Repent* (n.d.), p. 23, and *Extracts from State Papers relating to Friends*, pp. 42, 44.
[4] Nayler, *The Old Serpents Voice* (n.d., ?1656), p. 8.
[5] Coppe, *A Fiery Flying Roll*, II, chapter 3.
[6] J. N., *A Salutation to the Seed of God* (1656), p. 8. Cf. Milton: 'Consciences that Christ set free'.
[7] Nayler, *Something in answer to two letters sent from New England* (1658), in *Sundry Books*, II, p. 739; cf. p. 741.
[8] Swarthmore MSS, quoted by Cole, 'The Quakers and Politics', p. 26.
[9] *Sauls Errand*, Epistle to the Christian Reader.
[10] Nayler, *The Power and Glory of the Lord Shining out of the North* (1653), pp. 14–15.

Who could have believed [Nayler asked in 1654] that England
would have brought forth no better fruits than these, now after
such deliverance as no nation can witness?... The God of
Hosts ... hath subdued all our enemies, and hath delivered us
thus far. Awake, awake, all sorts of people; can you say you
have not had a power in your hands against these
abominations?... You have not proved faithful in the
promises to the Lord in the day of your fears.[1]

Like Fox, Nayler admitted that Quakers were accused of being 'about to
raise a new war'.[2] 'Want of justice cast kings from their thrones and
overturned nations',[3] but now (he had written in 1653) 'the rich are
exalted above the poor, and this is not done by any open enemy, ... but
... by those who pretend to be against oppression and for whom, under
that pretence, thou has adventured all that is dear to thee, to put power
into their hands.' 'Woe is me for you high ones, how are you fallen from
the tenderness I have seen in some of you when you were sufferers with
the people of God.'[4]

'You had a large day', he told them sadly in 1660, 'and time to have
done good.' 'If you had harkened to the light in your consciences', you
would not have 'set up what you had cast down, and got into their
estates, and so into their pride by unrighteous gain, whom God had cast
out'. 'You are now left as men in desolation and darkness.'[5] The sequence
is clear—divine deliverance by the instrumentality of the Army—avarice
and ambition of the leaders—oppression of the poor—tyranny not
dissimilar from what God had overthrown.[6] 'We have gone seeking the
Righteous One through Parliaments and Protectors (so called) ... but
his government we have not found.'[7] Repeating Winstanley's
denunciation of kingly power which had survived the King, Nayler
wrote: 'it is not merely the nature of a king nor of a bishop by which the
innocent people of God have suffered; but by the lordly, oppressing

---

[1] *Several Papers*, p. 23. I have changed 'notion' of the original to 'nation'.
[2] J. N., *A Few Words Occasioned by a Paper Lately Printed* (1657), p. 26. For Fox see pp. 157–8 below.
[3] Ibid., pp. 21–2.
[4] Nayler, *A Lamentation ... over the Ruins of this Oppressed Nation* (1653), in *Sundry Books*, I, pp. 99–101; cf. pp. 405–6, 574, 755, 769 (where the reference is specifically to Cromwell's betrayal); cf. also *A Few Words*, pp. 24–5.
[5] Nayler, *To those who were in Authority, whom the Lord is now Judging* (1660), in *Sundry Books*, II, pp. 591, 595.
[6] Cf. J. N., *Behold you Rulers* (1660), p. 1—written in Oliver's time, and to him. For avarice and ambition see pp. 281–2 below.
[7] Nayler, *An account for the Children of Light* (1660), in *Sundry Books*, II, p. 604.

cruel spirit.'[1] By 1660 he was advocating passive obedience to all governments.[2]

Nayler appears to echo Winstanley on many occasions—for instance his contempt for the man who 'worships a God at a distance, but knows him not, nor where he is, but by relation from others'.[3] He denied that the Bible was the Word of God.[4] Too much emphasis on the Christ that died at Jerusalem was a design of the Serpent, to make men 'believe that they are in a better condition than their fathers'.[5] Nayler's emphasis was always on the Christ within. He repudiated predestination to damnation: the light within was sufficient for salvation.[6] The only true ministers were those who preached perfection.[7] Nayler was severe against those whose religion was exclusively other-worldly: 'You profess a redeemer', but his 'redemption must be of another world', whilst 'the old work of the devil must stand in this world.'[8] He shared the radical distrust of human wisdom: 'take heed of searching into the hidden things of God by your own wisdom, which is carnal.' Instead, men must rely on 'the pure light of God dwelling in you and you in it'.[9]

Collier in 1657 identified Quaker principles with Ranters': 'no Christ but within, no Scripture to be a rule, no ordinances, no law but their lusts, no heaven nor glory but here, no sin but what men fancied to be so, no condemnation for sin but in the consciences of ignorant ones'. He was thinking especially of Nayler.[10] But John Whitehead had also been a Ranter; Burrough and other leading Quakers had leanings that way; Margaret Fell was alleged to have been one.[11]

Nayler's symbolic entry into Bristol was only a heightened example of the 'signs' in which many Quakers indulged. The beliefs which motivated him were 'near to that which is a most glorious truth', one MP admitted.[12]

---

[1] Nayler, *A Warning to the Rulers* (1659), in *Sundry Books*, II, p. 766; cf. *What the Possession of the Living Faith is* (1659), p. 31.

[2] *An Account for the Children of Light*, in *Sundry Books*, II, p. 607.

[3] J. N., *A Discovery of the first Wisdom from beneath and the second Wisdom from above* (1653), p. 11; cf. pp. 38–9 above. See also Nayler, *A Second Answer to Thomas Moore* (1655), p. 27.

[4] Nayler, *A Publike Discovery of the Open Blindnes of Babels Builders* (1656), pp. 9–10.

[5] *A Discovery of the First Wisdom*, p. 19.

[6] *Love to the Lost* (2nd edn, 1656), p. 32; G. F. and J. N., *A Word from the Lord* (1654), p. 3.

[7] *A Second Answer to Thomas Moore*, p. 29; cf. *Love to the Lost*, pp. 22–3; *A Publike Discovery*, p. 4.

[8] *A Salutation to the Seed of God*, p. 17.

[9] *A Discovery of the First Wisdom*, p. 6.

[10] [Collier], *A Looking-Glasse for the Quakers*, p. 7.

[11] C. Holmes, *Seventeenth-Century Lincolnshire* (Lincoln, 1980), pp. 232–3; *WTUD*, pp. 236–40.

[12] Burton, *Parliamentary Diary*, I, p. 69.

Fox had been addressed in terms no less extravagant than those which
Nayler's followers applied to him, and Edward Burrough had gone at
least as far in addressing Margaret Fell in 1655.[1] But Fox kept his head,
and was correspondingly irate with Nayler for not keeping his; and
Nayler timed his demonstration badly, when a Parliament bent on ending
religious toleration had just met. They seized the opportunity to make an
example of him as a declaration of hostility to the government's policy of
toleration.

After the event, Nayler accepted the official line, that he had given 'up
himself wholly to be led by others, whose work was wholly to divide us
from the children of light'.[2] 'A sort of people who pretend that they
owned me' and indulged in 'many wild actions' broke up Quaker
meetings in disorder, led apparently by Martha Simmonds. Nayler
rejected them as 'unclean ranting spirits'[3] and was henceforth careful to
differentiate himself from Ranters.[4] 'Most of those that had joined to
James [Nayler] fell in with John Perrot' later.[5] Robert Rich, who 'ran out
with James Nayler and John Perrot' was 'an old Ranter and opposer ...
who has remained in the destroying ranting opposing spirit ever since',
wrote Barbados Friends in 1678.[6] Mr McGregor sensibly remarks that
for Friends the word 'Ranter' 'was often a convenient description of the
unwelcome by-products of their missionary activities rather than an
autonomous movement or an endemic religious mood'. The name could
also be applied to 'doubtful converts ... who were reluctant to submit
themselves to Quaker discipline', especially as that became stricter after
1660.[7]

---

[1] Barbour and Roberts, *Early Quaker Writings*, pp. 477–8.

[2] Nayler, *To the Life of God in All*, p. 3. This became the official version; cf. *A Collection of Sundry Books*, I, pp. viii–ix, xvii.

[3] [Anon]., *A True Narrative of The Examination, Tryall and Sufferings of James Nayler* (1657), pp. 3–4; cf. Nayler, *To the Life of God in All*, p. 8, and *Sundry Books*, I, pp. xvi, xxxiii, liii; K. L. Carroll, 'Martha Simmonds: A Quaker Enigma', *JFHS*; 53 (1972), pp. 49–50.

[4] Nayler, *Wickedness Weighed: in an Answer to a Book ... by Ellis Bradshaw* (1656), p. 14; *An Answer to a Book ... by Richard Baxter* (1656), pp. 25–6.

[5] John Bolton, *Judas and his Treachery Still continued* (1670), pp. 18–19; Carroll, *Perrot*, pp. 10, 45, 50, 57, 60–1, 83–4, 86, 107–8.

[6] Quoted by Carroll, *Perrot*, p. 108.

[7] J. F. MaGregor, 'Ranterism and the Development of Early Quakerism', *Journal of Religious History*, 9 (1977), p. 345 and *passim*; cf. *First Publishers of Truth*, p. 261, and p. 162 below.

3 Edward Burrough (1634–62): Quaker Politician

Edward Burrough was born at Underbarrow, near Kendal, and died whilst still a young man. He was a precocious boy, who 'got up to be a Presbyterian, and followed the highest of the priests and professors of that form'. He was in consequence mocked by his 'former acquaintance' as 'a Roundhead'.[1] He passed through a period in which he 'followed only to hear the highest notionists', and himself talked 'of high things', but remained profoundly dissatisfied until he was converted by George Fox.[2] His parents, persons of some standing in their neighbourhood, disowned him when he became a Quaker: like Nayler, he took to the road as an itinerant preacher. In 1654 he came to London, to preach the light of God which had arisen in the North.[3] He was one of the first Quakers to appear in 'that great City ... where Satan's seat is'.[4] Around 1656 he went on a preaching tour to Ireland, and was forcibly shipped back to England; he was there again in 1660. In 1659 he visited Dunkirk. He died in an overcrowded and insanitary jail in 1662.

The most remarkable thing about Burrough is the authority he acquired whilst still a young man. From 1654 he was accepted as one of the Quaker leaders. Professor Cole saw him rather than George Fox as the political spokesman of the Quakers in the 1650s.[5] Burrough 'looked like a scholar', Ellwood tells us, contrasting him with Nayler, who 'looked but like a plain simple countryman'.[6] Burrough was always a fierce controversialist. In his *Memorable Works*, 340 pages out of 896 consist of replies (often savagely worded) to attacks on Quakers. Burrough rejected 'free-willers' ('which may be true in Christ but a lie unto you'),[7] Fifth Monarchists,[8] Ranters, Seekers and waiters, Levellers[9]

---

[1] 'It is the same man that was called Roundhead that is called Quaker', Edward Byllynge remarked in 1659 (*A Word of Reproof And Advice to my late Fellow-Souldiers and Officers*, p. 11); cf. Fox, *Journal* (1902), I, p. 368. This is a corrected reprint (ed. N. Penney) of the 8th edition of 1891.

[2] Edward Burrough, *The Memorable Works of a Son of Thunder and Consolation* (1672), pp. 14–15. 'Notionists' usually means Ranters: cf. R. Purnell, *Good Tydings for Sinners* (1649), p. 63.

[3] *Works*, pp. 11, 66.

[4] Burrough, *An Epistle to Friends of Truth In and about London* (1667), p. 4. Written 1661.

[5] A. Cole, 'The Quakers and the English Revolution', p. 45.

[6] T. Ellwood, *The History of the Life* (1906), pp. 18–19. First published 1714.

[7] Burrough, *A Trumpet Of the Lord Sounded out of Sion* (1656), pp. 24–5.

[8] Ibid., pp. 25–6; E. B., *Good Counsel and Advice Rejected by Disobedient Men* (1659), pp. 18–19; *Works*, p. 800.

[9] *Works*, pp. 15, 26, 138, 208, 279–80, 320, 548, 746; *A Trumpet Of the Lord*, pp. 26–30; E. B., *A Return to the Ministers of London* (1660), pp. 8–9; *Truth (the Strongest of all) Witnessed Forth* (1657), pp. 8–10, 18, 43; E. B., *A Vindication of the People called Quakers* (1660), p. 8.

and Presbyterians.[1] He also expended much energy in criticizing Richard Baxter and John Bunyan.[2]

Burrough had a continuing interest in social reform, which he sometimes expressed in language reminiscent of Winstanley. In 1659 Burrough denounced 'all earthly lordship and tyranny and oppression ... by which creatures have been exalted and set up one above another, trampling under foot and despising the poor'. 'Hath not the great and heavy oppressions of the law', he asked in the same year, 'been long felt and cried out against, the long delays in courts and the great fees of officers, which causeth many to be excessively rich out of the ruins of the poor, which hath brought odium upon the law itself?... Doth not he that respects persons commit sin?'[3] Even in 1661 Burrough was cautious about rejecting the doctrine that 'all things ought to be in common'.[4] But he had no sympathy for 'sturdy beggars and rogues and idle and disorderly persons'. The law against them 'is good, if it be duly and justly executed upon such as are truly guilty herein', and is not used against Quaker missionaries.[5]

Some of Burrough's political statements have a Leveller ring. More than once he—like Nayler and Fox, Bishop and Byllynge—claimed the rights of a freeborn Englishman, and asserted the Quakers' 'just and lawful right and title as such to possess and enjoy' their 'lives, liberties and estates'.[6] He pleaded Magna Carta against the imprisonment of Quakers in 1657.[7] 'The faithful subjects cannot enjoy their birthright privilege as they ought,' he complained to Oliver and his Council in 1658.[8] In 1659 he even asked Parliament 'to establish the Agreement of the People'—the officers' Agreement of 1649, apparently.[9] 'All governors and rulers ought to be accountable to the people', and to their successors in office. They should be elected each year, and even 'the highest of the rulers' should be as much 'subject under the law and

---

[1] 'Some who preached and prayed for the King and bishops do now preach and pray ... for those who destroyed King and bishops' (Burrough, *A Measure of the Times*, 1657, p. 11).
[2] *Works*, pp. 310–24, 136–52, 275–309.
[3] Ibid., p. 500; cf. p. 553.
[4] Ibid., p. 802.
[5] Ibid., p. 358.
[6] Ibid., pp. 85, 89 (when Burrough and Howgil were expelled from Ireland), 773, 813; Reay, 'The Quakers and 1659; Two Newly Discovered Broadsides by Edward Burrough', *JFHS*, 54 (1977), p. 105. For Nayler see *A Collection of Sundry Books*, I, p. 187.
[7] *Works*, p. 273.
[8] Ibid., p. 563; Reay, op. cit., pp. 105, 109.
[9] Ibid., p. 108. Vane and Salway seem to have seriously contemplated this in November 1659 (Wariston, *Diary*, III, p. 151).

punishable by it' as 'the poorest of the people'. 'The law ought to be known unto all people.'[1]

Burrough in his scholarly way had a deeper sense of popular tradition behind him than most Quakers, even if he got it mainly via Foxe's *Book of Martyrs*. Burrough defended Wyclif and the Lollards for views which the Quakers were alleged to have reproduced.[2] He accepted the analogy between Quakers and Marian martyrs.[3] He proclaimed those heretical shibboleths, the Everlasting Gospel and the anointing.[4] He shared traditional radical anticlericalism. Priests were 'the fountain of all wickedness abounding in the nations'. Consequently 'the seminaries of sin and Satan'—Oxford and Cambridge which trained the clergy—should be 'beaten down and suppressed', Burrough urged Charles II in 1660.[5] He estimated that the clergy collected £1½ million per annum in tithes, mainly from the poor.[6]

Burrough was in favour of the widest toleration for protestants. 'The laws of man can but settle a sect; ... true religion can never be settled by that means.'[7] Those who persecute for forms are apostate Christians; intolerance is antichristian; it necessarily leads to hypocrisy.[8] Toleration also made good political sense, Burrough assured Charles II, since it prevented discontents; he anticipated the economic argument in favour of toleration which was to become fashionable later in the century. Persecution 'must unavoidably tend to destroy and expel trading, husbandry and merchandize in these kingdoms, for a great part of trading and husbandry depends upon such kind of persons whose principles are for toleration in religion'.[9] Toleration was not however to be extended to papists, since 'their weapons are carnal and devilish.' 'The poor and common sort' of papists were to be pitied; but 'priests and Jesuits and clergymen, they are to be cut off with the edge of the sword of the Lord

---

[1] *Works*, pp. 442. Does this mean annual Parliaments?

[2] Ibid., pp. 801–4, 806, 809; cf. *State Papers Relating to Friends*, pp. 39–44—a paper addressed to Richard Cromwell, signed by Byllynge, Pearson, Samuel Fisher and others. Nayler recognized some medieval heretics as predecessors (*An Answer to a Book ... by Richard Baxter*, 1655, p. 12). Cf. pp. 175, 297, 302–3 below.

[3] Ibid., pp. 499, 806–9; cf. Barbour and Roberts, *Early Quaker Writings*, p. 117.

[4] *Works*, p. 724; cf. F. Howgil, *A Testimony Concerning the Life, Death, Trials, Travels and Labours of Edward Burrough* (1662), p. 15; cf. Barbour and Roberts, op. cit., pp. 191, 203; G. Whitehead and E. Burrough, *The Son of Perdition Revealed* (1661), p. 33. See pp. 303–6 below.

[5] *Works*, Sig. c, pp. 157, 233, 722–3.

[6] *A Just and Lawful Tryal* (1660), p. 16; cf. *Works*, pp. 234, 223–39, 509.

[7] *Works*, pp. 509–13; cf. pp. 495, 579, 716–19, 830–4.

[8] Ibid., pp. 800, 817, 842–5, 850–78.

[9] Ibid., pp. 771, 790–2, 818.

God ... and no pity.'[1]

Most interesting for our purposes are Burrough's political attitudes. In 1657 he described himself as 'a friend to England's Commonwealth'.[2] The civil war against Charles I, he said, had originally been justified by the 'great measure of iniquity filled up in monarchical government, and a great measure of oppression upon the poor people of this nation by their lords and great men'.[3] In 1655 Burrough warned Oliver Cromwell that although God had made him an instrument to punish his enemies, he and his Council had neglected 'to take off oppression and to ease the oppressed', ignoring 'the grievous cry of the poor'. 'The same laws stand still in force by which tyranny and oppression is acted.' But if Cromwell repented God would 'give thee the necks of princes to tread upon, and their dominion for thy inheritance'.[4]

From 1657 onwards Burrough pestered Oliver (and later his son), personally and by pamphlet, with 'good counsel and advice'. He told the Protector in 1657 that God had given him power 'to break [his] enemies to pieces'. The Lord had raised him up to be a plague upon royalists 'because of their unrighteousness, oppression and tyranny'.[5] If Oliver had remained faithful, by now 'the Hollander had been thy subject ... the King of France should have bowed under thee his neck; the Pope should have withered as in winter.'[6] About Oliver's war against Spain Burrough wrote 'something there is in it known to the Lord'—though this would not extend to an alliance with France.[7] Burrough told Richard Cromwell that his father 'was called of God into that great work, to subdue the grievous tyrannies once ruling over tender consciences; ... and the Lord was with him in victory and went before him ... and made him prosperous' against all his enemies. But Oliver 'did not wholly fulfil the will of the Lord, nor the work which he began'.[8]

In 1657 Burrough urged Oliver not to accept the crown.[9] His most moving tribute came when he saw Cromwell's effigy lying in state after his death.

---

[1] Ibid., pp. 361, 535, 619, 799–800, 808, 862.
[2] *A Just and Lawful Trial of the Teachers and Professed Ministers of England. By a friend to England's Commonwealth.* This last phrase was suppressed in *Works* (p. 223).
[3] *A Visitation and Presentation of Love unto the King and Those Called Royalists* (1660), p. 33.
[4] *Works*, p. 97. We may compare Winstanley upon 'kingly power' which survived the execution of Charles I. Cf. p. 87 above.
[5] *Good Counsel and Advice Rejected* (1659), p. 17.
[6] Ibid., pp. 26–7.
[7] Ibid., p. 35.
[8] Ibid., p. 53.
[9] Ibid., p. 9; cf. Cole, 'The Quakers and the English Revolution', p. 45.

> I knew the man when he was living, and had knowledge of his
> spirit.... Alas for him! who was once a great instrument in the
> hand of the Lord, to break down many idolatrous images....
> And did not once his children, officers and his brave soldiers
> and Army pull down all the images and crosses and suchlike
> popish stuff wherever they met it?

And now he is made an idol himself. This had happened, Burrough
reflected, because he 'too much sought the greatness and honour of the
world, and loved the praise of men, and took flattering titles'. So that 'all
men might see the first Cause is lost.... And I began to recall what a
gallant instrument for the Lord he once was, and how many glorious and
noble victories God once gave him.'[1]

On several occasions Burrough protested against 'putting of honest,
godly men out of the Army' or from the commission of the peace.[2] In the
summer of 1659 he was in correspondence with Sir Henry Vane, whom
he was trying to influence.[3] On behalf of 'the people called Quakers'
Burrough insisted on the provision of 'freedom and true liberty to
subjects'.[4] Some time in 1659 Burrough made (or drafted) what sounds
like a formal offer of political collaboration to the Rump of the Long
Parliament: 'that you speedily do order the choosing of a committee ...
consisting of six or eight or more of the ablest and soberest men of each
sort of profession in the nation'—Presbyterians, Independents,
Anabaptists, Quakers—'and likewise of the rest of all sorts of men as you
in wisdom shall think fit'. This committee would list the grievances and
oppressions which the freeborn of the nation suffered from and would
propose remedies to Parliament, as well as suggesting 'the way of an
equal and just government' for the future.[5] The Quakers would clearly be
prepared to participate in such a committee.

In a second memorandum the readiness of Quakers to undertake

---

[1] *Works*, pp. 458–61. Wither made similar comments in *Salt upon Salt* (1659), pp. 19–20, in
Miscellaneous Works, IV.
[2] *Good Counsel and Advice*, pp. 51–2; cf. p. 64, and the *Declaration of the People of God in
scorn called Quakers* (April 1659), pp. 5–7: signed by Edward Byllynge, Anthony Pearson and
eleven others.
[3] Cole, 'The Quakers and Politics', pp. 150–1.
[4] E. B., *A Declaration from the People called Quakers* (1659), p. 10.
[5] *To the Parliament of the Commonwealth of England Sitting at Westminster*, in Reay, 'The
Quakers and 1659', p. 107. Dr Reay points out that suggestions for a similar committee were
being made by non-Quakers as well as by other Quakers at this time: so Burrough was perhaps
not so unrealistic as one might think (op. cit., pp. 103–4, 106).

political and military employment was made even clearer. Burrough protested that Quakers had been 'cast out of places of all trust in the nation, as if we deserved no place of fidelity amongst you, no not to have any office, nor hardly to have been allowed us our birthright privilege, for we have been cast out of the place of justice, and out of the Army in which we would have been of service to you and our country'.[1] This policy 'hath sorely weakened you.... How can you expect any help from us to defend you?' Declaring that 'there is the spirit of ambition and oppression to break down in yourselves', Burrough proceeded to set out terms for military support.

> If we see that spirit amongst you that would advance righteousness and not seek yourselves but the good of the nation, oh then we should rejoice and our lives would not be dear to lay down.... We are lovers of your souls and friends to the seed of God amongst you and shall be assisters and helpers with you in all righteous things till righteousness and true judgement be established.[2]

The terms on which Quakers should accept 'places among men, for the service of the nation' are discussed in *A General Epistle to Saints*.[3]

'There is a government to be set up in this nation,' Burrough declared, 'even that which is of the Lamb.'[4] What exactly did he hope for? He clearly still had millenarian expectations. In 1654 he proclaimed that 'the Lord of heaven and earth is now turning the world upside down, all old things shall pass away.... By his sword will the Lord plead with all flesh, and the slain of him shall be many.'[5] 'The way of the coming of his kingdom hath seemed to be prepared,' he told the MPs of the Rump in 1659, by the 'mighty things' done in England during the Revolution.[6]

Like most early Quakers, Burrough used military metaphors in a way that might reasonably alarm his enemies. 'Put on your armour and gird on your sword ... and prepare yourselves for battle,' he told 'the Camp

---

[1] *To the Parliament and Army (in generall) of the Commonwealth of England*, in Reay, op. cit., p. 109. There are many complaints to the same effect—e.g. *Good Counsel and Advice Rejected*, pp. 15, 53, 59; cf. Cole, 'The Quakers and the English Revolution', pp. 46, 53; Barbour, *The Quakers in Puritan England*, pp. 221–2.

[2] Reay, op. cit., pp. 109–11; cf. *Works*, pp. 605–6.

[3] *Works*, pp. 389–91. Professor Cole plausibly dates this Epistle to 1659, rather than 1658, as in *Works* (Cole, 'The Quakers and Politics', pp. 144–5).

[4] *Works*, p. 621.

[5] Ibid., p. 12.

[6] Burrough, *To the Parliament of the Common-Wealth of England* (1659), single sheet.

of the Lord in England' in 1655. 'Stand upon your feet and appear in your terror as an army with banners and let the nations know your power.... Let not your eye pity nor your hand spare, but wound the lofty and tread under foot the honourable of the earth.'[1] That presumably is not to be taken literally, any more than Burrough's letter to Margaret Fell in the following year, in which he asked, 'How is the war prospering in England?'[2] But cumulatively such language becomes menacing. 'Our army is almost scattered and broken,' Howgil wrote to Margaret Fell in June 1655.[3] She herself called the Army the 'battle-axe in the hand of the Lord'—though she appears to be referring to times past.[4] 'Spare none', wrote Howgil, also in 1655, 'neither old nor young; kill, cut off, destroy, bathe your sword in the blood of Amalek and all the Egyptians and Philistines, and all the uncircumcised'.[5] 'The sword of the Lord is in the hands of the saints', John Audland reminded Friends in the same year, 'and this sword divides, hews and cuts down deceit.'[6]

And what are we to make of Burrough's *Woeful Cry* of 1657? What will happen, he asked, when Christ comes to reign, 'and the saints which you have oppressed receive the authority and dominion? It shall be said, "All that would not that Christ should reign, slay them before him."' 'The saints shall rule with a rod of iron.'[7] In 1656 Burrough had started a pamphlet with the words: 'The Lord from heaven, in this his day, is risen and come forth to make war with all his enemies, *being the fullness of time*.'[8] The title of a pamphlet of 1660 included the words 'in these last days of [Christ's] glorious appearance'.[9] In the same year Burrough proclaimed that 'Antichrist must fall.... God will exalt his kingdom upon earth' and will 'free his people, and they shall be happy *in this world*, and for ever'.[10] 'We look for a new earth as well as for a new heaven,' he told Parliament, also in 1660—echoing Erbery.[11]

---

[1] *Works*, p. 671, cf. *WTUD*, pp. 245–6.
[2] Ross, *Margaret Fell: Mother of Quakerism*, p. 54.
[3] Ibid., p. 51; cf. p. 54.
[4] M. Fell, *To the General Councill of the Officers of the English Army* (1659), quoted by Cole, 'Quakers and Politics', p. 167.
[5] Howgil, in Burrough, *To the Camp of the Lord in England*, p. 17.
[6] Audland, *The School-Master Disciplined* (1655), quoted in *Biographical Dictionary of British Radicals in the Seventeenth Century*, ed. R. B. Greaves and R. Zaller (Brighton, 1982), I, p. 30.
[7] E. B., *The Wofull Cry of Unjust Persecution* (1657), in *Works*, pp. 265, 259.
[8] Burrough, *Stablishing against Quaking Thrown down and overturned* (1656), p. 3 (my italics). The tract is directed against Giles Firmin.
[9] E. B., *To the Beloved and Chosen of God* (1660).
[10] *Works*, p. 766. My italics.
[11] Burrough, *To the Parliament of the Commonwealth of England* (1659), p. 3. See p. 88 above.

To understand Burrough's attitude to politics in the late 1650s we must grasp the context in which he saw the English Revolution, with which he had grown up. It seemed to him, as to Milton, a God-given opportunity which had been lost because of the avarice and ambition of men. God 'overthrew that oppressing power of kings, lords and bishops, both in church and civil state, and brought some tyrants and oppressors to just execution.'[1] (Is Burrough here approving regicide?) The Long Parliament had been 'the first assertors and contenders for England's liberty, ... whom the Lord hath honoured in beginning to remove tyranny and oppression and reaching after our long-lost liberty'.[2] Cavaliers 'are, and have been always, enemies to the very appearance of righteousness'.[3] Their sufferings during the interregnum had been God's punishment.[4] Burrough—like Nayler, Hubberthorne and Howgil—always assumed that Quakers had supported Parliament in the civil war.[5]

But as early as 1655 Burrough was discussing the Army's failure to live up to expectations.[6] 'The principle of sincerity, ... of opposing oppression and pressing after reformation' was soon lost, and many 'became self-seekers' and 'were oppressors even as others before them'.[7] Burrough called on Parliament in November 1658 to 'remember the Old Good Cause that is decayed; let it be once more revived in the nations.... Remember the first engagement ... was for freedom.'[8] 'Whosoever are against the Good Old Cause and perfect freedom ... we are against them and will engage our lives against them.'[9] 'The outgoings and dealings of the Lord have been and are mighty and wonderful in this nation,' Burrough told Parliament in 1656, admitting even that some MPs 'were partakers in a good degree of his power and outgoings ... while you stood in his counsel'.[10] 'The Lord God,' he repeated to the

---

[1] Burrough, *A Message to the Present Rulers of England* (1659), p. 6; partially omitted from *Works*, p. 586.

[2] Burrough, *To the Parliament of the Commonwealth of England* (1659), p. 4.

[3] Burrough, *A Trumpet of the Lord Sounded out of Sion* (1656), pp. 9–10.

[4] [Burrough], *A Visitation and Presentation of Love* (1660), pp. 4–5, 32.

[5] *A Trumpet of the Lord*, pp. 9–10; *Work*, pp. 671–3; cf. pp. 132–3, 140 above.

[6] *Works*, pp. 86, 97–9; cf. E. B., *The Wofull Cry of Unjust Persecutions* (1656), p. 20, Burrough, *A Measure of the Times* (1657), p. 5.

[7] *A Visitation and Presentation of Love*, pp. 13, 32; cf. E. B., *Good Counsel and Advice*, pp. 4–5; *To the Parliament of the Common-Wealth of England* (1659), single sheet; Burrough, *A Presentation of Wholesome Informations unto the King of England* (1660), Epistle; *Works*, pp. 458–60, 497–8, 506, 612–13.

[8] *Good Counsel and Advice*, p. 65; cf. *Works*, p. 523; Burrough, *Satans Designe Defeated* (1659), p. 17.

[9] Burrough, *To the Whole English Army and to Every Particular Member thereof* (1660), single sheet.   [10] E. B., *The Crying Sinnes Reproved* (1656), p. 3.

restored Rump in 1659, 'hath done great and honourable things by you; ... mighty things hath been brought to pass in our nations by the hand of the Lord.'[1]

The Army was crucial.[2] 'The Lord ... was with them in many things he called them to, and gave them victory and dominion over much injustice and oppression', until they turned to self-seeking. But there was still time for them to extend their activities beyond 'these few poor islands', to 'set up your standard at the gates of Rome', to avenge 'the blood of the guiltless through all the dominions of the Pope'. 'True honour ... doth consist in victory over all that which is contrary to God.'[3] 'Is there no hope of your return to the Good Old Cause?' he cried desperately in January 1659–60.[4] 'There is some great work to do ... in the nations,' he had written in May 1659, 'with their outward sword; that time is not long till a good thing may be accomplished by our English Army.'[5]

In May 1659 Burrough and Samuel Fisher were in Dunkirk holding meetings of 'some hundreds of officers and soldiers'. Some feared 'the whole Army should be seduced to follow us.'[6] Whilst the New Model continued to exist, Professor Cole rightly summed up, 'Friends never completely abandoned the hope that it might resume its old role as a "battle-axe in the hand of the Lord". But when it was dissolved, their military and political aspirations died with it.'[7]

1660 marked the end of hopes for reform at home or a military crusade against popery on the continent. How was Burrough to react? It was, he had to recognize, God's will that Charles II and the royalists should come back. But this did not necessarily imply any desert on their part: rather it was a just punishment for those former servants of God who had betrayed their trust.[8] Burrough was blunt about the terms on which he believed God had restored the King: 'This is your day that God hath

---

[1] Burrough, *To the Parliament of the Common-Wealth of England* (1659); *Satans Designe Defeated* (1659), p. 17.

[2] Cf. *A Trumpet of the Lord*, pp. 6–8; Burrough, *A Visitation and Warning Proclaimed* (1659), pp. 29–31.

[3] *Works*, pp. 537–40. Burrough had given similar advice to Oliver Cromwell to 'rock nations as a cradle' (*Good Counsel and Advice*, pp. 17, 26–7, 35–7, 53, 59).

[4] *To the Whole English Army*, single sheet; cf. *Works*, pp. 610–13.

[5] Reay, 'Early Quaker Activity', p. 117.

[6] Ibid., p. 129.

[7] Cole, 'The Quakers and Politics', pp. 226–7.

[8] *Works*, pp. 664–5; pp. 669–73, 684, 687, 706, 785; Burrough, *A Just and Righteous Plea Presented to the King of England and his Council* (1661), p. 23; *A Visitation and Presentation of Love*, pp. 4–5.

given you to try you.' He went on to argue, reasonably but ominously, that 'the strength and safety and prosperity of the King and his government stands in the union, good affections and love of his subjects.'[1] Despite expectations, the nation 'appears to be as far from settlement in an happy union in government as for many years'.[2] 'Force and cruelty,' he added even more ominously, 'will never make the King happy, but will work contrary, for the people are wise and understanding, and will not long bear any degree of the yoke of slavery.'[3] Persecution 'seems ... not the way of prosperity'.[4]

It would therefore be foolish as well as wrong to execute the regicides, Burrough told the King and his Council. 'It's probable they were raised up of God as a judgement and reproof upon you, because of your iniquities, which were many and great against God.... They had once a just Cause ... and the Lord blessed them in it. The providence of war was clearly on their side, which I call the hand of the Lord.'[5] But although 'the gates of hell at this time seem to be open against us', Burrough was confident that God 'will judge and avenge our persecutors in his season, and we shall be a people when the Egyptians lie dead upon the sea-shore'.[6]

It was in this spirit that Burrough acceded—with little enthusiasm, it would appear—to the peace principle of 1661. As long ago as 1657 he had warned against seeking to bring about Christ's kingdom with 'carnal weapons', presumably in reference to the Fifth-Monarchist uprising of that year.[7] It must come 'by the arm of the Lord alone'.[8] But he was not one of the original signatories to the peace *Declaration* of January 1661— almost the only leading Quaker whose name was missing.[9]

Writing to Friends in 1660 Burrough found it necessary to ask 'Why should we murmur against God? or say "Why hast thou done it?"' He stressed the importance of walking 'in all wisdom, so that your enemies have nothing against you'.[10] 'It is very just with the Lord' to let 'the men that now are in power ... have their day'. He leads up to the conclusion,

---

[1] *A Just and Righteous Plea*, Sig. A 2, p. 32.
[2] Burrough, *The Everlasting Gospel of Repentance and Remission of Sins* (1660), p. 29.
[3] *Works*, p. 783 (should be p. 791).
[4] Ibid., p. 792.
[5] Ibid., pp. 705–8.
[6] Ibid., pp. 766–7.
[7] Ibid., p. 201.
[8] Ibid., p. 247.
[9] Cole, 'Quakers and Politics', pp. 263–4.
[10] *Works*, pp. 663–4, 690.

in capitals, 'BABYLON MUST FALL WITH A GREAT NOISE.'[1] He died too soon for us to know whether he accepted pacifism as a temporary expedient or as a long-term principle.[2]

Burrough shared with Erbery, Sedgwick and Penington the idea that there has been apostasy since the Apostles' time, and that the church is in the Wilderness.[3] The various sects vainly cry up tradition, Scriptures or 'the practice of the saints before us'.[4] I suggested that there are echoes of Winstanley in Burrough. 'There is but only life and death in the whole creation.... Where life rules and reigns, death is held in captivity and bondage.'[5] Burrough claimed to receive messages from God,[6] and to 'judge by the infallible spirit' those who have received no command from Christ to preach.[7] The Bible, he asserted, was 'profitable', but not 'the most perfect rule of faith and life to the saints'.[8] Milton would have agreed. Burrough was thought to be too tolerant of the ideas of the near-Ranter John Perrot in 1661.[9] Burrough too looked to posterity. 'If you should destroy these vessels,' he told Charles II and the royalists, 'yet our principles you can never extinguish, but they will live for ever and enter into other bodies to live and speak and act.'[10]

4   George Fox (1624–91) and the Peace Principle

George Fox was ten years older than Edward Burrough. He too came of 'the middling sort', his father being a prosperous weaver. Descriptions of Fox as a weaver's son apprenticed to a cobbler underestimate his social standing. His master was a shoemaker who was also a grazier. When Fox left home in 1643 he 'had a great deal of gold and silver about him'—sufficient private means to enable him to lead an itinerant life. He was at

---

[1] Ibid., pp. 664–6.
[2] Ibid., pp. 842–3.
[3] Ibid., pp. 49, 185–94, 325, 413–14, 420–3, 623, 793–4; cf. Nayler, *A Warning to Rulers* (1659), in *Sundry Books*, II, p. 765. See pp. 297–302 below.
[4] *Works*, p. 417.
[5] Burrough, *A Discovery of Divine Mysteries* (1661), p. 7; cf. Winstanley, *The Law of Freedom*, p. 226, and p. 144 above.
[6] *Works*, pp. 196–7.
[7] Ibid., p. 51.
[8] Ibid., p. 541; cf. Fox. *Journal*, I, p. 36; *Gospel-Truth Demonstrated* (1706), pp. 131, 158.
[9] Carroll, *Perrot*, p. 63.
[10] *Works*, p. 677.

home with gentry sympathizers, and towards the end of his life he built and endowed a meeting house at Swarthmoor.[1]

From 1643 onwards he wandered all over the Midlands, discussing and arguing with religious radicals. He was often in despair.[2] But by 1647 he was having 'great openings concerning the things written in the *Revelation*', which he regarded as the most relevant book of the Bible.[3] The origin of the Society of Friends is usually dated from Fox's very successful tour of the North which began in 1651. In 1654 he announced that 'the Army is coming up from the North', and indeed in that year Quaker preachers swarmed all over the South and West of England.[4]

Like Burrough, Fox had a strong sense of social justice.[5] Denunciations of the rich and their oppression of the poor, in terms which seem to echo Abiezer Coppe, abound in Fox's early writings.[6] 'God hath made all of one mould and one blood to dwell upon the face of the earth,' he declared in 1654.[7] 'Thy treasure is here in the earth,' he told the rich, in words which recall Winstanley and Coppe; 'there thou worshippest the host of heaven, and it reigns over thee.' A rich man is 'the greatest thief', since he got his goods 'by cozening and cheating, by lying and defrauding.... And if the thief steal it, thou art undone ... and then thou hangest thy fellow creature contrary to the law of God.'[8] Inequality is abetted by the law. 'If a lord or an earl come into your courts, you will hardly fine him for not putting off his hat; ... it is the poor that suffer, and the rich bears with the rich.'[9] 'Some you have made to swear, some you have made to pay for swearing.'[10] Pamphlets like these were not reprinted in *Gospel-Truth* in 1706.[11]

William Penn in his Introduction to Fox's *Journal* said that 'the generality' thought the early Quakers were 'turners of the world upside

---

[1] *DNB*, 'George Fox'.

[2] Fox, *Journal*, I, pp. 4, 22.

[3] Ibid., I, p. 8.

[4] Fox, *Newes Coming up out of the North* (1654), title-page; cf. *Journal*, I, p. xlv.

[5] Ibid., I, p. 54 (1650); Fox, *Gospel-Truth Demonstrated in a Collection of Doctrinal Books* (1706), pp. 6 (1653), 12–13 (1654), 29–31 (1655), 128–9 (1658).

[6] As was clearly pointed out by Braithwaite, *Beginnings*, pp. 46–50.

[7] *Gospel-Truth*, p. 27 (1654). This seems to be a standard Quaker phrase; cf. Burrough, *Works*, p. 500. It was also used in Cromwell's Manifesto justifying his war with Spain in 1655, which may have been drafted by Milton (Abbott, *Writings and Speeches of Oliver Cromwell*, III, p. 880).

[8] Fox , *Newes Coming up out of the North*, p. 11. Not reprinted in *Gospel-Truth*.

[9] G. F. and P. M., *An Instruction to Judges & Lawyers* (n.d.), pp. 27–8. Not in *Gospel-Truth*.

[10] *Newes Coming up out of the North*, p. 20.

[11] An exception is a pamphlet of 1660, *To Both Houses of Parliament*, in which the demand that no one should be put to death for stealing cattle or money survives (*Gospel-Truth*, p. 219).

down, as indeed in some sense they were'.[1] In his pamphlets of the 1650s Fox called insistently for law reform, along lines similar to those advocated by Levellers and other radicals. Like Winstanley, Fox looked forward to the time when 'all the law books in the nation will be thrown away which are made in the will of men ... that everyone may know the law in short and plain [words?]'.[2] 'Every constable in every town' should 'have the law committed to him and call all the people together, that they may all know it'.[3]

In a programme which Fox put before Parliament in 1659 (whose main emphasis was to demand toleration for Quakers) he repeated traditional radical demands: all the law of England should be brought into a known tongue so that every countryman might plead his own cause. No one should be imprisoned because he could not or would not fee an attorney. Bills, writs and indictments should be simplified and shortened. The death sentence for stealing cattle or money should be abolished. 'This will be the way to take oppression off the poor people.... Away with lawyers.... This is the way to bring the nation like a garden, and a free nation, a free people.'[4] All fines and amercements should be given to the poor, together with former monastic lands, all glebe lands, and 'all those fines that belong to lords of manors, ... for lords have enough'. These last would have been major acts of expropriation, greater than any that Winstanley envisaged.[5] And in phrases which tell us a good deal about the condition of English gaols—with which Quakers were all too familiar— Fox insisted, 'Let all gaols be in wholesome places, that the prisoners may not lie in their own dung and piss.... Let there be a house of office in all gaols.'[6] The pamphlet also had provisions for poor relief, and wanted begging to be stopped.[7]

Fox was aware that poverty led men and women to steal.[8] Already in 1648 he 'exhorted the justices [of Derbyshire] not to oppress the servants in [fixing] their wages'.[9] In 1655 he denounced, in Digger style, those who call themselves lords of commons, wastes and forests, 'and keeps it

---

[1] Fox, *Journal*, I, p, xxxiv.

[2] G. F., *A Warning from the Lord* (1654), p. 24; cf. Fox, *Several Papers Given Forth* (1660), pp. 32–3. Neither reprinted in *Gospel-Truth*.

[3] *Newes Coming up out of the North*, p. 22. cf. Winstanley, *The Law of Freedom*, Chapter 6.

[4] G. F., *To the Parliament of the Comon-Wealth of England* (1659), pp. 3–5; cf. *Newes Coming up out of the North*, p. 22 and *An Instruction to Judges & Lawyers*, pp. 18–19, 31–40.

[5] *To the Parliament ...*, pp. 6, 8. Cf. Winstanley, *The Law of Freedom*, pp. 286, 374.

[6] Ibid., p. 13. Cf. Braithwaite, *Second Period*, pp. 16, 558–9.

[7] *To the Parliament ...*, pp. 9, 13.

[8] Fox , *To the Protector and Parliament of England* (1658), p. 12. Not in *Gospel-Truth*.

[9] *Journal*, I, p. 27.

from the people, when so many are ready to starve and beg'.[1] Among all
the other reasons for abolishing tithes, Fox told priests that they were 'as
bad as ever the Cavaliers, or rather worse, ... plundering people you do
no work for.... Your actions make you to stink in the country.'[2]
Opposition to the established church and its endowed clergy led Fox, as
it led Burrough, to oppose the universities. One of his earliest revelations
from the Lord was that 'to be bred at Oxford or Cambridge was not
enough to make a man fit to be a minister of Christ.'[3] 'The Whore set up
your schools and colleges ... whereby you are made ministers,' he told
the clergy in 1659, urging Parliament to put the universities down.[4]

Fox quoted a letter written to Chief Justice Glynne in 1656 by Edward
Pyott ('on behalf of us all') which started off: 'We are free men of
England, free born; our rights and liberties are according to law and
ought to be defended by it.'[5] Fox makes less of the heretical succession
than Burrough does, which is curious since his mother was 'of the stock
of the martyrs', and Margaret Fell was said to be the great-granddaughter
of Anne Askew.[6] Fox frequently refers to the Everlasting Gospel.[7]

Fox seems to have been no less opposed to kingship than was
Burrough. Charles I's 'family was a nurse for papists and for bishops'.[8]
Fox urged the Parliament of 1654 not to follow the 'laws and customs of
kings and queens' against the light.[9] Of the Presbyterians he said in 1654
'there is that nature that would have an earthly king to reign, in which
nature lodgeth the murderer.'[10] He advised Oliver Cromwell to reject the
crown offered to him in 1657.[11] In 1660, like Milton, Fox published a
passionately anti-monarchical tract, in which he declared that 'those who
desired an earthly king' were 'traitors against Christ'. 'Antichristians ...

---

[1] G. F., *A Declaration Against all Professions and Professors* (1655), p. 12.
[2] G. F., *Several Papers Given Forth* (1660), p. 20.
[3] *Journal*, I, p. 7; cf. *Newes Coming up out of the North*, p. 39; G. F., *The Lambs Officer* (1659), p. 2 (against Hebrew, Greek and Latin).
[4] *The Lambs Officer*, pp. 3, 18; Fox, *The Great Mistery of the Great Whore Unfolded* (1659), p. 154. *To the Parliament ...*, p. 8; cf. *Early Quaker Writings*, ed. Barbour and Roberts, p. 256.
[5] Fox, *Journal*, I, p. 287; cf. p. 318.
[6] Ross, *Margaret Fell*, pp. 5, 8.
[7] *Journal*, I, pp. 36, 110, 115, 121, 165, 176, 256, 338, 406, 418; II, pp. 8, 98, 360; *The Lambs Officer*, pp. 13, 21; *A General Epistle To be read in all the Christian Meetings in the World* (1662), p. 3; *Gospel-Truth*, p. 196. See p. 303 below.
[8] *Newes Coming up out of the North*, p. 19.
[9] *A Message from the Lord to the Parliament of England* (1654), p. 1.
[10] G. F. and J. N., *A Word from the Lord* (1654), p. 15. This passage was rather naturally not printed in *Gospel-Truth*.
[11] *Journal*, I, p. 432; Nickolls, *Original Letters and Papers of State*, p. 141.

will have a king', but 'true Christians' will have no king but Christ. 'Ignorant and foolish people that would have a king' will regret it, but 'the Lord will not hear you at that day.'[1]

Fox was very rude about the House of Lords. 'What a dirty, nasty thing it would have been,' he told the Council of Officers in 1659, 'to have heard talk of a House of Lords among them'—i.e. among supporters of the Parliamentarian Cause in the 1640s.[2] Byllynge in the same year asked his 'late fellow soldiers ... which amongst ye ... hath not said it would never be a good world so long as there was a lord in England? And likewise swore against a House of Lords?... Was there any of this stuff amongst ye some years since?' And in a passage which underlines his rejection of pacifism Byllynge added, 'Dukes and Marquises I deny, but the military chief or inferior captain or leader I own.... Knights of all sorts I deny, but the just soldier ... I own in his place.'[3]

Like Burrough, Fox long continued to have hopes of the Army. He too certainly had no objections to the soldier's trade in the 1650s. 'See that you know a soldier's place,' he told them in 1657, 'and see that ye be soldiers qualified, ... and that ye be content with your wages.'[4] He complained in 1659 that 'many valiant captains, soldiers and officers have been put out of the Army' and navy, as well as out of the commission of the peace.[5]

On many occasions Fox, again like Burrough, urged Cromwell and the Army to undertake a military crusade in Europe. In January 1658, when England was already at war with Spain, Fox told the Protector that if he had 'minded the work of the Lord as he began with thee at first, ... the Hollander had been thy subject and tributary, Germany had given up to have done thy will, and the Spaniard had quivered like a dry leaf; ... the King of France should have bowed his neck under thee, the Pope should have withered as in winter, the Turk in all his fatness should have smoked'. Oliver should 'let thy soldiers go forth ... that thou may rock nations as a cradle.'[6] In a paper of 1659 intended 'for the inferior officers and soldiers to read' Fox urged them to conquer Spain: 'If ever you

---

[1] Fox, *Several Papers Given Forth*, pp. 5–14.
[2] G. F., *To the Councill of Officers of the Armie* (1659), p. 7. Not in *Gospel-Truth*.
[3] Byllynge, *A Word of Reproof, and Advice to my late Fellow-Souldiers* (1659), pp. 9–10, 7–9.
[4] G. F., *This is to all Officers and Souldiers of the Armies in England, Scotland and Ireland* (1657), p. 2. Not in *Gospel-Truth*.
[5] G. F., *To the Councill of Officers*, p. 5; cf. *Journal*, I, p. 189, 409, and *passim*; *Short Journal*, p 53.
[6] Fox and Burrough, *Good Counsel and Advice Rejected by Disobedient Men* (1659), pp. 26–7 36–7.

soldiers and true officers come again into the power of God which hath been lost, never set up your standard till you come to Rome.'[1] In 1660 Fox threatened the King of Spain: 'as you have killed with the sword, so shall you perish by the sword.... Now shall the Lamb and the saints have the victory.'[2]

Like Burrough too, Fox used military metaphors especially frequently in his early writings. 'The saints of the most high God are coming to break them in pieces.... The mighty day of the Lord is coming', when 'God will rule in his saints above the heathen.'[3] 'A day of slaughter is coming to you who have made war against the Lamb and against the saints.... The sword you cannot escape, and it shall be upon you ere long.'[4] Since the early Quakers were not pacifists on principle, such words might well alarm their enemies.

Fox, no less than Burrough, thought that the popular revolution had been betrayed. 'Oh what a seriousness was in the people at the beginning of the wars, yea both small and great,' he recalled in 1659. 'Oh how is the sincerity choked and smothered and quenched by the fatness of the earth!'[5] 'There was a tenderness in many of you ... which have tasted of the mercies of God and deliverances.... But now you are got into ease and pride'; they have allied with former Cavaliers to oppress their former supporters.[6]

'God hath showed wondrous works in this island ... there is no nation hath tasted the like.... But in all nations there is not more persecution and imprisoning' than in England, where 'so many of the people of God ... are put in prison with them which was once open enemies against them while they were in arms'.[7]

> Oh England, England [Fox had cried in 1654] thou hast forsaken thy visitation; thou hast tasted of the love of God, and all people in it; but a-whoring thou hast gone after gold, after riches, after honour.... Wonderful deliverances God hath wrought, and given many victories, [but] the same nature, pride and covetousness and oppression got up again.... You

---

[1] G. F., *To the Councill of Officers*. pp. 2, 8.
[2] *Gospel-Truth*, pp. 196–7.
[3] *Newes Coming up out of the North*, pp. 3–6.
[4] Ibid., p. 31; cf. Fox. *The Vials of the Wrath of God Upon the seat of the Man of Sin* (1655), p. 7.
[5] *To the Councill of Officers*, pp. 6–7.
[6] G. F., *A Warning from the Lord* (1654), pp. 1–2. Not in *Gospel-Truth*.
[7] Ibid., p. 5. Note Fox's assumption that 'the people of God' had been 'in arms' for Parliament.

have promised many fair promises to the nation, but little you have performed.[1]

Like Winstanley, Fox saw oppression as a great spread tree, 'and all you underling officers, which have been as the arms of this great tree, ... all your branches must be cut down'.[2] 'All the whole creation groans under the burden of corruption.' 'God hath blessed this nation, and made himself manifest in it.' Yet now the rulers make riches their God.[3] 'Hath not men with the form of godliness long ruled without the power? Is not strife and wrath and brawling and racking and backbiting the fruits of it?'[4] 'When so many are seeking for greatness, honour and highness, how do you walk in humbleness of mind?'[5] 'O ye chief magistrates of England ... is this according to your promises and engagements unto the Lord in the day of your distress?' Beware lest God 'overturn you by the same arm and power as he did them that are gone before you'.[6]

Like Burrough and Nayler, Fox believed that he was living 'in the last times'.[7] 'Now do the prophets of the Lord begin to prophesy, sons and daughters.' 'The day doth appear that God will rule in his saints above the heathen.... Now is the Son of God come.' God 'is magnifying himself in his sons and daughters'.[8] Such pamphlets were not reprinted; similar millenarian passages in the *Journal* were suppressed—e.g. 'the mighty day of the Lord that was coming', 'the Lord was coming to teach his people himself by his spirit'; 'the mighty day of the Lord was coming upon all sin and wickedness.'[9] In May 1659, with the Rump restored, Fox called all priests to come up to the bar of judgement of the Lamb 'in this his day which is come'.[10] Since Fox believed that 'the saints shall judge the world, ... whereof I am one'; the clergy would hardly be amused.[11]

---

[1] *Newes Coming up out of the North*, pp. 18–19; cf. *This is to all Officers and Souldiers*, pp. 3, 6.
[2] *Newes Coming up out of the North*, p. 18; cf Winstanley, *The Law of Freedom*, pp. 161–2.
[3] *Newes Coming up out of the North*, pp. 23–4.
[4] G. F., *The Priests and Professors Catechisme* (2nd edn., ?1657), p. 16. Not in *Gospel-Truth*.
[5] *A Warning from the Lord*, p. 6.
[6] *An Instruction to Judges & Lawyers*, p. 40.
[7] *A Word from the Lord*, p. 9; cf. Nayler, *An Epistle to several Friends about Wakefield* (1653), in *Sundry Books*, I, p. 27; *The Lambs War* (1658), in Barbour and Roberts, *Early Quaker Writings*, pp. 109, 116.
[8] *Newes Coming up out of the North*, pp. 3–9. Winstanley constantly referred to sons and daughters.
[9] *Short Journal*, pp. 17, 21, 30; c f. pp. 6, 13.
[10] *The Lambs Officer*, title-page, pp. 1, 13. For the date see Reay, 'Early Quaker Activity', p. 113.
[11] G. F. and J. N., *Sauls Errand to Damascus* (1654), pp. 10–11; cf. *WTUD*, pp. 232–41, where I suggest that George Fox's millenarian teaching combined with his socially radical views had much to do with his early success.

From August 1659 to the beginning of 1660 Fox withdrew from all activity, and seems to have undergone some sort of spiritual crisis, if not nervous breakdown. He appears to have taken no part in the negotiations with republican politicians and Army leaders which Burrough and others undertook at this time, and to have been increasingly sceptical of them.[1] He was unenthusiastic about Quakers joining the militia, but did not come out against it even when asked. 'There is something in the thing,' he told Bristol Quakers, 'and you cannot well leave them seeing you have gone amongst them.'[2] Fox admits in his *Journal* that Quakers had been invited by the government in 1659 'to take up arms, and great places and commands were offered to some of us'.[3] He himself, it was said, was offered a colonelcy.[4] One may suspect that it was lack of confidence in the policies of the Committee of Safety as much as principled pacifism which caused Friends to reject these offers. They would not have been made if the Quakers were declared pacifists.

When Fox emerged from his 'time of darkness', he seems to have decided that political action must be renounced. 'Nothing but hypocrisy and falsehood and fair pretences were seen amongst you,' he told 'those that have been formerly in authority'; 'when you pretended to set up the Old Cause, it was but your silliness; so that you long stunk to sober people.'[5] Fox had presumably recognized during his period of abdication that the restoration of the Stuarts was inevitable. Perhaps indeed his withdrawal was due to recognition of the 'silliness' and irrelevance of the frenzied activities of the republicans.[6]

There can, I think, be no doubt that Fox had not committed himself to pacifism before the Restoration. In 1651 he had been offered—and had rejected—a commission in the Parliamentary Army. In his *Journal* Fox attributes this refusal to pacifist principle, but this must be retrospective mental adjustment. Several times under the early Protectorate Fox was asked for—and gave—undertakings not to take up arms against

---

[1] *Journal*, I, pp. 361–2; cf. A. Cole, 'The Quakers and Politics', 136–41, 204–5. Nayler seems at least to have thought some good might come of these discussions (Nayler, *A Collection of Sundry Books*, II, p. 758).

[2] Reay, 'Early Quaker Activity', p. 116. For Quakers as militia commissioners see ibid., pp. 125–30.

[3] Fox, *Journal*, I, p. 450; cf. Cole, 'The Quakers and Politics', pp. 64–6, 157–60.

[4] *Memoirs of James Gough* (1782), pp. 55–7.

[5] Fox, *To Those that have been Formerly in Authority* (1660), p. 2.

[6] I have benefited from discussing this point with Hugh Barbour, though he is in no way responsible for what I have written.

Cromwell's government.[1] There were plenty of reasons why Fox should not have wished to commit himself publicly to the Army or to Cromwell in the early 1650s, as there were again in 1659. The offer of a commission was rather like the offer of a Cardinal's hat to Laud in 1633. The Pope's offer would not have been made to Archbishop Abbott. In the early 1650s men like Joyce and Sexby were bought off, temporarily at least, by military promotion.

In January 1661 the 'peace principle' was announced, henceforward characteristic of Quakerism. 'The spirit of Christ,' Fox declared, 'will never move us to fight and war against any man with carnal weapons.'[2] John Reeve had declared a principle of absolute non-resistance, and John Lilburne after his conversion to Quakerism announced with typical flamboyance that 'carnal weapons of any kind whatsoever' had no place in Christ's spiritual kingdom.[3] Thomas Lurting, Quaker boatswain's mate on one of Blake's ships, adopted a similar position in 1657.[4]

Such manifestations were the product of growing disillusionment. But this was checked in 1659, when for a few months a revival of God's Cause seemed possible. Fox seems to have been exceptional in his scepticism. As late as December 1659 Hubberthorne rebuked Baptists for declaring that they would be obedient in civil matters to any government which was or might be established in England. 'If Charles Stuart come, or any other and establish popery and govern by tyranny, you have begged pardon by promising willingly to submit and live peaceably under it as the ordinance of God.... Some did judge that ye had been of another spirit.'[5] But as the cause of the Commonwealth crumbled Fox's new-found pacifism won rapid acceptance. Margaret Fell in June 1660 drafted a paper which was given to the King, subscribed by Fox, Hubberthorne, Fisher and ten others. This stated that Friends 'do deny and bear our testimony against all strife and wars and contests.... Our weapons are

---

[1] H. J. Cadbury, 'The *Editio Princeps* of Fox's *Journal*', *JFHS*, 53 (1974), pp. 216–17; Carroll, 'Quakerism and the Cromwellian Army in Ireland', ibid., 54 (1978), p. 143.

[2] G. F., *A Declaration from the Harmless and Innocent People of God called Quakers, Against all Plotters and Fighters in the World* (1661), pp. 2–3; cf. *Several Papers Given Forth* (1660), pp. 48–9.

[3] *The World of the Muggletonians*, p. 76, and references there cited; *The Resurrection of John Lilburne* (1656), pp. 10–13.

[4] Braithwaite, *Beginnings*, pp. 521–2; cf. Cole, 'The Quakers and Politics', pp. 6, 33–4 and *passim*: Carroll, 'Quakerism and the Cromwellian Army in Ireland', pp. 153–4.

[5] E. B. and R. Hubberthorne, *An Answer to a Declaration put forth by the general Consent of the People called Anabaptists in and about the City of London. Which Declaration doth rather seem a begging of Pardon of the Caveliers then a Vindication of that Truth and Cause once Contended for* (1659), p. 4.

not carnal but spiritual.'[1] Two months later a Quaker wrote to George Fox saying that it would have been better 'if all had been kept still and quiet in those times.... The forwardness and want of wisdom in some is one great cause of our present sufferings.'[2] The official Quaker proclamation of the peace principle appeared seven months later.

Whatever may have been the case with Fox himself the peace principle was certainly new to Friends as a whole, and some time was needed to impose it upon them. Edward Byllynge was one who was unhappy about the new principle. In 1660 and again in 1662 he refused to give an undertaking not to take up arms or plot against the King. It was alleged that he and his supporters wanted to call in the paper asserting the peace principle, and that he threatened to oppose it publicly if Quakers referred to themselves as the King's 'loyal subjects'. That particular phrase was withdrawn.[3] Byllynge remained a Quaker.

The tiny and unsuccessful but bloody Fifth-Monarchist revolt of January 1661 occurred a few days before the declaration of the peace principle was printed. It probably accelerated acceptance of the new policy. Quakers were arrested in large numbers at the time: Fox indeed issued a statement warning Friends against involvement in plots.[4] But as late as November 1662 some Friends disavowed Margaret Fell's paper of June 1660.[5] Isaac Penington continued to think the sword might lawfully be used in defence of one's country.[6] Dr Reay suggests, tentatively, that the Perrot schism may bear some relation to disputes over the peace principle. Fox rebuked Perrot for wearing a sword, and Robert Rich, Nayler's former supporter, defended him.[7] Fox admitted to Muggleton in 1667 that some Quakers had indeed been swordsmen and Ranters: so were some Muggletonians, Fox retorted, 'and they are so still'. Quakers have changed: have Muggletonians?[8] As late as 1685 a few Friends joined

---

[1] Ross, *Margaret Fell*, p. 128.

[2] Reay, 'Early Quaker Activity', p. 144, quoting Swarthmore MS.

[3] *State Papers relating to Friends*, pp. 153–4; G. Leslie, *The Snake in the Grass* (3rd edn., 1698), pp. 224–5, quoted by Reay, 'Early Quaker Activity', pp. 179–80. First published 1696.

[4] Fox, *Journal*, I, pp. 448, 450; cf. Cole, 'The Quakers and Politics', pp. 64–6, 157–60.

[5] Ross, *Margaret Fell*, p. 157; cf. pp. 165, 181.

[6] See p. 128 above.

[7] Reay, 'Early Quaker Activity', pp. 178–9.

[8] G. F., *Something in Answer to Lodowick Muggleton's Book ... the Quakers Neck Broken* (1667), p. 9. For opposition to the peace principle and Quaker participation in plots against the government, see Reay, 'Early Quaker Activity', esp. pp. 178–88; *Calendar of Clarendon State Papers*, ed F. J. Routledge (Oxford UP, 1970), V, p. 258—'four hundred pairs of pistols ... for the Quakers'.

Monmouth's rebellion.[1]

There are many comparisons to be made between the ideas of Fox and of Winstanley. In 1648 Fox was renewed 'to the state of Adam which he was in before he fell'.[2] Fox was accused of claiming to be one of the saints who would judge the world.[3] 'Every man that cometh into the world is enlightened with the light of Christ,' said Fox in a passage of the *Short Journal* which was excluded from the *Journal*.[4] Men could be freed from sin on earth.[5] Fox claimed to be the Son of God.[6] Christ gives power to those who receive the light 'to become the Sons of God; and this would bring them into unity with the Son and with the Father'.[7] 'Christ is risen,' Fox announced in 1653; 'Christ is come.'[8] Fox uses Cain and Abel, Esau and Jacob, symbolically, as Winstanley does.[9] The concept of anointing is common to both. Both conceived of God as a consuming fire.[10] Both employed the radical concept of the two seeds.[11] Fox gave this a specifically agricultural orientation in Scotland in 1657:

> I felt the seed of God to sparkle about me, like innumerable sparks of fire. Not but that there is abundance of thick, cloddy earth of hypocrisy and falseness above, and a briary brambly nature which is to be burnt up with God's wind and ploughed up with his spiritual plough before the seed brings forth heavenly and spiritual food to his glory. But the husbandman is to wait in patience.[12]

---

[1] D. R. Lacey, *Dissent and Parliamentary Politics in England, 1661–1689* (Rutgers UP, 1969), p. 172.

[2] Fox, *Journal*, I, pp. 28, 34; G. F., *Three General Epistles* (1664), p. 5. Cf. p. 138 above.

[3] *Sauls Errand*, pp. 10–11; Braithwaite, *Beginnings*, pp. 108–9; W. S. Mortimer, 'Allegations against George Fox by the Ministers of North Lancashire', *JFHS*, 39 (1947), pp. 16–17; cf. Barbour and Roberts, op. cit., p. 247.

[4] *Short Journal*, p. 41; cf. p. 21, another suppressed passage.

[5] Fox, *The Lambs Officer* (1659), pp. 15–16; cf. *WTUD*, p. 169.

[6] *Short Journal*, p. 17: not in *Journal*. Cf. *Sauls Errand to Damascus*, pp. 2–11.

[7] *Short Journal*, p. 31; cf. *The Lambs Officer*, p. 21.

[8] *Gospel-Truth*, pp. 4, 120.

[9] *Newes Coming up out of the North*, pp. 16–17, 26, cf. Winstanley, *The Law of Freedom*, p. 54.

[10] *Short Journal*, pp. 1, 4, 16; G. F., *An Epistle-General To those who are of the Royal Priesthood* (1660), p. 12; cf. *The Religion of Gerrard Winstanley*, p. 3.

[11] *Short Journal*, p. 32; cf. *Newes Coming up out of the North*, pp. 11, 18–19, 22.

[12] Fox, *Journal*, I, p. 412; cf. pp. 21, 35, 42, 183, 424.

5   After 1661

The Society of Friends survived where Fifth Monarchism did not. But its ideas changed in many ways. Burrough, who died in 1662, retained his millenarianism even after the restoration.[1] So did George Bishop, who in 1660 warned 'those who put the day of the Lord afar off ... lest it come upon them unawares.... It is even come.' His reason for believing this was 'this present calmness ... when the flood thought to have overwhelmed' God's people.[2] 'You have time to work,' he told King and Parliament next year, 'and it is not long.' The English are 'a nation of men, a warlike nation, a people whom the Lord hath owned above any people; a people whom the Lord hath appeared to save more than any people'.[3] 'Appeared to' is appropriately ambiguous for the English nation; but the Lord 'hath brought forth a people by whom he hath made known himself; he hath not dealt so by another nation'. No ambiguity here! Friends are those 'upon whom the ends of the earth are come, and in whom [God] is now come to finish his work'.[4] So 'all stand fast, unshakable, unmoveable.... For it is his great day and his great battle that is to be fought.... It is a work worth your while, the weightiest that ever was; it's that unto which all things have wrought since the world began.... Ye shall have power over the nations and rule them with a rod of iron.'[5] Bishop still believed in the possibility of recovering the pre-lapsarian state on earth.[6]

But this was soon put into the distant future.[7] By 1662 Bishop was offering the consolations of the after life as compensation for suffering on earth.[8] Robert Barclay's *Apology for the true Christian Doctrine* (Latin 1676, English translation 1678) provided the theological underpinning for this partial return to a more traditional, more other-worldly, theology.

---

[1] See p. 152 above.
[2] Bishop, *A Few Words in Season ... in this Hour wherein the Lord is drawing Nigh to Judgment* (1660), p. 2.
[3] Bishop, *A Book of Warnings*, p. 1.
[4] Bishop, *An Epistle of Love To All the saints scattered in these Nations* (1661), pp. 13, 23.
[5] Ibid., pp. 24, 26.
[6] Bishop, *A Tender Visitation of Love To both the Universities of Oxford and Cambridge and to the Inns of Court and Chancery* (1660), pp. 15–16.
[7] Bishop, *A Vindication of the Principles and Practice of the People called Quakers* (1665), pp. 5–7, 27, 75.
[8] Bishop, *A Treatise concerning the Resurrection* (1662), p. 23. For Bishop's return to a more traditional theology see ibid., pp. 71–115, 131–49.

It was published in the same year as his *The Anarchy of Ranters*.[1]

Whether or not defeat is the right word, the Society of Friends was something very different after the restoration from the loose body of Quakers which had existed before. Imposing the peace principle meant organizing, distinguishing, purging. The process had begun after the Nayler crisis when 'many wild spirits, Ranters and suchlike' had been disowned and excluded.[2] After Nayler and the Perrot schism, reliance on everyone's inner light had to be controlled by a new emphasis on 'the sense of the meeting'.[3] Organization meant exclusion, which necessitated machinery. The Quakers became a peculiar people, with their own discipline based on consensus. After 1660 many well-known Quakers, like Anthony Pearson, withdrew or emigrated. There were schisms— Perrot, the Story–Wilkinson separation of the 1670s. Fox said that Perrot 'preached the rotten principles of the old Ranters': he had had close relations with Nayler's followers.[4] But it was the same sort of separation, the same sort of discipline, as all other nonconformist sects (except the Muggletonians) had to adopt in order to survive in the hostile post-restoration world. (The Muggletonians could afford to be disorganized because they were not interested in proselytizing.) The Quakers came to adopt something like a preaching ministry, regular meeting times and places (to which Perrot particularly objected), a hierarchical structure of meetings, greater emphasis on sin and discipline (to which Story and Wilkinson objected), financial organization. Those who could not stand the pressure of persecution in the 1660s and 1670s fell off: those who survived dropped exuberances like interrupting church services and going naked for a sign. The Quakers survived, prospered and rewrote their history—as Muggleton rewrote the history of the sect which he took over.[5]

George Bishop, who remained a member of the Society of Friends, was one who protested against Fox's tightening of discipline over a group whose *raison d'être* had seemed to be absence of centralized control. 'It leads into the apostasy,' he said, 'and will seek to bring dark night in again.'[6]

---

[1] Yet Barclay went naked 'for a sign' in 1672, rather late (Lesley A. Higgins, 'The Apostatized Apostle, John Pennyman', *Quaker History*, 69 (1980), p. 102).

[2] *WTUD*, pp. 246–54, 371–8; Reay, 'The Quakers and 1659', 'The Quakers, 1659, and the Restoration of the Monarchy'; Braithwaite, *Beginnings*, pp. 278, 309–31; *Second Period*, pp. 247–59 and *passim*.

[3] Reay, 'Early Quaker Activity', p. 11.

[4] Fox, *Journal*, I, p. 519; Carroll, *Perrot*, pp. vii, 10, 50, 57, 60–1, 83–4, 86, 107–8.

[5] See pp. 47, 291–2.

[6] Braithwaite, *Second Period*, p. 312.

Emigration was one solution which seems to have appealed especially to those Quakers least happy about the direction in which Fox was leading them. Perrot and Rich went to the West Indies, Byllynge to New Jersey, which in 1676 saw his last attempt at constitution-making, the 'Conclusions and Agreements of the Proprietors of the Province of West Jersey'. This drew freely upon *A Mite of Affection*. Migration was thus one way out of defeat, travelling to establish the Leveller/Quaker republic in America. But in order to emigrate Byllynge needed the money of rich Quakers. And in the long run rich Quakers were little more interested in democracy than rich Independents had been. It is interesting to contrast Byllynge's constitution with William Penn's Frame of Government for Pennsylvania in 1682. There the representative assembly was not sovereign: there was an upper house composed of men of wealth. And even for the elective assembly there was a property qualification. Not yet, not yet...

The transition to the Society of Friends was assisted by the extraordinary mortality among leaders in the early 1660s—great tribute to the efficacy of English gaols in removing undesirables, and justification of Quaker complaints of their appalling state.[1] James Parnell had died in prison in 1656, at the age of 19, and John Camm in 1657. Lilburne also died (on parole from prison) in that year, aged only 42; if he had survived he might have been expected to exercise a powerful influence. Nayler died in 1660, aged 42, and Thomas Aldam in the same year; George Fox the Younger in 1661; Burrough and Richard Hubberthorne in 1662, aged 28 and 34 respectively; William Ames in the same year. John Audland died in 1664, aged 34, Samuel Fisher in 1665, Richard Farnsworth in 1666 (aged about 33?), Francis Howgil in 1669. Apart from Fox, only George Whitehead and William Deusbury of the original leaders lived on, and neither of them was of the calibre of Lilburne, Nayler, Burrough, Hubberthorne, Fisher or Howgil. Quakerism survived these heavy losses, unlike Fifth Monarchism.[2] But the leaders of the second generation were in no position to challenge Fox's leadership, even if they had wanted to. Many of them—Penington, Penn, Barclay—came of significantly higher social rank than the yeomen of the 1650s: this may have contributed to their acceptance of the new direction. The Wilkinson faction, Hugh Barbour tells us, 'was often composed disproportionately of the earliest convinced, who did not see

---

[1] See p. 155 above.
[2] See pp. 67–8 above.

as clearly as Fox the need for new patterns'.[1]

Rewriting the history meant demoting James Nayler, once regarded as at least Fox's equal—as Muggleton to a lesser extent demoted John Reeve in rewriting Muggletonian history.[2] Fox oversimplified their relationship when he wrote in 1667: 'the first that got up into this posture of keeping on their hats in prayer against Friends was the Ranter; the next was James Nayler (but quickly abandoned); and the next was John Perrot.'[3] The smear technique has become familiar in our century, and it is not pleasant: Nayler adopted a Ranter practice 'against Friends', but 'quickly abandoned' it; he is denigrated, not totally excluded from the party. In Fox's *Journal* Nayler receives minimal mention.[4]

The whole question of the principles on which Quaker self-censorship operated calls for further investigation. As early as 1660 George Bishop was urging that Quaker pamphlets should be censored before publication, so as to avoid occasion of offence or stumbling.[5] Edward Byllynge had disagreements with his colleagues about publication. Even before methods of controlling the contents of Quaker books were standardized in 1672, Fox appears to have exercised a *de facto* censorship, though Burrough managed on occasion to evade it.[6] It would be nice to know more about the editing of Burrough's works after his death. Some clauses were deleted from *A Declaration from the People called Quakers* (30 December 1659), because their rejection of violence seemed ambiguous by later Quaker standards.[7] *To the Whole English Army* and both addresses *To the Parliament of the Common-Wealth of England* were omitted.[8] John Pennyman, who may have been a Perrot sympathizer, who was disowned for burning books 'as a sign' in 1670, and who

---

[1] H. Barbour, review of R. T. Vann, *The Social Development of English Quakerism, 1655–1755*, in *Quaker History*, 60 (1971), p. 126.

[2] See p. 47 above.

[3] Fox, *A Testimony in that which separates between the pretious and the vile* (?1667), p. 3.

[4] Fox, *Journal*, I, pp. 107, 327–8, 343. For another significant silence of Fox's, about Elizabeth Harris, possibly a Perrot supporter, see Carroll, 'Elizabeth Harris, the Founder of American Quakerism', *Quaker History*, 57 (1968), pp. 110–11.

[5] Cole, 'The Quakers and Politics', p. 258, quoting Bishop's *A Few Words in Season* (1660).

[6] T. P. O'Malley, 'The Press and Quakerism, 1653–1659', *JFHS*, 54 (1979), pp. 173–4: '"Defying the Powers and Tempering the Spirit": A Review of Quaker Control over their Publications, 1672–1689', *Journal of Ecclesiastical History*, 33 (1982). Between 1674 and 1688 20 per cent of the manuscripts submitted for publication were rejected. The object of the censorship at this date was 'to prevent the distribution of any eccentric or inflammatory literature', to avoid extreme or political statements; the emphasis was all on Quaker sufferings ('"Defying the Powers"', pp. 83–4).

[7] Cole, 'The Quakers and Politics', p. 194.

[8] For omissions of Burrough's writings as published in *Works*, see Reay, 'Early Quaker Activity', pp. 12, 114.

invited 'all sorts of Ranters' to his wedding in 1671, quoted Burrough in 1675 to show how far the Quakers had strayed from their original vision.[1]

There had been 'much doubtings and questionings' about publishing *Good Counsel and Advice Rejected by Disobedient Men* in 1659, when Burrough was conducting negotiations with men who had formerly been 'disobedient'.[2] We know that Ellwood edited Fox's *Journal* in order that 'nothing may be omitted fit to be inserted, nor anything inserted fit to be left out'.[3] One suspects that the latter category may have seemed the more important to Ellwood. Many interesting omissions are noted in the 1925 edition of the *Short Journal*, including miraculous healings, Fox claiming to be the Son of God, Fox as Moses, Fox's millenarian expectations and his Cromwellian sympathies, the loan of a meeting house to soldiers.[4] Fox's *Book of Miracles* was suppressed; Penn and Ellwood do not refer to miracles to which Fox himself at the time attached considerable significance.[5]

Reprinting Nayler's works was deferred because some Friends feared they would give offence.[6] Many of his writings of 1655–6 were omitted from *Sundry Books*. Careful analysis of omissions and alterations would be interesting. Letters which used the same ecstatic language as had been addressed to Nayler were similarly censored.[7] I noted omissions from Isaac Penington's collected works, including some written in his Quaker period.[8]

There is of course nothing reprehensible in this practice. The object of reprinting Quaker works was to edify. It would have been wrong to reprint passages which would have seemed unedifying in a later age, in which tastes had changed. What is interesting is to note the changes. Muggleton doctored Reeve's works, and Toland pursued a similar policy when he edited Ludlow's *Memoirs* for publication in 1698, for the edification of radical Whigs. He omitted much millenarian material which would not have appealed to this public. Ludlow would have

[1] Lesley H. Higgins, 'The Apostatized Apostle', pp. 102–18.
[2] Cole, 'The Quakers and Politics', p. 52. 1659 was of course a politically sensitive year.
[3] Braithwaite, *Beginnings*, p. 532.
[4] Fox, *Short Journal, passim*, esp. pp. 17, 279 (Son of God), 243, 366 (Moses), 87, 304 (lending meeting house). See also Reay, 'Early Quaker Activity', p. 6; cf. Cadbury, 'The *Editio Princeps* of Fox's *Journal*', pp. 197–216.
[5] *George Fox's 'Book of Miracles'*, ed. H. J. Cadbury (Cambridge UP, 1948), p. 44 and *passim*.
[6] Nayler, *Sundry Books*, I, pp. xxi–xxii.
[7] Barbour and Roberts, *Early Quaker Writings*, p. 477.
[8] See p. 128 above.

approved.[1] But it creates problems for the historian. Professor Cole observed that collected editions of the writings of other Quakers as well as Burrough 'show marked variations from the originals', so that it is imperative to consult the first editions.[2] John Pennyman in 1691, and Dr Reay more recently, noted omissions from the collected editions of the writings of George Fox the Younger, Howgil and others.[3] Professor Cole also observed that some pages of manuscript letters preserved at Friends' House 'have either been lost or removed', especially for the year 1659. Since this was the year in which divisions between Friends were at their sharpest, it is hardly likely that this is entirely accidental.[4] More work is needed here.

---

[1] Ludlow, *A Voyce from the Watchtower*, Introduction, *passim*. Dr Worden is perhaps a little severe on Toland's editorial methods: he would have expected to be judged not by the standards of twentieth-century historical scholarship but by the demands of the Good Old Cause in the 1690s.

[2] Cole, 'The Quakers and Politics', p. 278.

[3] Reay, 'Early Quaker Activity', pp. 6, 117, 180; John P[ennyman], *The Quakers Unmask'd* (1691), pp. 8–13, 21–2, quoted by Dr Reay.

[4] Cole, 'The Quakers and Politics', pp. 280–1.

Chapter 6

Independents and Republicans

1 John Owen (1616–83): 'Cromwell's Archbishop'

John Owen was relatively young when civil war broke out. Under Laud he had held no living, so he did not have to conform to the ceremonies. He was fortunate enough to be employed as a private chaplain, first to Sir Robert Dormer, then to Lord Lovelace. Later he became Vicar of the Puritan town of Coggeshall, on the recommendation of the Earl of Warwick. Already he had useful patrons. In 1642 he had no hesitation in choosing sides. In *The Duty of Pastors and People Distinguished* (1643) he looked back at 'the iniquity of those times whereinto we were lately fallen; in which lord bishops and priests had almost quite oppressed the bishops of the Lord and ministers of the gospel'. 'Never so many errors and suspicions in a hundred years crept into ... the Roman apostasy ... as did into ours of England in sixteen.'[1] 'Were a man a drunkard, a swearer, a Sabbath-breaker, an unclean person, so he were no Puritan, and had money ... the episcopal heaven was open for them all.'[2] Owen initially associated himself with the Presbyterians, 'led by an opposition to episcopacy and ceremonies'; but on more careful consideration he decided—as Milton did—that his principles were more suited to Independency; he organized his Coggeshall church on congregational lines.[3] But he remained a Calvinist, unlike Milton.

The first Fast Sermon which Owen preached before the House of Commons was in 1646, when he was 30 years old. He used the opportunity to plead for unity between Presbyterians and Independents,

---

[1] Op. cit., in *Works* (1850–5), XIII, pp. 27–8; cf. *The Advantage of the Kingdom of God in the Shaking of the Kingdomes of the World* (1651), *Works*, VIII, p. 323: prelacy is 'a mere antichristian encroachment upon the inheritance of Christ'.

[2] *A Vision of Unchangeable free mercy*, preached before the House of Commons, 29 April 1646, *Works*, VIII, p. 29.

[3] *A Vindication of the Treatise on Schism* (1657), *Works*, XIII, pp. 222–7; cf. *The Death of Death in the Death of Christ* (1647), *Works*, X, pp. 140–1.

for tolerance of disagreements, and for abandonment of the death sentence against heretics.[1] He reminded MPs that Presbyterians had formerly been accounted sectaries; Milton made a similar point in *The Reason of Church Government* and *Areopagitica*.[2] Attempts to impose uniformity upon saints by external force, Owen told Parliament, were 'purely antichristian'.[3]

So Owen steered a middle course between 'the pit of democratical confusion and the precipitous rock of hierarchical tyranny'.[4] The godly were the middling sort. 'Not many great, not many wise, not many mighty after the flesh, are partakers of the heavenly calling'; but the gospel of Christ does not 'oppose or take away those many differences and distinctions among men in society', still less threaten property.[5] In 1648 Owen spoke against the election of elders by 'the people that have taken the covenant', preferring that the godly only should choose.[6]

Owen was appointed to preach before Parliament on the day after Charles I's execution, succeeding to the place of unofficial preacher-in-chief hitherto held by Stephen Marshall. In these sermons Owen continually stressed divine responsibility for the English Revolution. But no nation is chosen, he had argued in 1646; like human beings, all are equally undeserving. If one chances to be used for God's purposes, that is a matter of God's free grace, not his merit.[7] 'There are great and mighty works in hand in this nation,' he declared after the battle of Worcester; 'tyrants are punished, the jaws of oppressors are broken, bloody revengeful persecutors disappointed and (we hope) governors set up that may be just, ruling in the fear of God.... The hand of the Lord hath been wonderfully exalted in all these things.... A mighty monarchy, a triumphing prelacy, a thriving conformity' are all 'brought down'. 'God hath gone with you (I hope) now to the end of your work; leave him not until he comes to the end of his.'[8]

---

[1] 'A short defensative about Church Government' attached to *A Vision of Unchangeable free mercy, Works,* pp. 44, 28–30; 'A Country Essay for the practice of Church Government there', ibid., pp. 55–69.

[2] *CPW,* I, pp. 764–8, II, pp. 566–9.

[3] 'A Discourse about Toleration', in *A Sermon Preached to the Honourable House of Commons on 31 January 1649, Works,* VIII, pp. 163–206, esp. pp. 197, 205. Cf. William Dell, 'unity is Christian, uniformity antichristian', *Several Sermons and Discourses* (1709), p. 64. See also pp. 111, 113–14 above.

[4] *The Duty of Pastors, Works,* XIII, p. 5.

[5] *Eschol: A Cluster of the Fruit of Canaan* (1647), *Works,* XIII, p. 81; cf. pp. 177–8 below.

[6] *The Diary of Ralph Josselin, 1616–1683,* ed. A. Macfarlane (1976), p. 121.

[7] *Works,* VIII, pp. 5–41, *passim.*

[8] *The Advantage of the Kingdome of Christ, Works,* VIII, pp. 313, 319, 322, 327.

But the ways of God are 'unsuited to the reasonings and expectations of the most of men'.[1] When God 'caused your spirits to resolve that the liberties, privileges and rights of this nation ... should not ... be wrested out of your hands by violence, oppression and injustice', God had secretly entwined 'the interest of Christ with yours' and 'prospered your affairs on that account'.[2] Thus Owen's Calvinism gave him a strong sense that the English Revolution was part of a divine plan which worked irrespective of the wills of men. Like Oliver Cromwell (who no doubt got the idea from Owen), he would have thought it blasphemy to judge of God's revolutions as 'necessities of men's creations'.[3]

Owen saw God's purposes in an international perspective. 'In these latter days,' he proclaimed in April 1649, 'Antichristian tyranny draws to its period.'[4] MPs should ask themselves, 'why is it that the Lord shakes the heavens and the earth of the nations?' It is so that

> he may shake out of the midst of them all that Antichristian mortar wherewith, from the first chaos, they have been cemented.... The full time is come.... Therefore, say not ... this or that suits the interest of England, but look what suits the interest of Christ.... Thou mayest with far more ease turn and stop the current of nature than obstruct the bringing in of the kingdom of Christ.... Babylon shall fall.[5]

It is mere presumption to suppose that Christ's kingdom can be set up in England or any other country with 'the Jews not called, Antichrist not destroyed, the nations of the world generally wrapped up in idolatry.... Will the Lord Christ leave the world in this state and set up his kingdom here on a mole-hill?'[6]

Already Owen was contemplating the worst possibilities. Preaching on the day after Charles I's execution he noted the ominous fact that phrases like 'a Parliament of saints, an Army of saints' were being used ironically, 'derisions of God's ways'. The fault lay in the intolerance of

---

[1] Ibid., pp. 327–32, 336; cf. *A Sermon Preached to the Parliament, Octob. 13, 1652, Works*, VIII, pp. 379–83.

[2] Ibid., p. 381; cf. pp. 6–7, 14–19, 24–7, 31.

[3] See p. 187 below.

[4] *The Shaking and Translating of Heaven and Earth: A Sermon Preached to ... Parliament, April 19, 1649, Works*, VIII, pp. 256–64; cf. p. 374.

[5] *The Shaking and Translating*, pp. 277–9; cf. *The Stedfastness of Promises and the sinfulness of Staggering, Works*, VIII, p. 229; *The Correspondence of John Owen, 1616–1683*, ed. P. Toon (1970), p. 69. Was Owen original in seeing Antichrist in chaos?

[6] *A Sermon Preached to The Parliament, Octob. 13, 1652*, p. 376; cf. *Gods Work in Founding Zion* (a sermon preached to Parliament, 17 September 1656), *Works*, VIII, p. 409.

the victorious Independents. 'Are not groans for liberty, by the warmth of favour, in a few years hatched into attempts for tyranny?' Self-seeking was prevalent. 'We are a returning people', going back to the bad old ways against which the Revolution had protested.[1]

By the 1650s Owen was a pillar of the Commonwealth establishment. He preached to Parliament to celebrate the defeat of the mutinous regiments at ·Burford in May 1649—'an appendix of good will for the confirming the former work which God had wrought'—'the God of the Parliament'. The regiments had 'engaged against that authority which God will own and defend', and consequently had set up 'themselves against the Lord'. The Levellers were especially blameworthy for 'their declared enmity to the ministers of the gospel', as well as to magistracy.[2] Owen was held largely responsible for the state church, supported by tithes, which Cromwell inherited from the Commonwealth.[3] Milton's sonnets of 1652 to Cromwell and Vane appealed to them 'to save free conscience from the paw/Of hireling wolves, whose gospel is their maw'. Milton was especially concerned about the proposal to impose doctrinal articles. Owen disowned Fifth Monarchists in 1654,[4] and was ordered by the Council of State to refute Bidle and the Socinians, following the appearance of a translation of the Racovian Catechism—licensed by Milton—and a Life of Socinus.[5]

In 1651 Owen became Dean of Christ Church, and in 1652 Vice-Chancellor of Oxford. He was consequently involved in defending that establishment institution against radical attacks.[6] His replacement in 1658 by John Conant, a Presbyterian who was later to conform to the restored episcopal church, was part of a shift to the right all over England. In 1657, when Parliament offered the crown to Oliver, Marchamont Nedham told the Protector that the talk of the town was that Philip Nye was to be Archbishop of Canterbury and Owen Archbishop of York. Despite this witticism, both in fact opposed acceptance of the crown; and Owen drafted the decisive petition against

---

[1] *A Sermon Preached ... on January 31* (1649), *Works*, VIII, pp. 147–8.
[2] *Human Power Defeated*, a sermon preached before Parliament on 7 June 1649, *Works*, VIII, pp. 197, 205–16.
[3] Cf. S. Fisher, *Baby Baptism meer Babism* (1653), pp. 573–6.
[4] *Correspondence*, ed. Toon, pp. 85, 66–8.
[5] *The Mystery of the Gospel Vindicated and Socinianism Examined* (1655), *Works*, XII, p. 3; cf. ibid., X, pp. 538–9, 561; VII, pp. 6, 130; XI, pp. 13–15; XII, p. 52, 164, 581–7.
[6] *A Dissertation on Divine Justice* (1653), *Works*, X, pp. 493–4; *Correspondence*, pp. 59–61, 65–6 (1654); *The Oxford Orations of Dr John Owen*, ed. P. Toon (Callington, Cornwall, 1971), p. 35.

kingship from a majority of the officers in London. Owen also opposed
the Other House. He initially supported Richard Cromwell, but in April
1659 switched his allegiance to the generals' Wallingford House party and
supported the coup by which Richard was persuaded to abdicate. Baxter
indeed held Owen largely responsible for Richard's overthrow.[1]

In 1656 Owen had urged MPs to be 'the preservers of the Good Old
Cause of England'.[2] But by 1659 he detected 'rage and contempt of all the
work of reformation that has been attempted amongst us'.[3] 'We are like a
plantation of men carried into a foreign country. In a short space they
degenerate from the manners of the people from whence they came, and
fall into that of the country whereunto they are brought.'[4] From 1647
onwards Owen had committed himself to the Army as God's agent.
Their 'work was done in heaven before they begun it.... The work
might have been done by children', but God 'was pleased to employ such
worthy instruments'.[5] In 1657 Owen sided with the Army against
Oliver, in 1659 with it against Richard. In 1659–60 he tried desperately to
bring together Monck and the generals in London. So he was stranded
when the Army collapsed. It is easy to mock at Owen, as Quakers did in
1659–60 because he could 'so sordidly comply with every government':
the man who had recently outlawed Quakers as fanatics was now called a
fanatic himself.[6]

But there is a consistency in his attempt to maintain a middle-of-the-
road position. It goes back to those Elizabethan and Jacobean Puritans
who saw themselves as the best defenders of protestantism against
popery on the one hand, sectarian anarchy on the other. In 1657 Owen
proclaimed that the Calvinist succession of preachers was the true
Church of England,[7] later listed as Jewell, Whitgift, Abbott, Morton,
Ussher, Hall (and many others).[8] Owen emphasized this position even
more after 1660, with modifications; in 1662 he insisted that the early
English reformers had had to make concessions to popular ignorance.

---

[1] Lamont, *Richard Baxter and the Millennium*, pp. 220–1.
[2] *Gods Work in Founding Zion, Works*, VIII, pp. 419–26; cf. ibid., p. 416: 'the old and common
Cause'.
[3] *The Glory and Interest of Nations professing the Gospel, Works*, VIII, pp. 467–8; cf. IX,
pp. 153–5, 163–4, 171, 177–8. Again there are many parallels in Milton's writings. For the
dating of this sermon see Woolrych's Introduction to *CPW*, VII, p. 61.
[4] *Of Temptation, the Nature and Power of it* (1658), *Works*, VIII, p. 112. The only plantation
Owen knew at first hand was Ireland.
[5] *Eben-ezer* (1648), p. 24.
[6] *Correspondence*, pp. 117–18; S. Fisher, *The Testimony of Truth Exalted* (1679), p. 548.
[7] *Of Schism* (1657), *Works*, XIII, pp. 182–206; cf. VIII, p. 304.
[8] *Works*, II, p. 304; cf. p. 219 below.

Hence continuous reformation was necessary.[1] But it was a consistent attitude.[2] He and his like accepted the Thirty-Nine Articles and the Synod of Dort; it was the Church of England that had changed.[3] It was the government, discipline and ceremonies of the church which nonconformists were unable to accept, rather than its theology; though the 'daily inroads made upon the ancient doctrines of this church' in the direction of Socinianism and popery made Owen increasingly unwilling to adopt the practice of occasional conformity.[4]

Reaction against the Laudian interlude had pushed Owen to the left, prepared him to accept toleration for all except papists and blasphemers.[5] In October 1652 he had laid down limits to toleration: 'error and falsehood' have no *right* to toleration, though they may be allowed it 'solely upon a civil account'.[6] Owen went on record in December 1659 against 'a universal toleration'; he supported tithes and opposed Quakers, 'they being persons of such principles as are destructive to the gospel and inconsistent with the peace of civil societies'.[7] He was equally opposed to 'enthusiasm':[8] after the restoration he poured out books against popery and Socinian rationalism impartially, as well as mocking the Royal Society for its dilettantism.[9]

The consistency of Owen's theological position perhaps helped him to withstand the shock of the restoration. He showed few signs of feeling personal responsibility or guilt for the defeat of God's Cause. He was able to dismiss the millenarian hopes of the revolutionary decades with

---

[1] *A Discourse concerning Liturgies and their Imposition* (1662), *Works*, XV, pp. 29–32; cf. ibid., pp. 206–8. Owen in fact saw the Reformation going back to Wyclif, the Lollards and Hussites—the traditional radical succession (*The Shaking and Translating of Heaven and Earth*, p. 263).

[2] *A Peace-Offering in An Apology and Humble Plea for Indulgence and Liberty of Conscience* (1667), *Works*, XIII, pp. 551–2.

[3] *Works*, VIII, p. 501 (1669); III, pp. 243–5 (1674); cf. II, pp. 279–80, 326; VII, pp. 74–6, 133, 249 (1676); V, pp. 164, 174 (1677); XIV, pp. 520–7 (1679).

[4] *A Discourse concerning Evangelical Love, Church Peace and Unity* (1672), *Works*, XV, pp. 65–8, 102; cf. ibid., pp. 184–5, 345–58, 378; II, p. 363, IV, pp. 244–6; IX, p. 25; XVI, pp. 241–5. Cf. my 'Occasional Conformity', in *Reformation, Conformity and Dissent: Essays in Honour of Geoffrey Nuttall* ed. R. B. Knox (1977), pp. 199–220.

[5] *Works*, VIII, pp. 165–7.

[6] *A Sermon Preached to The Parliament, Octob. 13, 1652, Works*, VIII, pp. 394–5.

[7] P. Toon, *God's Statesman: The Life and Work of John Owen* (Exeter, 1971), pp. 118–19; cf. *Two Questions Concerning the Power of the Supreme Magistrate* (1659), *Works*, XIII, pp. 508–16; also III, pp. 556–7, XVI, pp. 424–76; Owen, *An Exposition of the Epistle to the Hebrews* (1668–84; repr. Edinburgh, 1854–5), IV, p. 118, V, pp. 321–7, 354–60. Fox replied in kind: see his *The Great Mystery of the Great Whore Unfolded* (1659), pp. 263–4.

[8] Owen, *A Discourse concerning the Holy Spirit* (1674), *Works*, III, pp. 225, 235.

[9] *Correspondence*, p. 132.

the words 'take heed of *computations*. How woefully, wretchedly, have we been mistaken by this!' Yet he knew that 'you will be tried with Antichristianism before you die.'[1]

Owen's Calvinism told him that God's doings might be incomprehensible to men: we could assert eternal providence even though we might not be able to justify God's ways to men in human terms. 'What know we hereof?'[2] So Owen could accept the fact of defeat more passively than Milton. Like Milton, Owen naturally rejected justification by success.[3] He attacked the Arian doctrine which Milton shared—that the Son was created in time and was 'the instrumental cause whereby God created all other things'.[4]

The constant factor for Owen was God's justice, which was so absolute that 'God must *necessarily* ... inflict punishment on sin.'[5] 'God could not ... pardon sin absolutely and without satisfaction.'[6] This blank assertion was part of Owen's case against Socinianism. In 1655 he had declared that 'the terror of the Lord ... and the threats of the wrath to come', of 'the eternity of punishment', were necessary to preserve mankind 'from the outrageousness and unmeasurableness of iniquity which would utterly ruin all human society'.[7] After the restoration Owen, like Thomas Goodwin, laid heavier emphasis on sin. In 1668 he published *The Nature, Power, Deceit and Prevalency of the Remainders of Indwelling Sin in Believers*.[8] This did not contradict *The Doctrine of the Saints Perseverance* (1654), belief in absolute assurance of salvation making possible a state of 'holy complacency',[9] though of course hypocrisy and self-deception were both possible.[10]

In 1643 Owen had expressed the conventional view that church and state were indissolubly linked.[11] But in 1652 he noted the danger of clerical aspirations to civil authority. 'The great design of grasping temporal power upon a spiritual account will prove to be the greatest

---

[1] *Works*, IX, p. 510 (1680).
[2] *An Exposition upon Psalm CXXX* (1668), *Works*, VI, p. 635.
[3] *Works*, XVI, p. 279.
[4] Ibid, XII, pp. 216, 220, 265–6, 271; cf. p. 164.
[5] *A Dissertation of Divine Justice* (1653), *Works*, X, pp. 507, 512, 516, 581, 614, 621; cf. XI, p. 140 (1654). My italics.
[6] *Works*, II, pp. 293–4 (1674).
[7] *The Mystery of the Gospel Vindicated*, *Works*, XII, pp. 586–7; cf. pp. 164, 412, 433; I, p. lvi, II, p. 154 (1657), X, p. 481.
[8] *Works*, VI, pp. 154–322.
[9] *The Grace and Duty of Being Spiritually Minded* (1681), *Works*, VII, p. 292.
[10] *An Exposition upon Psalm CXXX*, pp. 593–4, 602.
[11] *A Display of Arminianism*, *Works*, X, p. 6.

badge of Antichrist.'[1] Already he was stressing the *secular* reasons for the existence of government.[2] From at least 1657 he had his doubts about the very idea of 'an authoritative national church consisting solely in the power and interest of the clergy'. Such a church, Owen came to think, actually weakened protestantism in England. Whether episcopalian or Presbyterian, it would be destructive of peace and union among a people overwhelmingly protestant and 'with a detestation of popery'. But divisions among protestants undermined resistance to popery, especially since Laudian Arminianism had led to 'a great weakening of the whole interest'. In these circumstances the church depended on the monarchy and might tend to support absolutism.[3] It was always important to emphasize doctrinal differences between protestants and papists, to insist that the Pope is Antichrist, not to allow Englishmen to forget the horrors of popish persecution. Otherwise the door might be opened to an 'apostate Antichristian church-state', which would be no less dreadful than 'idolatrous paganism'. This was a reason for Owen's rejection of occasional conformity.[4] The line of thought runs interestingly parallel to that of Owen's former protégé Henry Stubbe. Owen's critical references to the Royal Society, which was hostile to 'fanatics' whilst tolerating papists, also recalls Stubbe.[5]

Owen's theological adherence to the middle way was paralleled by his social attitudes. He had not much use for the 'rude, godless multitude'.[6] 'Dissenters from the present establishment', he wrote in 1667, came from the middling sort, 'upon whose industry and endeavours, in their several ways and callings, the trade and wealth of the nation do much depend'.[7] He used this economic argument in favour of toleration.[8] Those 'who are industrious in their affairs' seemed to him in 1681 to be 'far more amiable and desirable' than the idle aristocracy, provided always that the

---

[1] *Christs Kingdom and the Magistrates Power*, *Works*, VIII, pp. 383–6. Milton would have agreed, notwithstanding his disapproval and Owen's approval of the Commonwealth's state church (p. 173 above).

[2] *The Labouring Saints Dismission to Rest* (memorial sermon for Ireton, 1652), *Works*, VIII, p. 350.

[3] *Some Considerations about Union among Protestants*, *Works*, XIV, pp. 519–27; cf. XV, pp. 193, 230–61. Though not published until 1680, this piece seems to have been written in or soon after 1665 (p. 522).

[4] *The State and Fate of the Protestant Religion* (1682), *Works*, XIV, pp. 540–7, 555.

[5] Owen, *Correspondence*, p. 132, quoted on p. 175 above. The date appears to be 1663. See also p. 265 below.

[6] *The Duty of Pastors*, *Works*, XIII, p. 3 (1647).

[7] *Works*, XIII, p. 571 (note the word 'present'); cf. pp. 367–8 (1669); III, pp. 263–4 (1674); VIII, pp. 649–50, 656 (1681). Cf. p. 171 above.

[8] *Indulgence and Toleration Considered* (1667), *Works*, XIII, pp. 534–5.

industrious sort remained spiritually-minded.[1] Many children, he observed, were undone by parents who gave them too large a stock to trade for themselves—an indication of his expected audience.[2]

Post-restoration survival was easier for Owen than for many. He retained old friendships—with Fleetwood and Desborough, for instance—but he managed to make new ones both at court and with the opposition.[3] He was no killjoy Puritan. At Oxford he had dressed foppishly, more like a layman than a divine, Wood thought. Like Bunyan he played the flute; like Milton he decried excessive scrupulosity 'which constantly produces the deplorable issues of superstition, self-righteousness and anxiety of conscience'.[4] Owen was cautious, publishing many of his post-restoration writings anonymously. In the 1650s he had protected the learned royalist Edward Pococke and also Thomas Willis; that now stood him in good stead.

Owen was more logical and consistent in his Calvinism than most. He was convinced of the hopeless sinfulness of the mass of mankind, and that God's justice worked absolutely independently of human merit and effort. So he could face reverses stoically. No government or society on earth was going to be perfect. If God withdrew his favour from England, men could only bow to the divine will. 'What know we hereof?' Scepticism and Socinianism indeed flourished, but they could be combated by intellectual argument: and to this Owen devoted himself.[5] The real danger came now from popery, because this was prevalent at court rather than among the people. In the 1670s Owen shared the alarm which Milton, Marvell, Stubbe and many others felt; and he too responded by intensified pamphleteering—politics continued by the only means now accessible to him. He would have appreciated 1688 if he had lived to welcome it.

---

[1] *The Grace and Duty of being spiritually minded* (1681), *Works*, VII, p. 389.
[2] *Eben-ezer*, p. 5.
[3] Ashley, *Wildman*, p. 207; Owen and Wildman were in Buckingham's cabal around 1670. See pp. 415–16 below: Owen and Marvell.
[4] *Of the Mortification of Sin in Believers* (1656), *Works*, VI, p. 3.
[5] *Works*, IV, p. 249 (1662); V, p. 3ˣ; VIII, pp. 27–8, 612 (1681); IX, pp. 365–6, 505.

2   Thomas Goodwin (1600–80)

It is interesting to compare and contrast the careers of John Owen and
Thomas Goodwin. Both were Calvinist Independents, both believed in
toleration, both were intruded as Heads of Oxford colleges. But the
differences are even more striking. Goodwin was sixteen years older than
Owen. He came up to Christ's College whilst memories of Perkins and
Ames were still fresh.[1] He was a friend of Richard Sibbes and helped to
edit Preston's sermons. By 1640 Goodwin had experienced exile, had
published half a dozen treatises and was a respected leader of the
Independents. He was naturally appointed to the Westminster
Assembly, and preached a Fast Sermon in 1642. He was a leading figure in
the Assembly, and had a hand in drafting *The Apologeticall Narration* of
the Five Dissenting Brethren. Owen meanwhile was a young man in his
twenties.

But Owen overtook Goodwin in the 1650s. He became Vice-
Chancellor of Oxford University whilst Goodwin was President of
Magdalen. Goodwin played little part in national politics, whilst Owen
was actively associated first with the Cromwells, then with the
Wallingford House party. Marchamont Nedham did not nominate
Goodwin for an archbishopric.[2] After the restoration, Goodwin's
nineteenth-century biographer tells us, 'Owen associated with the
surviving statesmen of the Commonwealth, and numbered among his
friends the Earl of Orrery, the Earl of Anglesey, the Lords Willoughby,
Wharton and Berkeley. Goodwin passed the serene evening of his life in
the intimate friendship of learned theologians.'[3]

So Goodwin's ideas were formed earlier than and in very different
circumstances from those of Owen. Goodwin was a covenant theologian
in the tradition of Perkins and Preston. His experience of struggle against
the Laudian regime, and of exile, gave a special slant to his ideas. In 1639
he wrote *An Exposition of the Revelation* in which he foresaw the
revolution that was to come. 'Fear not the Cause of God in England.
There is a battle to be fought.' Satan is 'growing worse and worse'. But
'Christ will not be foiled. The primitive Christians, although their light
grew dimmer and dimmer, yet they conquered heathenism. These now

---

[1] *Memoir of Dr Thomas Goodwin* by his son, in *Works* (1861–3), II, pp. lviii–ix.
[2] See p. 173 above.
[3] *Works*, I, p. xlvii.

must needs conquer much more.'[1] Goodwin was very fierce against the Laudians' 'apostasy'. They were 'setting up an image of old popery in a protestant reformed way, even as popery is an image of heathenish worship in a Christian way'.[2] He found in Revelation a description of 'the ruin of Rome' by an 'insurrection or rising of the people in the tenth part of the city', which he took to mean Great Britain. Following Brightman, Finch and Mede he dated this 'insurrection' to the 1650s; but it 'may fall out sooner than we are aware of',[3] since 'we live in the last days.'[4]

If *A Glimpse of Sions Glory* (1641) is correctly attributed to Goodwin[5] his millenarianism at that date took very democratic forms, under the influence no doubt of the plebeian revolt in London in 1640–1. 'It is the work of the day to cry down Babylon, and to give God no rest till he set up Jerusalem as the praise of the whole world.' (How different from the ineluctably just and unmoved God of Owen!) 'The voice of Jesus Christ reigning in his church comes first from the multitude, the common people ... that are so contemptible, especially in the eyes of Antichrist's spirits and the prelacy.' Such words have almost a Leveller ring. 'You that are of the meaner rank, common people, be not discouraged.'[6] But Goodwin was no Leveller. God did not rely on the common people to bring the revolution 'to perfection'. He will move 'the hearts of the great ones, of noble, of learned ones', whose 'spirits have been set against the saints of God', counting them 'factious and schismatic and Puritans'. But they will come to see that they are 'the best commonwealthsmen'. The reign of God and his saints on earth will last a thousand years. 'When the adoption of the Sons of God shall come in the fullness of it, the world shall be theirs.' 'It is a quibble whether there shall be need of ordinances, at least in the way that now there is.'[7]

In *The Keys of the Kingdom of Heaven*, published in 1644, Goodwin and Philip Nye testified to the revolution that had taken place. Until very recently power had been

---

[1] Ibid., III, p. 35.
[2] Ibid., III, pp. 70–1, 107–8, 131, 161, 174, 178–9, 184–5, 190–1.
[3] Ibid., III, pp. 184–205. Winstanley also interpreted 'the tenth part of the city' as referring to England (*The Religion of Gerrard Winstanley*, p. 10).
[4] *Works*, III, pp. 120, 157, 189; *A Sermon of the Fifth Monarchy* (1654), p. 29.
[5] J. F. Wilson, 'A Glimpse of Syons Glory', *Church History*, 31 (1962), pp. 66–73; A. R. Dallison, 'The Authorship of the *Glimpse of Syons Glory*', in *Puritanism, Eschatology and the Future of Israel*, ed. P. Toon (1970), pp. 131–6.
[6] Op. cit., in Woodhouse, *Puritanism and Liberty*, pp. 233–4.
[7] Ibid., pp. 235–40.

in so great a remoteness from the people that the least right or interest therein was not so much as suspected to belong to them. But ... it hath now in these our days been brought so near unto the people that they also have begun to plead and sue for a portion and legacy bequeathed them in it. The saints (in these knowing times) ... begin more than to suspect that some share in the key of power should likewise appertain unto them.

But the authors were anxious that the people should not claim the *whole* power: in church government the middle way between Brownism and Presbyterianism was to be pursued, power was to be shared between people and elders.[1]

Goodwin's *Sermon of the Fifth Monarchy* must come from this period. It was published in 1654 by a Fifth Monarchist for his own purposes. The title-page, for which Goodwin was presumably not responsible, claimed that the sermon proved 'by invincible arguments that the saints shall have a kingdom here on earth ... after the Fourth Monarchy is destroyed by the sword of the saints'. The sermon itself declared that 'all the same privileges that are in Christ himself are in the saints; we are Sons as he, we are kings as he.' 'We shall one day be the top of nations and ... we shall reign on earth.' The saints 'do now govern the world invisibly'; soon they will 'do it visibly'.[2] 'The imprisonment of the saints,' said the publisher of the sermon in 1654, 'speaks another kind of language.'[3] The implication was that Thomas Goodwin had abandoned his former millenarianism.

Certainly in the 1640s Goodwin had been full of confidence. In February 1646 he told the House of Commons that the saints 'are privy counsellors to the great King of Kings; ... and God doth give these saints a commission to set up and pull down by their prayers and intercessions'.[4] The astonishing events of the English Revolution had been God's handiwork. 'We have seen [God] do that in a few years in England that he hath not done in an hundred years before.'[5] No nation

---

[1] In Woodhouse, op. cit., pp. 293–8. Professor Woolrych reminds me that this middle way had been laid out in *The Apologeticall Narration* by the Five Dissenting Brethren, of whom Goodwin was one, in 1643 (Haller, *Tracts on Liberty*, III, p. 332). Owen made similar distinctions: see p. 171 above.

[2] Op. cit., pp. 3, 18, 29; cf. *Works*, III, p. 26: the saints reigning on earth (1639). John Tillinghast was still quoting Goodwin with approval in 1655 (*Generation-Work*, Part III, Sig. A 8v).

[3] *Sermon of the Fifth Monarchy*, Sig. A 2v.

[4] *The Great Interest of Saints and Kingdoms* (1646), pp. 42–3.

[5] Ibid., p. 46.

since the Apostles' time was more desirable to live in than England 'in respect of the enjoyment of the gospel and the communion of saints.' Hence toleration of the saints was essential to national well-being.[1] In 1647, so we are told, Goodwin presented 'to some members of the Army' an account of a vision of a crusade which overthrew monarchy in England, France, Spain 'and after in all Christendom'.[2]

In the euphoria of the 1640s Goodwin perhaps strayed in the direction of antinomianism. He believed, with Quakers and other radicals, that 'the person of the Son doth dwell in our persons'. The elect, he thought, 'now actually sit with Christ in heaven'.[3] He believed in progressive revelation and thought that in his age 'a new world of divinity hath been found out', and that more might be.[4]

Goodwin had seen 'the greatest outward alterations that were in any age'.[5] With the 1650s 'when you may judge the world favours religion' he contrasted 'the price of the market ... in our days'. 'The learning then cried up and the way of preaching' could not appeal to a godly man; for him 'conversion was a great shipwreck' in worldly terms, after which he could hope only 'to be a poor schoolmaster or a Levite in a private gentleman's house'.[6]

Goodwin, like Owen, preached a thanksgiving sermon for the suppression of the Levellers.[7] But his tone was changing too. In and after the 1650s he preached much to encourage those tempted to despair.[8] After the restoration we hear no more about the rule of the saints on earth: the stress lies on the consolations of the after life. In *Patience and its Perfect Work* (?1666), describing those who have been 'bereft of their inheritance in their native country' and are in banishment, Goodwin urges contentment with our lot in this life, whatever it may be. The restitution of all things comes only at the day of judgement.[9] If I get to heaven, Goodwin concluded, 'I care not ... what befalls me in this world.'[10] He justified predestination by the argument that 'kings and

---

[1] Ibid., pp. 51–9.
[2] [Anon.], *A Vision which One Mr Brayne (One of the Ministers of Winchester) had in September 1647* (1649, single sheet).
[3] *An Exposition of Various Portions of the Epistle to the Ephesians, Works*, II, p. 396. But contrast *Works*, I, pp. 478–9; VI, pp, 189, 330—all much later.
[4] *Works*, IV, p. 237.
[5] *Works*, VI, p. 157.
[6] *Works*, VI, p. 484.
[7] *Works*, II, p. xxx.
[8] *Works*, III, pp. 315–40, IV, p. 208, VI, pp. 157, 385–9.
[9] *Works*, II, pp. 429–55; cf. I, pp. 77–9.
[10] *A Discourse of the Punishment of Sin in Hell* (1680), p. 347.

princes ... have favourites whom they will love, and will not love others, and yet men will not allow God that liberty, but he must either love all mankind or he must be cruel and unjust.'[1] 'To fight for religion, there is no warrant in the Word of God for it.'[2] Goodwin, like Owen, henceforth devoted a great deal of energy to controverting Socinianism.[3] But, unlike Owen, Goodwin was in favour of occasional conformity.[4]

The terrible *Discourse of the Punishment of Sin in Hell*, published posthumously in 1680, sees 'the great God as an enraged enemy'. He and Christ 'account it a part of their glory' to execute punishment themselves. There are nearly 200 pages of this, which the divines who published it thought 'not ... unseasonable in so secure and atheistic an age'.[5] (Contrast Goodwin's earlier reflections on the necessity of convincing men of God's love, 'men naturally having hard and suspicious thoughts of God and Christ'. 'Men are apt to think that God had a design upon them as upon enemies.')[6]

Like Owen, Goodwin—married to an alderman's daughter—addressed a middle-class audience. Commercial metaphors abound.[7] Thoughts are vagrants: we cannot stop them passing through our minds, but we must be diligently on the watch for them, catch them, examine them, whip them and send them on their way.[8] Particular churches, wrote Goodwin, echoing Roger Williams, are like trading companies—part of the city yet entire and distinct in their government.[9] He anticipates a Miltonic argument for free trade in ideas—'Let the market stand open, take heed how you prohibit any truth to be sold.... Let wisdom cry all her wares.... Revenues of God's glory ariseth out of the custom of these wares.' England 'hath been the greatest mart of truth for this last age, of any part of the world'.[10]

Miltonic too is Goodwin's belief that through the covenant of grace we

---

[1] *Works*, II, p. 163.
[2] *Works*, V, p. 218.
[3] *Works*, I, pp. 125, 460; IV, pp. 304, 407, 520–1.
[4] *Works*, I, pp. 557–8; cf. p. 177 above.
[5] Op. cit., pp. 10, 78.
[6] *Works*, IV, p. 208.
[7] *Works*, I, pp. 37, 123, 254–5; III, pp. 356–7, 398, 473; IV, pp. 215, 247–8, 313; cf. p. 173.
[8] Ibid., III, pp. 527–8.
[9] Ibid., I, p. 540. Cf. *WTUD*, p. 101. Wither used the same metaphor (*An Improvement of Imprisonment*, 1661, p. 103, in *Miscellaneous Works*, III; *Parallelogrammaton*, 1662, pp. 104–5). Edward Byllynge argued that all churches should be open in the sense that shops are open: there should be no compulsion to buy the goods which they offer (Byllynge, *A Word of Reproof*, pp. 16–17). For Williams see *WTUD*, p. 101.
[10] *Works*, IV, pp. 244, 313 (1625); cf. *Areopagitica*, *CPW*, II, p. 548.

can enter on earth 'a heaven in comparison of [Adam's] Paradise'.[1] He went beyond Milton in arguing that Eve was taken out of Adam's side 'to show the equality of the wife to the husband'.[2] 'Eve was the Mother of all Living, she was the first believer. We have a warrant that she believed, we have not a certain ground that Adam did; for the covenant is made with her.... She first trusted in Christ.'[3] If Goodwin had worked out the implications of this, it could have subverted the universally accepted assumptions of male supremacy.

3   Oliver Cromwell (1599–1658) and the Revolutions of Christ

It may seem incongruous to speak of Oliver Cromwell's *experience* of defeat. He died in his bed, the most powerful man in the British Isles. Many of the characters in this book were in his gaols when he died. At the restoration his corpse was disinterred and mutilated, together with that of Ireton, his regicide son-in-law. But it is unlikely that Oliver ever saw this as a possibility, so secure did Army rule still appear to be in September 1658. Yet Oliver did, I think, experience defeat on at least two occasions. The first was Barebone's Parliament; the second the case of James Nayler.

Cromwell always had a strong sense that the Parliamentarian Cause was the Cause of God, and that God looked with special favour on England. He made this clear in his contributions to the Putney Debates in 1647. God has determined to destroy Babylon 'and will not have her healed'. Cromwell was waiting for 'some extraordinary dispensations, according to those promises that he hath held forth of things to be accomplished in the later times, and I cannot but think God is beginning of them'. But the Scriptures are difficult to interpret, and Cromwell's understanding of what exactly Babylon was did not coincide with that of his opponents in the Putney Debates.[4]

For Cromwell the fact that Parliament's Cause was God's had been a

---

[1] *Of the Creatures*, quoted by D. R. Danielson, *Milton's Good God: A Study in Literary Theodicy* (Cambridge UP, 1982), p. 209.
[2] *Works*, II, p. 422.
[3] Ibid., I, p. 222; cf. II, p. 244.
[4] Woodhouse, *Puritanism and Liberty*, pp. 103–4.

stimulus to action in the civil war. ('As if God should say, "Up and be doing, and I will help you and stand by you",' he wrote to the Suffolk Deputy Lieutenants in July 1643.)[1] In 1648 he argued that rebels from the Parliamentarian Cause flew in the face of 'so many evidences of divine providence going along with and prospering a righteous Cause'.[2] To the wavering Robin Hammond he argued that God's 'presence hath been among us, and by the light of his countenance we have prevailed'. The Army was 'called by God'.[3] He used similar arguments to Wharton in January 1650. We must not pay too much attention to the fallible instruments through whom God has acted 'these nine years: we must look at what God has wrought.'[4] 'Arbitrary power', he told the Irish in December 1649, 'men begin to be weary of in kings and churchmen. . . . Some have cast off both, and hope by the grace of God to keep so. Others are at it!'[5]

Cromwell and the Council of Officers justified the dissolution of the Rump by recalling 'this Cause which the Lord hath so greatly blessed and bore witness to', culminating in his marvellous appearance for his people at Worcester. The Rump 'would never answer those ends which God, his people and the whole nation expected from them', would never complete 'that work the foundations of which God himself hath laid'. Consequently the Army leaders had been 'led by necessity and Providence to act as we have done, even beyond and above our thoughts and desires'.[6]

So when he greeted Barebone's Parliament in July 1653 Cromwell was following a well-worn track, though he spoke with unusual enthusiasm about 'those very great appearances of God'. But he struck a new note when he told his audience, 'You are called by God to rule with him and for him.'[7] 'This may be the door to usher in things that God hath promised and prophesied of, and set the hearts of his people to wait for and expect. . . . I do think something is at the door, we are at the

---

[1] Abbott, *Writings and Speeches of Oliver Cromwell*, I, p. 245.
[2] Ibid., I, p. 622.
[3] Ibid., I, pp. 696–8.
[4] Ibid., II, pp. 189–90; cf. II, p. 453.
[5] Ibid., II, p. 200. R. G. in 1654 summarized Cromwell tendentiously as having said, 'You did believe that God was entering into a contest with kings and priests, and would suddenly open the eyes of the nations, so that within a few years there should not be either left in the whole world' (R. G., *A Copy of a Letter from an Officer of the Army in Ireland*, 1656, p. 17). For R. G. see pp. 192–3 below.
[6] Abbott, op. cit., III, pp. 5–8.
[7] Ibid., III, pp. 60–1.

threshold.'[1] 'You are at the edge of the promises and prophecies.'[2]

This speech has led some to suggest that Cromwell shared, at least temporarily, the millenarian hopes of the Fifth Monarchists. Austin Woolrych's careful analysis, however, makes it clear that, although Cromwell was influenced by the euphoria of the moment, he did not expect Barebone's Parliament to usher in the millennium. 'You manifest this ... to be a day of the power of Christ', not *the* day; his hope that God would soon 'fit the people' to elect a Parliament[3] suggests a longer perspective. Barebone's was a temporary expedient to cope with the problem set by failure to agree on how elections for a new Parliament were to be controlled—and indeed how any Parliament could be elected which would accept Army rule.[4]

Nevertheless, the fact that even the handpicked members of Barebone's Parliament had dissolved in acrimonious squabbles was a serious setback. Oliver referred to it ruefully later as 'a story of my own weakness and folly'.[5] It marked, I think, a psychological turning-point. Oliver went on speaking of 'the Cause', but even in his opening speech to Barebone's Parliament 'those great appearances of God' to which he referred had occurred in the Second Civil War of 1648, in Ireland and at Worcester. Formerly 'the Cause of the people of God was a despised thing'; 'now even our enemies confess that God was certainly engaged against them.'[6] The Cause has become the Army. Its might was irresistible: but the increasingly purged and disciplined Army of the 1650s moved steadily away from 'the people of God'.

In March 1654 George Fox was indignant at Cromwell's call for a fast, in which he looked back to the days when God worked 'the deliverance of the nation from their bondage and thralldom, both spiritual and civil, and promising for them a just liberty by his own people'.[7] 'God hath showed wondrous works in this island,' Fox agreed. 'But how is it that so many of the people of God ... are put in prison with them which was once open enemies against them?'[8]

From now onwards Oliver was on the defensive. Having broken with

---

[1] *The Lord General Cromwells Speech* (1653), p. 24, quoted by Woolrych, *Commonwealth to Protectorate*, p. 147.
[2] Abbott, op. cit., III, p. 64.
[3] Woolrych, op. cit., pp. 147–9.
[4] Cf. p. 289 below.
[5] Abbott, op. cit., IV, p. 489.
[6] Ibid., III, pp. 53–7.
[7] Ibid., III, pp. 225–8.
[8] George Fox, *A Warning from the Lord* (1654), pp. 5–6.

the radicals in 1649 and 1653, political logic demanded a deal with the natural rulers of the countryside, with those who elected Parliament. In his opening speech to the 1654 Parliament Oliver told MPs what they wanted to hear about the wickedness of 'that levelling principle' which would 'tend to the reducing all to an equality'; and of Fifth Monarchists who 'tell us that liberty and property are not badges of the kingdom of Christ'. He agreed even 'to put a stop to that heady way ... of every man making himself a minister and a preacher'.[1] When he dissolved the Parliament he said reassuringly that 'if a commonwealth ... must needs suffer', it is better that 'it should rather suffer from rich men than poor men.'[2]

Oliver continued to resort to traditional rhetoric about the Cause, though increasingly identifying it with his government. 'This Cause', he told Parliament at the dissolution of January 1655, is either 'of God or of man.... If it be of God, he will bear it up.' 'Those mighty things God hath wrought in the midst of us' are 'the revolutions of Christ himself'. 'The Lord hath done such things amongst us as have not been known in the world these thousand years.' 'Let men take heed and be twice advised, how they call his revolutions, the things of God and his working of things from one period to another, ... necessities of men's creations.... They vilify and lessen the works of God and rob him of his glory.'[3]

But for Oliver the Cause remained closely linked with religious toleration. In Ireland in December 1649, at the height of his radical enthusiasm, he had written of 'so antichristian and dividing a term as clergy and laity';[4] next year he was widely believed to have promised to abolish tithes. Even in 1655 he declared that God has 'spoken very loud on behalf of his people by ... restoring them a liberty to worship with the freedom of their consciences and freedom in their estates and persons'. He attacked those who long to 'put their fingers upon their brethren's conscience to pinch them there.... What greater hypocrisy than for those who were oppressed by the bishops to become the greatest oppressors themselves as soon as their yoke was removed.'[5] He was digging in his toes on liberty of conscience for those with 'the root of the matter in them'.

---

[1] Abbott, op. cit., III, pp. 435–40.
[2] Ibid., III, p. 584.
[3] Ibid., III, pp. 590–3.
[4] Ibid., III, p. 197.
[5] Ibid., III, pp. 583–6.

In the Protector's opening speech to his second Parliament (17 September 1656) he proclaimed, 'we would keep up the nobility and gentry.' His emphasis now was on *national* interests, not God's. He frequently mentioned God, but mostly in connection with reformation of manners, restriction of horse-racing, cock-fighting, etc.[1] The Major-Generals were sacrificed. Yet this attempt to meet Parliament half-way did not save James Nayler. Oliver's henchmen in the House did their best, but the hysteria was such that they could do no more than argue against sentence of death. Most MPs were determined to finish with toleration. Oliver's defeat was symbolized in the fact that he did not make his deadly request for the House to 'let Us know the grounds and reasons whereupon they have proceeded' until after Nayler had been sentenced.[2] But Oliver used the opportunity to expedite negotiations for the Petition and Advice which—it was hoped—would win Parliament's support for the Protectorate at the price—among other things—of a very substantial retreat on religious toleration: tithes to be maintained, a confession of faith to be agreed by Protector *and Parliament*; no toleration for anti-Trinitarians (like Milton), blasphemers (like Nayler) or those who defend licentiousness (Ranters and perhaps other antinomians).[3]

Firth suggested that Cromwell saw himself as a blind instrument in the hands of a higher power: he did not have revelations, but he sought to interpret the dispensations of Providence in a way that gave him a great deal of latitude for pragmatic action.[4] 'Let us all not be careful what use men will make of these actings. They shall, will they, nill they, fulfil the good pleasure of God, and we shall serve our generations.'[5] Hence he could tell Commonwealthsmen in 1648 that monarchy, aristocracy or democracy might each 'be good in themselves or for us, according as Providence should direct us'.[6]

Cromwell was no intellectual, and by comparison with most of those discussed in this book he lacked stable convictions or objectives. 'I can tell you, sirs, what I would not have,' he said in 1641, 'though I cannot what I would.'[7] His helpless question to Ludlow, 'I am as much for

---

[1] Ibid., IV, pp. 273–8. [2] Ibid., IV, p. 366.

[3] *Constitutional Documents of the Puritan Revolution, 1625–1660*, ed. S. R. Gardiner (3rd edn., 1906), pp. 454–6.

[4] C. H. Firth, *Oliver Cromwell and the Rule of the Puritans in England* (Oxford UP, 1953), pp. 470–2: first published 1900.

[5] Abbott, op. cit., I, pp. 644–5.

[6] Ludlow, *Memoirs*, I, pp. 184–5.

[7] Sir Philip Warwick, *Memoirs of the Reign of King Charles the First* (1813), p. 194.

government by consent as any man, but where shall we find that consent?'[1] was the reasonable comment of a pragmatist who had taken upon himself to control the uncontrollable, to solve the insoluble. When Edmund Calamy told him there would be nine in ten against the Protectorate, Oliver replied 'But what if I should disarm the nine and put a sword in the tenth man's hand? Would not that do the business?'[2] It depended, of course, on what the business was: one feels that Cromwell had less and less of a positive policy as his rule continued. He had been hailed as the Moses of his people; but his final vision of himself was as a good constable to keep the peace of the parish. The metaphor is perhaps illuminating in the light of Wrightson and Levine's description of the parish constable as one of the representatives of the village élite whose main concern was to discipline and control the labouring poor.[3]

Oliver was perfectly sincere in his denunciation of Levellers. He may have wanted to make MPs' flesh creep; but in 1647, when he was trying to be conciliatory, he had left the Army Council in no doubt that he saw 'very great mountains in the way' of the Agreement of the People, which would give a vote to 'men that have no interest but the interest of breathing'.[4] And in 1649 he told the Council of State (or so Lilburne assures us) that if they did not break the Levellers 'they will break you; yea and bring all the guilt of the blood and treasure shed and spent in this kingdom upon your heads and shoulders, and frustrate and make void all that work that with so many years industry, toil and pains you have done.'[5] In that outburst God's Cause becomes something like a commercial investment.

Cromwell experienced defeat in the failure of Barebone's Parliament; he consequently suffered a further defeat when polarization between Army and Parliament led to the victimization of Nayler and the compromise of the Petition and Advice. But the first defeat had been made possible by the isolation of the generals from any basis of mass support, as a result of the events of the winter of 1648–9. The rhetoric of God's Cause could not conceal that there was no longer agreement as to what the Cause was. Francis Osborne was uncharitable but not far from the mark when he wrote in 1656, ostensibly of Mahomet, that he 'rolled

---

[1] Ludlow, Memoirs, II, p. 11.
[2] Firth, op. cit., p. 411.
[3] Wrightson and Levine, Poverty and Piety in an English Village: Terling, 1525–1700, passim; Abbott, op. cit., IV, p. 471.
[4] Woodhouse, op. cit., pp. 8, 59.
[5] J. Lilburne, The Picture of the Counsel of State (1649), in Haller and Davies, op. cit., p. 204.

on his untutored rabble by mixing profit and rapine with his religion, which he left uncertain, grounding his precepts upon success, once owned as dropped upon them out of heaven; making himself still confident of the event'.[1]

Marvell's 'Horatian Ode', Milton's *Defences of the People of England*, as well as the reproachful addresses of Quakers later in the 1650s, show that others as well as Cromwell looked upon him as the representative of God's Cause. 'God hath made you a successful instrument to cast out that conqueror, and to recover our land and liberties again by your victories,' Gerrard Winstanley wrote, dedicating *The Law of Freedom* to Cromwell in 1652. God had shown Cromwell 'the highest honour of any man since Moses's time'.[2] Oliver's very great, and well-earned, prestige was an invaluable asset in the years after 1654. John Rogers, who in the summer of 1653 called Cromwell 'the great deliverer of his people',[3] soon changed his mind. But others did not, fearing the increasingly desperate tactics employed by Fifth Monarchy Men and Quakers. Owen and Goodwin felt that the essentials of God's Cause had been attained (so far as they ever could be in a sinful world). Robert Bennett in June 1654 regarded Oliver as the best guarantee against 'the common enemy', whose return to power was 'the greatest fear of many good men'.[4] Newcome and Baxter also came to look on him as the lesser evil; Baxter's retrospective view was positively enthusiastic.[5] Marvell, like Owen, continued to praise Cromwell whilst attacking Levellers. Neither wanted Oliver to accept the crown.[6] Milton never publicly criticized Cromwell. Wither thought the Protector had made more progress towards God's kingdom on earth than any 'since Christ ascended'.[7] Reeve in 1656 still expected God to 'make use of Oliver Cromwell': Clarkson in 1659 gave lavish praise to his continued defence of toleration.[8] I cited above Edward Burrough's tribute to the Protector who had so often rejected his 'good counsel and advice'. Addressing Oliver's effigy lying in state, Burrough asked, more in sorrow than in anger, 'Must this be all the monument? ... A dead image, whereby the man and his nobility was

---

[1] F. Osborne, *Miscellaneous Works* (11th edn., 1722), I, p. 94.
[2] Winstanley, *The Law of Freedom*, p. 275.
[3] See p. 55 above.
[4] Quoted by Woolrych, *Commonwealth to Protectorate*, pp. 389–90; cf. p. 396.
[5] See pp. 210, 214, 216, below, and Sedgwick, pp. 106–8 above.
[6] See p. 173 above, pp. 246–7 below.
[7] Wither, *A Suddain Flash* (1657), p. 16, in *Miscellaneous Works*, II
[8] See p. 48 above.

abused?... And shall we have no other representation of once noble Cromwell?' 'He did too much forget that good Cause.'[1]

4   James Harrington (1611–77), Henry Neville (1620–94) and the Harringtonians

I

James Harrington was not a regicide. He had not been a prominent leader during the Revolution, as Vane and Lambert had been. Yet in November 1661 he was arrested and imprisoned without trial on a charge of plotting against the government. We do not know when he was released nor on what conditions. He published nothing after the restoration.

Why was he subjected to such exceptionally severe treatment? His theories, though very influential, seem academic rather than incendiary. Part of the answer must lie, I think, in the existence of the Rota Club, which became in 1659–60 a fashionable centre for discussion of Harrington's political ideas. The Rota was a forum in which bright young men like Henry Stubbe and Samuel Pepys aired their views; under the chairmanship of Milton's friend Cyriack Skinner it also contained Henry Neville, member of the Rump and an active republican; and John Wildman, the ubiquitous plotter whose presence at the Rota together with Maximilian Petty reminds us that Leveller propaganda in 1659–60 was virtually indistinguishable from that of the Commonwealthsmen. After the restoration ''twas not fit, nay treason' for the Rota to meet, Aubrey tells us.[2] The Rev. John Ward had heard that the King initiated the Royal Society in opposition to the Rota Club, where Harrington 'and such strange fellows as he ... talked about a Commonwealth'; Charles 'not thinking fit to put down the other by open contradiction'.[3] There was panic fear of plots in the early 1660s and continuing suspicion of any centres of discussion. In 1675 the government tried to close down coffee-houses. The Whig Green Ribbon Club played a significant role in the Exclusion crisis of the later 1670s.

---

[1] Burrough, *Works*, pp. 458–61; see p. 146 above; cf. Bishop, quoted on p. 133 above.

[2] For Levellers see p. 34 above. For the Rota, see Aubrey, *Brief Lives*, ed. A. Clark (Oxford UP, 1898), I, p. 291. Others who attended the Club included Milton's friend Andrew Marvell, William Petty, Roger Coke, the royalist John Berkenhead and Aubrey himself (Aubrey, op. cit., II, p. 148).

[3] *Diary of the Rev. John Ward, Vicar of Stratford-upon-Avon, 1648–79*, ed. C. Severn (1839), p. 116. I am not supporting this theory of the origins of the Royal Society.

We know nothing of Harrington's reaction to defeat, except that he remained silent—apart from drafting the unfinished *The Mechanics of Nature*—and is alleged to have gone mad. He had already appealed to posterity 'if this age fail me'.[1] A summary of Harrington's main ideas had been published in 1656—before *Oceana*—in *A Copy of a Letter from an Officer of the Army in Ireland to his Highness the Lord Protector*, signed by R. G. and said to have been written in June 1654. There are mysteries about this pamphlet. John Toland, Harrington's first biographer, said that Wildman or Neville published it.[2] Another suggestion is that R. G. is Richard Goodgroom, a yeoman who became an Army chaplain. He was a signatory to one of the Digger pamphlets in 1649, became a Fifth Monarchist, was plotting with Colonel Okey in 1656, was recommissioned in 1659 and became chaplain to Robert Overton. After the restoration he was in jail from 1661 to 1667 and again in 1671.[3] R. G.'s presentation of Harrington's work is competent,[4] and he was no mere plagiarist. He made one significant point which is not to be found in Harrington's works: 'among many other accidents' which led to 'increasing the power of the Commonwealth' was 'the settling the militia in Deputy-Lieutenants' under Henry VIII.[5]

R. G. generalized what was to be Harrington's argument: not land only but 'the riches of the people in general is the natural cause of destruction to all regal states'. The civil war had resulted from a long-standing 'state disease'. And he added that under the Commonwealth the sale of the King's, bishops', deans' and chapters' and delinquents' lands, and of fee-farm rents, meant that England was 'farther off from a capacity of being governed by monarchy again'. Even if monarchy was restored, it could be maintained only by a standing army.[6] R. G. anticipated Harrington's distinction between political 'foundation' and

---

[1] *The Political Works of James Harrington*, ed. J. G. A. Pocock (Cambridge UP, 1977), pp. 600, 602. Cited henceforth as Pocock, op. cit.

[2] Harrington, *The Oceana and Other Works*, ed. J. Toland (1737), p. xviii.

[3] Winstanley, *The Law of Freedom*, p. 95; *Thurloe State Papers*, V, p. 197; Pocock, op. cit., pp. 11–12; Capp, *The Fifth Monarchy Men*, p. 250.

[4] The essential passage is reproduced in Pocock, op. cit., p. 11.

[5] R. G., op. cit., p. 9; cf. Pocock, op. cit., p. 45.

[6] Ibid., pp. 10–11. Professor Pocock regards this as a misinterpretation of Harrington's argument (op. cit., pp. 57–8); it might however be seen as a clarification. It does not fit, indeed, with Pocock's interpretation of Harrington; but contemporaries are not necessarily wrong when they disagree with later historians. Stubbe and Albertus Warren were also to develop a more commercial version of Harringtonianism (Jacob, *Henry Stubbe*, pp. 142–3, quoting Warren's *An Apology for the Discovery of Humane Reason. Written by Ma[rtin] Clifford Esq.*, 1680). See pp. 275–6, 324–5 below.

'superstructure'.[1] R. G.'s reference to 'friends to the Good Old Cause' and to the 'freeborn people of England' might have been made by Wildman; but 'the just God of heaven and earth, who hath appeared so visibly and miraculously for this Cause of freedom',[2] sounds more like a preacher than either Wildman or Neville. Harrington, Goodgroom and Wildman were arrested in 1661, in the flurry which led to the execution of Vane and the imprisonment of Lambert for life, of Wildman for six years.[3] If R. G. does turn out to be Goodgroom, he forms an interesting link between Winstanley and Harrington.[4] Perhaps the Diggers were not all poor labourers and squatters from the Cobham neighbourhood? Perhaps intellectuals like Goodgroom, the poet Richard Coster, Everard and possibly Clarkson came down from London to demonstrate solidarity? Perhaps William Covell had a similar relationship to the colony at Enfield?[5]

I shall not attempt to summarize Harrington's views again.[6] Rarely can so few pages as those in which he discussed English history have had so great and lasting an effect.[7] Interesting for us is that, although Harrington's thought is not primarily theological, he shares with millenarians, with Cromwell, Owen, Ludlow, Stubbe, Fifth Monarchists, Milton, Quakers and Marvell a sense that the English Revolution had marked a turning-point in history. In it the political superstructure had been adjusted to match changes in the balance of property. So complete was the rupture with the past that 'the right of kings, the obligation of former laws, or of the oath of allegiance, is absolved by the balance.'[8] The Engagement theorists spilt much ink in trying to find justifications for what Harrington so summarily explained. He cuts through traditional platitudes as sharply as Hobbes.

'The Gothic balance'[9] had been upset by the land transfers of the

---

[1] R. G., op. cit., p. 15.
[2] Ibid., pp. 21–3.
[3] Pocock, op. cit., p. 125. R. G.'s reference to those who had to recant the doctrine that 'the saints were the Lord's anointed ... and say it's the Lord Protector' (p. 14) might be written either by a sceptic like Wildman or Neville, or by a saint shocked by the *volte-face* of some of his fellows.
[4] Russell Smith long ago suggested that Harrington may have been influenced by Winstanley (*James Harrington and his Oceana*, Cambridge UP, 1914), an idea which historians have not so far taken seriously.
[5] See p. 41 above.
[6] See my 'James Harrington and the People', in *Puritanism and Revolution* (Panther edn., 1968), pp. 289–302; or, better, Tawney's *Harrington's Interpretation of his Age*, reprinted in *History and Society: Essays by R. H. Tawney*, ed. J. M. Winter (1978), pp. 66–84.
[7] Pocock, op. cit., pp. 196–9, 606–9.
[8] Ibid., p. 203; cf. pp. 85–6: Filmer dismissed.
[9] Ibid., pp. 164, 191–3.

century and a half before 1640, from crown, aristocracy and church to
gentry and yeomanry. This shift in the balance made it impossible for
government to function in the traditional way. In Harrington's oft-
quoted words, 'the dissolution of this government caused the [civil] war,
not the war the dissolution of this government.'[1] Henry Marten and
others elaborated this in *The Armies Duty* (1659):

> The dying pangs of a monarchical power in England caused our
> wars.... The Parliament's Army did indeed prevent a
> possibility of the resurrection of that power by a forcible
> changing the property in the lands and so reviving a new
> monarchy; but the old was dead by a kind of natural dissolution
> before the Parliament voted it useless, burdensome and
> dangerous:[2]

In these circumstances the government, Harrington wrote, recalling
1645, 'must of necessity be new-modelled'.[3] In this sense the Good Old
Cause had, in Marvell's phrase, been 'too good to have been fought for':
Charles I ought to have seen the inevitability of power passing to what
Harrington called 'the people', meaning the men of property, those who
could buy land.[4]

Harrington's starting point was feudal ('Gothic') society, in which
landownership entailed military power because tenants owed military
service. The transfer of land to 'the people' at and after the dissolution of
the monasteries brought 'so vast a prey to the industry' of 'the people'
that the feudal military system was undermined.[5] But Harrington had,
however reluctantly, to recognize the changes that came with the rise of
capitalism. 'Natural revolution happeneth from within, or by commerce,
as when a government erected upon one balance ... comes to alter to
another.'[6] 'Where there is a bank, ten to one there is a commonwealth.'[7]
Although capitalism in England was mainly rural, 'innumerable trades'
allowed merchants to become richer than landowners, and therefore
'purchasers of great estates'. (Harrington's brother was a City

---

[1] Ibid., p. 198.
[2] I owe this reference to the kindness of Professor C. M. Williams.
[3] Pocock, op. cit., p. 187.
[4] Ibid., p. 776; the passage almost anticipates Marvell (see pp. 249–50 below). Cf. Neville, *Plato Redivivus* (1681), in *Two English Republican Tracts*, ed. Caroline Robbins (Cambridge UP, 1969), pp. 140–2.
[5] Pocock, op. cit., pp. 43, 198.
[6] Ibid., p. 405; cf. pp. 56–61.
[7] Ibid., p. 409.

merchant.) 'The revenue of industry in a nation, at least in this, is three-
or fourfold greater than that of the mere rent.' (Industry for Harrington
includes agrarian capitalism, for which the way must be cleared.) 'If the
people then obstruct industry they obstruct their own livelihood.'[1]
Political power can therefore be safely entrusted to 'the people'; they will
protect themselves from 'robbers or Levellers'.[2] 'Industry of all things is
the most accumulative, and accordingly of all things hates levelling.'[3] By
the same token the rule of the saints, 'without election by the people',
would of necessity be founded on military force, and so would be unjust,
indeed irreligious.[4] Felix Raab saw *Oceana* as a polemic against
Cromwell's rule;[5] his later pamphlets were aimed impartially against a
restoration of monarchy and an oligarchy of saints.

So Harrington's is no mere determinist theory of history. The shift in
the balance only creates conditions without which; it produces no
automatic solutions. Human prudence is necessary to establish an
appropriate new constitution. Until this is done politics remains 'a
wrestling match'.[6] Queen Elizabeth established something like a
'principality in a commonwealth', but her successors tried to revive
'sovereign power in a monarchy', by which Harrington meant
absolutism.[7] Until good, scientifically-based laws are established, the
new commonwealth will not be stabilized; still less will an equal
commonwealth be set up which will survive. The agrarian balance
ensures that no stability is possible under any government except a
commonwealth, whether or not it has a prince as its figure-head.[8]

We must attend carefully to Harrington's use of words here. Only
those who own property are 'people'. Servants, who lack 'wherewithal to
live of themselves', *cannot* be free, *cannot* share in the government of a
commonwealth: such is the nature of the balance. 'People' have servants.[9]
Harrington declared that monarchy and House of Lords could never be

---

[1] Ibid., p. 293; cf. pp. 304–5, 406, 470–2.
[2] Ibid., p. 292; cf. pp. 292, 429–30, 657–60.
[3] Ibid., pp. 122, 430, 840.
[4] Ibid., p. 796; cf. pp. 744–5, 838–9.
[5] Raab, *The English Face of Machiavelli: A Changing Interpretation, 1500–1700* (1964), p. 188; cf. Pocock, op. cit., p. 859.
[6] Pocock, op. cit., p. 196.
[7] Ibid., pp. 608–9.
[8] Cf. J. C. Davis, *Utopia and the Ideal Society: A Study of English Utopian Writing, 1516–1700* (Cambridge UP, 1981), pp. 213–17.
[9] Pocock, op. cit., pp. 212, 430, 665–6, 786–8. The *locus classicus* for the exclusion of the poor from 'the people' is the Harringtonian Captain Adam Baynes's speech in Richard Cromwell's Parliament (Burton, *Parliamentary Diary*, III, pp. 147–8). Baynes had, consistently enough, been one of Nayler's defenders in 1656.

restored in England. The restoration made him appear wrong; but kings after 1660 were not monarchs in Harrington's sense, but princes in a commonwealth.[1] There could be no going back to the sort of monarchy that Charles I had tried (and inevitably failed) to establish. 'When no Parliament,' Harrington used to say, 'then absolute monarchy: when a Parliament, then it runs to Commonwealth.'[2]

Similarly the peerage restored in 1660 was very different (in Harringtonian terms) from that which had existed under 'the Gothic balance'. The peerage had been undermined economically long before 1640. 'A King governing now in England by Parliaments would find the nobility of no effect at all.' Parliament had become 'a mere popular council'.[3] Feudal tenures had been under attack from the gentry long before 1640; their abolition during the Revolution completed the transformation of land into a commodity. This was, in Professor Perkin's words, 'the decisive change in English history, which made it different from that of the continent'.[4] Abolition of feudal tenures was confirmed by Parliament in 1656; further confirmation of this abolition was the first business the Convention Parliament turned to in 1660 after agreeing to recall Charles II.[5] Abolition of the feudal levy in 1661 confirmed the peerage's loss of independent military power.[6] Financial control passed from monarch to lower house.[7] As early as 1656 Francis Osborne had grasped the fact that a House of Lords could not oppose the wishes of the gentry—whether he got it from Harrington or (less likely) Harrington from him.[8] Henry Neville also realized what had happened. 'Tenures are so altered that they signify nothing towards making the yeomanry dependent upon the Lords.... The natural part of our government, which is power, is by means of property in the hands of the people;

---

[1] Pocock, op. cit., pp. 351–2, 608. This is one of the few points on which Pocock's Introduction seems to me misleading.

[2] Aubrey, *Brief Lives*, I, p. 291. For Harrington on absolute monarchy see also Pocock, op. cit., pp. 844–53.

[3] Pocock, op. cit., pp. 608, 770; cf. L. Stone, *The Crisis of the Aristocracy, 1558–1641* (Oxford UP, 1965), *passim*.

[4] H. J. Perkin, 'Social Causes of the British Industrial Revolution', *TRHS*, 5th Series, 18 (1968), pp. 134–5.

[5] C. B. Macpherson appreciated the importance of the abolition of feudal tenures for Harrington (*The Political Theory of Possessive Individualism: Hobbes to Locke*, Oxford UP, 1962, pp. 172–3). Cf. Pocock, 'Authority and Property: The Question of Liberal Origins' in *After the Reformation: Essays in Honor of J. H. Hexter*, ed. B. Malament (Manchester UP, 1980), p. 347.

[6] C. G. Robertson, *Select Statutes, Cases and Documents* (6th edn., 1935), p. 28.

[7] Ibid., pp. 198, 703, 770. Samuel Butler had grasped this point clearly (*Prose observations*, pp. 163, 282–4).

[8] F. Osborne, *Miscellaneous Works*, I, pp. 174–5.

whilst the artificial part, or the parchment ... remains the same.'[1] Let
the King come in, Harrington said, 'and call a Parliament of the greatest
Cavaliers in England, so they be men of estates, and let them sit but seven
years, and they will all turn commonwealthsmen'. Punctually within
seven years the Cavalier Parliament drove the King's minister,
Clarendon, into exile.[2]

So the restoration of King and Lords was no obstacle to the
establishment of a Harringtonian commonwealth: the balance made it
inevitable. 'Your lordships and the people have the same cause, and the
same enemies,' Shaftesbury told the upper house in 1675. There were
only three possibilities: rule by standing army, 'tumbling into a
democratical republic' or rule through peers and people. Peers were now
little more than rich citizens. The civil war had shown that they had no
special military abilities.[3] Generals no longer commanded armies because
they were peers; they became peers because they successfully
commanded armies. If they were very successful they became dukes.
Harrington did not say that after seven years the *House of Commons*
would turn commonwealthsmen: he said Parliament, including the lords,
for 'it is the great interest of the present peerage that there be a well-
ordered commonwealth.' The nobility could be 'a guard for the people'.[4]

So England had inevitably to be a commonwealth in Harrington's
sense. 'Or to speak more properly and piously, a commonwealth is not
made by men but by God; and they who resist his holy will ... cannot
prosper.'[5] But Harrington had hoped to show his countrymen how to
stabilize an *equal* commonwealth. His concept of 'equality' was as
limited as his conception of 'the people'. In Oceana fundamental laws
protected property. Harrington assumed that 'the natural rulers' would
continue to rule so long as their economic superiority was protected
against absolute monarchy or military dictatorship.[6] Men follow their

---

[1] Robbins, op. cit., p. 133; cf. Selden, *Table Talk* (1847), pp. 105–6.
[2] Aubrey, op. cit., I, p. 291; cf. Pocock, op. cit., pp. 351–2, 744–5. The fact that the King
connived at Clarendon's disgrace only confirms, Harrington would say, that he was in the last
resort totally dependent on Parliament. Cf. Clive Holmes, *Seventeenth-Century Lincolnshire*,
pp. 235–7.
[3] Pocock, op. cit., pp. 132–3; Stone, op. cit., pp. 263–70. Saye and Sele had grasped this point as
early as 1657: see C. H. Firth, *The House of Lords during the Civil War* (1910), pp. 250–1.
[4] Pocock, op. cit., pp. 703, 698.
[5] Ibid., p. 704.
[6] In 1647 Laurence Clarkson had written a pamphlet to try to persuade the lower and middling
sort to revolt against the assumption of the nobility and gentry that they might with impunity
'oppress the persons of such that are not as rich and honourable as themselves' (*A Generall
Charge*, pp. 10–18; see pp. 42–3 above). Clarkson did not succeed in changing the social
assumptions on which Harrington relied.

reason, which is the same thing as following their interests,[1] though they may not interpret these interests correctly. We may contrast Winstanley, whose reason taught not self-interest but co-operation: an interesting difference of starting-point for thinkers who have some things in common. Winstanley wanted to establish universal democracy: for Harrington only a leisured class can attain the political understanding necessary to determine what laws are best. Oceana weighted the representation of men with more than £100 land *per annum*, and had an upper chamber which propounded laws on which the lower decided. Government itself was greatly decentralized, as it was to become in England, especially after 1688. The gentry ran local government in virtual independence: the executive was closely dependent upon the landed class from which it was drawn.[2]

Harrington wanted to preserve what Professor Macpherson calls an 'opportunity state' whilst preventing the emergence of 'that foul beast, the oligarchy'.[3] Here the two most radical elements in his system came into play, the agrarian law and secret ballot. Something like an agrarian law had been advocated by Gabriel Plattes in *Macaria* (1641).[4] In September 1646 and again in October 1648 the lower ranks in the Army were said to be putting forward schemes for an upper limit to the amount of landed property which any one individual could hold, similar to Harrington's agrarian law.[5] Harrington's object was to prevent social polarization by restricting the number of the very rich, and so to establish a relative equality among 'the people' in his sense of property-owners.[6] Secret ballot (the other device which Harrington regarded as fundamental to Oceana)[7] was common practice in merchant companies in the City of London. Charles I prohibited its use in 1637, but it was introduced into City government by Lord Mayor Penington in 1642.[8] A ballot had been proposed in the House of Commons in 1646, for motions involving either the granting of money or appointment to office.[9]

---

[1] Pocock, op. cit., pp. 171–2.
[2] Cf. Davis, op. cit., pp. 220–9.
[3] Pocock, op. cit., pp. 231, 744–5, 786, 838–9.
[4] Op. cit., p. 4.
[5] Ed. J. A. F. Bekkers, *Correspondence of John Morris with Johannes de Laet* (Assen, 1970), pp. 122, 149.
[6] Pocock, op. cit., pp. 230–7, 328, 459, 664.
[7] Ibid., p. 231.
[8] Valerie Pearl, *London and the Outbreak of the Puritan Revolution* (Oxford UP, 1961), pp. 61, 92, 246, 286; cf. R. B. Davis, *George Sandys: Poet and Adventurer* (1955), p. 101. Waller was apprehensive about the introduction of secret ballot in the House of Commons in 1641.
[9] *The Diary of John Harington, MP, 1646–53*, ed. M. F. Stieg (Somerset Record Soc., 1972), pp. 42–3.

Rejected then, it was introduced for elections to the Council of State in 1651:[1] the construction of a ballot box was apparently voted.[2] The ballot was later used for voting in the Royal Society. For similar reasons Harrington made the radical recommendation that MPs should be paid.[3]

Harrington's version of English history is a secularized providentialism.[4] It was not the sins of the old regime which led God to overthrow it: shifts in the balance of property caused its demise—'as natural as the death of a man'.[5] And yet there are parallels, analogies, between Harrington's scheme and radical theological theories. Church, crown and aristocracy had lost their lands because as landowners they had been feckless, extravagant, unimproving; the purchasers were the prudent, careful, thrifty men of whom Puritan preachers approved, who would increase the wealth of the Commonwealth. Harrington wanted to see a mean between racking of rents and rational improvement.[6]

The consequence of the shift of political power was a new commercial imperialism, of which the old regime had been incapable. Harrington expressed this in millenarian terms as a realization of the manifest destiny of the chosen English people. 'The late appearances of God unto you', he wrote, have not 'been altogether for yourselves'. If 'called in by an oppressed people ... in the dregs of the Gothic empire' (Scotland? Ireland? France?), England has a duty to respond. 'If the cause of mankind be the Cause of God, the Lord of Hosts will be your captain.' The first European nation 'that recovers the health of ancient prudence ... shall assuredly govern the world'; if we don't, France will. 'If you add unto the propagation of civil liberty ... the propagation of liberty of conscience, this empire, this patronage of the world, is the kingdom of Christ.' 'If our religion be anything else but a vain boast, ... here is that empire wherein justice shall run down like a river.' 'What is in our way?' Harrington asked apocalyptically. 'The dragon, that old serpent?'[7] The harnessing of millenarianism to imperialism could not be more explicit— nor more successful. Hugh Peter in 1646 had expressed a similar

---

[1] G. E. Aylmer, *The State's Servants: The Civil Service of the English Republic* (1973), pp. 21, 352.
[2] J. Frank, *The Beginnings of the English Newspaper, 1620–1660* (Harvard UP, 1961), p. 330.
[3] Pocock, op. cit., p. 708.
[4] Cf. ibid.; 'The ordering of a restored republic might be identified with the resurrection of Christ in a sense more reminiscent of Winstanley than of Hobbes' (p. 80; cf. p. 75).
[5] Ibid., p. 203.
[6] Ibid., p. 304.
[7] Ibid., pp. 329–30, 332–3.

expansionist commercial foreign policy in religious terms.[1] Among other
things, Harrington's commonwealth for increase would satisfy the land
hunger of those members of the ruling class who would be restricted by
his agrarian laws. Harrington was the first to envisage the British Empire
as a system of outdoor relief for younger sons.[2] England, Harrington
predicted, 'will bear a prince in a commonwealth far higher than it is
possible ... to bear a monarch'.[3]

Harrington's thought drew on and meshed with what contemporaries
were thinking and doing. The agrarian law and the secret ballot were
being discussed at least a decade before Harrington took them up. The
concept of the balance is of course a commercial one, and goes back long
before Harrington's time. Use of the lot to solve disputed problems was
common practice among Puritans: Johnston of Wariston, for instance,
and Pepys.[4] All this suggests to me that Harrington's theories were based
on involvement in as well as deep thought about the political problems of
his day. His realism, despite the utopian form of *Oceana*, is impressive. I
venture to disagree with Professor Pocock's vision of Harrington as an
armchair academic theorist who got his ideas from reading Machiavelli.
Harrington did read Machiavelli; but he mingled Machiavelli's ideas with
others drawn from current political practice and speculation—including,
as Professor Pocock valuably demonstrates, the ideas of Marchamont
Nedham. The fact that Harrington produced analyses of English history
and programmes for political action which remained influential for a
century bears witness to his careful study of and reflection on his subject
matter. His intense political activity from 1656 onwards again suggests
more than an academic interest in politics.[5] The Rota was not just a
talking shop; its closure after the restoration, and Harrington's arrest,
confirm that.

What is interesting is the direction of Harrington's political activity in
1659. He associates with politically active republicans like Ludlow,
Neville and Wildman. But—unlike Milton and Stubbe—Harrington's
main concern in 1659–60 is not only to keep the Stuarts out. Harrington
is hardly less concerned to argue against Rogers, Stubbe and perhaps
Milton.[6] For an alliance of the saints with the Army could have prevented

---

[1] *Mr Peters Last Report of the English Wars* (1646), pp. 6, 9–11; *Good Work for a Good Magistrate* (1651), pp. 78–109. Cf. p. 181 above.
[2] Cf. Davis, op. cit., pp. 230, 235, and pp. 246–8 below.
[3] Pocock, op. cit., pp. 351–2.
[4] See p. 83 above.
[5] Cf. p. 192 above; R. G.'s political involvement.
[6] See p. 78 above; *CPW*; VII, pp. 518–21.

the balance from asserting itself, could have given fresh life to the 'wrestling match' that English politics had been for so long. Whereas a restoration of monarchy, provided it was accompanied by disbandment of the Army, would mean return of the power of the gentry and the City of London, in accordance with the balance. Whether or not monarchy and House of Lords came back was a relatively minor matter; England without an Army could only be a commonwealth, in Harrington's sense of the word.

Environment has always seemed to me more important than inheritance in the evolution of political thought. Significant new political ideas emerge in periods of political and social change. Thus the English Revolution produced Hobbes, the Levellers, Winstanley as well as Harrington, and ultimately Locke. Tawney convincingly established that analyses like Harrington's had been circulating in unorganized form for a generation before he published. Tawney instanced Ralegh, Bacon, Sir Thomas Wilson, John Selden and Bishop Goodman;[1] we may add Sir John Davies, Sir Henry Spelman, Francis Quarles, Henry Parker, Tom May and the anonymous author of *A Certificate from Northamptonshire* (1641).[2] But the events of the 1640s and 1650s gave food for thought too. The abolition of feudal tenures and wardship, the land confiscations and sales to which R. G. drew attention, the new economic power and political influence of the City of London, the new power of the English state, based on a new system of taxation—all these (as well as Machiavelli) went to the planning of Harrington's 'commonwealth for increase'. It was not its Machiavellian virtue that made Harrington's model so convincing to his and succeeding generations; it was its deep roots in the historical reality of the England about which he wrote. The debates on the Other House in Richard Cromwell's Parliament already show a wide acceptance of Harrington's principles.[3]

II

Historians rightly distinguish between Harrington and the Harringtonians, who after 1660 taught a modified form of the master's doctrines. But perhaps sufficient allowance has not been made for

---

[1] Tawney, *Harrington's Interpretation of his Age*, in Winter, op. cit., p. 78.
[2] *A Certificate*, pp. 16–18. The unknown author quotes Bacon and Ralegh in discussing the effects of the dissolution of the monasteries on the balance of landed property.
[3] Burton, *Parliamentary Diary*, III and IV *passim*.

experience of the defeat of the Revolution in this modification: the utopian moment was over.[1] Throughout 1659 and the early months of 1660 Harrington, like Stubbe and Milton, continued pamphleteering desperately; he still hoped that 'political prudence' might be applied to establishing an 'equal commonwealth' and preventing the emergence of oligarchy. Pocock makes the interesting point that Harrington's style in these later pamphlets is much clearer and more readable than in *Oceana*. He suggests that this change may have been due to Neville's influence.[2] But Milton too simplified his prose style in 1659–60: perhaps the urgency of the political situation was a common cause.

Former Levellers like Wildman and Maximilian Petty attended the Rota Club, and many Leveller pamphlets of 1659 had a strong Harringtonian flavour. The Levellers had argued a different case against Ireton in 1647, but now Harrington's republicanism represented the best they were likely to get. Wildman and others had been in touch with dissident Commonwealthsmen like Okey and Saunders since 1654, and Professor Pocock is surely right to say that *Oceana* attempts to provide a theory that would mediate between the positions in the Putney Debates of Ireton on the one hand and Rainborough and the Levellers on the other.[3] Harrington discerned that the clamour for monarchy in 1660 really reflected a desire for 'a government of laws and not of men'.[4]

But after 1660, with Harrington silenced and a totally new political situation, his disciples were concerned to see *a* stable commonwealth established: few continued to dream of an *equal* commonwealth. The threat now came not from an oligarchy of saints but from a revival of military rule, this time under the King with French backing. Harrington had regarded a standing army as a temporary aberration, for 'an army is a beast that hath a great belly and must be fed.' He could not see how any but a revolutionary government prepared to confiscate the land of its opponents could afford to maintain such a beast for long.[5] But sinister possibilities emerged in the 1670s, which Neville and later Harringtonians had to face.[6]

I shall be looking later at the revision of Harringtonianism by Henry

---

[1] *MER*, p. 199; cf. pp. 202–3, 225.
[2] Pocock, op. cit., p. 101.
[3] Ibid., pp. 27, 42–3. This hardly fits with Professor Pocock's guess that Harrington was politically isolated.
[4] Ibid., pp. 497, 762.
[5] Ibid., p. 165.
[6] Ibid., pp. 61, 165. For land confiscations see pp. 284–5 below.

Stubbe.[1] The outstanding document of Harringtonian revisionism was Henry Neville's *Plato Redivivus* of 1681. Neville, 'more affected by Cicero than the Bible', had been described as Harrington's representative in the Rump, the member for the Rota.[2] In February 1659 Richard Cromwell's Parliament had spent much time discussing whether Neville was guilty of atheism and blasphemy. But when the Rump was restored he became a member of its Council of State, and brought in a motion for an oath renouncing Charles Stuart.[3] After the restoration he was suspected of being in contact with the imprisoned Colonel Hutchinson, and was himself jailed for alleged complicity with the Northern Plot.[4] In 1664 he was released and obtained permission to go abroad, returning only in 1667 or 1668.[5] His associates at this period included Wildman, Algernon Sidney, Ashley Cooper and the Duke of Buckingham.[6]

Before 1681 Neville had published only scurrilous squibs on *The Parliament of Women* and the jovial glorification of polygamy in *The Isle of Pines* (1668). But he had proclaimed his Harringtonian beliefs in 1659 to Richard Cromwell's Parliament.[7] He was a political thinker 'whose originality should not be lightly dismissed'.[8] In *Plato Redivivus* he produced a 'possibilist' document, not his ideal, but 'the best that the people would or could receive'.[9] He stressed the historical aspects of Harrington's theory. Military despotism would necessarily be unstable because not in accordance with the balance. To set up 'parchment' ('in which the form of government is written') against economic power would perpetuate the instability which had bedevilled English politics for 200 years.[10] In the new circumstances the agrarian law and the secret ballot, essential to Harrington's scheme for an *equal* commonwealth, were played down.[11] Neville was well aware how anxious 'the people' were to avoid any repetition of civil war.[12] As Shaftesbury appreciated,

---

[1] See pp. 275–6 below.
[2] F. P. G. Guizot, *History of Richard Cromwell and the Restoration of Charles II*, trans. A. R. Scoble (1856), I, p. 308.
[3] Burton, *Parliamentary Diary*, III, pp. 296–305; *Commons Journals*, VII, p. 800.
[4] Lucy Hutchinson, op. cit., pp. 249, 254–5.
[5] Robbins, op. cit., pp. 12–13.
[6] Ashley, op. cit., pp. 217–18, 222–3; Burton, *Parliamentary Diary*, IV, p. 324. Neville may well have read *Paradise Lost*: see Robbins, op. cit., p. 127.
[7] Burton, *Parliamentary Diary*, III, pp. 132–5, 229, 330–1; IV, pp. 23–5.
[8] Pocock, op. cit., pp. 134–6, cf. pp. 100, 145.
[9] Robbins, op. cit., p. 200.
[10] Ibid., pp. 88–90, 133–5, 140–7, 159, 173–5.
[11] The agrarian was mentioned, but only obliquely: ibid., p. 97.
[12] Ibid., p. 80.

the peers, the richest members of the Commonwealth, were now natural allies of 'the people' against military rule. So Harrington's analysis was revised, and fused with a modification of the traditional Parliamentarian theory of the Norman Yoke. This had in radical usage come to be directed against monarchy *and aristocracy*. But now the enemy is only potential military absolutism. The new role of the peers as 'protectors' of the people[1] was projected back into the age when, for Harrington, lords and king had been inseparable allies, indistinguishable parts of the Gothic balance.[2] This was possible only because the feudal power of the peerage had so completely disappeared in England.

Neville, in 1681, also knew that fear of military absolutism was closely linked with fear of 'Giant Popery';[3] against which, he said, the best defence was 'a company of poor people called fanatics, who are driven into corners as the first Christians were'.[4] Neville drew on their tradition that the Pope was Antichrist, that the apostasy had started in the Apostles' days; he recalled the revolutionary theories of 'honest John Calvin'.[5] In his second edition he added a fierce attack on the clergy of the established church, and called for them to be elected. Harrington had regarded the clergy as bulwarks of reaction. Civil liberty demanded toleration: yet Harrington thought that a state church and an endowed clergy were essential to civil government. So ministers must be elected by the people in their parishes.[6]

Neville too appealed directly to 'the middle sort of people'.[7] He insisted that a settled republic would wield much greater military power than a monarchy striving to become absolute, under which—as the noble Venetian in Neville's dialogue delicately put it—England had become 'of so small regard, and signifies so little abroad'. Democracy 'is much more powerful than aristocracy, because the latter cannot arm the people for fear they should seize upon the government'.[8] Philip IV of Spain and Cardinal Mazarin had argued vehemently in the 1640s against permitting the establishment of a republic in England, on similar grounds to

---

[1] Ibid., pp. 87–8, 194; cf. p. 192.
[2] Ibid., pp. 130, 133–4, 193–4; cf. Davis, op. cit., p. 242.
[3] Robbins, op. cit., p. 132. Is this an echo of *Pilgrim's Progress*?
[4] Ibid., p. 158; cf. p. 76—praise of Independent congregations. Cf. Milton's comparison of Familists to the early Christians—*CPW*, I, p. 788.
[5] Robbins, op. cit., pp. 112, 116, 118, 160–1; cf. the reference to 'the seed of the serpent and the seed of the woman', ibid., p. 177.
[6] Pocock, op. cit., pp. 752, 764–7, 844–6.
[7] Robbins, op. cit., pp. 116–19, 137, 181; cf. pp. 82, 154–5, 158–60, 164.
[8] Ibid., pp. 79, 92–3, 95–6, 173–4, 200.

Neville.[1] The main planks of Neville's platform became Whig orthodoxy: Parliamentary control of foreign policy, of the army, of ministers, of the church and of finance.[2] For Neville the exclusion of James Duke of York and the claims of the Duke of Monmouth were irrelevant to England's major problems. To exclusion he preferred limitations on the power of any popish successor to Charles II: for this would confirm the monarch in his status of a prince in a commonwealth, or 'a Doge'. Neville tactfully put this description of his most sacred majesty into the mouth of the noble Venetian.[3]

I noted the possible influence of Harrington on Osborne.[4] It is more obvious on Saye and Sele, Stubbe, Algernon Sidney,[5] Marvell,[6] Dryden,[7] Lucy Hutchinson,[8] Shaftesbury, Denzil Holles, Halifax,[9] Sir William Temple,[10] Penn, Locke, Toland, *The Free State of Noland* (1696) and Steele.[11] The University of Oxford included his works in the great burning of the books in which Hunton, Hobbes, Milton and Baxter suffered in 1683.

Neville popularized Harrington in the revised form in which his ideas were passed on to the eighteenth century, though economic realities reinforced Stubbe's more directly commercial emphasis.[12] But eighteenth-century Harringtonianism had lost the radicalism which had attracted Levellers and Henry Marten in the 1650s, Vane, Stubbe and the author of *Chaos* in 1659.[13] William Sprigge, also in 1659, proposed an agrarian law to limit accumulation: significantly he called his book

---

[1] Ibid., pp. 92, 181–6; A. J. Loomie, 'Alonso de Cardenas and the Long Parliament, 1640–1648', *EHR*, XCVII (1982), p. 292; *Recueil des instructions données aux ambassadeurs de France*, ed. J. J. Jusserand, Vol. 24, *Angleterre* (Paris, 1929), i. (*1648–65*), pp. 35–8.

[2] Robbins, op. cit., pp. 185–6.

[3] Ashley, op. cit., p. 223; Robbins, op. cit., pp. 124, 167–72. (This is another addition in the second edition of *Plato Redivivus*.)

[4] See pp. 196–7 above.

[5] Sidney, *Discourses on Government* (1698), p. 420.

[6] See pp. 248–51 below.

[7] R. Nevo, *The Dial of Virtue: A Study of Poems on Affairs of State in the Seventeenth Century* (Princeton UP, 1963), p. 258.

[8] Hutchinson, *Memoirs*, pp. 15, 40–1.

[9] Raab, op. cit., pp. 227–8, 242–54.

[10] Temple, *Works* (1740), I, pp. 69–70; *Essays*, ed. J. A. Nicklin (n.d.), p. 258.

[11] J. P. Kenyon, *Revolution Principles: The Politics of Party, 1689–1720* (Cambridge UP, 1977), pp. 167–8.

[12] See pp. 275–6 below.

[13] See pp. 253–4, 256 below for Stubbe and Vane. Stubbe thought that 'the Petition of Right and other laws in being ... had already deposed monarchy, and we were only to improve, not create, a republic' (*An Essay in Defence of the Good Old Cause*, 1659, Sig. ×5; cf. Sig. ××2v, *A Letter to an Officer of the Army*, 1659, pp. 60–4, and *An Account of the Rise and Progress of Mahometanism*, 1911, p. 71: interest rules): Davis, *Utopia and the Ideal Society*, pp. 243–53.

A Modest Plea for an Equal Commonwealth.[1] Walter Moyle thought liberty and colonization went together; that 'the balance of dominion changes with the balance of property' had been 'fully demonstrated by the great Harrington'.[2] American and French revolutionaries took the theory over, again without the radicalism of the original. 'The great art of lawgiving consists in balancing the poor against the rich,' wrote the American Harringtonian John Adams; interest in Harrington became widespread in France, we are told, only after Thermidor.[3]

So the experience of defeat silenced Harrington and led his disciples, necessarily, to eviscerate his theories.[4] They succeeded in making him a great figure after 1688, a prophet of the rule of the propertied and of the British Empire. Harrington's attempt to restrain 'that foul beast, the oligarchy', and his hope that the British Empire would be 'the kingdom of Christ' were, alas, not realized.[5]

---

[1] Op. cit., pp. 84–6. Note 'equal'.
[2] Moyle, *An Essay upon the Constitution of the Roman Government* (c.1699), in Robbins, op. cit., p. 232; cf. pp. 237–40, 247.
[3] See my *Puritanism and Revolution*, pp. 296–7.
[4] The early Defoe was perhaps a surviving radical Harringtonian of .sorts: see *WTUD*, pp. 381–2.
[5] Pocock, op. cit., p. 786; cf. pp. 744–5.

Chapter 7

Some Conservative Puritan Ministers

I

For the sake of completeness I want to look at some of those moderate Puritans and Presbyterians who supported Parliament at the beginning of the civil war, drew back from regicide and toleration of radical sectaries, and then came to terms with the government of the Protectorate. Terrified by what they saw as the 'anarchy' of 1659–60, they supported the return of the King; but then found that their last state was worse than their first. There must have been many such. I have chosen five ministers who left an articulate record: Ralph Josselin, Adam Martindale, Henry Newcome, Philip Henry and Richard Baxter.

Josselin was born in 1617 and lived until 1683. From 1641 to his death he was vicar of Earls Colne. He supported Parliament from the beginning of the civil war and during the second civil war. He rejoiced in November 1644 that now 'alehouses are in the power of the well-affected and the ministers of the parish'—the establishment of the power of local élites which the Laudian hierarchy had challenged.[1] In 1649 Josselin took the Engagement 'to be true and faithful to the Commonwealth', apparently without hesitation. He even appears to have approved of the execution of Charles I, though 'very many of the weaker sort of Christians' were 'passionate concerning it, but so ungroundedly that it would make any bleed to observe'. He believed that 'the Lord hath some great thing to do; fear and tremble at it, oh England.'[2] He refused to sign *The Essex Watchman's Watchword* (February 1649), which deplored Pride's Purge

---

[1] *The Diary of Ralph Josselin, 1616–1683*, ed. A. Macfarlane (1976), pp. 13, 126–8, 27, For parish élites, see K. Wrightson, *English Society, 1580–1680* (1982), Chapter 1.
[2] *Diary*, p. 155

and the execution of the King as well as the toleration proposed in the Agreement of the People.[1] By this date Josselin was reading millenarian books, and his thoughts were 'much that God was beginning to ruin the kingdoms of the earth and bringing Christ's kingdom in, and we English should be very instrumental therein'.[2] The younger Charles Stuart, Josselin hoped, would 'die an untimely death ... in good time for his kingdoms'.[3] 'The last days draw near,' he observed in 1653.[4]

But by then he was beginning to have new doubts. From September 1648 to the new year he complained of unpaid tithes. He was reading Socinian books, and began keeping a notebook in which he tried to reconcile the contradictions of the Bible[5] —presumably in order to be able to cope with sectaries who stressed them. News of 'quashing the Levellers' at Burford in May 1649 seemed to him 'a glorious rich providence of God to England', and after June we hear no more of his 'reconciler'. But in 1653 he feared 'a storm on the ministry',[6] and he was still having trouble with sectaries in his own parish. From 1655 onwards he was worried by Quakers. In that year he began to express doubts about the imminence of the millennium. In April 1657, at the time of Venner's rising, he reported that 'divers men bustle to make Christ king; truly Cromwell will carry it from him at present, but surely there is a time when Christ shall reign more than inwardly.'[7] Next year 'Cromwell died, people not much minding it.'[8] 'A spirit of slumber and remissness is wonderfully upon the nation,' he observed in January 1659; a year later the nation was 'looking to Charles Stuart, out of love to themselves not him'.[9] 'May we think there was nothing in all the saints' expectations in England?' he asked in August 1660; or 'may not one arise, and woe to him that is the person to be the Man of Sin. Horresco when I think, and who it is.' Could Charles Stuart have been in his mind?[10]

---

[1] Ibid., p. 157. For *The Essex Watchman's Watchword* see Harold Smith, *The Ecclesiastical History of Essex under the Long Parliament and Commonwealth* (Colchester, n.d.), pp. 102–7.

[2] *Diary*, pp. 119, 219–21. Henry Newcome was readng Joseph Mede in 1654 (*Autobiography*, ed. R. Parkinson (Chetham Soc., 1852) p. 52).

[3] *Diary*, p. 223; cf. pp. 223–30, *passim*, 257, 269–70, 289, 295.

[4] Ibid., p. 307.

[5] Ibid., pp. 134–53.

[6] Ibid., pp. 167, 303.

[7] Ibid., pp. 352, 365, 397–8.

[8] Ibid., p. 430.

[9] Ibid., pp. 436, 457–8. Cf. Wither: Charles was restored not from 'love unto his person or his cause,/Or zeal to true religion or the laws', but for social and economic reasons (*Speculum Speculativum*, 1660, pp. 81–3, in *Miscellaneous Works*, V).

[10] *Diary*, p. 467; cf. pp. 478–80.

After the restoration Josselin managed to hold on to his living, and even to avoid wearing the surplice for twenty years.[1] In 1667 the Dutch war gave him 'hopes of England recovering out of troubles'; Parliament, he noted, was 'high against a standing army'.[2] Macfarlane points out that there is not a single reference to hell or to damnation in Josselin's *Diary*, and that 'belief in the after life does not play an important part in his private thoughts' as there recorded.[3] In both respects he compares with Milton and conflicts with the traditional stereotype of a Puritan minister.

Adam Martindale (1623–86) and Henry Newcome (1627–95) may be paired as Lancashire Presbyterians. In the civil war Martindale served in the Parliamentarian Army as chief clerk in a foot regiment. 'All the ministers in our neighbourhood ... and all serious Christians generally declared themselves satisfied for the cause of that party,' he tells us, though Martindale did not enjoy military life and left to become a schoolmaster in 1644.[4] He took the Covenant, and in 1646 he was appointed to a living.[5] Although he is accounted a Presbyterian he had some sympathy for the Independent position.[6] But he disapproved of Pride's Purge and 'many other villanies' which the Army acted,[7] and thought little of 'a young man of pregnant parts' who 'trod much in Milton's steps'.[8] He took the Engagement, albeit reluctantly.[9]

Like Josselin, Martindale had trouble with sectaries, anti-Trinitarians and Quakers.[10] He published in 1649 *Divinity Knots Unbound*, directed against antinomians and Anabaptists; and in 1653 *An Antidote against the Poyson of the Times*, attacking anti-Trinitarians.[11] In 1659 he was at least ambivalent in his attitude towards Booth's rising.[12] Martindale said at the time (or so he would have us believe) that even if he were sure that 'the usurpers' would continue his liberty ('as they had hitherto done') and 'that a King and a free Parliament would throw me out', yet he would

---

[1] Ibid., pp. 627–8.
[2] Ibid., pp. 536–7.
[3] A. Macfarlane, *The Family Life of Ralph Josselin: A Seventeenth-Century Clergyman* (Cambridge UP, 1970), p. 168.
[4] *The Life of Adam Martindale*, ed. R. Parkinson, (Chetham Soc., 1845), pp. 37, 41; cf. p. 35.
[5] Ibid., pp. 38, 59.
[6] Ibid., pp. 61–74.
[7] Ibid., pp. 74–5, 89.
[8] Ibid., p. 99.
[9] Ibid., pp. 93–100.
[10] Ibid., pp. 106, 110, 114–15.
[11] Ibid., pp. 70, 85–6, 110.
[12] Ibid., pp. 131–41.

prefer the latter.[1] He believed, indeed, that he would retain his living, but he had reckoned without the vengefulness of the local gentry. After a spell in jail he was outed in 1662.[2] Even after the restoration Martindale remained opposed to toleration, and tried to dissuade dissenters from separating from the state church.[3]

Henry Newcome was only 15 when civil war broke out. He went up to Cambridge in 1644. In 1647 he succeeded his brother as schoolmaster at Congleton. Another brother became 'a zealous sectary'. In 1648 Newcome was ordained.[4] He was—or claimed to have been—very upset by 'the horridness' of the execution of the King, but he took the Engagement.[5] He was a traditional Puritan in the school of Preston; he was less tolerant of Independency than Martindale.[6] He met with sectaries who rejected Sabbatarianism, thought that 'there was neither heaven nor hell but in a man's own self' and that 'the soul within a man was God': so he welcomed the Rump's Blasphemy Act, and preached against antinomianism.[7] The Protectorate of Cromwell seemed to him the salvation of the ministry[8]—though later he looked back less enthusiastically at Oliver's 'atheistical carriages'.[9] In 1656 he and Baxter were still discussing the danger that tithes might be abolished.[10]

In 1659 Newcome welcomed Booth's rising, and after its defeat feared he was in danger of sequestration.[11] He regarded the restoration as 'a deliverance never to be forgotten', and published the sermon in which he welcomed the King's return, with dedication to Booth. But to no avail: he was ejected from his living. Yet 'it is enough to receive approbation and acceptance in heaven.'[12] Even though 'I was but coarsely used upon his majesty's restoration', and though the Presbyterians 'saw ourselves the despised and cheated party ... yet if I knew it would be so, and had the same to do again, I would do as I did'. For in 1659–60 'we lay at the

---

[1] Ibid., p. 133.
[2] Ibid., pp. 143–51, 159, 163
[3] Ibid., pp. 139, 198, 234.
[4] H. Newcombe, *Autobiography*, pp. xi, 9, 11.
[5] Ibid., pp. 13, 214–15.
[6] Ibid., pp. 2, 12, 19, 26, 95, 106.
[7] Ibid., pp. 32, 37, 103.
[8] Ibid., p. 46.
[9] Ibid., p. 104.
[10] Ibid., p. 330.
[11] Ibid., pp. 109–10, 116–17.
[12] Ibid., pp. 121, 154.

mercy and impulse of a giddy, hot-headed, bloody multitude.'[1] It was not God but the King 'who cast us down'.[2] Newcome worried lest he should leave nothing for his family 'and men will say, "This was his strictness, and this is Puritanism! See what it gets them! What it leaves to wife and children!"'[3] Yet he and his Lancashire Presbyterian friends determined 'to stick close to the public ordinances and not to separate' from the national church.[4]

In fact Newcome prospered more after his ejection than previously.[5] But he was not perhaps quite as happy as he tried to persuade himself. At the end of 1661 he had frequent temptations to what he called atheism, by which he presumably meant doubts about God's goodness. 'Will not the Lord help his poor servants?' he asked on Christmas Eve. 'Mr. Baxter against atheism stood me in some stead.' Newcome was preaching much of patience around this time.[6] In 1666 he was worrying about the possibility of a general massacre of protestants.[7] Next year he reflected on the powerlessness of Puritans at elections, in which they had formerly been so influential.[8] In 1674 he thought 'the condition of the nation and church is very sad.... God's hand remarkably against us.'[9] In 1683 he sheltered Robert Ferguson the plotter, on the run after the Rye House Plot.[10] Even his pleasure at the Revolution of 1688, which he lived to see, was marred by 'the rabble throwing snowballs.... Alas, it is but what these late times has bred them to.'[11]

Philip Henry (1631–96) was the son of a royalist official who had also served the Earl of Pembroke; as a child Philip played with Princes Charles and James. This did not affect his political outlook. After the restoration he declared, privately, that 'though particular instruments might miscarry', yet the cause of Parliament 'was in general the Cause of God, and will in due time be made so to appear'.[12] He saw the execution of

---

[1] Ibid., pp. 118–19, 154.
[2] *The Diary of the Rev. Henry Newcome, 30 September 1661 to 28 September 1663* (Chetham Soc., 18, 1849), p. 117.
[3] *Autobiography*, pp. 135–6; cf. *Diary*, p. 130.
[4] *Diary*, pp. 119–20.
[5] *Autobiography*, p. 155.
[6] *Diary*, pp. 14–41.
[7] *Autobiography*, p. 159.
[8] Ibid., p. 168.
[9] Ibid., p. 207.
[10] Ibid., pp. 249–50.
[11] Ibid., p. 271.
[12] *Diaries and Letters of Philip Henry*, ed. M. H. Lee (1882), pp. 11, 102.

Charles I.[1] He graduated from Christ Church and was ordained by the
Shropshire classis in 1657.[2] He participated in its monthly conferences,
discussing such subjects as 'How may it be proven that there is a God?'[3]
Apparently the conferences continued until February 1662: the last
meeting 'we are likely to have till God mend things in the nation; would
we had prized and improved them while we had the liberty of them'.
Ominously, the subject for discussion was 'an sit transubstantiatio in
sacra coena?'[4]

Henry refused to be reordained, and was ejected from his living. In
1661 he spoke of the restoration rather tepidly, 'which I cannot yet but
call mercy considering his right, also the sad condition we were in,
through usurpers, and the manner of his coming in without bloodshed'.
Nevertheless, the fact that the summer was very wet suggested to him
that 'God is angry with us'.[5] He was shocked when the post-restoration
minister of Wrexham administered the sacrament to the gentlemen of the
parish one Sunday and to the poor the week after.[6] But he was 'loath ...
to encourage the people to separate'.[7] The Declaration of Indulgence of
1672 seemed to him to threaten 'our parish order which God hath
owned', and to 'beget divisions and animosities amongst us'.[8] The
Congregationalists, he thought, 'unchurch the nation; they pluck up the
hedge of parish order.'[9] Even when he had a congregation of his own after
1689 he remained an occasional conformist and was buried in the parish
church of Whitchurch.[10]

II

The evidence left by Richard Baxter (1615–91) is more complex than that
left by the others whom we have been considering in this chapter. Baxter
was an eager controversialist throughout his life, and over time he shifted
his ground on many issues. He left, in *Reliquiae Baxterianae*, an
autobiography whose literary charm and appearance of moderation and

---

[1] Ibid., p. 12.
[2] Ibid., p. 34.
[3] Ibid., p. 61.
[4] Ibid., p. 77.
[5] Ibid., pp. 87, 85.
[6] Ibid., p. 103.
[7] Ibid., p. 99.
[8] Ibid., p. 250.
[9] Ibid., p. 277.
[10] Ibid., pp. 329, 379–82.

sweet reasonableness owes something to the wisdom of hindsight, more perhaps to the editorial blue pencil of Matthew Sylvester. These characteristics sometimes obscure its polemically defensive intention. But since we are trying to find out how men explained their actions, this perhaps does not matter.

Baxter, son of a declining gentleman, did not go to a university. He commenced his long ministry at Kidderminster in 1641, and took a clear and positive stand in defence of Parliament from the beginning of the civil war. 'I made no doubt but both parties were to blame.... But then I thought that whosoever was faulty, the people's liberties and safety could not be forfeited', and that 'the subjects should adhere to that party which most secured the welfare of the nation. I thought it a great sin for men that were able to defend their country to be neuters.'[1] Baxter had been brought up in the tradition of Perkins, Sibbes and Ames,[2] and he saw the war partly in religious terms: the serious, sober, godly sort who wanted 'a just parochial discipline' against the hierarchy of the church supported by 'the vulgar rabble of the carnal and profane', who did not want a discipline which would interfere with their 'ignorance, carelessness and sins'.[3] Long afterwards Baxter looked forward to meeting Lord Brooke, Pym and Hampden in heaven. He prudently 'blotted out' this passage from all editions of *The Saints Everlasting Rest* published after 1659.[4] Yet even in 1659 he did not repent of his support for 'the main Cause': he would do it again 'in the same state of things'. For in the background was the popish threat, which Baxter never forgot. Charles's 'impious and popish armies would have ruled him and used him as other armies have done those that entrusted them'.[5] Like Ludlow, Baxter had not expected the civil war to last more than a few weeks.[6]

But Baxter saw the issues in social as well as religious terms: some gentry and the solid middling sort were for Parliament, most lords, knights, gentry (and their tenants) for the King. 'The great cause of Parliament's strength ... was that the debauched rabble throughout the land, emboldened by his [Charles I's] gentry and seconded by the common soldiers of his army, took all that were called Puritans for their

---

[1] *Reliquiae Baxterianae*, ed. M. Sylvester (1696), p. 39.
[2] Ibid., pp. 4–5, 14, 131.
[3] Ibid., pp. 30–5.
[4] Ibid., III, p. 177.
[5] Baxter, *A Holy Commonwealth* (1659), pp. 486–7, 478; cf. pp. 382–4. See also Lamont, *Richard Baxter and the Millennium*, Chapter 2, and pp. 293–6.
[6] *Reliquiae Baxterianae*, p. 43; Ludlow, *Memoirs*, I, p. 38.

enemies.' This filled the Parliamentary armies with 'sober, pious men'.[1]
It was 'the fury of the rabble' that made Baxter withdraw from
Kidderminster to Parliamentary territory.[2]

But from the start Baxter was worried by the 'headiness and rashness
of the younger unexperienced sort of religious people'.[3] The 'old Cause'
began to change 'with the new-modelling of the Army'. Baxter joined it
as a chaplain, and was horrified by the subversive political and religious
views of the sectaries who had come to dominate it.[4] With a paranoia
shared by William Prynne, Baxter came to think that Levellers, Vanists,
Seekers, Quakers and Behmenists were all actuated by Jesuit principles,
even if they were not actually secret papists. Robert Everard, 'a busy
preaching seeker' (in appearance) in fact admitted his popery about the
restoration; 'but they permit but now and then one thus to detect
themselves'.[5]

Baxter did his best to stem the tide, supplying evidence for Thomas
Edwards's *Gangraena*.[6] But he found that 'the antinomian doctrine'
came naturally to 'the common profane multitude'. From now onwards
his main concern was to get discipline re-established.[7] Hence his hatred
of Vane, Owen and other defenders of religious toleration.[8] Baxter took
the Covenant but not the Engagement, and not untypically tried to
dissuade others from taking the Covenant. He was appalled by the
execution of the Presbyterian minister Christopher Love in 1651.[9]

Yet gradually in the 1650s he shifted ground again. He realized that
Cromwell could 'conjure up at pleasure some terrible apparition of
Agitators, Levellers or such like'. Yet Cromwell seemed the only defence
against seeing 'both tithes and universities overthrown'. Baxter thought
it his duty 'to commend the good which a usurper doth'. He approved of
Triers and Ejectors, who 'saved many a congregation from ignorant,
ungodly, drunken teachers'.[10] Baxter took the initiative in establishing the

---

[1] *Reliquiae Baxterianae*, pp. 30–3, 44, 85, 89, 91, 94.
[2] Ibid., pp. 42–3.
[3] Ibid., p. 39.
[4] Ibid., pp. 49–52.
[5] Ibid., pp. 54–6, 78. The Quakers retaliated on Baxter in kind. See e.g. Burrough, *Works*,
pp. 310–24; Nayler, *An Answer to a Book ... by Richard Baxter* (1656). For Everard see p. 20
above. His surname is that of an old Catholic family.
[6] *Reliquiae Baxterianae*, p. 56.
[7] Lamont, *Richard Baxter and the Millennium*, pp. 128, 143.
[8] *Reliquiae Baxterianae*, pp. 75, 101, 103, 111. Baxter's references to Owen were much
bowdlerized by Sylvester. See G. F. Nuttall, 'Richard Baxter's *Apology*, its Occasion and
Composition', *Journal of Eccesiastical History*, IV (1953), pp. 69ff.
[9] *Reliquiae Baxterianae*, pp. 64–5, 67, 408–22.
[10] Ibid., pp. 70–2, 74.

Worcestershire Association, a voluntary disciplinary system built up from below, which supplied the model for at least thirteen other counties. It is interesting, as Professor Lamont points out, that Baxter looked back to Grindal as his inspiration.[1]

Baxter tried hard to enlist support in the Parliaments of 1656 and 1659 for a state-backed national system of discipline and for a franchise limited to church members.[2] Even without such support, he claimed in 1659, 'many thousands have been converted to a holy, upright life, thanks to the promotion of godliness.'[3] For 'the success of the wars' had made a change 'in the public affairs which removed many impediments to men's salvation', aided by 'the presence and countenance of honest Justices of the Peace'. 'When it became a matter of reputation to be godly, it abundantly furthered the success of the ministry.'[4] As Henry Newcome put it in a letter to Baxter in 1656, 'though the good are the lesser party, yet the other party is kept under more than heretofore'.[5] When Richard Cromwell succeeded his father, Baxter became 'a great pillar to Cromwell and his way'[6]—a 'pensioner', in Henry Stubbe's less flattering phrase, though he admitted the possibility that Baxter was 'such a novice as to be insensibly drawn in by court-artifices' without a bribe.[7]

In 1659 Baxter dedicated his *Key for Catholics* to Richard Cromwell, declaring that he was 'one that rejoiceth in the present happiness of England and earnestly wisheth that it was but as well with the rest of the world'. He honoured 'all the providences of God by which we have been brought to what we are'—a phrase which a post-restoration critic took, maliciously, as justifying the execution of Charles I.[8] It was on Richard Cromwell's behalf that Baxter wrote in *A Holy Commonwealth* 'all this stir of the republicans is but to make the seed of the serpent to be the sovereign rulers of the earth'. 'Every man is by nature a rebel against heaven, so that ordinarily to plead for a democracy is to plead that the sovereignty may be put into the hands of rebels.' He agreed with Newcome that 'were not this multitude restrained they would presently

---

[1] Lamont, op. cit., pp. 165–6.
[2] R. B. Schlatter, *Richard Baxter and Puritan Politics* (Rutgers UP, 1957), pp. 51–4, 64–6; cf. *A Holy Commonwealth*, pp. 218–19, 249–57.
[3] *A Holy Commonwealth*, p. 48.
[4] Ibid., pp. 85–8.
[5] Newcome, *Autobiography*, p. 327.
[6] Josselin, *Diary*, p. 431.
[7] Stubbe, *An Essay in Defence of the Good Old Cause* (1659), Sig.ˣxˣ, 2v–A 2v.
[8] [Anon.], *Evangelium Armatum: a Specimen or Short Collection of Several Doctrines and Positions Destructive to Our Government Both Civil and Ecclesiastical* (1663), p. 41.

have the blood of the godly.'[1] The rabble, Baxter thought, was kept under only by the Army.[2] Hence, when the Army collapsed, he had to support the restoration of monarchy in the interests of discipline.[3] 'Charles II gets in; and Mr Baxter cries hallelujah' was the sour comment of a contemporary.[4] Baxter himself might have said that Charles was more likely than anyone else after Richard Cromwell to recover the ideal Christian monarchy which Constantine had established and the papacy had subverted. Discipline was an essential precondition for the advent of his conservative millennium.[5]

For a brief period Baxter in 1660 seemed influential, 'intimate with Lord Chancellor Hyde, who was courting him to receive a bishopric', friendly with Lord Broghill,[6] and appointed a royal chaplain. Yet Baxter was disappointed, and deprived of his Kidderminster lectureship. 'In times of usurpation', he wailed, he 'had all this mercy and happy freedom'. Under 'our rightful King ... I and many hundreds are silenced, ... suspected and vilified, ... accounted as the scum and sweepings or off-scourings of the earth'.[7] With the wisdom of hindsight, Baxter thought that under the Protectorate 'England had been like in a quarter of an age to become a land of saints, and a pattern of holiness to all the world, and the unmatchable Paradise of the earth. Never were such fair opportunities to sanctify a nation lost and trodden underfoot.'[8] He even spoke of the end of the Protectorate as the time of 'the fall of Adam'.[9]

So Baxter came to value what Philip Henry called 'a face of godliness',[10] even to the extent of defending hypocrisy: 'though they cannot be truly religious against their will, it will make them visibly religious.'[11] And—by a different route—he came to the conclusion of so many nonconformists,

---

[1] *A Holy Commonwealth*, pp. 92–4; cf. pp. 65, 103, 203, 226–31, and pp. 210–11 above.

[2] Ibid., pp. 236–7, 244.

[3] *A Sermon of Repentance* (1660), preached to the House of Commons, April 1660.

[4] *Memoirs of the Life of Mr Ambrose Barnes*, ed. W. H. D. Longstaffe (Surtees Soc. Publications, L, 1866), p. 19.

[5] Lamont, op. cit., *passim*. See also a perceptive review by J. R. Jacob in *Eighteenth-Century Studies*, XVI (1982), pp. 457–61.

[6] *Life of Adam Martindale*, p. 152; *Reliquiae Baxterianae*, pp. 105, 197, 205–6; II, p. 109.

[7] *Reliquiae Baxterianae*, pp. 84–5.

[8] Ibid., p. 97.

[9] Quoted by Lamont, op. cit., p. 300; cf. ibid., pp. 270, 315–16.

[10] M. Henry, *The Life of the Reverend Philip Henry* (1825), p. 89.

[11] Baxter, *Practical Works* (1830), XIII, p. 459; *Catholick Communion Defended* (1684), pp. 12, 15, 17, quoted by Lamont, op. cit., p. 260; cf. my *Society and Puritanism*, p. 249. George Wither took a different point of view when he argued that religious toleration was the only alternative to state-imposed hypocrisy (*Westrow Revived*, 1653, pp. 8–9, in *Miscellaneous Works*, III; *Vox Vulgi*, 1661, P. 17: I quote from the edition edited by W. D. Macray, 1880).

that 'suffering must be the church's most ordinary lot.' Saints should not dream of a kingdom of this world, or flatter themselves with the hopes of a Golden Age, or reigning over the ungodly'.[1] For 'the rich will rule in the world, and few rich men will be saints'. 'We shall have what we would, but not in this world.'[2] The clergy should preach more of 'the joys of heaven' than of this-worldly matters.[3]

III

One common factor in the lives of these conservative Puritan ministers is the crucial importance for them of tithes. Tithes meant a state church, and with it ideological control over the lower classes, all too rebellious in the revolutionary decades. But tithes were also essential for the subsistence of these ministers. Josselin was in grave difficulties in the hard winter of 1648–9, when his parishioners were not paying the tithes due.[4] His *Diary* provides also ample evidence of his economic dependence on neighbouring gentry.[5] It was difficult for him to be objective about sectarian attacks on hireling ministers. We should bear this in mind when we think that Newcome, for instance, sometimes seemed inclined to bargain a little too fiercely with his congregation.[6] To be left to the voluntary good will of parishioners would, in the long run, mean a declining income; and parsons were family men, few of them with private means like Baxter. For them it was a duty and a matter of pride and self-respect to provide decently for their families.[7] There was rea¹ panic in 1653, and again in 1659, when it seemed possible that tithes might be abolished. The comments I have quoted from Newcome and Martindale must be read in the light of this anxiety.[8] Milton was less than sympathetic when in 1659 he asked: will they 'bring back again bishops, archbishops and the whole gang of prelatry ... to keep their tithes'? By 1660 it seemed the only way.[9]

The creation of Baxter's Worcestershire Association and other voluntary associations was thus a way of sustaining the morale of

---

[1] *Reliquiae Baxterianae*, p. 132.
[2] Ibid., p. 297; cf. p. 133.
[3] Ibid., p. 129.
[4] Josselin, *Diary*, pp. 148–85 *passim*.
[5] Ibid., pp. 125, 151, 186–8 and *passim*.
[6] E.g. Newcome, *Autobiography*, pp. 70, 115, 349–65, etc.
[7] See p. 211 above.
[8] See pp. 209–10 above.
[9] *CPW*; VII, p. 283; cf. Baxter, *A Sermon of Repentance* (1660), and p. 306 below.

clergymen at a time when they badly needed it, of giving them a professional confidence which soon led them to lobby MPs and governments. The obverse of this was the reluctance of Martindale, Newcome and Henry to allow 'parish order' to be disrupted: even when they had been ejected from their livings they did not want their former parishioners to desert the parish church.[1] They disapproved of the governors of the church, as they had done under Laud; but in each case they clung to their belief in the possibility of an anti-Catholic Church of England. The Cause of Parliament had been justified for them not least by its overthrow of the Laudians. We may compare Oliver Heywood (1630–1702), another northern Presbyterian divine, who preferred Perkins and Sibbes above Aristotle and Plato, and who spoke of 'the Good Old Cause of Puritanism and nonconformity'.[2]

Baxter and Newcome had high hopes of the Protectorate's modified state church, which infuriated those who felt with Milton that religious liberty demanded the abolition of tithes. Such a church might ultimately have offered an alternative to the Army as an instrument of social control. Cromwell was reported to have thought that 'no temporal government could have a sure support without a national church that adhered to it'.[3] If the Triers and Ejectors could have installed disciplined and ideologically sound ministers in all livings, it might have worked: 'people are governed by the pulpit more than the sword in time of peace,' Charles I had said.[4] But such a church would have been little more to the liking of the gentry than an army. Their control of their local churches would have been undermined by an efficient new system of ordination and discipline for the clergy.

If attitudes to tithes formed the great dividing line between conservative and radical Parliamentarians, these five divines remind us of what nevertheless linked them: protestantism. Newcome and Baxter looked back to the tradition of moderate, non-Presbyterian Puritanism within the Church of England, to the school of Perkins, Preston, Sibbes; but so too did Erbery, Owen, Goodwin and Stubbe.[5] Like many nonconformists after 1660, Baxter invoked the name of Archbishop Grindal, whose tradition Archbishops Abbot and Ussher had

[1] See pp. 210–12 above.
[2] Heywood, *Autobiography, Diaries, Anecdotes and Event Books*, ed. J. H. Turner (1882–5), I, p. 162, III, p. 297.
[3] Burnet, *History of My Own Time*, I, p. 114.
[4] Charles I, *Letters*, ed. Sir C. Petrie (1935), pp. 200–6.
[5] See pp. 85–6, 174–5, 177, 179, 210, 213 above, p. 269 below.

continued.[1] This tradition had bound together conservative and radical Puritans against Laud, against Catholicism. Baxter believed that support for Parliament in the civil war had been justified by the popish danger. He persuaded himself that the execution of Charles I had been due to papists, and that many sectaries were crypto-papists. Intellectually this is as silly as the view that the hand of Moscow today moves the campaign for nuclear disarmament; but it helped to free protestantism from the stigma of regicide and heresy.

The continuing strength of popular protestantism is worth emphasizing. In the 1650s the English Army in occupation of Ireland and Scotland did its best to detach the Irish from the Church of Rome, the Scots from the Presbyterian Kirk. It was completely unsuccessful: the native churches were popular institutions, with deep roots. But the episcopal Church of England? When in 1640 it lost the support of the state, it collapsed without trace; its few defenders argued on social rather than religious or patriotic lines, in 1641 and in 1660.[2] But though bishops disappeared unlamented, *protestantism* did not: through all the confusion and changes of the 1640s and 1650s anti-popery remained synonymous with patriotism. And this continued at least until Roxana echoed Nell Gwyn to say 'Though I was a whore, yet I was a protestant whore.'[3] This strong sense of *protestant* patriotism, associated with fear of Spanish or French invasion via Ireland, extended from the radical sectaries, through conservatives, lay and clerical, well into the ranks of the episcopalians. That is why Milton in *Of True Religion, Heresy, Schism, Toleration* (1673) quoted the thirty-nine Articles in an attempt to unite protestants from Arians and Anabaptists to Anglicans against the threat of popery and absolutism. In moments of crisis—1640, 1688—this protestant solidarity proved an irresistible force.

---

[1] For this tradition see Peter Lake's admirable *Moderate Puritans and the Elizabethan Church* (Cambridge UP, 1982), *passim*. Stubbe added Jewell, Whitgift and Whitaker to the list.
[2] See Edmund Waller in *Old Parliamentary History* (1763), IX, pp. 388–9; Baxter, *A Sermon of Repentance*.
[3] D. Defoe, *Roxana: or, The Fortunate Mistress* (Oxford, 1840), p. 71. First published 1724.

Chapter 8

Survivors

1   John (1607–81) and Samuel Pordage (1633–?91): The Epic of the Fall

I

John Pordage, the son of a grocer, was born in London a year before Milton. He may have practised medicine, unlicensed, in London during the 1630s.[1] In 1644 he was in Reading, curate to Thomas Gilbert, later an Independent. By 1647 he had been appointed to the rectory of Bradfield, Berkshire, by Elias Ashmole, who would appreciate his interest in astrology. Bradfield was one of the richest livings in the county. Pordage had to overcome his scruples about taking tithes: he said, rather feebly, that he had tried without success to return them to the magistrate. He cannot have tried very hard. Some of his parishioners thought him excessively covetous.[2] He soon made enemies in Berkshire, who accused him of heresy to the Committee for Plundered Ministers. In 1651 he was acquitted on all counts. One of his opponents 'threatened me that at the sitting of the next Parliament he would throw me out of my living'.[3]

The changes of 1653 worked to Pordage's disadvantage. The Protector's ordinance for ejection of ministers was (in Pordage's words) 'entrusted into the hands of many fierce, rigid and narrow-spirited men', and his enemies were successful at their second attempt. After many hearings Pordage was ejected in December 1654 as 'ignorant and very insufficient for the work of the ministry'. The ordinance, Pordage told

---

[1] G. N. Clark, *A History of the Royal College of Physicians of London* (Oxford UP, 1964), I, pp. 247–8, 276.
[2] J. Pordage, *Innocencie Appearing, Through the dark Mists of Pretended Guilt* (1655), pp. 16, 18, 30–4, 71, 109–110.
[3] Ibid., p. 103.

Cromwell, was 'an engine of persecution to condemn saints and throw them out of their estates and livelihood'.[1]

As early as 1645 Pordage had been noted as a teacher of Familism.[2] The accusations against him, in 1651 and 1654, were that he was a Familist and that he held 'notions of Ranterism, which at that time [1650–1] were everywhere frequently discoursed of'. These notions included rejection of the Trinity, denial of the divinity of Christ and the historicity of his life on earth, believing that God was in every man, rejecting water baptism, saying that 'it was a weakness to be troubled for sin.'[3] Pordage was further alleged to have said that marriage was a very wicked thing, contrary to the Word of God, and that a man might keep company with more than one woman; he had defended polygamy.[4] He was also accused of frequent and familiar converse with angels and spirits.[5]

Pordage denied most of the allegations, many of which were no doubt based on malicious gossip; but he does seem either to have annoyed or very much confused many of his parishioners. He admitted to seeing visions, and seized the opportunity of his trial to expound his philosophy at some length.[6] But it was well known that Familists would 'say or unsay anything' if it suited them.[7] For good measure Pordage was alleged to have said that there would soon be no Parliament, magistrate or government in England; the saints would take over the estates of the wicked and the wicked should be their slaves; he cared no more for the higher powers than for the dust beneath his feet.[8] He had heard William Erbery preach, and he praised Richard Coppin's writings.[9]

At his house in Bradfield Pordage had entertained, for longer or shorter periods, a remarkable collection of flamboyant radicals—Abiezer Coppe, William Everard (or Robert Everard the Agitator and Socinian), Thomas Tany (Theaureaujohn). Coppe and Tany specialized in shocking the respectable, Everard in raising apparitions—'a giant with a great

---

[1] Ibid., Epistle Dedicatory.
[2] John Etherington, *A Brief Discovery of the Blasphemous Doctrine of Familisme* (1645), p. 10. Etherington was an ex-Familist himself.
[3] *Innocencie Appearing*, pp. 2, 6, 9, 14, 16, 23–5, 27, 47, 56–8, 84–6, 102; cf. pp. 42–4, 46–7 above.
[4] Ibid., pp. 14, 18–19, 30–4, 91.
[5] Ibid., pp. 16, 26.
[6] Ibid., pp. 65–6, 72–9.
[7] Ibid., pp. 24, 102.
[8] C. Fowler, *Daemonium Meredianum. Satan at Noon, or Antichristian Blasphemies* (1655), pp. 32, 53–61, 135–6. Fowler was an old enemy of Edward Burrough. See the latter's *Works*, pp. 625–41.
[9] Pordage, *Innocencie Appearing*, pp. 9, 12, 22. Fowler compared Pordage's evasiveness with that of Erbery (*Daemonium Meredianum*, pp. 29, 31, 41, 61, 132). See also pp. 45–6 above.

sword in his hand', 'a great dragon' breathing fire, accompanied by
noisome smells.[1] Thomas Bromley, another of Pordage's 'communion',
was 'much against property'. (The source is Richard Baxter, who knew
Bromley well.)[2]

After the restoration Pordage was rather surprisingly restored to his
living. But he was outed under the Act of Uniformity in 1662; soon we
find him leading a Behmenist congregation in London.[3] He suffered
heavy losses in the Fire of London, and in 1669 he was back in Reading
running a conventicle attended by 'tradesmen of every parish of the town
and near'.[4] Baxter described Pordage as chief of the Behmenists. From
the mid-1650s he had been making Behmenist pronouncements. He
claimed that 'that inward spiritual eye, which hath been locked up and
shut by the Fall' had 'been opened in an extraordinary way' in the
members of his community.[5] Pordage later became closely associated
with Jane Lead (1623–1709), Behmenist and Philadelphian. She too had
almost nightly prophetic visions. Pordage assisted with her work on
Boehme. Philip Herbert, fifth Earl of Pembroke, who had been
associated with Pordage's community at Bradfield, was another keen
Behmenist who took Pordage under his protection.[6] Pordage's *Theologia
Mystica, or The Mystic Divinitie of the Aeternal Invisible*, was published
in 1683, two years after his death. It is a hodge-podge of Boehme's less
coherent ideas, dealing with questions like 'What in God is pure eternal
nature's essence?'[7]

II

Samuel Pordage, John's eldest son, was born in 1633. He was a witness
on his father's behalf in 1654. He later described himself variously as 'of
Lincoln's Inn' and 'a student of physic'. Roger L'Estrange, whom
Samuel Pordage had lampooned in his *Azariah and Hushai* called him
'limping Pordage, a son of the famous Familist about Reading'. Dryden

---

[1] *Innocencie Appearing*, pp. 15, 69–80; cf. *WTUD*, pp. 225–6.
[2] *Reliquiae Baxterianae*, p. 78; G. F. Nuttall, *James Nayler: A Fresh Approach* (Supplement No. 26 to *JFHS*, 1954), pp. 3–4.
[3] S. Hutin, *Les Disciples Anglais de Jacob Boehme* (Paris, 1960), p. 89.
[4] A. G. Matthews, *Calamy Revised* (Oxford UP, 1934), p. 395.
[5] *Innocencie Appearing*, p. 73. Erbery had quoted Boehme approvingly (*Testimony*, p. 333).
[6] Hutin, op. cit., pp. 87–9, 252–3; Nuttall, op. cit., p. 12.
[7] Op. cit., p. 1. The book was edited by Edward Hooker, whose 100-page Prefatory Epistle is a deplorable mish-mash of anecdotes, facetiousness and chat.

in the second part of *Absalom and Achitophel* versified this as 'Lame
Mephishobeth the wizard's son'.[1] At one time Samuel Pordage was chief
steward to the Earl of Pembroke, his father's patron.

In 1660 the forward youth who would appear had to write panegyrics
to Monck or Charles II, especially if he had things to cover up, like
Dryden, Locke and Sprat, who had composed panegyrics to Oliver
Cromwell in 1654. Samuel Pordage had his father's reputation to live
down; he wrote poems on both Monck and the King, as well as 'An Elegy
on the Matchless Murther of Charles the First of Happy and Blessed
Memory':

> He must forget the rugged times the while,
> That can indite aught in a polished style.[2]

These were published, together with a number of pastoral love poems, in
Poems upon Several Occasions (1660). In his 'Panegyrick to ... Monck'
Pordage wrote:

> We 'ave tried, and too too long, a Commonwealth,
> Such as it was, a bane to England's health,
> When fifty tyrants with one mouth agree
> To eat up law, religion, liberty,
> Monsters that Kings' and bishops' lands devour,
> Kept by extorted sums the nation poor...[3]

Cromwell however is the villain of the piece, not the Long Parliament.
Oliver usurped

> All what our heroes once contended for
> With the sad tempest of a civil war.[4]

Also in 1660 Samuel Pordage published Seneca's *Troades Englished*: he
later took to tragedy in heroic rhymed couplets, made fashionable by the
Earl of Orrery, dedicating by preference to duchesses. There were
disagreements about the authorship of *Herod and Mariamne* (1673), a

---

[1] *DNB*. Aubrey on the other hand, a less partial witness, called Samuel Pordage a 'handsome
man' (*Brief Lives*, II, p. 161). Oldham's *Imitation of the Third of Juvenal* sneers at Pordage's
poverty.
[2] S. P[ordage], *Poems upon Several Occasions* (1660), Sig. E. 3v.
[3] Ibid., Sig. B 2–B 3.
[4] Ibid., Sig. B 3v.

tragedy of love and war, death or honour, in Jesus Christ's Jerusalem. Pordage said that the play 'hitherto passed under the name of another, whilst I was out of the land'. The other was Elkanah Settle, who claimed to have 'put a finishing hand' to a 'first copy ... given me by a gentleman to use and form as I pleased', the Prologue tells us. Samuel Pordage put his name on the title-page of *The Siege of Babylon*, published in 1678 by 'the author of the *Tragedy of Herod and Mariamne*'. The tone of the play is conveyed by Roxana's speech:

> The crimes I did commit the gods above
> Will easily pardon, because crimes of love...
> To kill a rival I account no sin.[1]

In 1679 Samuel Pordage revealed a new allegiance by dedicating to the Earl of Shaftesbury his edition (the sixth) of John Reynolds's *Triumphs of Gods Revenge against the sin of Murther*. This was followed in 1681 by *A New Apparition of Sir Edmundbury Godfrey's Ghost to the E—— of D—— in the Tower*. The printer of this thoroughly Whig broadsheet had to make a public apology for the reflections on Danby. We now begin to see why L'Estrange, Dryden and Oldham disliked Samuel Pordage. In 1682 Pordage published a parody of Dryden's *Absalom and Achitophel*, *Azariah and Hushai: A Poem*, followed by *The Medal Revers'd, a Satyre against Persecution*, in the same year.[2]

Azariah and Hushai is the most competent of Samuel Pordage's poetical productions. Its opening lines parody the beginning of Dryden's *Absalom and Achitophel* agreeably:

> In impious times, when priestcraft was at height,
> And all the deadly sins esteemed light...

Pordage's handling of his counter-allegory is not unskilful. Amazia, who represents Charles II,

> ...though he God did love,
> Had not cast out Baal's priests, and cut down every grove.[3]

Pordage is outspoken about the evil influence of Eliakim (James II) and

---

[1] S. Pordage, of Lincoln's Inn, Esq., *The Siege of Babylon* (1678), p. 58.
[2] 'Persecution is [the devil's] cloven foot' (*The Medal Revers'd*, p. 8).
[3] [S. Pordage], *Azariah and Hushai: a Poem* (1682), p. 1.

'the Egyptian concubine' (the Duchess of Portsmouth, Egypt being naturally France).[1]

One of the more delicate areas that Dryden had to cover was the relationship between Charles II and his bastard son, the Duke of Monmouth. He carried off this, and his allusions to the King's active sex life, with skill and panache. But Dryden was after all writing on the royal side. Pordage was not, and he had to walk a tricky tightrope as he described a (Jesuit) plot against Amazia. When discussing Azariah (Monmouth) he emphasized throughout the hero's 'youth, beauty and the grace with which he spoke'.[2] But there were ticklish passages such as those in which Hushai (Shaftesbury) advises Azariah:

> You should without a crown for ever live
> Rather than get it by the people's lust.[3]

Azariah's support was socially impeccable:

> Most of the Jews he gained to his side,
> Not factious sects, the rabble or the rude
> Erring, unthinking, vulgar multitude,
> But the chief tribes and princes of the land,
> Who durst for Moses' ancient statutes stand,
> The pious, just, religious and the good,
> Men of great riches and of greater blood.

There were of course a few vulgar social climbers on to this bandwagon:

> Among the rout perhaps there some might blend
> Whose interest made them public good pretend....
> These and some others for a Commonwealth
> Among the herd, unseen, might hide by stealth....
> And Azariah, though they used his name,
> Disdained their friendship with a loyal shame.[4]

But there were time-serving opportunists on the other side too:

> Some priests and Levites too among the rest,
> Such as knew how to blow the trumpet best:

---

[1] Ibid., p. 26. [2] Ibid., p. 35.
[3] Ibid., pp. 17, 21. [4] Ibid., pp. 22–3.

> Who with loud noise and cackling cried like geese,
> 'Twixt God and Baal these priests divided were...

Dryden, naturally, was the main target of Pordage's wit:

> Shimei, the poet laureate of that age,
> The falling glory of the Jewish stage,...
> Tell me, Apollo, for I can't divine,
> Why wives he cursed, and praised the Concubine;
> Unless it were that he had led his life
> With a teeming matron ere she was a wife;
> Or that it best with his dear Muse did suit,
> Who was for hire a very prostitute.[1]

There was a certain skill, too, in the way in which Pordage managed to give his most revolutionary doctrines a conservative covering:

> By laws kings first were made, and with intent
> Men to defend, by heaven's and man's consent....
> If kings usurped a power, by force did sway,
> The people by no law was bound t' obey....
> For innovation is a dangerous thing,
> Whether it comes from people or from king.[2]

Pordage's conclusion pulls all the stops. Amazia recalls

> I am my people's father and their King....
> And though I think they may have done me wrong
> They are my children and I must forgive....
> And I remember now I have a son

who acts as mediator between the God/King and his children.

> Thus Amazia was once more restored:
> He loved his people, they obeyed their lord.[3]

This second restoration of the King recalled the happy union of 1660, after the death of 'the tyrant Zabed' (Oliver Cromwell); God and man

---

[1] Ibid., p. 27. Cf. *The Medal Revers'd* (1682): 'When Oliver he for an hero drew/ He then swam with the tide—appeared a saint' (pp. 1–2).

[2] Ibid., p. 31. Pordage may have taken this point from Marvell: see the passage quoted on pp. 250–1 below.

[3] *Azariah and Hushai*, pp. 37–8.

were reconciled. Left unsaid was that a King cannot be restored to his throne unless he has been deprived of it, or threatened with deprivation; God and man can be reconciled only after they have been alienated from one another. Pordage did pretty well on the whole, but his control of his subject matter is not as invariably tactful as Dryden's.

III

Samuel Pordage's longest poem, *Mundorum Explicatio: Or, The Explanation of an Hieroglyphical Figure*, was published in 1661. This Behmenist epic presents problems of authorship similar to those of *Herod and Mariamne*. For the 'hieroglyphical figure of the world' which the poem explains 'came into my hands, another being the author'.[1] This other must surely have been Samuel's father John, a well-known Behmenist. The poem is prefaced by an Encomium on J. B. and his interpreter J. Sparrow, Esq.[2] Samuel's interest in Boehme is not clearly demonstrated apart from this poem, but his relationship to the fifth Earl of Pembroke may hint at it. My guess would be that father and son collaborated on the poem, but that Samuel did most of the writing, which is not much worse than the rest of his published verse. There is no indication that John Pordage had poetic aspirations.

The significance of *Mundorum Explicatio* for us lies not in its poetic merit but in its themes. The poem starts from the triumph of evil in the world; Pordage set himself to justify the ways of God to men, to assert eternal Providence against scoffers who argue that there is no God, to explain why the wicked flourish in this world. Beginning with the Fall of Adam and Eve, Pordage asserts human freedom and the possibility of recovering Paradise on earth.[3] Like Milton, Pordage rejects traditional heroic themes of love and war in 'this epic poem' (though he was to deal with them in his dramas):

> I sing no hero's doughty gests in wars...
> Nor the dread fury of the wars I sing..

---

[1] S. P., armiger, *Mundorum Explicatio*... (1661), Sig. a 3.
[2] Ibid., Sig. a 4–5, p. 16.
[3] Ibid., pp. 2–3.

Nor

> With Mars or Venus doth my Muse conjoin,
> Her name's Urania, and her song's divine.[1]

Milton's Muse was likewise Urania. Pordage indulges in several Miltonic invocations:

> O thou eternal everlasting day!
> Illuminate my darker soul, I pray.[2]

The influence of John Pordage is suggested by the general Behmenism of the poem, by the ubiquity of spirits and angels—though, like Milton's, they are corporeal angels. It is Satan who suggests that there are no spirits.[3] The philosophy behind *Mundorum Explicatio* is never very systematically put before us: we pick it up as we go along.

> God from eternity
> Did generate two principles, which be
> Contrary to each other. God alone
> Cannot (but by these principles) be known.

Neither of them in itself is God,

> Yet he's the root from whence they flow.

Pordage's note adds that this root is 'the unsearchable *ens increatum*, or nothing abyss. God is God only in the Second Principle.' The first Principle is

> An angry jealous God
> And full of wrath, vengeance and ire.

This is not simply evil, but it is the life and essence of the dark world, without which there can be no hell. In it is Lucifer's kingdom. Hell is the absence of the Second Principle, which is love and light. The Father is the First Principle, Justice; the Son is the Second, Mercy.[4]

'God ne'er intended to awake' the principle of wrath. That principle was useful so long as it was subordinated to the principle of light and

---

[1] Ibid., Sig. b 8; cf *MER* p. 409.
[2] *Mundorum Explicatio*, p. 310; cf. pp. 123–5.
[3] Ibid., pp. 30–54. ('Laugh not at fairies, pygmies, gnomies, sylphs/Truths are counted old wives' idle tales'—p. 37).
[4] Ibid., p. 318.

love, but Adam's Fall allowed the wrath-fire principle to obscure the Second Principle.[1] All things therefore proceed from one root: heaven is the cause of hell. These two Principles extend throughout the universe: Sodom and Babylon oppose Sion and Jerusalem. 'Ours', Satan told the rebel angels, 'rocks, stones, flints, mines of iron and lead;/ His rivers, trees, air, gold and silver bred'.[2] But the Principles are not merely opposites: they are also inextricably intermingled. 'Hell and heaven blended are together':

> While you dwell in Babylonish state...
> Your next near neighbour (in the world's account)
> May dwell upon thrice sacred Sion's mount....
> He ploughs, he sows, he reaps the earth: so you...
> But yet your aim and end and his infers
> He is God's steward, you are Lucifer's.[3]

Hell's kingdom is in this world. Heaven is not 'a place above the starry sky', but within man; it is where Christ is.

> O mount not now beyond the clouds, for where
> The Second Principle remains, 'tis there
> That heaven is.[4]

Paradise too is hidden throughout the world, as Boehme had suggested—and may be found. With Milton's 'A Paradise within thee, happier far' we may compare Pordage's 'Paradise doth open in the heart'.[5]

> Nothing is more near than heaven to thee
> Wert thou not blind...
> The deeper thou into thyself dost go
> The nearer thou still heaven approachest to.[6]

Satan, Pordage observes, likes especially to win the great of this world to his side in the battle against the Second Principle. Satan's own titles

---

[1] Ibid. pp. 71–3, 77, 88, 108; cf. p. 113. The two principles had been discussed by John Pordage in *Innocencie Appearing* (p. 73).

[2] *Mundorum Explicatio*, p. 77.

[3] Ibid., p. 30.

[4] Ibid., p. 174. Cf. *The Religion of Gerrard Winstanley*, pp. 29, 47–8.

[5] *Mundorum Explicatio*, p. 321. For Boehme see a review by Alan Rudrum in *English Language Notes*, XIX (1982), p. 285.

[6] *Mundorum Explicatio*, pp. 27–30, 311–13; cf. p. 321.

suggest that rulers, prelates and aristocrats are likely to be of the devil's party:

> Hell's mighty monarch, Prince of Acheron,
> Grand Duke of Styx, Primate of Phlegeton,
> Of Lethe Earl...
> Hell's Nuncio thus speaks.[1]

Ignorance of the principles leads to the errors of all sects. There is a 'fantastic region ... out of this earth', a circle of fools, in which,

> Blinded and groping, wanting heat and sun...
> All sects, as in a misty circle run.

—Presbyterians, Independents, Baptists, Ranters, Quakers, Fifth Monarchists, Enthusiasts.[2]

Ranters, Pordage adds in an interesting note, from not clearly comprehending the distinction of the two principles, 'fall into that erroneous notion of all things proceeding from God, as well the evil as the good, and that they served him in all manner of wickedness and sins as well as in uprightness and love, seeing he was the author of all'. In fact they serve the First Principle.[3]

In *A Treatise of Eternal Nature* John Pordage tells us that God created eternal nature out of himself.[4] Samuel Pordage's universe, unlike his father's and Milton's, was created out of nothing.[5] The fall of the rebel angels preceded that of man: Adam was created to take Lucifer's place.[6] God created Adam

> a king
> And lord and ruler over everything,[7]

promising him immortality if he managed to survive for forty days without falling.[8] Like Milton, Pordage has difficulties in accounting for

---

[1] Ibid., pp. 99–100.
[2] Ibid., pp. 95–6.
[3] Ibid., p. 108.
[4] Op. cit., pp. 8–10.
[5] *Mundorum Explicatio*, p. 56. This is an additional reason for supposing that John Pordage did not write *Mundorum Explicatio*.
[6] Ibid., p. 59.
[7] Ibid., p. 12.
[8] Ibid., p. 60.

the fall of a perfect being: he must already have fallen to be able to fall. Pordage adopts Boehme's solution: Adam fell, in his sleep, before eating the fruit, before the creation of Eve. Before this Fall

> Such members as we have now he had none
> To propagate.[1]

As for Boehme, the original Adam was a hermaphrodite:

> He should both father be and mother then
> For male and female God created man.

Adam would have brought forth children by celestial birth. *After* Adam had fallen in his dream God gave him sexual organs, and Eve to go with them.[2] At this stage they were in a curious intermediate state.

> In Paradise as yet they were, for sin
> Actually had not yet entered in. . . .
> God's blessed image in their souls was set
> Though much obscured . . .
>   Could they so have stood
> They had been blessed, for their state was good.[3]

God, however, saw 'their pronity unto a farther fall'; so he warned Adam again and set him the test of the forbidden fruit.[4] The tree of life was the Second Principle, light or love of God. The tree of death was 'the awakened properties of the dark world', the First or wrathful Principle of death.[5]

From the tree of life come judgement, wit, property, self-interest, love to relations, doing right, riches, beauty, sports, honours, promotions, goods, possessions, pleasures, morality, good carriage, parts, civil honesty, degrees of state—kings, earls, etc.—power and authority, concupiscence, manual arts and trades, grammar and the liberal arts (including natural magic and theology), poetry, politics, etc., etc. Of this extraordinary jumble Pordage wrote:

> This is the food
> Which man's soul eats, and finds it very good.

---

[1] Ibid., p. 62.

[2] Cf. *Considerations on the Scope of Jacob Behmen's Writings*, pp. 100–1 (not by John Pordage), in *A Compendious View of the Ground of the Teutonic Philosophy*, and *The Works of Jacob Behmen Covering God and the Divine Nature*, pp. 100–4, 110, ibid.

[3] *Mundorum Explicatio*, pp. 60–3.

[4] Ibid., pp. 63–4.

[5] Ibid., pp. 40, 60, 66, 69.

Beauty is not evil, though Satan may convert it to poison. Nor is poetry:

> The end of poesy is the praise of God
> Used to that end, it is exceeding good.

And Pordage enters into a conventional diatribe against those who 'make poesy hateful by their wanton rhymes'.[1]

The Serpent's seduction of Eve was Miltonic in its courtly flattery:

> Great mistress of this world, our gracious queen,
> Commandress of this mighty orb terrene.

The Serpent pretended that Eve was trying to warn him off the forbidden fruit:

> That you this fair tree might alone possess...
> I by experience know no lust lies here,
> And you know that.

Eve denied it, but the point went home.[2] Brushing aside her qualms with a 'Pish! Don't believe 't', the Serpent explained that he got all his wisdom from the tree.

> You would be wise and like the gods...
> They did prohibit you this tree
> Lest you by eating like themselves should be.

(How many gods were there?) And Eve told Adam

> I shall a goddess be, and thou a god.

Samuel Pordage wastes no time in explaining why Adam accepted this story:

> Adam invited thus receives the fruit,
> And without long delay falls rashly to 't...
> Strait operates the fruit, a shivering cold
> Upon their naked carcasses takes hold.[3]

---

[1] Ibid., pp. 89–90, 93.
[2] Ibid., pp. 66–7.
[3] Ibid., pp. 67–70.

Pordage here skirts round the problem of human freedom in rather a facile manner

> Man's will cannot be forced...
> He choose may what he will...
> And yet you see most wills seem captivate
> To ill.

Pordage's gloss is that if (by God's permission) a man is possessed with an evil spirit which forces his lips to speak blasphemy, that cannot be imputed to him for sin.[1] Most men are led by good or evil demons.[2] But the seed of God is in all men.[3]

God's reaction to what had happened was abrupt and final. 'Hence, pack away!' 'Now have the stars a power over thee'—astrology a consequence of the Fall.

> From Paradise they go, or Paradise
> Rather departs from them.[4]

In Pordage's poem, as in Milton's, Satan then returns to hell to boast of his triumph:

> Princely vassals! Who is like to us?

He proclaimed eternal enmity to love and harmony.[5] God in his counter-speech to the good angels asks (of Adam)

> Shall we desert him? Leave him to his foe?
> Strict justice might, but love cannot do so.[6]

Pordage returns to the Fall later in the poem, suggesting the allegorical nature of the story.

> But less obscure and trulier thus it is...
> After that unity had broken been

---

[1] Ibid., p. 87.
[2] Ibid., pp. 53–4.
[3] Ibid., p. 79.
[4] Ibid., pp. 71–2.
[5] Ibid., pp. 76–81, 107. Hell, Pordage notes, is 'here after a poetical manner described', but it is not 'in any particular place, but throughout the whole world' (p. 102).
[6] Ibid., pp. 83–7. Cf. Milton's 'Die he or justice must' (*PL*, iii. 210).

And discord introduced by the sin,
Of Adam,

the Second Principle withdrew to its own centre:

The world bereft
Of 't was as well as Adam naked left.

The First Principle of wrath took over, symbolized by the wall of brass and flame surrounding Paradise, 'which till Christ no man could ever pass'.[1]

So Samson's strength did Jesus' typify
Who at his feet bowed hell's great majesty.

Jesus pulled down the

wall, which as a bar did stand
Between the world and Paradise...
and then
A way was made to Paradise again...[2]

If Part I of Samuel Pordage's epic anticipates *Paradise Lost*, Part II anticipates *The Pilgrim's Progress*. It tells the story of a pilgrim, whom we first meet

Like one who lost upon a wild heath sees
A hundred ways...
All sects he has tried: his eye
More blinded is by their formality.

He can only pray 'I truly seek thee, Lord'.[3] An angel starts him off on his pilgrimage:

I the way that thither leads will show;
Narrow and strait at first appear it will.

---

[1] Ibid., pp. 231–2.
[2] Ibid., pp. 233–4. Samson typifying the humanity of the Son of God recalls the links between *Paradise Regained* and *Samson Agonistes*, which Milton published together.
[3] *Mundorum Explicatio*, p. 126.

The pilgrim falls asleep in a beautiful valley; he is awakened by
Conscience, stabbing and flogging him, crying, 'Awake from sin.' But
during his sleep a mist has arisen; only the angel gives out a little light.
The pilgrim crosses the stream of repentance (Jordan), where he is
baptized, and his pardon for sin is flown down from heaven.

'Two heavenly nymphs', Faith and Hope, are sent to guide and
support him, and they lead him to a kind of Paradise called 'God's free
grace'. Here he thinks himself safe, and sleeps.

> And whilst he sleeps, he dreams he travels on
> With that swift pace with which he first begun.

But this is an illusion. Faith and Hope leave him: dark clouds descend.[1]
He is attacked by a 'troop of shadows merely notional'.

> His busy brain now full
> Of these pert imps, do set his tongue on wheels.

He talks and talks—like any over-confident would-be saint. A beautiful
lady, Misapprehension, leads him through 'the bower of deceit', where
he meets a crowd of people sitting chained to their chairs—'seats of
security'—all persuaded that 'their regeneration was complete', that
'they could not fall from grace'. He is just about to sit in one of 'those
bird-limed chairs' when his tutelar angel reveals the truth.

> Prostrate upon the ground he falls, his cries,
> With true contrition winged, mount the skies.

God will never deny grace to those who sincerely seek it. Grace herself
appears, showing the Pilgrim 'the heavenly, the true way'.[2] This way
seems to him

> To lie here over rocks, through valleys there;
> Here dark black caves, there seas of blood appear;
> Here precipices thick, here thorns, here steep
> And stony places, there strong watchmen keep
> The passages: a thousand dangers show
> Themselves along the way that he must go.

---

[1] Ibid., pp. 129–37.
[2] Ibid., pp. 138–41.

But Hope and Faith are standing on the path when he gets there. They left him, they explain, because he was sleeping so soundly that they thought he was dead.[1]

Abstract entities continually have to rescue the Pilgrim. Truth, Watchfulness and Humility guide him. Grace reappears when prayed for. Chastity helps him to overcome Lust. Meekness saves him from Wrath, whose 'right hand bore a pine, his left a shield'.[2] When Deceit tempts him with the world's riches, honours, pleasures, a chariot conveniently descends from heaven, and in it the Pilgrim routs Deceit and her show. But this sudden success goes to his head, and he starts to thrash about in mad zeal and haste until Prudence restrains him:

> Thou must commit the reins of zeal to me...
> Zeal drives so fast that he will quickly err
> Unless my dove and serpent draw the car.[3]

Zeal then explains that the Pilgrim must sacrifice his 'Delilah', defined as 'whatsoe'er it be/ Thou'rt loath to part with'.

> 'And must she die',
> Cries he, 'who did within my bosom lie?'
> 'Yes', answered Zeal, 'God will with none dispense.'

Delilah gets short shrift:

> She slain,
> He posteth forward without stop amain.

Now he conquers 'the rebel passions', and sacrifices 'carnal affections'.[4] 'By this same light' the Pilgrim also sees that he

> Can in the earth own no propriety.
> All that he hath he offers to the Lord;
> He's but a steward and must nothing hoard
> Contrary to his Master's will; but here
> Prudence directs him how his goods to share;

---

[1] Ibid., p. 144.
[2] Ibid., pp. 146–55. Cf. Satan in *PL*, I. 292–4; but the comparison is common in epic.
[3] Ibid., pp. 175–6.
[4] Ibid., p. 178.

> Else subtle Satan would step in the while
> And with his tricks would him of all beguile....

That is a remarkably ambiguous conclusion after starting with such a flat statement. The Fall, Pordage tells us, 'begat self-interest and propriety': Adam and Eve owned no property.[1]

After further adventures, the Pilgrim experienced a trance:

> This is the state, in which the soul's blest eye
> Sees God (beyond thoughts) intellectually...
> What in this state she [the soul] doth or hear or see
> Must needs be true.[2]

'As in the building of a house' stones come together, so the Pilgrim felt joined in 'a mysterious union' with other saints.

> Saints thus combined are like a tower...
> O blessed love, from which true union flows.[3]

But even after this mystic experience temptations still beset the Pilgrim. He became too complacent about his spiritual gifts and graces. Envy makes him

>   not content
> To see another be more eminent
> In visions, raptures or the like....
> He jealous is lest his lights be outshone.[4]

Opportunely his guardian angel appears with the antidote to this spiritual pride, so familiar among the sects of the revolutionary decades: a pill of true resignation. The 'high adored deity' of 'Reason's foolish schools' is 'cast down and on the earth must lie'.

> The first degree in Wisdom's sacred school
> Is to be wise, by first becoming fool....
> I'd not have Reason banished from men:

---

[1] Ibid., pp. 179, 202.
[2] Ibid., pp. 196–7.
[3] Ibid., p. 198. When, in *Paradise Regained*, the Son of God stands on the pinnacle of the Temple where Satan has placed him, he is perhaps held up by the union of the faithful. See *MER*, p. 300.
[4] *Mundorum Explicatio*, pp. 201–2.

> Mere animals indeed they would be then...
> But that our Reason should its weakness own,
> Confess that heaven's arcanas are unknown
> To her...
> And not to dare, with a proud scrutiny,
> To search heaven's secrets with her purblind eye.[1]

The Pilgrim took the point and 'subjects his Reason to divinity'.[2]

The way to heaven lies through Paradise, which is itself approached through death and hell. Death nailed the Pilgrim to the cross in 'true mortification'.[3] Paradise is his native land, even more than 'mine own native Albion' is for Pordage,

> though there poor and mean
> I still should dwell.[4]

But heaven can be attained on earth: 'Paradise doth open in the heart'.[5] From Paradise the Pilgrim was taken to an even higher state, 'into th' eternal world'.

> Here he becomes a true magician,
> Here he becomes in Jesus Christ a man.[6]

In *A Treatise of Eternal Nature* John Pordage insisted that 'the spirit of the Holy Trinity is magical' and 'acts magically'. 'There is no use of reason in the still eternity, for the divine magia fills its place; neither is reason made use of in Paradise, nor in the angelical world, nor in the New Jerusalem.'[7] In Samuel Pordage's epic God promises after the Fall that 'my power and magic shall you still assist'.[8] By mastery of magic we can escape from Aristotle and get back to the state Adam was in before the Fall.[9] Those who feast on the fruits of the tree of life

---

[1] Ibid., pp. 205–10.

[2] Ibid., p. 211. Cf. Milton, 'Down Reason then, at least vain reasoning down'. Pordage had already said that Reason is what distinguishes man from animals (p. 11). Cf. Penington, p. 124 above.

[3] *Mundorum Explicatio*, pp. 212–15, 217–18, 226–9, 232, 243, 255–67.

[4] Ibid., p. 252.

[5] Ibid., p. 321.

[6] Ibid., pp. 323–30.

[7] [Anon.], *A Compendious View of the Grounds of the Teutonic Philosophy* (1776), Part I, J. P[ordage], *A Treatise of Eternal Nature*, pp. 40–1.

[8] *Mundorum Explicatio*, pp. 35, 87.

[9] Ibid., pp. 283–96.

> Shall only God's true sacred magi be....
> Heaven's magicians can do
> More than Belzebub or his magi too.

The age of miracles was not past, Pordage proclaimed. The gifts of tongues, of healing, prophecy, prayer, poetry, of interpreting Scripture and dreams, of miracles, were all open to men. The discerning of spirits, union and communion with holy spirits departed, with angels—all this might come from eating the fruits of the tree of life, through regeneration, purity of heart.[1]

John Pordage's eternal nature is created out of the still divine chaos in the abyss at the bottom of the universe, which itself is generated out of God's essence.[2] Among many other parallels between the Pordages and Milton, the following are perhaps worth noting. Samuel Pordage allowed Adam and Eve in Paradise to 'enjoy the pleasures of eternal love ... like angels (though in flesh they move)'.[3] He shared Milton's rejection of conventional human learning, of abstract intellectual speculation and discussion. More positively he concluded:

> No vain disputes shall studied be by thee
> But God and Reason shall thy study be,

rather than the learning of the schools.[4]

Milton suggested that heaven might be more like to earth than men think; Pordage tells us that 'Heaven's bliss and joy, hell's pain ... come from one deep root'. Heaven and hell are both within man.

> Hell hid in heaven, heaven in the midst of hell;
> And yet so great a gulf between.[5]

---

[1] Ibid., pp. 268–84, 292–6. We should not be too superior about seventeenth-century references to magic, which often mean something like 'natural philosophy'. John Dee, Sir Frances Bacon, Sir Walter Ralegh and Gerrard Winstanley used the phrase approvingly. The latter and the would-be reformer John Webster, Erbery's disciple, wanted to see magic taught at the universities.

[2] J. Pordage, *A Treatise of Eternal Nature*, pp. 8–19. Samuel Pordage used the conventional argument from design to show that a creator God must exist; nature or chaos cannot explain the existence of the universe (*Mundorum Explicatio*, pp. 4–5).

[3] *Mundorum Explicatio*, p. 125; cf. *PL*, IV. 741–9.

[4] *Mundorum Explicatio*, pp. 236, 318; cf. Preface, Sig. av, and *MER*, pp. 423–4.

[5] *Mundorum Explicatio*, pp. 317–19. Cf. pp. 228–9 above.

Heaven and hell are therefore not geographical locations, above the sky or below the earth.[1] Heaven is 'the abode/ Of Jesus and of all the Sons of God'.[2] Pordage, like Milton, mentions the telescope: 'the perspective we look through'.[3] He refers to 'these palpable dark clouds' which cover the entrance to hell.[4] Pordage seems to share Milton's literary preferences. He mentions with approval Tasso, Du Bartas and Sylvester, Spenser and Quarles.[5] Unlike Milton, but like Cowley, Pordage has lengthy descriptions of the noise and torments of hell.[6] Like Milton, Pordage believed in inspiration:

> God's spirit's the key: th'art b'inspiration's shewed.[7]

We do not know whether Samuel Pordage shared his father's Miltonic approval of polygamy; he spoke however against Milton's heresy of mortalism, and accepted the Trinity.[8]

Pordage anticipates Milton's fusion of events which took place at widely separated historical periods. Christ's death and resurrection are precisely parallel to the Fall of Adam and Eve, and both to Christ's temptation in the wilderness:

> So long as Adam slept when Eve was made,
> So long he in the grave and anger stayed.

By 'breaking through with an human soul' into Paradise, Christ 'recovered what Adam had lost and so unbarred that way ... for all those that shall follow him'. Christ remained forty days in Paradise before the Ascension, during which period he withstood Adam's temptations during his forty days in Paradise, as he had previously for forty days in the wilderness resisted temptations like those which Deceit offered the Pilgrim—the theme of *Paradise Regained*. Pordage refers to Christ as 'the Great Exemplar'.[9]

Since Marlowe's Mephistophilis anticipates Milton's Satan in saying

---

[1] Ibid., p. 10; cf. p. 113, and *MER*, p. 309.
[2] *Mundorum Explicatio*, p. 329; see pp. 305–6 below.
[3] Ibid., p. 313.
[4] Ibid., p. 102.
[5] Ibid., p. 235.
[6] Ibid., pp. 102–21, 227–9.
[7] Ibid., Sig. A 4v.
[8] Ibid., pp. 7, 318, 327. For polygamy see pp. 221–2 above, 262 below.
[9] Ibid., Sig. A 2v, pp. 60, 172–3. Cf. p. 228 above.

'where we are is hell', it is interesting that Pordage refers to 'Faustus' who ate the apples of the tree of death,[1] and that he makes a devil tell the Pilgrim, in Mephistophilean vein.

> We know more than you think we do, although
> We it to mortals very seldom show.[2]

Unlike Milton, Samuel Pordage did not think Christ's coming imminent. It might be in the age of the world 7000—i.e. AD 2051. But it might be sooner.[3]

After quoting so much of Pordage, I do not need to say that I am not advancing him as a hitherto unrecognized great poet. Some of his lines have a metaphysical vividness:

> The crested cock,
> The housewife's watch, the sturdy ploughman's clock.[4]

> The spongy lungs, the bellows of the heart,
> The stomach cook, by whom the food is dressed.

Teeth are 'the mill and grinder of the body's meat'.[5] There is a splendid non-sequitur in

> Seeing that there a God immortal is,
> It follows then there are more worlds than this...
> ...I do believe there's four
> And never was and never shall be more.

But these are internal, not physical worlds: Pordage specifically declares that the moon and the stars are not worlds.[6]

Pordage has no use for the excessive reliance on human reason which he attributes to Ranters. He anticipates *Paradise Lost* in his treatment of the Fall, and Bunyan in his use of the age-old theme of pilgrimage, updated to meet the temptations of the mid-seventeenth-century world. But only the plot suggests Bunyan: all Pordage's characters are allegorical

---

[1] Ibid., p. 121.
[2] Ibid., p. 112.
[3] Ibid., p. 84, Pordage's note.
[4] Ibid., p. 20.
[5] Ibid., pp. 23–4. Even this, it must be admitted, is derivative. Similar passages are to be found in Sylvester's Du Bartas, in Phineas Fletcher's *The Purple Island*, and even in Spenser (H. Jenkins, *Edward Benlowes (1602–1676): Biography of a Minor Poet*, 1952, pp. 69–70).
[6] *Mundorum Explicatio*, pp. 7–8.

abstractions, cardboard figures. They are totally lacking in life and personality. There is none of the class-conscious awareness of oppression, poverty and suffering which makes Bunyan's narrative so vivid.

In the Preface to his epic Pordage sums up what he takes to be its theme. 'Acts and statutes ... are all contracted into the one word, LOVE.... The strongest love causes the strictest obedience.... But man being created a free agent, whilst in Paradise, this natural appetite grew weak, and through his disobedience became depraved and fell to lower objects.' 'Since to love and serve God is the end of all religion', disputes, alterations, ceremonies, forms of religion, are all superfluous. We should therefore live with a good conscience under such 'laws and forms as our superiors by the special Providence of God are permitted to impose upon us', provided only that 'such laws and forms are no ways a hindrance to this end of loving God'. 'That disputative and wrangling spirit which has lately seized on this part of the world ... has damped man's love to God and charity towards his neighbour; everyone imposing on the liberty and conscience of another what appears truth to himself.'[1]

As with Sedgwick, post-revolutionary exhaustion prepared Pordage for the return of the episcopal church; but it also created a climate hostile to religious intolerance. How committed Samuel Pordage had ever been to the revolutionary cause we do not know. His panegyrics of 1660 suggest that he was not much of a Parliamentarian. On the other hand, even when addressing Monck he referred to 'our heroes of the civil war'.[2] Many were taking cover in that remarkable landslide. In *Mundorum Explicatio* Samuel seems to share many of his father's ideas. *Azariah and Hushai* also suggests a continuing loyalty to the Good Old Cause. Whether or not Samuel Pordage himself retained Parliamentarian loyalties, *Mundorum Explicatio* certainly deals, among many other things, with the problems facing ex-Parliamentarians, and to that extent it is useful for our purposes. Samuel Pordage lived in the same world as Milton, as Bunyan—and as Henry Stubbe.[3]

---

[1] Ibid., Preface, Sig. a, a2.
[2] See p. 228 above.
[3] Curiously, Pordage and Stubbe share one eccentricity—belief in a Purgatory of sorts (*Mundorum Explicatio*, pp. 219–25; J. R. Jacob, *Henry Stubbe: Radical Protestantism and the Early Enlightenment in England*, 1983, p. 70).

2   Andrew Marvell (1621–78): Millenarian to Harringtonian

I have written a good deal on Marvell on various occasions, trying to establish his political consistency, his full participation in the politics of his time,[1] and his close political relationship to Milton.[2] I shall deal here only with aspects of Marvell's prose and poetry which seem to me relevant to his experience of defeat. From at least 1649 or 1650 he had accepted the revolution in which (so far as we know) he had not participated. In 1653 he lauded the Commonwealth as the 'darling of heaven and of men the care'.[3] Like Milton, Dryden and Pepys, Marvell became a Cromwellian civil servant. As with Milton, his acceptance of the Protectorate did not extend to wishing to see Oliver Cromwell become King.

As many commentators have noted, the 'Horatian Ode' conveys a deep sense of destiny, of portentous changes having come about by means not entirely within human control:[4]

> 'Tis madness to resist or blame
> The force of angry heaven's flame.

We can now perhaps relate this to the sense among so many radicals that their Cause was God's, that its achievements had come almost without human volition. Oliver Cromwell ruined

> the great work of time
> And cast the kingdom old
> Into another mold.
> Though justice against fate complain,
> And plead the ancient rights in vain.

Milton's sonnet had the same vision of an active Cromwell ploughing his way 'through a cloud/ Not of war only but detractions rude' to rear 'God's trophies'.[5] Marvell has some sympathy for 'the royal actor',

---

[1] 'Society and Andrew Marvell', in *Puritanism and Revolution*, pp. 324–50.
[2] 'Milton and Marvell', in *Approaches to Marvell: The York Tercentenary Lectures*, ed. C. A. Patrides (1978), pp. 1–30.
[3] 'The Character of Holland', line 146.
[4] R. Nevo, *The Dial of Virtue: A Study of Poems on Affairs of State in the Seventeenth Century* (Princeton UP, 1963), pp. 98–106. The point is well made by Judith Richards, 'Literary Criticism and the Historian: Towards Reconstructing Marvell's Meaning in "An Horatian Ode"', *Literature and History*, 7 (1981), p. 44.
[5] Milton, 'To the Lord General Cromwell'.

playing out his part in 'that memorable scene' on 'the tragic scaffold'.[1]
But Cromwell and his Army have successfully subverted traditional
hierarchy. Naked power has overcome Charles's 'helpless right'. A new
state is being founded on 'a bleeding head', just as the Roman state had
been—though neither state's founders perhaps foresaw quite how
'happy' its fate was to be. (Rome, no one would need reminding in 1650,
had been the Fourth Monarchy; the successor to that conquering power
could only be the Fifth Monarchy.)

The millenarian note is continued in

> As Caesar he ere long to Gaul,
> To Italy an Hannibal.

France and Italy were the targets of all who thought it England's duty to
overthrow the Roman Antichrist: in Fast Sermons to Parliament,[2] in
Josselin's millenarian dreams,[3] in Quaker admonitions to the Army,[4] in
jests about Hugh Peter preaching in St Peter's chair at Rome.[5] Hugh
Peter, Robert Blake and Sir Edward Peyton all predicted the end of
monarchy in Europe.[6] Cromwell

> to all states not free
> Shall climacteric be.

James Harrington, Marvell's friend, was soon to be advocating the
export of freedom.[7]

The new state is, however, different from the traditional monarchies
which have become 'helpless'. Cromwell 'urges his star', collaborates
with destiny, has blasted his way through the great chain of being, not in
order to replace one personal power by another.[8] He is 'still in the
republic's hand', presenting his spoils 'to the Commons' feet'; his fitness

---

[1] But not perhaps as much sympathy as some sentimentalists have thought. Dr Richards rightly
   points to Marvell's careful choice of words. 'For any gentleman', she writes, 'let alone a king,
   judgement that he had done nothing "common" or "mean" on the scaffold could well be
   minimal praise: gentlemen were expected to die well' (op. cit., pp. 41–3).
[2] Cf. Thomas Goodwin, quoted on p. 181 above; Hugh Peter, *Gods Doing and Mans Duty*
   (1646), pp. 24–5, 30; John Owen, *A Vision of Unchangeable Free Mercy* (1646), p. 31.
[3] Josselin, quoted on p. 208 above.
[4] Burrough and Fox, quoted on pp. 146, 151, 157–8 above.
[5] J. Spittlehouse, *Rome Ruin'd by Whitehall* (1650), p. 339.
[6] See my *Puritanism and Revolution*, pp. 133–4, 144, and references there cited.
[7] Aubrey, *Brief Lives*, II, p. 54. See p. 199–200 above.
[8] R. Selden, 'Historical Thought in Marvell's *Horatian Ode*', *Durham University Journal*, LXV
   (1972), p. 46. I have benefited by discussing this point with Dr Cicely Havely.

to sway derives from his obedience to the Commonwealth whose servant he is.

We have noticed the role of the Army in radical thinking, its link with hopes for millenarian aggression abroad and for religious liberty at home. This may illuminate Marvell's concluding emphasis on the necessity of Cromwell still keeping his sword erect. Power has been gained by the Army and must be maintained by it. So the conclusion of the poem reinforces the point from which it started: 'the forward youth ... must ... oil th'unused armour's rust'. We must make our destiny our choice.

In much lighter vein the millenarian note is sustained in 'To his coy mistress'. I have argued elsewhere that the lines

> I would
> Love you ten years before the Flood:
> And you should if you please refuse
> Till the conversion of the Jews

refer to the well-known argument that the conversion of the Jews (the signal for the arrival of the millennium) would happen in AD 1656 because Noah's Flood had occurred in the year 1656 from the Creation.[1] We may compare Marvell's love for his coy mistress which grew 'vaster than empires and more slow' with the 'heavy monarchs' of the 'First Anniversary' whose 'earthy' projects are 'more slow and brittle than the China clay'. In both cases the reference is to rulers of the first four monarchies. The conversion of the Jews will come at the same time as the overthrow of the papacy, heir of the fourth (Roman) empire, and will usher in the Fifth Monarchy.

Five years after the 'Horatian Ode' Marvell followed up the millenarian theme in 'The First Anniversary of the Government under O.C.'. Again the poet depicted Cromwell as an instrument of God, this time with a more confident acceptance.

> An higher power him pushed
> Still from behind, and it before him rushed.

---

[1] In my forthcoming Clark Lecture, '"Till the Conversion of the Jews"'.

Only the vulgar 'think these high decrees by man designed'.[1] Unlike 'heavy monarchs' Oliver

> the force of scattered time contracts,
> And in one year the work of ages acts....
> And though they all Platonic years should reign,
> In the same posture would be found again....
> For one thing never was by one king done.

They 'only are against their subjects strong'. 'Heavy monarchs' 'neither build the temple in their days' nor care about trying to fulfil the prophecies. Cromwell by contrast 'cuts his way still nearer to the skies' and tunes in to the music of the spheres in order to build 'th' harmonious city of the seven gates'.

The Protectorate had established true liberty where Cromwell's predecessors had failed. ''Tis not a freedom, that where all command.' The feat was done by balancing in equality the conflicting components of the state, 'fastening the contignation which they thwart'.[2]

> And they, whose nature leads them to divide,
> Uphold, this one, and that the other side...
> While the resistance of opposed minds,
> ... on the basis of a senate free,
> Knit by the roof's protecting weight agree...
> Founding a firm state by proportions true...
>
> For to be Cromwell was a greater thing,
> Than ought below, or yet above a king.

Cromwell did himself 'depress/ Yielding to rule, because it made thee less'.

From this secure base in controlled freedom Oliver turns to the world abroad. If the 'observing princes' had only the sense to follow Cromwell,

> Where holy oracles do lead,
> How might they under such a captain raise
> The great designs kept for the latter days

—i.e. for the approach of the millennium. Instead

---

[1] Cf. Cromwell's speech quoted on pp. 186–7 and Owen on p. 172 above.
[2] 'Contignation' = (1) a framework, (2) a timber floor (Margoliouth's note).

> Unhappy princes, ignorantly bred,
> By malice some, by error more misled....
> Still they sing Hosanna to the Whore.

Marvell promises that, given leisure and strength, he will undertake a further exposure of the 'long slumbers' of 'kings that chase the Beast'. In this he will be following 'angelic Cromwell', who 'pursues the monster thorough every throne' until it shrinks 'to her Roman den impure ... Nor there secure'.

But this is 1655, not 1650. Millenarian expectations dwindled with the passing of the years in which the Second Coming had been expected. Now it is a dim and doubtful hope.

> If in some happy hour
> High grace should meet in one with highest power,
> And then a seasonable people still
> Should bend to his as he to heaven's will,
> What might we hope?...
>
> Sure, the mysterious work, where none withstand,
> Would forthwith finish, under such a hand:
> Fore-shortened time its useless course would stay
> And soon precipitate the latest day.
> But a thick cloud about that morning lies....

The most we can say is

> If these the times, then this must be the man.

Oliver 'girds yet his sword, and ready stands to fight'. But the men are lacking,

> unconcerned or unprepared;
> And stars still fall, and still the Dragon's tail
> Swinges the volumes of its horrid flail....
>
> Hence that blest day still counter-poised wastes,
> The ill delaying what th'elected hastes.

—and Marvell sinks bathetically to rejoice that Cromwell was not hurt when his coach-horses ran away with him, and to attack religious radicals—Fifth Monarchists, Quakers, Ranters.

Marvell inserts an apparent warning to Oliver not to accept the crown.[1] Gideon conquered two kings and had greater strength than any king. 'Yet would not he be Lord, nor yet his son.' (Ludlow and Milton were also to use Gideon as a symbol of the great ruler who was not a king.)[2] Cromwell 'refused to reign': 'At home a subject, on the equal floor.' Only his enemies would wish him to become a king. The more perceptive among them recognized that the terrifying strength of England's navy was the basis of national power.

> The ocean is the fountain of command;
> But that once took, we captives are on land.

'On the Death of Oliver Cromwell' is less of a public poem. But in it too Marvell praised the late Protector for establishing England's sea power, as he had done in 'On the Victory obtained by Blake over the Spaniards' (if that poem is by Marvell). He stresses Oliver's religious motivation:

> He first put arms into religion's hand,
> And tim'rous conscience unto courage manned:
> The soldier taught that inward mail to wear,
> And fearing God how they should nothing fear...
> In all his wars needs must he triumph, when
> He conquered God still ere he fought with men.

By 1660 millenarianism had lost the urgency of its appeal, not only for Marvell. What remained was a sense of England as the chosen nation, and a belief in sea power as the means to support England's greatness. So Charles II himself could speak not only of trade as 'the great and principal interest of the nation', but also of the English as God's 'own chosen people'; and Dryden could take over the theme of national power and national trade with no hint of an anti-Catholic crusade. 'The conventional view of the English as God's chosen people echoes through *Annus Mirabilis*,' Professor McKeon says: so does the parallel between

---

[1] Here I am decidedly with J. N. Zwicker, 'Models of Government in Marvell's "The First Anniversary"', *Criticism*, XVI (1974), pp. 1–12, and Annabel Patterson, 'Against Polarization: Literature and Politics in Marvell's Cromwell Poems', *English Literary Renaissance*, V (1975), pp. 264–8. I cannot understand how Professor J. M. Wallace came to think otherwise (*Destiny his Choice: The Loyalism of Andrew Marvell* (Cambridge UP, 1968), pp. 108–14, 122–3). Cf. my 'Milton and Marvell', p. 8, and W. L. Chernaik, *The Poet's Time: Politics and Religion in the Work of Andrew Marvell* (Cambridge UP, 1983), esp. pp. 6–7, 51–2, 101.

[2] Ludlow, *A Voyce from the Watchtower*, p. 135; *MER*, p. 173.

Londoners and Jews.[1] Pseudo-millenarian predictions of glorious times to come for London and England became common form.

We saw earlier how James Harrington had advocated 'a commonwealth for increase', a secularized millenarian future for the British Empire.[2] So it is no surprise that Marvell passed from millenarianism to acceptance of Harrington's historical theories. *The Rehearsal Transpros'd* (1672) was an attack on the renegade Samuel Parker, who had turned high Anglican and had published a defence of persecution. Marvell's principal and congenial task was to make Parker (Mr Bayes) look ridiculous. 'Henceforward [after Charles II had issued the Declaration of Indulgence] the King fell into disgrace with Mr Bayes .... Our author did not afford His Majesty that countenance and favour which he had formerly enjoyed.'[3] But Marvell's book also contains a dignified defence of Milton's political record, and of the Good Old Cause. The latter has sometimes been misunderstood, so I reproduce it at length:

> 'Whether it were a war of religion or of liberty is not worth the labour to enquire. Whichsoever was at the top, the other was at the bottom; but upon considering all, I think the Cause was too good to have been fought for. Men ought to have trusted the King with that whole matter. ... The King himself, being of so accurate and piercing a judgement, would soon have felt where it stuck. For men may spare their pains where Nature is at work, and the world will not go the faster for our driving. Even as his present Majesty's happy restoration did itself, so all things else happen in their best and proper time, without any need of our officiousness.[4]

In view of Marvell's recorded words and actions in the 1650s, and of his continued oppositionist activities in the 1660s and 1670s, it is difficult to believe that he is disavowing the Good Old Cause, as some have suggested. Nor, if we read him carefully, is this a possible interpretation of what he actually wrote.[5] Marvell chose his words with care as well as with wit and irony. Recall the situation in 1672. Marvell was ostensibly

---

[1] A. P. Thornton, *West India Policy under the Restoration* (Oxford UP, 1956), p. 16; M. McKeon, *Politics and Poetry in Restoration England* (Harvard UP, 1975), pp. 232, 63, 159; cf. pp. 153, 174–5, 249, 268–81.

[2] See pp. 199–200 above.

[3] *The Rehearsal Transpros'd*, ed. D. I. B. Smith (Oxford UP, 1971), p. 62.

[4] Ibid., p. 135.

[5] The passage is so carefully ambiguous that it appears to start by referring not to the English civil war but to the Scottish war of 1639.

defending Charles II's Declaration of Indulgence and the policy of toleration against high-flyers like Parker. So it was important not to alienate the King—who indeed vastly enjoyed Marvell's book. Marvell's balanced vindication of the Cause recalls Baxter's, and we have already seen Marvell's appreciation of the English Revolution as a historical turning-point. Marvell, clearly enough, is expressing a Harringtonian view of history.[1] The victory of the Parliamentarian Cause was in the long run inevitable, whether or not men officiously try to drive the world faster. But if 'the Cause was too good to have been fought for', it must have been far too good to fight against—as the royalists had done.[2] 'Men ought … to have trusted the King' can only be interpreted ironically: it was notorious that Charles I was impervious to rational argument on this subject: that was why he ultimately had to be executed.[3] Charles II's 'happy restoration' came about because his former enemies decided to recall him—'for their sakes, not for his'[4] —another irony. In the Second Part of The Rehearsal Transpros'd Marvell argued that popular revolt, though unlawful, was a natural and unavoidable reaction to corruption in government.[5] He had already observed, urbanely, that 'some usurpers, because of the tenderness of their title, have thought fit to carry with the greatest clemency and equality to the people, and to make very good and wholesome laws for the public.'[6] That need not necessarily apply to Cromwell; but who else could Marvell have been thinking of ? In 1677 he wrote, with similar irony, 'As none will deny that to alter our monarchy into a Commonwealth were treason, so by the same fundamental rule the crime is no less to make that monarchy absolute.'[7]

---

[1] For Baxter, see p. 213 above. Cf. Hobbes: 'Methinks the King is already outed of his government, so as they needed not have taken arms for it. For I cannot imagine how the King should come by any means to resist them' (Behemoth, in English Works, ed. Sir W. Molesworth, VI, 1839, p. 169). For Harrington and Harringtonians see Chapter 7 (4) above.

[2] Parker and other contemporaries saw this point clearly enough: S. Parker, A Reproof to the Rehearsal Transpros'd (1673), p. 443; [Anon.], A Commonplace Book out of the Rehearsal Transpros'd (1673), pp. 51–2; Edmund Hickeringhill, Gregory Father Grey-Beard, With his Vizard off (1673), pp. 135–6.

[3] On the preceding page Marvell had referred to Charles's 'imaginary absolute government, upon which rock we all ruined' (p. 134). In 1677 he said that the Irish rebellion of 1641 'ended in the ruin of his Majesty's reputation, government and power' (An Account of the Growth of Popery and Arbitrary Government in England, Amsterdam, 1677, in Complete Works, ed. A. B. Grosart, IV, p. 259).

[4] See p. 208 above.

[5] The Rehearsal Transpros'd, p. 240.

[6] Ibid., p. 225.

[7] An Account of the Growth of Popery and Arbitrary Government in England, in Complete Works, IV, p. 261.

We should read Marvell's remarks in the light of his previous career. We need not believe Richard Leigh's accusation that Marvell thought monarchy antichristian;[1] equally we need not take seriously Marvell's urbane support on occasion for Charles II. His very funny parody of the King's speech in 1675 shows that (by then at least) he had no illusions about Charles's feckless shiftiness.[2] The Cavalier Parliament's intolerance and Charles's hankering after indulgence for Catholics offered the possibility of persuading the King to take over the Cromwellian policy of tolerance. But in the later 1670s Charles's pro-French and absolutist leanings became apparent, and Marvell's anonymous satires became more and more outspokenly republican.[3] What Marvell wrote about the Good Old Cause makes sense as a Harringtonian interpretation of the English Revolution: a basic argument, indeed, of *The Growth of Popery and Arbitrary Power* (1677) was that the protestant religion in England is inextricably interwoven with the secular interests of 'the people'.[4] Richard Leigh more than once associated Marvell with Harrington.[5] In 1677 Marvell wrote an epitaph for Harrington; but such was Marvell's reputation then that it was not used for fear of giving offence.[6] As we shall see, Henry Stubbe likewise supported Charles II's Declaration of Indulgence but swung away from the court in 1673: so did many others. Stubbe argued that the interests of monarchy were inextricably intertwined with protestantism.[7] Marvell, who managed to retain the friendship of both John Owen and Richard Baxter,[8] believed like them (and Stubbe) that the Calvinist tradition in the Church of England was the true one and that the Laudians had been schismatical innovators.[9]

---

[1] Leigh, *The Transproser Rehears'd* (1673), pp. 95–6.

[2] Usefully printed in M. G. Bradbrook and M. G. Lloyd Thomas, *Andrew Marvell* (Cambridge UP, 1940), pp. 125–7.

[3] I have not quoted from these, since in some cases attribution is disputed; but contemporaries were prepared to think they were Marvell's.

[4] There are Harringtonian echoes in 'Upon his Majesties being made free of the City' (line 106), and 'Britannia and Rawleigh' (lines 179–81). Cf. my *Puritanism and Revolution*, p. 340.

[5] [Leigh], *The Censure of the Rota On Mr. Dridens Conquest of Granada* (Oxford UP, 1673), p. 1, etc.; *The Transproser Rehears'd*, p. 146.

[6] Aubrey, *Brief Lives*, I, p. 293.

[7] See pp. 270–3 below; cf. also pp. 111–13 above.

[8] The association with Owen must have been close: Marvell's printer is recorded as saying that 'nobody but Dr Owen ... had the proofs in his hands' of the second impression of the First Part of *The Rehearsal Transpros'd*—op. cit., p. xxiv.

[9] Ibid., p. 33; cf. p. 237. For Owen, Baxter and Stubbe see pp. 175, 177, 213 above, and p. 267 below.

3   Henry Stubbe (1632–76): Private Rethinking

Henry Stubbe was born at Partney, Lincolnshire, where his father, also Henry (?1606–78) was rector. Said to have been 'Anabaptistically-inclined' in his younger days, Stubbe senior became a Presbyterian and held various livings in Somerset and Gloucester. He was ejected in 1662 but continued to preach. In his last years he conformed (or was connived at by the Bishop of Gloucester) and occupied the miserably poor living of Horsley. He published religious works of the greatest conventionality. His wife was a Purefoy, possibly related to the regicide William Purefoy, a 'Presbyterian-Independent' MP.[1]

Henry Stubbe junior became a protégé of Sir Henry Vane, whose views he echoed in the 1650s. But after 1660, as Stubbe bluntly put it, 'the late changes in our nation had disengaged me from my former adherencies; and I have no longer a regard or concern for Sir Henry Vane or General Ludlow than is consistent with my sworn allegiance'.[2] Henceforth his career was to be curious, not to say paradoxical: Stubbe has until recently been consistently misunderstood.

Stubbe had no first-hand experience of the Parliamentarian Cause which he defended in 1659; he was not quite 17 when Charles I was executed. After graduating from Christ Church in 1653 Stubbe spent two years with the Army in Scotland. In 1655 he was appointed Under-Library-Keeper at the Bodleian Library and became a controversial Oxford figure. He supported the Independent group in the university against the Presbyterians, who in 1658–9 seemed to have the ear of the new Protector, Richard Cromwell.[3] Stubbe's particular bête noire in the university was John Wallis, whom he was perhaps encouraged to attack by John Owen, Dean of Christ Church and Vice-Chancellor. Stubbe was

---

[1] This is suggested by Onofrio Nicastro, Lettere di Henry Stubbe a Thomas Hobbes (8 Iuglio 1656 – 6 maggio 1657) (Siena, 1973), pp. 1, 37. Purefoy (d. 1659), descended from an old Lincolnshire and Warwickshire family, was MP for Warwick in the Long Parliament. Stubbe settled in Warwickshire after his ejection from Oxford, though he regularly visited the south-west.

[2] Stubbe, The Indian Nectar, Or a Discourse concerning Chocolate (1662), Sig. A 3v–A 4. I have found no information about Stubbe's relation to Edmund Ludlow, but the latter was very close to Vane in the 1650s (Ludlow, A Voyce from the Watchtower, pp. 12–13, 311–15). Stubbe was no doubt ironical in attributing his radical views to Vane's patronage: he was certainly no advocate of such dependence.

[3] Nicastro, op. cit., p. 9 (Stubbe to Hobbes, 7 October 1656): Stubbe needs Independent support 'for else the Presbyterians had outed me long ago'.

indeed referred to in 1657 as Owen's 'amanuensis'.[1]

But here we come upon one of Stubbe's many paradoxes. He was—or professed to be—a fervent disciple of Thomas Hobbes at this stage. They had a mutual enemy in Wallis, with whom Hobbes was in controversy: and Stubbe eagerly aided and abetted him in this conflict.[2] But the alliance was to all appearance more than one of convenience. The 25-year-old Stubbe wrote frequently and in very admiring terms to the septuagenarian Hobbes, and made considerable progress with translating *Leviathan* into Latin.[3] Hobbes for his part, Aubrey tells us, 'much esteemed' Stubbe 'for his great learning and parts'.[4] The alliance is perhaps less odd than it seems. Hobbes's Erastianism, his dislike of clerical pretensions, whether catholic or Presbyterian, was combined with an admission that 'the Independency of the primitive Christians' might be the best form of church government.[5] For an avant-garde intellectual like Stubbe, Hobbes's uncompromising anti-clericalism, his combination of tolerance with authoritarianism, had its attractions. Stubbe may have helped to introduce Hobbes's works to a group of like-minded Oxford dons.[6]

But Stubbe was an eclectic thinker. In addition to being 'amanuensis' to Owen and 'journeyman' to Hobbes,[7] he was influenced by Harrington, whose model he thought 'above praise' and well-adapted to 'the posture of our nation';[8] and he retained his loyalty to Vane.[9] His main enemy in the period 1658–60, when his political pamphleteering began, was the alliance which Richard Cromwell and his 'courtiers' were forming with the Parliamentary gentry and the Presbyterian clergy, led

---

[1] *The Savilian Professours Case Stated* (1658), pp. 6, 22; Nicastro, op. cit., pp. 11, 17, 55–6, 58; Owen, *Works* (1850–5), XIII, p. 300. Owen indignantly rejected the suggestion.

[2] See Stubbe's *Clamor, Rixa, Joci, Mendacia, Furta, Cachini, Or, A Severe Enquiry into the late Oneirocriticon Published by John Wallis* (1657), *passim*; cf. Nicastro, op. cit., p. 29, Stubbe to Hobbes, 6 May 1657.

[3] Nicastro, op. cit., pp. 6–7, 16, 22–3, 25, 31. Owen tried to discourage him (ibid., p. 28).

[4] Aubrey, *Brief Lives*, I, p. 371.

[5] Hobbes, *Leviathan*, ed. C. B. Macpherson (1968), p. 711.

[6] Nicastro, op. cit., p. 4.

[7] Ibid., pp. 26, 75.

[8] Stubbe, *Malice Rebuked, Or A Character of Mr Richard Baxters Abilities and a Vindication of the Hon. Sir Henry Vane from his Aspersions* (1659), p. 42. Stubbe however said that *Oceana* 'never issued from the same study' as Harrington's later writings, which Stubbe preferred (*The Common-Wealth of Oceana Put into the Ballance and found too light*, 1660, To the Reader). Harrington replied sharply in *A Letter unto Mr Stubbe* (1660) (Pocock, op. cit., pp. 828–31). Harrington had already criticized Stubbe's *A Letter to an Officer* (1659) in *A Sufficient Answer to Mr Stubbe* (1659) (Pocock, op. cit., pp. 804–6).

[9] Thomason described Stubbe in 1659 as '"a dangerous fellow"; Sir Henry Vane's adviser' (quoted by Woolrych in his Introduction to *CPW*, VII p. 56).

in Oxford by Wallis and John Wilkins.[1] (Vane, like Milton, had warned that 'since the fall of the bishops and persecuting presbyteries, the same spirit is apt to arise in the next sort of clergy that can get the ear of the magistrate' and establish an 'antichristian tyranny'.)[2] The Independents lost control of Oxford: in May 1658 Stubbe had to make a public apology to Wallis for accusing him (correctly) of illegally feathering his own nest.[3]

Like Milton at the same time, Stubbe tried desperately to rally the supporters of the Good Old Cause: like Milton and Vane, he saw that the Cause's supporters were a minority and that the problem was to devise a constitution which would preserve their hegemony. Stubbe quoted 'that excellent pen of Mr Milton', the 'glory of our English nation', at least twice.[4] Like Milton, Stubbe ultimately came to believe (or at any rate to say) that the 'debauched and ungenerous nation' was not capable of 'democratic contrivances'. ('New governments, though good, create advantages for after-times, and not those wherein they were erected.')[5] Having served his patron Vane faithfully, Stubbe adjusted to the new realities of the restoration.[6] One of Vane's beliefs which Stubbe rejected was millenarianism. Vane thought he was living in 'the last times', and that the thousand-years' rule of the saints was imminent.[7]

In 1659–60 Stubbe published at least six tracts designed to rescue the Good Old Cause. *Malice Rebuked* (April 1659) was at once a defence of Vane and a counter-attack on Richard Baxter, who had criticized Vane. 'It were not fitting,' Stubbe said in reference to Baxter, 'that court parasites should be more forward and fervent to enslave us than we to defend our liberty.'[8] Stubbe, like Milton again, claimed to be defending 'the most glorious Cause in the world'; like Owen, Goodwin and Ludlow, like Penington, Burrough and Venner, he saw 'the actings of our God' in this age of happy 'miracles', in 'the overturning of a monarchy' and of the church and the nobility.[9] But now 'all is but as the wandering Jews in the desert'; men had been misled.[10] Stubbe saw hope in

---

[1] For Wilkins's hostility to Stubbe, in 1658 and 1670, see Nicastro, op. cit., pp. 82, 71.
[2] Vane, *A Healing Question* (1656), in *Somers Tracts*, VI (1809), p. 307; cf. *MER*, p. 190.
[3] Nicastro, op. cit., pp. 32, 82.
[4] *Clamor, Rixa....*, p. 16; *A Light Shining out of Darknes*, pp. 174–5.
[5] Stubbe, *Legends no Histories* (1670), Sig. ˣ2, †2–2v.
[6] *Malice Rebuked*, p. 5; cf. S. Butler, *Prose Observations*, p. 113.
[7] *Thurloe State Papers*, I, pp 265–6; Vane, *The Retired Mans Meditations* (1655), p. 380 and Chapter 26 *passim*; *An Epistle General to the Mystical Body of Christ on Earth, the Church Universal in Babylon* (1662), pp. 2–3, 53.
[8] *Malice Rebuked*, Sig. A2–2v.
[9] Ibid., pp. 1–2. See pp. 63–4, 78–9, 125–6, 150–1, 173, 181–2 above.
[10] *Malice Rebuked*, p. 5.

Vane's *The Retired Mans Meditations*, which revealed 'the most glorious truths that have been witnessed unto these 1,500 years and more', presumably since the apostasy. These truths are difficult for the modern reader to find in Vane's turgid tract, but they must include his republicanism and the view which Milton shared and to which Stubbe remained constant: 'the magistrate's intermeddling with Christ's power over the judgements of men' is 'the mystery of iniquity working in men of a legal conscience'. That Christ is sole lord over the conscience is a supreme law; consequently all men have 'right and title' to complete religious freedom 'by the purchase of Christ's blood'.[1] (We recall Milton's 'consciences that Christ set free'.) This principle Baxter opposed—and was punished for it through Stubbe's next fifty pages.[2] Baxter himself, Stubbe suggested, was guilty of Arminian and Socinian heresies.[3]

The anonymous *A Light Shining out of Darknes* (almost certainly by Stubbe) has sometimes been attributed to Vane; but on stylistic grounds alone this seems impossible. Its vices are those of excessive erudition rather than of elevated obscurity. But the fact that contemporaries could be unsure of the authorship suggests that at the time Stubbe and Vane were believed to have closely similar views. The tract is a mass of quotations from authorities—a procedure which Stubbe defended as intended to show how many questions were open: he tried especially to select 'such testimonies as made for the negative and heterodox part'.[4] Stubbe rejected, on familiar radical grounds, the idea of a separate parochial clergy, tithes and episcopal ordination. Anyone with God's spirit may preach. The Apostles were craftsmen.[5] The very principles of protestantism, Stubbe argued, oppose any authoritative public interpreter of Scripture.[6] He was especially severe on the universities. Unknown to the primitive Christians, they are popish and antichristian.[7] Most interesting perhaps is Stubbe's defence of the Quakers against his former patron, John Owen. The Quakers—whom Stubbe compares to the early Christians, as Milton had compared Familists—really only carry Owen's principles to a logical conclusion: Owen used to be against

---

[1] Ibid., pp. 7–10. For republicanism see pp. 40–1.
[2] Ibid., pp. 10–60.
[3] Ibid., pp. 10–12. See pp. 268–9 below for Stubbe and Socinianism.
[4] *A Light Shining out of Darknes* (1659), p. 169.
[5] Ibid., pp. 1–54, 100–5, 112–50, 176–86.
[6] Ibid., pp. 92–9. Stubbe seems to have forgotten his Hobbism here!
[7] Ibid., pp. 139–50, 156–63.

tithes when he was in the Army.[1] George Bishop later claimed to have drawn many of his own Quaker ideas from *A Light Shining out of Darknes*.[2]

An Essay in Defence of the Good Old Cause (September 1659) also defended Vane and attacked Baxter. The latter had been 'instigated by the courtiers to revile … the abettors of a Commonwealth'. Unlike Milton, Stubbe appears to have regarded 'the more learned and judicious Episcoparians' as possible allies against the dangers of the new Presbyterianism.[3] The Good Old Cause, 'often mentioned with detestation, reproach and scorn' in Oxford, was especially old and good when compared with the Instrument of Government or 'that most nonsensical paper called the Petition and Advice'. The Good Old Cause had been concerned with 'liberty, civil and spiritual' against 'the corruptions of a king'. Our bondage under the Norman Yoke was comparable with that of the children of Israel in Egypt.[4] Yet, in Harringtonian vein, Stubbe argued that 'the Petition of Right and other laws in being had already deposed monarchy' before the civil war; 'we were only to improve, not create, a republic.'[5]

The sovereignty of the people is Stubbe's implicit starting point. But who are the people?[6] He believed—as realistically as Milton—that 'the universality of this nation is not to be trusted with liberty at present'. They must grow up to be worthy of an equal commonwealth (note the Harringtonian phrase): to establish one now would mean 'subversion of all that God hath been thus long a-building amongst us'. Since it is not lawful for Christians to commit power over religion to the magistrates,[7] we must 'limit our Commonwealth unto the honest and faithful party': the words echo Vane as well as Milton.[8] Even though at the moment tolerationists 'are possessed with the militia of the nation', opponents of toleration—greater landed men and the clergy—easily outnumber them. We should not underestimate the influence of the clergy, who 'possess weak spirits with the hopes of prospering here and assurance of

---

[1] Ibid., pp. 19–20, 81–92. Vane appears sympathetic to the Quakers in *The Retired Mans Meditations*, p. 211; *MER*, pp. 95–6.

[2] George Bishop, *A Looking-Glass for the Times* (1668), p. 217. Professor Woolrych compares *A Light Shining* with Milton's *Considerations Touching the Likeliest Means to remove Hirelings out of the Church*, published two months later (*CPW*, VII, pp. 55–7).

[3] *An Essay*, Sig. ˣ3, ˣₓˣ, 2v–A 2v, pp. 131–3.

[4] Ibid., Sig. ˣ4–4v, 5v, 7v.

[5] Ibid., Sig. ˣ5; cf. Pocock, op. cit., p. 608.

[6] *An Essay*, pp. 4, 9, 17.

[7] Ibid., pp. 31–50. Contrast pp. 253–4 above.

[8] Ibid., Sig. ˣˣ2v–3, ˣˣ5–8.

salvation hereafter'.[1] But Stubbe's pamphlet then degenerates into a rambling and ramshackle narrative of the early history of Christianity in the Roman empire after Constantine briefly established a universal toleration.[2] This material was to be reworked later, much more effectively, for *An Account of the Rise and Progress of Mahometanism*.[3]

Stubbe's proposals were made more specific in *A Letter to An Officer of the Army concerning a Select Senate* (22 October 1659). But again they are concealed in a mass of historical learning, much of it seemingly irrelevant. Repeating that it is impossible 'to step forthwith into an equal commonwealth', Stubbe distinguished between 'the people' and 'the nation', the latter including all men except servants.[4] Vane had recognized in this year that 'the depraved, corrupted and self-interested will of man, in the great body which we call the people', could hardly 'be prevailed with to espouse their true public interest'. He argued that sovereignty resides 'in the whole body of adherents to this Cause', who should choose 'a general council or convention of faithful, honest and discerning men'.[5] 'They only are the people,' ran Stubbe's version, 'who upon the erection of a government have empowered the legislators to act, being avowedly ready to stand by and uphold them in their actings.' (This is reminiscent of the intended refounding of the state by the Leveller Agreement of the People.) In England, consequently, 'the people' are those who opposed Booth's rebellion and actively supported Parliament.

Stubbe's definition conveniently excluded Presbyterians and included all the sectaries. All of 'the people' in this sense should receive full toleration: others 'according to their composibility'. The active 'people' should all 'be registered as the Liberators of their country', and they alone would be 'capable of places of power and profit', they alone would be armed: they would be (revealing phrase) 'as the prime gentlemen'; for 'to be a part of the people it is not necessary that one actually have land in such and such a country'.[6] This body of the militia, including the armies in Ireland and Scotland, would choose deputies who would in turn ballot for the members of a Select Senate, to be drawn from Independents, Anabaptists, Fifth-Monarchy Men and Quakers—'the patriots'.

---

[1] Ibid., Sig. ˣˣ8–ˣₓˣ, v. Winstanley said similar things.
[2] Ibid., pp. 55–99.
[3] See pp. 259–264 below.
[4] *A Letter*, pp. 53–5. 'An *equal* commonwealth' again.
[5] Vane, *A Needful Corrective* (1659), p. 6; *A Healing Question*, p. 311.
[6] *A Letter*, pp. 52–4. 'Country' presumably equals 'county'.

Members of the Senate would sit for life and would secure 'the
fundamental constitutions'. A Parliament was 'to be chosen by the whole
nation, not the people only'. It would include the select senators.
Parliament could legislate in all spheres except fundamentals (reserved for
the Senate), concerning the militia, the ministry or the universities. The
Senate would appoint sheriffs (presumably because they supervised
elections), though Parliament was to nominate JPs.[1]

Parallels between Stubbe's tract and Milton's *The Ready and Easy Way
to Establish a Free Commonwealth*, published two months later, are
clear. But, more realistically than Vane or Milton, Stubbe recognized
that a minority government must have a secure military basis. 'All
government is by an army'; a standing army was necessary to enforce
toleration and to control the City of London—at least for a transitional
period until 'the nation' was capable of self-government.[2] His was a
realistic attempt to redress the Harringtonian balance. In a very just
analysis Professor Woolrych puts Stubbe far above any other
commonwealthsman publishing in 1659–60 for intelligence and
constructiveness.[3] Not least significant, perhaps, of the parallels between
Stubbe and Milton is that *The Ready and Easy Way, An Essay* and *A
Letter* all advocate government by a minority as the only guarantee of
that first essential, religious toleration; but all agree that power should
ultimately return to a wider electorate when the people become capable
of self-government. This may throw light on the conclusion to *Samson
Agonistes*, where 'the people' escaped the destruction which Samson
wrought upon the Philistine aristocracy and clergy.[4] Another parallel
between the two men is the desperation with which they poured out
pamphlet after pamphlet in these last months of the republic.

In the post-restoration period Stubbe is famous, or notorious, as the
leading propagandist against the Royal Society and the leading defender
of Aristotle against the Society's spokesmen. Since Stubbe also praised
monarchy and defended the policy of Charles II's government in the
Third Dutch War, it has generally been assumed that he turned his coat at
the restoration and either acted as a paid hack or as an unpaid aspirant for
court favour. There appear to be similarities between his behaviour and
that of Marchamont Nedham, who had already changed sides three times

---

[1] Ibid., pp. 59–63. Note the importance Stubbe attaches to Oxford and Cambridge.
[2] Ibid., p. 64. Wither had advocated a perpetual Parliament to safeguard liberty (*The Dark
Lantern*, 1653, pp. 1, 37–74, in *Miscellaneous Works*, III).
[3] *CPW*, VII, pp. 55–7, 82–3, 126–8.
[4] *MER*, pp. 438–9; cf. pp. 314–15 below.

before the restoration and made a fourth turn then. But recently Professor J. R. Jacob has put forward another explanation. His interpretation is complex and cumulative, and cannot be adequately summarized here: anybody interested must read his fascinating book, *Henry Stubbe: Radical Protestantism and the Early Enlightenment in England*. But we can begin with a work that Stubbe did not publish, *An Account of the Rise and Progress of Mahometanism, with the Life of Mahomet*.[1] This is an astonishingly powerful book—tough-minded, sceptical, vastly learned but written with a real historical sense. Most of Stubbe's other books carry a heavy baggage train of irrelevant classical learning which distracts the reader from his main argument.[2] But in *The Rise and Progress* this learning was put to controlled use.

The early Christians, so runs Stubbe's argument, did not regard Christ as divine, though they expected his Second Coming in the near future; nor did they deify the Holy Ghost.[3] They had no temples, no altars; their presbyters were laymen. They practised adult baptism by total immersion. (Infant baptism, Stubbe thought, was a Roman pagan custom.)[4] The Christianity we have inherited, Stubbe insisted, is a mixture of 'Essene and Egyptian (Jewish) Therapeutai'; the tenet that Jesus is the Messiah derives from Gentile philosophy and from pagan rites and ceremonies. The Lord's supper was of pagan origin.[5] From the very beginnings of the church there was a split between Judaizing and Gentile Christians, between Peter and Paul. Arian Christians had a low opinion of Paul. 'His juggling carriage and his trimming with all parties' laid 'the foundation of perpetual schisms and heresies'. To those who accepted Jesus as the Messiah, Paul 'permitted any superstition'.—'And who knows how sincere or how complacential he was in his writings, whose deportment is thus related?'[6]

The influx of Gentiles into the church swamped the monotheists of Jewish origin. Lower-class Gentile Christians could more easily believe in the divinity of Christ 'being so accustomed to the deifying and

---

[1] Ed. Hafiz Mahmud Khan, op. cit. (1911); cf. Jacob, op. cit. (Cambridge UP, 1983), Chapter 4 *passim*, and J. R. and M. C. Jacob, 'The Anglican Origins of Modern Science: the Metaphysical Foundations of the Whig Constitution', in *Isis*, 71 (1980), pp. 260–1.

[2] This is true of *A Light Shining out of Darknes, An Essay in Defence of the Good Old Cause, A Letter to an Officer* and especially *A Further Justification of the Present War against the United Netherlands*, to which the history of the early Roman Empire seems particularly inappropriate.

[3] *Rise and Progress*, pp. 11–13, 15–16.

[4] Ibid., pp. 18–21.

[5] Ibid., pp. 22, 53.

[6] Ibid., pp. 55–6.

conferring divine honour and worship upon men'.[1] Persecution led Christians to abandon the doctrine of the imminent Second Coming, and to stress the other-worldly element in their creed. 'Subjection to the pagan magistrate' was preached, 'many dissolute and enormous assemblies disowned and declared heretical'.[2] (It is difficult to think that the analogy of English sectaries after 1660 could have escaped Stubbe.) Ultimately Constantine came to power with the support of armies mostly composed of foreigners, men of mercenary spirits and hostile to the established clergy, who 'cared not if a new religion were introduced so that they might share the spoils of the old'.[3]

Under Constantine pagan habits of dedicating temples, erecting altars, maintaining a priesthood, were introduced. Christians who adhered to the earlier traditions—Donatists, Novatians, Arians (the 'Puritans ... of those ages'), were persecuted as heretics.[4] Stubbe leaves it to his readers to draw the analogy with Laudian and restoration persecutions. Once the church was established there was an inundation of barbarism and ignorance.[5] The church came under the control of Trinitarians, 'enemies to all humane learning'. The leaders were 'a sort of people who followed the court religion and believed as their prince ordained'. They taught implicit faith, external ceremonies rather than inward piety, with the result that 'Christianity was ... degenerated into ... a kind of paganism'—with superstitious worship of the Virgin Mary, the saints, images, belief in miracles.[6] It became popery in fact.

Stubbe recognized that his description of the early centuries of the church differed greatly 'from the usual accounts ... delivered to us by divines and vulgar historians'. But all early Christian accounts are tainted as sources. They tell us nothing of the Syriac or Judaizing churches. Casaubon has shown how little the Fathers are to be relied on.[7] 'There has never yet been a general council' of the church: those so called were

---

[1] Ibid., pp. 22–9.
[2] Ibid., pp. 30–4.
[3] Ibid., pp. 33–4.
[4] Ibid., pp. 35–43. Marvell in 1676 also called the Novatians 'the Puritans of those times', which would suggest that he might have seen Stubbe's manuscript (*A Short Historical Essay Touching General Councils, Creeds and Impositions in Religion*, printed with *Mr Smirke, or the Divine in Mode*, in *Complete Works*, ed. Grosart, 1872–5, IV, p. 107). Bishop Parker presumably cribbed the phrase from Marvell (*History of His Own Time*, 1728, p. 196). Cf. S. Butler, *Prose Observations*, p. 119.
[5] *Rise and Progress*, p. 7.
[6] Ibid., pp. 43–7.
[7] Ibid., pp. 49–53; cf. Milton's distrust of the Fathers. Stubbe also cites Selden lavishly: ibid., pp. 25, 107–14 and *passim*; cf. *Rosemary & Bayes* (1672), p. 19.

summoned to register the victory of one faction over another.[1] (The contentions between Athanasians and Arians were 'about trifles', Stubbe wrote in *A Further Justification*.)[2] Interest, he declared in a Harringtonian phrase, 'is the secret spring that governs the motions of mankind'.[3]

So the world went on, 'to good malignant, to bad men benign'.[4] Bishops were too occupied with political factions to look after their flocks; the latter were 'overrun with ignorance and immersed in debauchery'.[5] The time was ripe for Mahomet. Stubbe thought he was 'a convert to the Judaizing Christians, and formed his religion as far as possible in resemblance of theirs'. Mahomet believed that Jesus would save his people in the last day, but that all Trinitarians would be condemned to hell.[6] An advantage of Mahometanism was

> not clogging men's faith with the necessity of believing a number of abstruse notions which they cannot comprehend, and which are contrary to the dictates of reason and common sense; nor ... loading them with the performance of many troublesome, expensive and superstitious ceremonies, yet enjoining a due observance of religious worship as the surest method to keep men in the bounds of their duty both to God and man.[7]

It is almost a description of the way in which sixteenth-century English protestants saw themselves as distinguished from Catholics.

No people are more averse to idolatry than Mahometans. All the traditional Christian criticisms of the Koran, Stubbe wrote blandly, 'may be urged with the same strength against our Bible'. We may compare 'the popish legends, or the fables recorded in our Fathers *and believed by the primitive Christians*'.[8] (The words I have italicized give a lot away!) 'I cannot distinguish between the Paradise of the Jews and Christians and that which Mahomet promiseth to his followers.' 'Our notions on the torments of the wicked in a lake of fire and brimstone somewhere

---

[1] *Rise and Progress*, p. 52.
[2] Op. cit., p. 63.
[3] *Rise and Progress*, p. 71.
[4] *PL*, XII. 538.
[5] *Rise and Progress*, p. 72.
[6] Ibid., pp. 145–6.
[7] Ibid., p. 166.
[8] Ibid., pp. 155, 159. Stubbe thought little of the 1649 translation of the Koran, made by Alexander Ross from the French (ibid., pp. 149, 237).

underground' are as absurd as 'any fables of the Mahometans'.[1] Their few
and plain articles of faith preserve them 'from schisms and heresies'.
Mahomet stressed frugality, so that his followers should not be
'debauched by riches'; and yet obliged them to give large sums in alms—
'a kind of Grecian levelling law'.[2] The doctrine of predestination—shared
by Jews and primitive Christians—contributed to military victory, as
Oliver Cromwell very well understood.[3] One reason for Mahomet's
success was that—unlike the Christian emperors—he was 'so remote
from ambition and avarice'.[4]

Polygamy, Stubbe observed, has been held against the Mahometans;
but it 'doth exactly agree with the law of nature', as well as being accepted
in the Old Testament. Whether Christianity prohibits polygamy 'to all or
only bishops ... may be a question'. Divorces were allowed by the early
Christian emperors.[5] We recall Milton and the many others who were
interested in polygamy and divorce in seventeenth-century England.[6]
Mahometan slavery was bad, Stubbe admitted; but 'in the West Indies we
keep infinite number of poor creatures in a most cruel slavery and debar
them and their posterity from the benefits of the Gospel to secure
ourselves the benefits of their labour.' That is an early protest against
slavery: like Aphra Behn, Stubbe had seen it at first hand.[7]

So Mahomet recovered true primitive Christianity,[8] including what
Stubbe always thought one of its most important tenets—absolute
toleration. 'It is indeed,' he wrote, 'more the interest of the princes and
nobles than of the people which at present keeps all Europe from
submitting to the Turks.'[9] This remark makes me wish we knew more
about what people were saying privately in the post-restoration years.
Ralph Josselin in November 1663 noted that 'many' were 'over-desirous
the Turks should overrun Christendom to gain their liberty'. Josselin
himself 'abhorred that principle' of gaining 'any outward liberty'
through Turkish success, but he nevertheless thought that 'God may do

---

[1] Ibid., p. 167.
[2] Ibid., pp. 168, 170; cf. pp. 174–7 (prohibition of usury).
[3] Ibid., p. 179.
[4] Ibid., pp. 112–13. For ambition and avarice see pp. 281–2 below.
[5] Rise and Progress, pp. 170–4.
[6] Leo Miller, John Milton among the Polygamophiles (New York, 1974), Chapters 4–5, 7–10,
   Appendix 3, p. 321, and passim; MER, pp. 136–9.
[7] Rise and Progress, pp. 187–8.
[8] For Mahomet as the heir of Gnostic Christianity see Norman O. Brown, 'The Prophetic
   Tradition', in Studies in Romanticism, 21 (1982), drawing on the work of Henry Corbin.
[9] Rise and Progress, p. 183.

good by them.'[1] Men were thinking of these things. The 1649 translation of the Koran seems to have worried Bunyan: 'how can you tell but that the Turks had as good Scriptures to prove their Mahomet the Saviour as we have to prove our Jesus is?'[2] In 1656 Henry Oldenburg was disturbed by the growing 'raillery of the profane' who asked awkward questions about Mahometanism.[3] That was the year in which Francis Osborne's *Political Reflections upon the Government of the Turks* eulogized Mahomet, and praised the Turkish government on Hobbist Erastian grounds for its control of religion. Osborne also had a good word for polygamy. Stubbe knew Osborne's book.[4] A scurrilous royalist song of 1659 referred to 'Alcoran Vane',[5] but I have found no other evidence that Vane shared his protégé's interest in Mahometanism.

Stubbe's approach inevitably reminds us of Gibbon; but also of Erbery's and the early Quakers' denunciations of the 'apostasy' of the early Christian church from the time of the Apostles. It also recalls the scholarly biblical criticism of Clement Wrighter and the Quaker Samuel Fisher, both insisting that the Scriptures were not a sacrosanct Word of God but a historical document to be interpreted like any other.[6]

Professor Jacob sees Stubbe's *Rise and Progress* as a milestone on the road which leads from the sceptical rationalism of the revolutionary radicals to the early English deists—Blount and Toland—and on to the Enlightenment. He is surely right. Stubbe's book was not published—could not be published—but it circulated in manuscript, perhaps widely. Charles Blount read it and quoted it (without acknowledgement) in a letter to the poet Rochester, who was unlikely to keep such ideas to himself.[7] At least six manuscript copies survive.[8] More important, perhaps, there is evidence that Stubbe was preaching similar doctrines in the south-west of England in the late 1660s and 1670s. Milton, Locke and Newton likewise held anti-Trinitarian views which they dared not

---

[1] Josselin, *Diary*, p. 502.
[2] Bunyan, *Works*, ed. G. Offor (1860), I, p. 17.
[3] Oldenburg, *Correspondence*, I, p. 91; cf. pp. 383, 385–6.
[4] Op. cit., in Osborne's *Miscellaneous Works*, II, esp. pp. 207–23, 236, 256. Cf. his Hobbist aphorism, 'Thus are subjects no less vain that do rebel than governments mad that provoke them to it' (p. 234). For Stubbe's knowledge of *Political Reflections* see Jacob, *Henry Stubbe*, p. 188.
[5] [Anon.], *Rump: or an Exact Collection Of the Choycest Poems and Songs relating to the Late Times* (1662), I, p. 162.
[6] Erbery also used biblical criticism in the interest of anti-Trinitarianism (see p. 91 above).
[7] Blount to Rochester, December 1678, in *The Letters of John Wilmot, Earl of Rochester* ed. J. Treglown (Oxford UP, 1980), pp. 206–16.
[8] *Rise and Progress*, pp. viii–xiii.

publish.[1] How many more were there? How much of what contemporaries branded as 'atheism' was in fact intellectual anti-Trinitarianism of this type? Professor Jacob has demonstrated that Boyle's corpuscular theory was designed to obviate the dangers of atheism which he saw in the ideas of Hobbes and Descartes, as well as of the religious radicals. Boyle trod a narrow path between the materialist atheism (as he saw it) of these two philosophers and the pantheistic materialism (as he saw it) of the radical sectaries. A narrow path, but one essential to keep to if socially necessary doctrines of established Christianity (as he saw them) were to be maintained.[2]

Oldenburg and Boyle, Wallis and Wilkins: does this throw some light on Stubbe's hostility to the Royal Society from the late 1660s? Professor Jacob thinks it does. Stubbe was influenced by Vane (executed in 1662), by Harrington (in gaol from 1661), by Hobbes (whom the Royal Society disliked). Stubbe was never an establishment man: the Royal Society was the Establishment *par excellence* in restoration England. Professor Jacob argues on the basis of *Rise and Progress* that Stubbe's main enemy continued to be 'popery', though that is for him a code word for Trinitarianism; that by 1669 he saw the Royal Society as a conspiracy of former Presbyterians—now called Latitudinarians—and near-papists to preserve Trinitarianism against its critics. Stubbe's defence of Aristotle was not mere obscurantism, nor was it cynical opportunism. Stubbe's Aristotle is not the Aristotle of Aquinas and the scholastics; it is the Aristotle of the Islamic scientists.[3] Defence of Aristotle is part of Stubbe's secret advocacy of Arianism.

There was of course an element of naughtiness in Stubbe's polemic against the Royal Society. The propaganda of Sprat's *History* and the class-conscious piety of the Hon. Robert Boyle were perhaps fair game; so was what Charles Webster calls 'the tendency of the Royal Society from the outset to lapse into uncritical appraisal of the absurd'.[4] But Professor Jacob's analysis makes better sense of Stubbe's career as a whole than anyone else's. (Not that anyone else has seriously tried to

---

[1] All three were strongly anti-Catholic, and Milton at least thought polygamy lawful. Blount was also an Arian.

[2] J. R. Jacob, *Robert Boyle and the English Revolution: A Study in Social and Intellectual Change* (New York, 1977), Chapter 3.

[3] Stubbe, *The Plus Ultra Reduced to a Non Plus* (1670), pp. 15–16; Jacob, *Henry Stubbe*, Chapter 5, *passim*. Samuel Butler thought the bishops were leading England back to Catholicism (*Prose Observations*, pp. xxvii, 50).

[4] C. Webster, *The Great Instauration: Science, Medicine and Reform, 1626–1660* (1975), pp. 494–5.

rationalize Stubbe's apparently outrageous self-contradictions.) We recall too that Stubbe's former patron John Owen jeered at the Royal Society's dilettantism and attacked its hostility to 'fanatics' whilst tolerating papists.[1]

Let us look at Stubbe's post-restoration career in this light. He decided, with Milton, that the English people had demonstrated their incapacity for sustaining a republic. Like William Sedgwick, he recognized that the alliance of church, crown and gentry had come to stay. The Church of England, Stubbe proclaimed, 'is the least defining and consequently the most comprehensive and fitting to the nation'. It is significant that the reasons he gave for adhering to the national church were not primarily religious.[2] If, as Stubbe probably calculated, the only alternative was a Presbyterian state church, he was right. Like Walwyn, Coppe, Webster and Rogers, Stubbe devoted himself to medicine as a profession. He was later accused of being hired by the College of Physicians to attack the Royal Society. This seems improbable, since Stubbe was in 1670 (simultaneously with his attack on the Royal Society) advising apothecaries how to outwit the College of Physicians, and criticizing the 'Frauds and Abuses committed by Doctors Professing and Practising Pharmacy'.[3]

Stubbe had somehow won sufficient favour at court to be appointed royal physician in Jamaica in 1662,[4] where he remained until 1665. Not perhaps the most glamorous of jobs, and one which did not suit his health; but the 'royal' in his title had the same symbolic significance as in 'the Royal Society'. He had made good, and the past was (temporarily at least) forgotten. Letters from Stubbe in Jamaica were published in the *Philosophical Transactions* of the Royal Society in 1667 and 1668.

One continuing emphasis in all Stubbe's pamphlets—as in all Milton's—was the absolute necessity of complete toleration for all protestants. Here the influences of Vane, Harrington and Hobbes combine. The main threat to toleration in the 1660s and early 1670s came from Parliament and bishops: formal protestants, Vane's biographer said in 1662, ally with papists against men like Vane.[5] As Marvell saw, the

---

[1] See p. 177 above.
[2] Dedication to Stubbe's translation of Joannes Casa, *The Arts of Grandeur and Submission* (1665), quoted by Jacob, *Henry Stubbe*, p. 45.
[3] Stubbe, *Lex Talionis* (1670), title-page.
[4] See Stubbe's Dedication of *The Lord Bacons Relation of the Sweating Sickness Examined* (1671) to Sir Alexander Frasier (op. cit., Sig. A 2–4).
[5] [G. Sikes], *The Life and Death of Sir Henry Vane, Knight* (1662), pp. 126–31.

main hope for toleration came from the King, heir in this of Oliver Cromwell. So Stubbe, rationally, gave his support to monarchy and opposed the alliance of Latitudinarian bishops and gentry in Parliament and in the Royal Society. Especially did this make sense after the fall of Clarendon in 1667.

In the ten years before his attacks on the Royal Society Stubbe published only two pamphlets and one translation.[1] During this period he had been cautious in his relations with Boyle, whom together with Oldenburg he had known since his Oxford days,[2] and whose patronage may have been helpful. They were still apparently on friendly terms in 1665.[3] Stubbe's *The Miraculous Conformist* of 1666 takes the deceptive form of a letter to Boyle about Valentine Greatrakes, who caused a sensation in the mid-1660s by a series of cures apparently wrought by the laying on of hands ('stroking'). This led to controversy on several grounds. First, the healing touch was supposed to be restricted to the anointed King. Secondly, the whole question of miracles was involved. Were they still possible, as Quakers and Samuel Pordage insisted? Or had they ceased since the time of Christ and the Apostles? Or had they never been possible, as some interregnum sceptics had argued? If they were still possible, could they nevertheless be explained in scientific and rational terms? If so, in what respects did modern 'miracles' differ from those described in the Bible?

Stubbe enjoyed himself here. His title goes out of the way to emphasize that Greatrakes was a former radical Puritan, who like Stubbe himself had conformed to the Church of England.[4] But Stubbe placed 'the gift of healing in the temperament or composure of his body',[5] thus calling in question the uniqueness both of Christ's miracles (and by implication his divine nature)[6] and of the royal touch. Queen Elizabeth, Stubbe pointed out, 'did for some time discontinue the touching for the King's evil, doubting either the success or the lawfulness of that way of curing. But she soon quitted that way of *Puritanism*' when papists suggested that she had lost the gift of healing 'because she had withdrawn

---

[1] One pamphlet was *The Indian Nectar* (1662), a product of Stubbe's trip to Jamaica. In it he emphasized the aphrodisiac properties of chocolate, a claim made in 1654 by James Wadsworth in *Chocolate: Or an Indian Drink*.

[2] *The Plus Ultra Reduced to a Non Plus*, p. 117; Nicastro op. cit., p. 29.

[3] Oldenburg, *Correspondence*, II, p. 402.

[4] Greatrakes at one time seems to have been interested in Muggletonianism (*The World of the Muggletonians*, pp. 47–8).

[5] *The Miraculous Conformist*, p. 11.

[6] Cf. Jacob, 'Robert Boyle and Subversive Religion', p. 287.

herself from the Roman church'.[1] To deny the royal gift of healing, David Lloyd suggested, amounted to 'levelling'.[2] What Stubbe *did* regard as miraculous, even more provokingly, was 'the grace of God in him [Greatrakes], ... a strong and powerful impulse' to use his gift. Greatrakes heard 'a voice within him (audible to no one else).'[3] Milton's Samson had 'powerful impulses'; Winstanley and many others heard voices; George Fox performed miraculous cures. Stubbe was endorsing precisely the sort of uncontrolled 'enthusiasm' which Boyle most feared.

Stubbe's pamphlets against the Royal Society started with *A Censure upon Certeine Passages Contained in the History of the Royal Society, as being Destructive to the Established Religion of the Church of England* (1670). In its successor, *Legends no Histories* (1670), Stubbe admitted that his readers might be surprised to find him defending the Ancients and Aristotle; twelve years' medical practice, he said, had convinced him of the value of traditional physic.[4] But his real reason for writing, he insisted, was to uphold the fundamental policy of these kingdoms by defending monarchy against popery on the one hand and against 'democratical contrivances' on the other. Stubbe himself had abandoned the latter because they could not 'take effect without such variety of changes as no sober man will think upon without horror, nor any that is wise pursue as feasible'.[5] 'Our church', he declared in 1671, 'is framed principally in opposition' to the papist, 'and the monarchy subsists only by that opposition'.[6] Those were strong words.

Stubbe's examples of 'the fundamental policy of these kingdoms' are all uncompromisingly protestant—'Henry VIII demolishing abbeys and rejecting papal authority, or Queen Elizabeth's exploits against Spain, or her restoring the protestant religion, putting the Bible into English, and supporting the protestants beyond sea'.[7] Her actions were 'warranted by the deportment of the Christians from the Apostolic and primitive times to the revolution under Constantine'.[8] But the 'authors of the *History of the Royal Society* have more of Campanella in them than Boyle'.[9]

---

[1] *The Miraculous Conformist*, p. 9 (my italics). The irony is transparent here, as in Stubbe's insistence that Greatrake's urine smelt like violets (ibid., p.11).

[2] D. Lloyd, *Wonders No Miracles* (1666), quoted by Jacob, 'Robert Boyle and Subversive Religion', p. 287.

[3] *The Miraculous Conformist*, pp. 2–3.

[4] *Legends no Histories*, Sig. ˣ⁻ˣᵛ.

[5] Ibid., Sig. ˣ2.

[6] *The Lord Bacons Relation*, Preface to the Reader, p. 29.

[7] *Legends no Histories*, p. 5.

[8] Ibid., p. 121.

[9] Ibid., Sig. ˣ3–3v.

This was the theme of *Campanella Revived, Or an Enquiry into the History of the Royal Society* (1670). The Society's avoidance of religious controversies meant 'laying aside all memory of the French and Irish massacres, and Marian persecutions, the Gunpowder treason, the firing of London'. 'Adieu... to all that King James writ ... to prove the Pope to be Antichrist'. Campanella had proposed to banish all theological questions from the schools, with the same insidious intent.[1] Long quotations from Campanella demonstrated his schemes to split the English in preparation for a restoration of Catholicism, schemes which the Royal Society had taken over.

Stubbe was thus continuing the battle against Presbyterian clergy and Presbyterian universities which he had started (as Owen's protégé) under 'the usurpations of Oliver and Richard', and which he modestly claimed had contributed to the restoration. Again he had no quarrel with 'the learned and judicious episcoparians'. The danger now was from 'those Cromwellian Renegadoes' and 'the Latitudinarians (upon whom neither religion, morality or generosity have any obligation).'[2] Stubbe thus implied that the Latitudinarians, so prominent in the Royal Society, were former Presbyterians (as indeed many of them were). Robert South, fellow member of Christ Church (of which Owen had been Dean) was a leading enemy of the Royal Society: Stubbe may have been exploiting his Oxford contacts here. Thomas Barlow, Stubbes's senior at the Bodleian in the 1650s, who was at that stage an 'episcoparian' ally for Hobbes against Wallis, in 1674 attacked the pursuit of scientific knowledge as a Jesuit plot, on Stubbian lines, and in particular a lecture given by Sir William Petty as impious if not atheistical.[3] Wallis alleged that in 1670 Stubbe received gifts of plate from various members of the university:[4] but Wallis of course is not the most objective of witnesses. By accusing the Latitudinarians of Socinianism Stubbe was able, to his own satisfaction, to bring them under the general umbrella of popery.[5]

On Socinianism Stubbe as usual had it both ways. It was a useful stick with which to beat the Latitudinarians.[6] On the other hand he argued that

---

[1] *Campanella Revived*, pp. 2-3.
[2] *The Lord Bacons Relation*, Preface to the Reader, p. 9; cf. Nicastro. op. cit., pp. 86–7.
[3] Jacob, *Henry Stubbe*, pp. 22–3; *The Genuine Remains of ... Dr. Thomas Barlow* (1693), pp. 151–9, quoted by P. W. Thomas, *Sir John Berkenhead, 1617–1679: A Royalist Career in Politics and Polemics* (Oxford UP, 1969), p. 234.
[4] Oldenburg, *Correspondence*, VI, p. 137; VII, p. 225.
[5] *A Censure, passim.*
[6] Ibid., p. 3.

to base religion purely on Scripture would lead to the victory of Socinianism, the implication being that Trinitarianism was not to be found in the Bible.[1] He was similarly unscrupulous about politics. The Act of Indemnity and Oblivion, he maliciously insisted, had been 'necessary to many of the Royal Society' because of their co-operation with the Cromwellian regime.[2] Stubbe argued that Bacon, the Society's hero, had inspired Englishmen with 'such a desire of novelty as rose up to a contempt of the ancient ecclesiastical and civil jurisdiction and the old government, as well as the governors of the realm', and so was responsible for the civil war.[3] We may suspect that Stubbe did not think Bacon's role as reprehensible as he pretended.

In support of this carefully defined protestantism which represented 'the fundamental policy of these kingdoms' Stubbe remained consistent. In *An Essay in Defence of the Good Old Cause* he had aligned himself with 'Perkins's doctrine in the chain of salvation', whilst rejecting Béza's advocacy of persecuting heretics.[4] In his contribution to the controversies arising from Marvell's *The Rehearsal Transpros'd* Stubbe referred to 'Bishop Whitgift and Jewell, Whitaker and Perkins' as the true succession of the Church of England. Were they alive now, 'they would be accounted fanatics, heretics and brambles' 'You see I retain the sentiments of the age of old Elizabeth,' he said, though remarking parenthetically that even she sent Peter Wentworth to the Tower and executed some nonconformists. Under Elizabeth there had been no revolt because no fear of 'a total subversion of the laws and liberties of the people', with the implication that there was such a threat under her successors.[5] Baxter looked to the same line of descent from Elizabethan Calvinists: so did Owen and Goodwin. For Baxter the danger of Catholicism had been a major justification for supporting Parliament in the civil war. Stubbe was appealing here to a formidable body of traditional protestant feeling.[6]

With his tongue again clearly in his cheek Stubbe echoed a phrase of

---

[1] Ibid., pp. 50–2, 58. Vane had won notoriety in 1646–7 by speaking up (together with Levellers) for the Socinian John Bidle (*MER*, p. 290).

[2] *Legends no Histories*, Sig. *2.

[3] *The Lord Bacons Relation*, Preface to the Reader, p. 6. Aubrey suggested that Hobbes parted company with Stubbe because of his attacks on Bacon and the Royal Society (*Brief Lives*, I, p. 371). Cf. Jacob, *Henry Stubbe*, p. 80.

[4] *An Essay*, Sig. *3v.

[5] *Rosemary & Bayes: or, Animadversions upon a Treatise Called, The Rehearsal Transprosed* (1672), pp. 16, 21–2.

[6] See pp. 213, 218–19 above.

Samuel Parker's which Marvell had pilloried,[1] only to draw from it the conclusion that Parker was trying to rebut:

> The civil peace (if not our common salvation) doth depend upon a reverence unto the clergy; and they are in times of peace the great support of government;[2] whilst their dictates are regarded awefully, the people are tractable, and the Prince may with ease manage them; but when they become contemptible, and are inodiated, then standing armies, arbitrary power and suchlike contrivances must secure the peace and monarchy. It is more safe and consonant to the old prudence to exact that the priests of all religions shall be equally reverenced than that none should be.[3]

Like Marvell, Stubbe defended Charles II's Indulgence policy against high-flyers such as Parker. The government of the Cabal was at least more liberal than those which preceded and succeeded it. In 1669 Stubbe claimed to be in touch with the Duke of Buckingham and the King, who (he said) encouraged him to attack the Royal Society.[4] So there is nothing surprising in Stubbe's *A Justification of the present War against the United Netherlands*, published in 1672. Charles's Declaration of Indulgence had been the necessary concomitant of the Dutch War, in order to win the support of nonconformists; the First Dutch War, as Stubbe pointed out, had been waged by the government of the Commonwealth to enforce the Navigation Act. So Charles's religious and foreign policy approximated in 1672 more closely than anything since 1654 to the policies of Vane's Commonwealth. No man who approved of the Dutch War of 1652–4 could logically disapprove of this one: or so Stubbe argued.[5]

Stubbe assumes the mask of a man ignorant of 'transactions of state', governed by 'that epidemical jealousy of court designs' and by 'all those surmises and misapprehensions' of 'an English malcontent'. He

---

[1] Marvell, *The Rehearsal Transpros'd*, p. 139, quoting Parker: 'Put the case, the clergy were cheats and jugglers, yet it must be allowed they are necessary instruments of state to awe the common people into fear and obedience.'

[2] This phrase echoes Charles I: *Letters ... of King Charles I*, ed Sir C. Petrie (1935), pp. 201–6.

[3] *Rosemary & Bayes*, pp. 18–19. If it is necessary to point out the irony of the passage, consider the subordination of 'our common salvation' to 'the civil peace', the words 'dictates', 'tractable' and 'manage', and the assumption that monarchy must depend either on the clergy or on an army. For the Harringtonian concept of 'the old prudence' see J. R. Jacob, *Henry Stubbe*, Chapter 6. Eachard's *Grounds and Occasions of the Contempt of the Clergy* had been published in 1670, so the reference to it would be clear.

[4] Oldenburg, Correspondence, VI, p. 138.

[5] In *Harleian Miscellany* (1744–6), VIII, p. 139.

originally opposed a war 'projected by some courtiers and others' for their own financial advantage. Especially, he tells us, he was 'jealous of the growth of popery'.[1] But after studying the question seriously he changed his mind. The Dutch were out to crush England, relying 'not so much upon their own strength, as upon our divisions, animosities and poverty'.[2] Elizabeth's support of the Netherlands, which Stubbe had so recently praised, arose 'not from concern for the protestant religion' but from 'a feminine humour, carried away by their flatteries and humble applications'.[3] The quarrel now is not between republican Dutch and the English royal court; 'the interests of the people, King and court are all one.'[4] Stubbe slips in a good deal of praise for the Long Parliament and Oliver Cromwell; Dutch criticisms of the English monarchy are cited at perhaps unnecessary length.[5]

Stubbe resumed his parallels between the First and Third Dutch Wars in *A Further Justification of the Present War against the United Netherlands*, published in 1673.[6] Trade, he argued, was necessary to England's prosperity. But trade depends on sea power.[7] Addressing himself even more openly to former Parliamentarians than in his *Justification*, Stubbe sharply contrasted the glories of the former age, when Oliver *'se faisoit craindre'*, with England's weakness now, discreetly attributed to 'our divisions, factions, lack of confidence in the government'.[8] Charles had been too busy 'composing his distracted kingdoms, re-establishing the government' and advancing England's trade against Dutch competition to have had 'leisure to regard the growth of the French monarchy'.[9] Blame for the sudden rise in French strength Stubbe (like the old Rumper Slingsby Bethel) attributed to Oliver Cromwell.[10] By contrast Stubbe quoted a statement attributed to members of the Barebone's Parliament: 'Antichrist, the Man of Sin, could never be destroyed in Italy whilst the Dutch retained any considerable strength in the United Provinces.'[11] So he shrugged off the difficult

---

[1] Ibid., p. 129.
[2] Ibid., pp. 124–5.
[3] Ibid., p. 137.
[4] Ibid., p. 139.
[5] Ibid., pp. 149–51.
[6] *A Further Justification*, pp. 57–70 (should be pp. 87–100), 73–122 (should be pp. 103–52).
[7] Ibid., Sig. A 4–4v.
[8] Ibid., Sig. A 4v, pp. 5, 7.
[9] Ibid., p. 18.
[10] [Bethel], *The Worlds Mistake in Oliver Cromwell* (1668), also defended Sir Henry Vane.
[11] *A Further Justification*, p. 91 (should be p. 121).

question of allying with the greatest Catholic power against fellow-protestants. It is safer, he suggested, to 'acquiesce in the royal word and honour of the King of France than in any promise of the Hollanders'. If popery should be restored in the Netherlands that will not be our fault.[1]

Stubbe then turned to the links between the Dutch War and the Declaration of Indulgence. By comparison with the interregnum, he told nonconformists, 'the government is only varied to a monarchy, under which they possess their former indulgence.'[2] He reminded the clergy that it was to their interest too 'that the nation be puissant, populous and rich ... and rents duly paid; but these ends could not be accomplished without the Declaration [of Indulgence] ... If there be no trading, how little will the difference be between the alienation of church lands and the receiving no rents from them.'[3] So both parties were better off than they had been in the 1650s, if only they would recognize the fact. Nonconformists had learnt, the hard way, how impossible it was 'to overthrow an hereditary monarchy, and how impossible it was for a nation inured to monarchy, divided in interests, discriminated by degrees of honour, debauched in its manners, irreconcilable in its factions, to retain its liberty.' Abandonment of resistance by 'fanatics' had given Charles a better opinion of them and had led to the Declaration of Indulgence.[4] So the King had revived 'the primitive policy of Constantine', the policy of toleration.[5] 'The sectaries are irreconcilably divided one against the other: the penal laws unite their interest against the government. But Indulgence continues them disjoined. Which is the most secure course?'[6]

Some of Stubbe's major ambiguities result from his attitudes towards Constantine. He praised Charles for reviving Constantine's tolerationist policy. Yet earlier he had quoted Dante, as translated by 'the excellent Mr. John Milton':

> Ah Constantine, of how much ill was cause
> Not thy conversion, but those rich domains
> That the first wealthy Pope received of thee![7]

---

[1] Ibid., pp. 18–24.   [2] Ibid., Sig. Bv.
[3] Ibid., pp. 28–9.   [4] Ibid., pp. 30–1.
[5] Ibid., pp. 32–50.   [6] Ibid., p. 72.
[7] *A Light Shining out of Darknes*, pp. 174–5, quoting Milton's *Of Reformation* (1641): *CPW*, I, p. 558; cf. *MER*, pp. 84–6. In the same work Stubbe cited (probably via Milton) Spenser's Eclogue of May from *The Shepheards Calendar* against Presbyterian ministers (loc. cit.): cf. *CPW*, I, pp. 722–3.

For Milton in 1641 Constantine's reign marked the beginning of the Apostasy. Erbery and many Quakers put the Apostasy far earlier, in the days of the Apostles.[1] Stubbe argued both ways. In *The Rise and Progress* the corruption of Christianity was only completed by Constantine.[2] He criticized Sprat for accepting the traditional view of Constantine.[3]

Stubbe was paid £200 for his two defences of royal policy. But his commitment to the court lasted no longer than the indulgence policy. When that came to an end, and Shaftesbury left the government, Stubbe became conscious again of the evils of popery and of the dangerous possibility of an alliance between crown and papists leading to absolutism. Marvell similarly swung from acceptance of the King's indulgence policy in *The Rehearsal Transpros'd* of 1672 to the fierce *Account of the Growth of Popery and arbitrary Government in England* in 1677. Milton, Traherne, Benlowes, Du Moulin and Penn were among those who took up the pen against popery after 1673.[4]

Stubbe's *The Paris Gazette* (1673) produced historical precedents for annulling the marriage between James Duke of York and the Catholic Mary of Modena. Again Stubbe resorted to translation to convey his message. In his version of Jacques Godefroy's *The History of the United Provinces of Achaia* he suggested the superiority of the republican Netherlands to absolutist France by the title, and by using words like Stadholder and States-General. By implication he attacked the royal power of prorogation and dissolution of Parliament, secret diplomacy (what did Stubbe suspect about the secret Treaty of Dover?) and the taking of French pensions.[5]

A Caveat for the Protestant Clergy, attributed to Stubbe, gave a lurid account of the Marian martyrdoms, and observed ominously that 'the Pope doth reckon upon our kingdom as held in fee of the papacy'. But the author, with Stubbian irony, was 'resolved not to doubt the integrity and prudence of his Majesty or our Parliament.... Nothing informs so much as history, and to be forewarned is in a measure to be fore-armed.'

---

[1] See pp. 297–301 below.
[2] *Rise and Progress*, pp. 35–48; *The Plus Ultra Reduced*, p. 16.
[3] Jacob, *Henry Stubbe*, p. 129.
[4] Milton, *Of True Religion, Heresy, Schism, Toleration* (1673), in *CPW*, VIII; Thomas Traherne, *Roman Forgeries* (1673); Harold Jenkins, *Edward Benlowes (1602–1676): Biography of a Minor Poet* (1952), p. 292; Peter Du Moulin, *Englands Appeal from the Private Cabal at Whitehall to the Great Council of the Nation* (1673); William Penn, *One Project for the Good of England* (1679). For the outburst of pamphleteering from 1673 onwards see Haley, *William of Orange and the English Opposition, 1672–4*, pp. 59, 97–8, 107.
[5] Op. cit., sig. A2.

The gentry were discreetly reminded of the threat which popery would offer to their monastic lands.[1]

As Professor Jacob succinctly puts it, all Stubbe's post-restoration writings 'hold up models of ancient practice wherewith to charm King and nation back ... to primitive purity ... The goal ... is not a new heaven and earth, but a workaday world of Erastian rule, peace and prosperity—tolerant, secularising, sober, industrious, perhaps polygamous and moderately levelling.' Monarchy was for Stubbe not the best form of government—no government is best 'abstracting from the circumstances'; but monarchy was the government most likely to provide stability in post-revolutionary England.[2] In 1659 Stubbe had observed that monarchy at present suited France, 'but an extraordinary revolution may so order things that it may be as little feasible there as amongst us'.[3] The change went the other way, but Stubbe's point remains.

The collapse of the Cabal thus brought Stubbe's radicalism back to the surface: the ideal of a tolerant absolutism, which Marvell too had perhaps temporarily espoused, now yielded to fear of French-backed Catholic absolutism. Stubbe made what J. R. Jacob regards as a significant contribution to the country opposition in the autumn of 1673, so much so that he was imprisoned, ostensibly because of *The Paris Gazette*. An unsuccessful attempt was made to pack him off to Jamaica again. Jacob even raises the question of whether Stubbe's death in 1676 may not have been murder. He was alleged to have fallen from his horse one evening and was drowned in very shallow water. But Stubbe—though no ascetic—was not a notorious drinker, and he was only 44 at the time. He was a potentially dangerous man with many years of activity in front of him—like Vane in 1662. Jacob's is only a hypothesis, but it is worth thinking about.[4]

Professor Jacob has recovered some of Stubbe's forgotten activities in taking radical politics to the lower classes, including 'dirty coalmen', as he travelled up and down Somerset. He preached in conventicles and alehouses, held forth at coffee-houses—where 'each man seems a

---

[1] Op. cit. (2nd edn., 1678), pp. 15–16. No first edition has been found. The posthumous attribution to Stubbe may therefore be false; but it reads like him. See Jacob, *Henry Stubbe*, pp. 139–40.

[2] Ibid., pp. 126–8.

[3] Stubbe, *The Commonwealth of Israel* (1659), p. 4. This is an interesting example of the word 'revolution' poised between its traditional and its modern sense: cf. Cromwell's 'revolutions of Christ'.

[4] Jacob, *Henry Stubbe*, pp. 137–8.

Leveller'—and 'drew the apron-men about him, as ballad-singers do the rout in fairs and markets'.[1] Early in 1670 Stubbe 'hath made most of the common sort [of Bristol] believe that the [Royal] Society is a company of atheists, papists, dunces...'.[2] Jacob gives examples of possible subjects for Stubbe's eloquence: Edward Chamberlayne, FRS, wanted to increase taxes in order to keep the common people poor and make them more industrious; John Beale, FRS, favoured enclosure though afraid that there might be 'insurrections' from 'common tenants'.[3] Against such schemes Stubbe's propaganda might well be acceptable to small farmers and tradesmen: the Royal Society, full of courtiers, bishops, peers and gentlemen, was associated with social privilege.[4] Stubbe himself was said to give medical treatment to the poor on cheap terms; in *Medice Cura Teipsum* (1671) he had recommended free medical treatment 'when there is occasion'.[5]

Professor Jacob sees Stubbe as the connecting link between the pantheistic materialism of Diggers and Ranters and the deism of Blount, Toland and the eighteenth century. Certainly Stubbe inherited many mid-century heresies. He was a mortalist—a heresy of which Vane had been accused.[6] He went out of his way to record that some of the earliest Christians denied the resurrection.[7] He was said not to believe in hell, and to make no distinction between God and nature.[8] By 1682, six years after Stubbe's death, the egregious John Beale was writing to Boyle regretting the prevalence of 'Hobbians and Stubbians', the most malignant enemies of all religion.[9]

One of the novelties of Professor Jacob's *Henry Stubbe* is his picture of Stubbe as a Harringtonian revisionist, publishing before Neville's *Plato*

---

[1] Ibid., pp. 83–4, quoting Glanvill; and Chapter 5 *passim*.

[2] Jacob, *Henry Stubbe*, p. 102, quoting Oldenburg, *Correspondence*, VI, pp. 444, 456. Is Stubbe the 'red-headed champion' referred to on p. 456?

[3] Jacob, *Henry Stubbe*, pp. 89–91.

[4] Ibid., p. 7.

[5] *Medice Cura Teipsum*, p. 19; Stubbe, *Directions for Drinking the Bath Waters*, Preface to the Reader, in John Hall, *Select Observations* (trans. J. Cook, 1679), Sig. A 5: 'Money is scarce and country-people poor.'

[6] Jacob, *Henry Stubbe*, p. 146. For Vane see J. R. Jacob, 'The Ideological Consequences of Robert Boyle's Natural Philosophy', *Journal of European Studies*, 2 (1971), p. 18; *Robert Boyle and the English Revolution*, p. 172.

[7] *Rise and Progress*, p. 25.

[8] Jacob, 'Robert Boyle and Subversive Religion', p. 284. Vane was said to know nothing of a material hell, and to believe in universal salvation (Burnet, *History of My Own Time*, I, p. 285).

[9] Boyle, *Works* (1744), V, p. 505. With 'Stubbian' compare Baxter's coinage of 'Vanist'. There were also 'Miltonists' (*MER*, p. 226).

Redivivus and with a different emphasis. By contrast with Neville's mainly secular approach, Stubbe used Harrington's vocabulary of ancient and modern prudence with reference to religion rather than politics. Ancient prudence is for him the toleration established by Constantine, or the civil religion of Mahomet. For a moment Stubbe thought Charles II was 'reviving' such a tolerant regime by the Declaration of Indulgence: hence his temporary support for royal absolutism.[1] Like Harrington, Stubbe envisaged an imperial future for Britain. Mahomet's stress on frugality and his encouragement of industry resulted in 'a great and lasting empire'. One advantage of polygamy was that it led to 'the multiplying of subjects, which are the sinews of empire'.[2] In *A Further Justification* Stubbe advocated use of sea power to maintain and advance national greatness—to make England 'the top of nations', in Thomas Goodwin's phrase.[3] The Hobbist Albertus Warren picked up this line of thought in 1680—again before Neville had published—though with a greater emphasis on links between the commercial classes and dissent and on the need to take account of the new balance of wealth which had arisen in England by 1680.[4]

Consideration of Henry Stubbe's career reinforces the necessity of remembering the censorship throughout this period.[5] J. R. Jacob was able to reconstruct Stubbe's ideas because *The Rise and Progress of Mahometanism*, unpublishable in his lifetime, happened to survive. The same is true of Milton's *De Doctrina Christiana*, of Locke's and Newton's papers. All three cherished secret heresies which would have been regarded as blasphemous in the societies which they adorned. Stubbe seems to have been more courageous, or rasher, than his fellow anti-Trinitarians in allowing his manuscripts to circulate privately.

Using this key Jacob has shown how faithful Stubbe remained to radical ideas. 'You see, O ye patriots of the Good Old Cause,' cried Glanvill in 1671, 'Mr Stubbe is constant to you.'[6] Jacob has skilfully unravelled the satire and subterfuge, the caricature, double meaning, irony and mockery, which run all through Stubbe's writing. But Stubbe

---

[1] Jacob, *Henry Stubbe*, pp. 116–18, 125–6, 203.
[2] *Rise and Progress*, pp. 170–5.
[3] *A Further Justification*, p. 79. Stubbe quoted John Dee on sea power, ibid., p. 83.
[4] [A Warren], *An Apology for the Discourse of Human Reason written by Ma.[rtin] Clifford Esq.*, pp. 83, 89–90, 116–20. This tract is dedicated to Shaftesbury. Cf. Jacob, *Henry Stubbe*, pp. 141–2.
[5] The point was made vigorously over thirty years ago by H. J. McLachlan, *Socinianism in Seventeenth-Century England* (Oxford UP, 1951), pp. 225–6, 303–7, 327–31, 338.
[6] Glanvill, *A Praefatory Answer*, Sig. A 5, quoted by Jacob, *Henry Stubbe*, p. 98.

is almost unique in that the key survived. Jacob concludes that we should be much more wary than scholars usually are when reading restoration tracts. It would be foolish to assume that they always mean what they say.[1] Stubbe may have been by temperament excessively devious. At Oxford in 1657 he denied in public the allegiance to Hobbes which he professed in private.[2] But perhaps it was wise to be cautious in those days when the political scene might change overnight. Stubbe too sometimes found it difficult to resist scoring points, even when he might be the only one who could see the joke. Men associated his red hair with a fiery temperament.[3] But he was also a serious scholar and thinker, a historian whose achievement has been wrongly neglected. We are all enormously indebted to Professor Jacob for restoring his reputation.

---

[1] Jacob, op. cit., pp. 3, 42, 58, 139–42, 159–64.
[2] Nicastro, op. cit., pp. 30, 79.
[3] *The Lord Bacons Relation*, Preface to the Reader, p. 11.

Chapter 9

Army, Saints, People

1 The Army and the Radicals

One point that forced itself upon me whilst writing this book was the continuing importance of the Army for the radicals.[1] Their ideas could have emerged only in the fluid state of society which existed during the revolutionary decades. We should not underestimate—as historians perhaps too easily do—the significance of rank and file and junior officers in London as members of gathered congregations, often as preachers themselves around whom such churches formed. Outside London it was normally under the Army's protection that separatist churches and groups could gather and survive. The Digger community at Cobham lasted as long as it had Army backing; and no longer. In January 1650 Winstanley was still hoping for Army support, and even in 1652 he appealed to Cromwell.[2] The Ranters drew on support from Army officers in their brief heyday. That the 'northern Quakers' owed much to Army protection is clear from Fox's *Journal*, and from the Nayler Debates in 1656. Removing the garrison from Bristol in 1654 at once reduced support for the Quakers.[3] In Ireland it was in the Army that Quakers 'found their greatest response'.[4] When Burrough and Howgil were expelled from Ireland in 1656, the guards taking them to the coast 'were loving to them and suffered them to have meetings where they came'.[5]

---

[1] Professor Cole came to the same conclusion in his pioneering essay on Quakers and Politics (see p. 151 above).
[2] Winstanley, *The Law of Freedom*, p. 209; cf. pp. 275–90.
[3] Horle, 'John Camm', in *Quaker History*, 71 (1982), p. 6.
[4] Carroll, 'Quakerism and the Cromwellian Army in Ireland', *JFHS*, 54 (1978), pp. 135–9 and *passim*; 'Quakerism in Connaught', ibid., pp. 187–8; Horle, 'John Camm', *Quaker History*, 70 (1981), p. 83.
[5] W. Edmundson, *Journal* (1715), p. 17.

The fluidity of the society was the product of the Army's victory. For nearly fifteen years the Army was the effective source of authority in the country; to it JPs and other local authorities in the last resort owed such backing as they received. Religious toleration, manifestly, would last only so long as the Army lasted. No elected Parliament in the mid-seventeenth century could conceivably accept it. But the Army of 1659–60 was not the Army of 1647–8. From 1649 onwards its character was slowly changing. The radicals' continuing hope in the Army was a rationalization of their despair. Their expectations had been raised to a peak by the execution of Charles I and the proclamation of the Commonwealth, only to be dashed by the forcible suppression of Levellers, Diggers and Ranters in 1649–51.[1] A second crisis of expectation came in 1653, with the dissolution of the Rump and of Barebone's Parliament. Again disappointment followed. A few Fifth Monarchists were driven into greater militancy, since the only hope for their sort of revolution lay in a personal intervention by Jesus Christ. The rest seem to have continued to pin their hopes on a new change of heart in the Army which had once been God's instrument.

Meanwhile radical regiments were purged or sent to Ireland. Just as successive Elizabethan Archbishops used Puritans to evangelize the dark corners of the North, so radical officers like Ludlow and Fleetwood were sent to Ireland, where their anti-popery could be put to less peaceful but equally profitable uses. The Western Design of 1655 was manned by troops chosen by commanding officers in England: this was presumably another way of getting rid of undesirables. Fighting in Ireland, Scotland, the West Indies and Flanders weeded out the original New Model. Cromwell's captains resigned in 1657. Monck purged and purged again his army in Scotland, Henry Cromwell his army in Ireland. Those who remained are likely to have been those least motivated by radical political or religious ideals.

There was in the long run no social basis of support for a non-radical Army. In 1649 'the people' (in Harrington's sense) and the saints accepted the rule of the generals in preference to Levellers (with a background fear of an Army controlled by junior officers and rank and file). In December 1653 'the people' acquiesced in the Protectorate as against a rule of the saints, who seemed to be reviving extremist policies against a background of London demonstrations in favour of Lilburne. By 1660 most of 'the people' had learnt their lesson: the old constitution

---

[1] See Chapter Two above.

would protect their interests, including those gained during the Revolution, better than an Army, whether led by generals, the godly or a democratic Army Council. The Cause had initially seemed to be that of simple people against the rich and powerful. But, as Winstanley pointed out, tyranny was tyranny whether exercised by men of inherited wealth or by men who had won their way to wealth by fighting.[1] When the next chance for the radicals came in 1659–60 the Army had become a police force protecting the gains of its commanders. Hopes of godly rule had been deferred so many times that there was something feverish in the activity of the militants now that a restoration of monarchy was an increasingly alarming possibility. Divisions in the Army at least offered hope that some generals, for opportunist reasons, might make common cause with the radicals, and so recreate a power base in the Army similar to that which had emerged in 1647. It was a forlorn hope, but no more obviously forlorn than Winstanley dedicating *The Law of Freedom* to Cromwell in 1652, or Harrington *Oceana* in 1656. There was a long-standing protestant tradition of co-operation with ungodly rulers to further God's purposes—Henry VIII, the Duke of Northumberland, the Earls of Leicester and Essex, the Duke of Buckingham, were all at one time the centre of the hopes of the godly. We know that all this bustle in 1659–60 came to nothing, but for drowning men quite a sizeable collection of straws offered themselves. Certainly conservatives were worried.

But the miracle was not to happen. God had abandoned the Army which had abandoned him. 'If your condition would enable you to do it,' one of Hyde's correspondents told him in July 1659, 'it were not difficult to buy the whole Army.'[2] That exaggerates, no doubt; but it would have been an inconceivable remark a decade earlier. Wariston was to say something similar seven months later.[3] 'When those, being instated in power, shall betray the good thing committed to them,' Moses Wall lamented, 'and by that force which we gave them to win us liberty hold us fast in chains, what can poor people do?' It was soldiers who kept Christ from rising.[4] The Army, so long the hope of the Revolution, now became its betrayer, allowing itself to be quietly disbanded. Anti-militarism,

---

[1] Sabine, op. cit., p. 198.
[2] *Clarendon State Papers*, III, p. 526.
[3] Wariston, *Diary*, III, p. 162; cf. p. 81 above.
[4] Letter to Milton, 25 May 1659, quoted in Masson, *Life of Milton*, V, pp. 602–3. See p. 53 above.

rejection of any kind of army rule, became fixed in radical mythology from 1660 to this day.

Wall was writing to Milton, who had repeatedly warned the rulers and people of the Commonwealth against the danger of degeneration, from his sonnets to Fairfax ('avarice and rapine'), Vane and Cromwell to *The Ready and Easy Way to Establish a Free Commonwealth* of 1660. So, we have seen, did many others—Levellers, Winstanley, Coppin, Fifth Monarchists, Hugh Peter, Vane, Erbery, Sedgwick, Quakers, Owen. So did the Socinian MP John Fry, John Cook, William Dell, John Goodwin, Henry Purnell, George Wither.[1] Wariston differed in warning himself.[2]

In 1649 Levellers had used the phrase 'ambition and avarice' about the generals.[3] For Milton, but not only for him, it came to be almost a technical term to describe the besetting sins of rulers and people in the 1650s. It was used by Ludlow, Spittlehouse, Erbery and Sedgwick.[4] Henry Oldenburg, writing to John Beale in September 1660, asked 'What is it that cuts nations and men asunder but ambition, mastery of wit and avarice?' This resulted, he stated, from looking for heaven in this world only. Hence 'the extreme necessity of plucking up above all that atheism so deeply rooted in the spirits of the ruling men of the world. We must establish the divine origin and truth of the Bible, its account of the creation, Fall and the Mosaic Law.' We must establish Christianity as against a religion of 'right reason'. Oldenburg was particularly concerned about Mahometanism and unorthodox accounts of the early history of Christianity.[5] Henry Stubbe, who was to write on precisely these subjects, stressed Mahomet's freedom from 'ambition and avarice'.[6]

I suspect that use of the linked words comes into prominence in the 1650s. Under the Commonwealth government was more public and

---

[1] See pp. 56, 100–1, 139–40, 150, 158–9, 262. Cook, *Redintegratio Amoris*, p. 71; *MER*, pp. 189–97; *CPW*, VII, p. 61; Woolrych, *Commonwealth to Protectorate*, pp. 132–3; cf. p. 51; Wither, *Vox Pacifica* (1645), p. 196 (*Miscellaneous Works*, II); *Prosopopeia Britannica* (1648), pp. 54–69 (*Miscellaneous Works*, IV); *The Dark Lantern* (1653), pp. 20–1, 28–9 (*Miscellaneous Works*, III); *Westrow Revived* (1653), pp. 69–70 (*Miscellaneous Works*, III); *Vaticinium Causuale* (1655), pp. 12–13 (*Miscellaneous Works*, I); *A Triple Paradox* (1661), p. 63 (*Miscellaneous Works*, II); *Three Private Meditations* (1666), p. 36 (*Miscellaneous Works*, IV); *Ecchoes from the Sixth Trumpet* (1666), p. 102 (*Miscellaneous Works*, VI).

[2] See pp. 82–3 above.

[3] *The Levellers (Falsly so called) Vindicated*, in *Freedom in Arms: A Selection of Leveller Writings*, ed. A. L. Morton (1975), p. 312; cf. p. 243.

[4] See pp. 93–4, 111 above; *MER*, pp. 194–5; Ludlow, *A Voyce from the Watchtower*, pp. 115–16.

[5] Oldenburg, *Correspondence*, I, p. 385; cf. p. 263 above.

[6] See p. 262 above.

those who observed the activities of their governors had higher expectations. 'Good commonwealthsmen' were expected to be less corrupt as well as more efficient than their predecessors; some expected them to be more godly and therefore more virtuous. Many fees and perquisites were abolished in favour of regular salaries, sale of some offices was prohibited. Vane made significant reforms in the Navy Office, which Samuel Pepys was to inherit.[1]

Avarice and ambition were not unknown in the country's governors before the interregnum: Cecil, the Howards, Buckingham and Wentworth were avaricious and ambitious on a scale that put Rump politicians and Major-Generals to shame. But now standards of judgement were different. Before 1640 governors came to office either because they were well-born, or through the special favour of the King and his favourites. There were complaints of the excessive greed of 'low-born' councillors, back to Thomas Cromwell and further. But, for them, all depended on the King's bounty, and the King was not to be criticized. When there was no fountain of honour, the quest for self-enrichment was exposed in all its nakedness. In this as in so much else, 1660 saw no full reversion to 1640. Greater Parliamentary control after the Restoration led to continuing criticism of 'avarice and ambition'. So much of a cliché had the phrase become that the poet Thomas Traherne, in a book which he prepared for publication just before his death in 1674, made a paradox of it. 'It is the glory of man that his avarice is insatiable and his ambition infinite'; 'avarice and ambition' are not 'evil in their root and fountain'; they create the dissatisfaction which leads man to God.[2]

The restoration then came about, in Milton's view, because of the avarice and ambition of the revolutionary leaders, because of lack of virtue and civic morale among the body of the people, and because of divisions among the godly themselves. 'Every faction hath the plea of God's Cause,' Milton wrote in the *Ready and Easy Way*.[3] Regicides complained bitterly of lack of unity among the Parliamentarians; some

---

[1] Aylmer, *The State's Servants*, pp. 145–7. Cf. pp. 93–4 above.
[2] Traherne, *Christian Ethicks*, pp. 65, 190, 283; contrast the more conventional use of the cliché on p. 235. (I quote from the 1962 reprint, entitled *The Way to Blessedness*, ed. M. Bottrall). Traherne, interestingly enough, disapproved of sale of offices (ibid., p. 109). Defoe gave the phrase to one of his pirates (*A General History of the Pyrates*, 1724, ed. M. Schonhorn, 1972, II, p. 390). Philip Greven noted in the later eighteenth century 'the constant linkage in [John] Adams's writings of avarice and ambition', and that they had been joined earlier by Benjamin Franklin (Greven, *The Protestant Temperament: Patterns of Child-Rearing, Religious Experience and the Self in Early America*, 1977, p. 253).
[3] *CPW*, VII, p. 380.

felt that they had been sold or victimized by their former colleagues.[1]

But contemporaries were also aware of the social causes of the restoration, none more than Sedgwick.[2] Most commentators saw only two alternative possibilities in 1660: the King or the 'bloody Anabaptists'. 'The old spirit of the gentry' was 'brought to play again' to suppress 'the growing light of the people by God' by an 'earthly, lordly rule'.[3] In July 1659 a Puritan anticipated peace and quiet 'unless a conquest be made by Quakers, who can never last a month in settlement, or by Charles Stuart', which he also thought improbable.[4] In August Sir George Booth took up arms lest a 'mean and schismatical party' should 'depress the nobility and understanding commons'.[5] Rumbold warned Hyde on 25 September that the government might fall to the Anabaptists, which 'gives great apprehensions' to big landowners.[6] Failing a restoration of the King, Mordaunt in November saw the alternatives as a Commonwealth with Presbyterian support, or the extermination of the nobility and gentry.[7] 'Can you at once suppress the sectaries and keep out the King?' asked *A Coffin for the Good Old Cause*.[8] W. C.'s *A Discourse for a King and a Parliament* (1660) argued that in order to set up a free commonwealth it would be necessary to reduce the gentry 'to the condition of the vulgar'. Then London would overawe the whole country. But, he said, no one can or dare resist the rule of the gentry.[9] Venner's *A Door of Hope* in 1661 did in fact denounce 'the old, bloody, popish, wicked gentry of the nation.'[10]

All this helps to explain the social anxieties which Newcome, Martindale, Baxter and others felt.[11] Clarendon saw the crucial moment as coming in February 1660 when control of the militia passed from 'persons of no degree or quality' to the nobility and principal gentry.[12] Similarly

---

[1] See *A Complete Collection* (of regicides' speeches), pp. 45, 55, 84–5, 87.
[2] See pp. 110–11, 113, 115–16 above: the restoration put servants and peasants back in their place.
[3] [Anon.], *The Cause of God and of these Nations*, quoted by Woolrych, Introduction to *CPW*; VII, p. 22. Cf. pp. 60–1 above.
[4] *Thurloe State Papers*, VII, p. 704.
[5] *Tracts relating to the Civil War in Cheshire, 1641–59*, ed. J. A. Atkinson (Chetham Soc., New Series, 65, 1909).
[6] Guizot, *Richard Cromwell*, I, p. 186.
[7] Carte, *Original Letters and Papers*, II, p. 230.
[8] Samuel Butler, *Posthumous Works* (6th edn, 1754), p. 300. The attribution to Butler of this tract is almost certainly wrong.
[9] Op. cit., pp. 4–6.
[10] See p. 60 above.
[11] See Chapter Seven above.
[12] Clarendon, *The History of the Rebellion*, ed. W. D. Macray (Oxford UP, 1888), VI, p. 176.

Pepys on 18 April wrote that 'either the fanatics must now be undone, or the gentry and citizens ... and clergy must fall in spite of *their* militia and army.'[1] Fuller, who thought that violence had 'stood ready to invade our property, heresies and schisms to oppress religion', observed that the Convention Parliament of 1660 was composed of 'persons (blessed be God) of the primest quality in the nation'.[2]

Traditionally the militia, officered by the gentry, with yeomen as rank and file, was the natural rulers' 'fortress of liberty', to quote a phrase used in 1646.[3] The militia had been subordinated to the Army in a series of stages, from 1650 to the Major-Generals. After Parliament had rejected the latter in 1656, the natural rulers slowly recovered their control over local government. Professor Pocock suggests that the Parliamentary classes saw in the militia their ultimate guarantee of power. 'The fact that they were well able to draw the connection between proprietorship and the control of the sword probably did more than anything else to preserve Harringtonian doctrine.'[4] The struggle for the militia, as yet uncharted by historians, became intense in 1659. The militia was not yet a force which could be set up against the Army unless the latter suffered internal disintegration; but that did not seem impossible. Henry Stubbe recognized the importance of the issue, and put forward a scheme for restricting the bearing of arms, whether in the Army or in the militia, to reliable adherents of the Parliamentarian Cause.[5]

Richard Cromwell's Parliament had insisted on its control over the militia.[6] Throughout 1659 and the early months of 1660 correspondents of the exiled court emphasized that the militia was the key to a restoration.[7] In June 1659 the restored Rump started reorganizing the militia as a counterpoise to the Army.[8] But Booth's rising in August, and the rallying of radicals to oppose it, reversed the trend towards restoration of gentry control. After the Army takeover in October, Mordaunt reported that 'Fleetwood arms all the Anabaptists'; he feared

---

[1] My italics.
[2] T. Fuller, *Mixt Contemplations in Better Times* (1660), in *Good Thoughts in Bad Times* (1830), pp. 331, 248.
[3] *Thurloe State Papers*, I, p. 54; cf. Burton, *Parliamentary Diary*, III, p. 169, IV, pp. 33, 474. See also p. 192 above.
[4] Pocock, op. cit., p. 131.
[5] See pp. 257–8 above; cf. John Sadler, *The Rights of the Kingdom* (1649), p. 76, and Burton, *Parliamentary Diary*, IV, p. 474.
[6] Burton, op. cit., III, pp. 450–93..
[7] Carte, *Original Letters and Papers*, II, pp. 310, 313 and *passim*.
[8] Guizot, *Richard Cromwell*, I, pp. 184, 199, 432.

that 'an Anabaptist militia' would overawe the country.[1] We saw earlier how active Quakers were as commissioners for the militia;[2] Mordaunt did not distinguish between them and Anabaptists. Only when the Rump came back in December could the Common Council of London set about establishing the City's militia under royalist officers.[3] In February Monck accepted the situation and granted the City the choice of its own militia.[4] There were 'murmurings' among the soldiers at this development, which clearly presaged the Army's downfall.[5] But by now the Army was so divided and scattered that resistance was impossible to organize.[6]

Throughout the late 1650s the natural rulers felt panic fear of any revival of Leveller or Army radicalism. The Nayler Debates in 1656 sufficiently reveal this, and the forces of law and order then won a significant victory. But in 1659–60 there was even more genuine cause for alarm. The Army itself seemed to be disintegrating. Most ominous of all was the reappearance of Agitators. Men recalled vividly the summer days of 1647 when Agitators had taken the initiative in the Army's mutiny, from the ejection of non-compliant commanders to the seizure of the King by Cornet Joyce and his 500 in June—the first blunt demonstration that the King's person was not sacrosanct. The cry 'Ye can create new officers'[7] was not forgotten. Henry Neville in 1681 recalled how Agitators in 1647 'did ... necessitate their officers to join with them', and afterwards drove away the Parliament too. Although 'the Army was afterwards cheated by their general', the example showed 'how easily an army of natives is to be deluded with the name of liberty, and brought to pull down anything which their ring-leaders tell them tends to enslaving their country'.[8]

Agitators and rumours of Agitators in the Army in 1659 caused great alarm. Between May 1649 and April 1659 the only mention of Agitators that I have come across was in June 1653, when a remonstrance presented

---

[1] *Letter Book of John Viscount Mordaunt*, ed. M. Coate (Camden Soc., 3rd Series, LXIX, 1945), pp. 44, 97; cf. *Clarke Papers*, IV, pp. 91–3, 113.
[2] See pp. 134–5 above; Gwynn Williams, 'The Quakers of Merioneth during the Seventeenth Century, Part I', *Journal of the Merioneth Historical and Record Soc.*, VIII (1978), p. 133.
[3] *Clarendon State Papers*, III, p. 634; Guizot, *Richard Cromwell*, II, p. 323.
[4] *Clarendon State Papers*, III, p. 689; cf. pp. 681–2, and Guizot, *Richard Cromwell*, II, pp. 359, 365, 382; Burton, *Parliamentary Diary*, III, pp. 403–596, IV, pp. 1–148.
[5] Guizot, op. cit., II, p. 383.
[6] Ibid., II, pp. 426–7.
[7] [Anon.], *A Call to all the Souldiers* (October, 1647), p. 7.
[8] Robbins, op. cit., pp. 179–80.

to Cromwell and the Council of Officers was said in one report to be 'by the Agitators of the Army'.[1] Godfrey Davies misled historians by stating categorically that 'the occasional rumours' in 1659–60 that the rank and file 'had chosen agitators as in 1647 were false'.[2] In fact Agitators were meeting at the Nag's Head tavern as early as April 1659.[3] An address to Fleetwood signed by 680 inferior officers and soldiers of what had formerly been Pride's regiment caused considerable excitement in Parliament in the same month.[4] In May 'Agitators in the Army' were calling for new commanders:[5] 'the soldiers know their strength', it was reported.[6] In September Parliament was again concerned about unauthorized activities of common soldiers.[7] 'The soldiers are independent of their officers,' Mordaunt wrote to the King on 16 January 1660; 'an Agitator will do more in an hour than all the officers in a day.'[8] 'Under-officers and soldiers would not stand by their superiors,' Wariston observed in December 1659.[9] Arise Evans confirmed that 'the under-officers and Agitators doth all.'[10] In February 1660 four Agitators were said to have been appointed from each troop in Colonel Rich's regiment: he was accused of introducing 'men of dangerous principles, as Quakers and the like', and of 'discountenancing old and faithful soldiers and preferring the Agitators'.[11] In the same month there were mutinies in London among the infantry, though the cavalry were not involved.[12] The Council of State issued a proclamation against Agitators in the Army on 24 March: £10 reward was offered for information against them.[13] There were Agitators in York in April, two of whose names we know;[14] and there were 'plots among some Agitators'.[15] At about the same time Hartlib

---

[1] Woolrych, *Commonwealth to Protectorate*, p. 141.
[2] G. Davies, *The Restoration of Charles II, 1658–1660* (San Marino, 1955).
[3] *Calendar of Clarendon State Papers*, ed. F. J. Routledge, IV, *1657–1660* (Oxford UP, 1932), pp. 191–3.
[4] Burton, *Parliamentary Diary*, IV, pp. 388, 451, 456–9.
[5] *Calendar of Clarendon State Papers*, IV, p. 210.
[6] Guizot, *Richard Cromwell*, I, p. 184.
[7] *Commons' Journals*, VII, p. 734.
[8] *Clarendon State Papers*, III, pp. 651–2.
[9] Wariston, *Diary*, III, p. 160.
[10] Arise Evans, *A Rule from Heaven: Or Wholesome Counsell to A Distracted State, Wherein is Discovered, The onely Way for settling the Good Old Cause* (1659), p. 50.
[11] HMC, *Leybourne-Popham MSS*, p. 168.
[12] *Diurnal of Thomas Rugge*, ed. W. L. Sachse, pp. 34–5.
[13] *Tudor and Stuart Proclamations*, I, No. 3174; *Clarendon State Papers*, III, p. 715; Rugge, *Diurnal*, p. 66.
[14] *Leybourne-Popham MSS*, p. 176.
[15] *Calendar of Clarendon State Papers*, IV, p. 640; Rugge, *Diurnal*, p. 74.

told Boyle that 'the common soldiers ... have chosen to themselves new Agitators.'[1]

By contrast with 1647 there was never any organized representation of the rank and file (except perhaps in Rich's regiment), no Agitator pamphlets. But evidence for the existence of Agitators is not just a matter of gossip among foreign envoys and royalist agents: most of the above reports come from English and Parliamentarian sources. These reports may have exaggerated, though it is equally possible that some activity went unrecorded. But for our purposes what men thought was happening is as important as what actually happened. The reappearance of Agitators seemed to hold out the possibility that the Army might after all serve God's Cause, or at least the Cause of the people. But Harrington's 'beast that hath a great belly' could survive only so long as the taxpayers could be coerced into paying for it.[2] None of the three Parliaments of the Protectorate voted adequate taxes; and at the first opportunity the taxpayers went on strike in 1659–60, as they had done twenty years earlier.

The fear in 1659–60 was that a desperate or a radicalized Army, rather than submit to the financial control of City and Parliament, might turn to a policy of confiscations and sales of land. After 1649 the Commonwealth had been financed very largely by sales of church, crown and royalist lands. In *The Poor Mans Advocate* (1649) Peter Chamberlen had urged that crown and church lands should be used to create public employment and end taxation. Lilburne, Hugh Peter, Erbery, Fox, Howgil and other Quakers took up the idea.[3] Robert Purnell, also in 1649, suggested using confiscated lands to abolish the excise and assessment. 'They forced you to raise an Army, let their estates pay for the Army,' he argued.[4] The decimation tax of 1655 was a half-hearted and unsuccessful attempt to do just that.[5] The Fifth Monarchist rebels of 1657 promised to abolish taxation. They did not say how, but the men of property could guess. It was a long-standing accusation that the real objective of the saints was to seize the property of the ungodly.[6] Harrington had suggested that a standing army would have to be maintained by confiscating the land of those 'remaining unconformable'.[7] Such confiscations were discussed

---

[1] R. Boyle, *Works* (1744), V, p. 287. Cf. Butler, *Hudibras*, Part III, canto ii, l. 272.
[2] Pocock, op. cit., p. 165; see pp. 104–5, 202 above.
[3] See pp. 87–8, 130, 155 above.
[4] Purnell, *Good Tydings for Sinners*, pp. 73–5.
[5] Cf. Sedgwick, p. 107 above.
[6] See pp. 64–5, 221–2 above.   [7] Pocock, op. cit., p. 347.

after the defeat of Booth's rising in 1659.[1] If we compare the English with the French, Russian and Chinese Revolutions we are struck by the absence of a revolution in landownership in the first (if we leave Ireland out of account). This helps to explain the ease with which the restoration of 1660 was achieved.

The reappearance of Agitators in the Army must have reinforced the determination of the natural rulers henceforward to keep control of military force in their own hands, lest there should be a revival of social radicalism.[2] The only way to do this in 1660 seemed to be by restoring a prince to head the Commonwealth. The Army was peacefully disbanded, paid off by loans from the City, with the gentry-controlled militia on guard. The Militia Act of 1661 put the militia under the King, but his control was to be exercised through lords-lieutenant. In 1663 even this was modified, and to the chagrin of the court the gentry's control over the militia was reasserted.[3] The unreliability of the militia in 1685 was one of the danger signals which prompted James II to build up an army. In 1688 the militia deserted him *en masse*. The Bill of Rights insisted on the right of protestant gentlemen to bear arms.[4]

2 The Saints and 'the People'

Milton believed in 1644 that Moses's wish had been fulfilled: 'all the Lord's people are become prophets.'[5] But the Moses of the English Revolution admitted sadly in December 1648 that 'we are not all saints.'[6] The relationship between saints and 'people' posed problems which we have often encountered in this book. Thomas Goodwin in 1639 had argued that 'the saints of God' would come to be recognized as 'the best commonwealthsmen'.[7] *A Door of Hope* in 1661 asserted that 'whatsoever can be named of a common or public good we mean by the Kingdom of Christ'.[8] But the question asked in 1649, 'How can the kingdom be the

---

[1] Covell, quoted on p. 41 above; cf. pp. 61–2 above.
[2] Cf. Pocock, quoted on p. 202 above.
[3] Lois G. Schwoerer, *'No Standing Armies!': The Anti-Army Mythology in Seventeenth-Century England* (Johns Hopkins UP, 1974), p. 89. Cf. R. G., quoted on p. 192 above.
[4] J. H. Plumb, *The Growth of Political Stability in England, 1675–1725* (1967), pp. 17, 20–1, 64.
[5] *CPW*, II, pp. 555–6.
[6] T. Spencer, 'The History of an Unfortunate Lady', *Harvard Studies and Notes in Philology and Literature*, XX (1938), p. 56. For Cromwell as Moses see pp. 189–90 above.
[7] See p. 180 above.
[8] See p. 65 above.

saints' when the ungodly are electors and elected to govern?'[1] was never satisfactorily answered, though *A Standard Set Up* tried.[2] Christopher Feake spoke of 'the people (I mean the faithful among them).'[3] Fifth Monarchism at least provided a justification for rule by an oligarchy.

Sedgwick had seen the Army as 'truly the people'.[4] John Spittlehouse in 1653 associated the saints and the Army: 'the real members of this commonwealth are included in the congregational churches and their well-wishers.'[5] In 1659 the claim was revived that 'the Army are the people in an active body', the 'principal body of the people, in whom the sovereignty doth at present reside', rather than in 'the people's representatives in Parliament'.[6]

There was a real problem here. The people, wrote the government propagandist John Hall in 1653, cannot be permitted 'a choice of their own governors, they being so divided and discomposed as for the present they are'.[7] Throughout the 1650s the search went on to find an electorate which would vote for an Army-dominated republic, or to find a definable group of adherents to the Good Old Cause, or constitutional devices which would safeguard essential freedoms against 'the people'. Levellers, Thomas Scott, John Jones, John Cook, Ludlow, Vane, Byllynge, Harrington, Stubbe, Milton, Baxter and many others took part in it.[8] No solution was found: an illiterate, uneducated people would no more vote for a sophisticated commonwealth of virtue than the natural rulers would. Yet an oligarchical commonwealth could be maintained only by an Army whose virtue could not be relied on.[9]

One advantage of Harrington's theory was the assumption that men of property will support a commonwealth not because they are virtuous but out of self-interest. Hobbes and the *de facto* theorists had earlier argued that men follow their own interests, in so far as they understand them; Harrington drew specific social conclusions with the important proviso that 'robbers and Levellers' are excluded from 'the people'.

---

[1] *Certain Queries Presented by many Christian People*, quoted in Woodhouse, op. cit., p. 246.
[2] See pp. 63–5 above.
[3] Feake, *A Beam of Light*, p. 51.
[4] See pp. 104–5 above. For other examples, see Woolrych, *Commonwealth to Protectorate*, pp. 131–2, and references there cited.
[5] Spittlehouse, *The Army Vindicated* (1653), pp. 2–3.
[6] [Anon.], *The Armies Vindication of this Last Change* (1659), pp. 3–9.
[7] Hall, *Sedition Scourg'd*, pp. 3, 8, quoted by Woolrych, *Commonwealth to Protectorate*, pp. 260–1.
[8] See pp. 76–7, 137 above; Baxter, *A Holy Commonwealth*, *passim*, and Lamont, *Richard Baxter and the Millennium*, pp. 183, 187.
[9] Cf. Stella Revard, quoted on p. 314 below.

Later revolutionary theorists were to substitute the rule of a minority through membership of a political party. This avoided one problem of the 1650s—knowing who the saints were; but it did not avoid another, the omnipresence of hypocrites and bandwagon jumpers. From Roger Williams, Coppe and Winstanley through Erbery, Sedgwick, Burrough and Fox to Milton and Bunyan, the real radicals regarded hypocrisy as the unpardonable sin. Disillusioned conservatives like Baxter and Henry found 'a face of godliness' acceptable as the price for suppressing upper- and lower-class vices and irreligion.[1]

'The people' turned against the Army before the saints had abandoned hope in it. For this there were many reasons. Worst of all was the Army's burdensome and unprecedented cost in taxation and free quarter. Secondly, it imposed a degree of godliness and a degree of toleration. It interfered with the running of local government by the natural rulers, and with the maintenance of traditional standards of deference. Even those who wanted godliness and toleration did not want to pay for them at the rates demanded; and of course there was disagreement on how much godliness, how much toleration. Barebone's Parliament mirrored the disagreements even among more radical Parliamentarians. As Baxter became reconciled to the Protectorate because it imposed godliness, so Quakers became increasingly hostile; as Quaker hopes rose in 1659, so Baxter and his like could see no alternative to a restoration, even if bishops came back too.

3   Folds for Scattered Sheep

The fluid society did not survive the Army. The natural rulers resumed their local hegemony. Parliament legislated against nonconformists and against mobility.[2] Religious radicals could survive only by organizing in congregations. This completed a process already under way. Once the Army had ceased to be the focus of unity, only the congregations united God's scattered people: and these in the long run could survive only by linking into sects. Yet forming sects also proved divisive: it united some

---

[1] See pp. 43–5, 96–7, 114, 158–9, 163 above. For Roger Williams see p. 183 above. Cf. Lamont, *Richard Baxter and the Millennium*, pp. 245, 260.

[2] P. Clark, 'Migration in England during the Late Seventeenth and Early Eighteenth Centuries', *P. and P.*, 83 (1979), esp. pp. 84–90.

by excluding others. Presbyterians and many Independents regarded themselves as part of the national church, reluctantly forced into sectarianism after 1660. But once they had been spewed out, the dissenting churches had to organize and discipline their members in order to survive in the society they had failed to transform.[1] It must have led to an enormous diversion of labour and energy on the part of their leaders. Excommunication appears to be one of the main activities of early Baptists, and conduct came to matter no less than doctrine, the external image no less than the inner state.

All the sects ultimately came to enforce the morality appropriate to a rapidly developing capitalist society. 'Debt ... sounds terribly,' wrote Henry Newcome. 'It is an appearance of injustice and of reproach, especially to religion.'[2] Bunyan's church at Bedford was very severe against those who could not pay their debts: Bunyan himself advised deacons to use poor relief to encourage industry and discourage idleness.[3] Such attitudes, and the sects' heavy emphasis on Bible-reading and therefore on literacy, confirm that they had little appeal for the very poorest classes in the community.

The Quakers, who had continued longest to rely on Army support, got the least toleration after 1660. Before winning toleration they had adapted themselves to the new society like other sects. The Quaker Stephen Crisp 'being called of God and his people to take the care of the poor', exhorted and reproved any that were slothful and encouraged those that were diligent when relieving their necessities.[4] To adapt Lenin's metaphor, the dissenting churches became schools of capitalism—inculcating the virtues of hard work, responsibility, thrift; deploring indebtedness, extravagance and bankruptcy. The fluid society of the 1640s and 1650s had given these voluntary societies the chance to establish themselves side by side with traditional geographical communities. But they proved to be endlessly quarrelsome and fissiparous because of the inherently anarchical tendency of the really radical ideology. Once the shield of the Army had gone, the dissidence of

---

[1] I tried to argue this in *Society and Puritanism in pre-Revolutionary England*, Chapters XIV and XV, and in *WTUD*, pp. 373–8. I hope readers will refer to these, especially if they find my shorthand remarks here unconvincing.

[2] Ed. Heywood, *Diary*, p. 150; cf. p. 211 above.

[3] *The Minutes of the First Independent Church (now Bunyan Meeting) at Bedford, 1656–1766*, ed. H. G. Tibbutt (Bedfordshire Historical Record Soc. publications, 55, 1976), pp. 76, 83, 182; Bunyan, *Works*, II, pp. 582–3, III, pp. 628–33.

[4] Barbour and Roberts, op. cit., p. 205; cf. R. B. Schlatter, *The Social Ideas of Religious Leaders, 1660–1688* (Oxford UP, 1940), Part II, Chapters 3 and 4 and pp. 233, 242–3.

dissent prevailed. Throughout the 1650s we come across Penington's imagery of the scattered sheep.[1]

When religious toleration came, it was not because the persecutors had become kinder and nicer, though no doubt some of them had. It was because the persecuted, even Quakers, had become more domesticated to capitalist society; and in the process had become assets too valuable to be thrown away. Quakers survived thanks to the peace principle and their adaptation to the world around them. Muggletonians survived too: they were also pacifists. Levellers, Diggers, Ranters and Fifth Monarchists did not survive. None of them formed a sect, none of them were absolute pacifists.[2] Erbery, we recall, noted that there were losses as well as gains in the organization which the sects adopted in order to survive.

I cannot suppress a certain sympathy for Erbery's feeling that all attempts to organize a church in the wilderness would merely mean a new apostasy. Rejection of all churches, by early Quaker dissidents and Milton as well as by Erbery, seems arrogant and anarchic. Yet if we contemplate the history of English nonconformity in the centuries after Erbery's death, his strictures of self-righteousness and pettiness are not entirely without foundation. If one's object is to attain worldly ends, then there is everything to be said for union among like-minded men and women. If the object is to save one's soul, it seems less obvious. The wholly informal organization of the Muggletonians perhaps came nearest to Erbery's ideal. They had no ministry, no organized worship, minimal discipline. But they remained a tiny, non-proselytizing group. Of the larger sects, the Quakers held out longest against organization, under the harmless name of the Society of Friends—not a church. Organization came too late or too early: it was part of their defeat. Perrot and others thought that with it came apostasy. The internal consensus of the radical congregations, based on Bible-reading, tended to exclude the illiterate. Winstanley, like the disowned John Pennyman, was buried as a Quaker;[3] but there is no evidence that he was ever an active member of the Society. Penington became a Quaker, with disastrous consequences for his prose style. The wilderness remained a wilderness, and Erbery could see no point in pretending it was anything else.

The secularization of politics during the revolutionary decades,

---

[1] See pp. 121–6 above. Cf. Clarkson, *The Lost sheep*, and Martha Simmons, *A Lamentation for the Lost Sheep Of the House of Israel* (1656).
[2] The Diggers practised non-resistance, but Winstanley was not a pacifist. For Erbery see p. 92 above.
[3] Higgins, 'The Apostatized Apostle, John Pennyman', p. 18.

emphasized by Margaret Judson, Felix Raab and Olivier Lutaud,[1] was reinforced when the crucial millenarian dates of the early 1650s and 1666 passed without event. The idea that England was the chosen nation lost all but a residual religious flavouring: the concept of progress was not so far ahead. Whether or not Oliver Cromwell saw himself as a saint ruling, he was the last who could aspire to that role in England, because the last who had an army to enforce his rule. Dr Morrill has suggested that Cromwell really did refuse the crown in 1657 because no visible Providence of God pointed in that direction.[2] The gulf between secular supporters of the Good Old Cause and millenarians became obvious in 1659, when Neville parted company with Vane, and Wariston was shocked that the arguments for and against a Senate were discussed 'without Scripture'.[3] One of the casualties of the revolutionary decades was providential history. When Providence ordained both 1649 and 1660, then Hobbist and Harringtonian theories of political obligation made better sense than arguments drawn either from divine right or from the immediate Providence of God. *De facto* theories bore the same relation to a providentialist interpretation of history as secular millenarianism did to the rule of the saints. The secular content of many Puritan doctrines—the calling, the work ethic, sabbatarianism—was taken over, again with a minimum of religious content.[4] Locke's was a philosophy of secularized, respectable Puritanism. Winstanley and Stubbe, on the other hand, pointed the way to a radical deism.[5]

After the restoration the saints were excluded from politics and higher education by the Clarendon Code. They settled down as a second-class people, folding themselves into sheep-pens, setting up their own educational institutions. Yet the established church remained necessary in the eyes of its defenders, perhaps even more necessary than before 1640. A church with no High Commission could not threaten the authority of the gentry, who had been badly scared by the attack on tithes and on social subordination. The doctrinal and ceremonial excesses of Laudianism were quietly dropped: preaching and Sabbath observance had episcopal approval. So there were no obstacles to the re-formation of

---

[1] M. A. Judson, *The Crisis of the Constitution* (Rutgers UP, 1949), pp. 423, 433; Raab, *The English Face of Machiavelli*, pp. 234–8, 261–3; O. Lutaud, *Socialisme et Christianisme sous Cromwell* (Paris, 1976), p. 336.
[2] J. Morrill, 'King Oliver?' in *Cromwelliana* (1981–2), pp. 20–5.
[3] Wariston, *Diary*, III, pp. 120–1; cf. ibid., III, p. 71 and p. 81 above.
[4] See my *Society and Puritanism*, pp. 490–3.
[5] See p. 275 above; *The Religion of Gerrard Winstanley*, pp. 55–7.

the alliance between gentry and established church, whose power so impressed Sedgwick and Stubbe.[1] 'If there was not a minister in every parish,' Robert South told the lawyers of Lincoln's Inn just before the restoration, 'you would quickly find cause to increase the number of constables.'[2] Though many towns were lost to nonconformity or irreligion, the alliance of parson and squire resumed its domination of the countryside. The Clarendon Code was the work of the gentry in the House of Commons rather than of the bishops. The ecclesiastical censorship continued to do an invaluable job in the three decades after 1660.

Milton and Winstanley had denounced the role of the priesthood in deceiving the people, and the point was made by Fox and most radicals. Though sin survived the Ranters who had abolished it, and returned even in the post-restoration Quaker theology of Robert Barclay (dedicated to Charles II), anticlericalism did not die with the return of the episcopal church. Not only Stubbe and Neville, but eighteenth-century radicals like Trenchard and Thomas Gordon were still obsessed with the power of priests to instil deference into the minds of their uneducated hearers.[3]

4   Other Losers

Finally, a difficult question. This book deals with some members of the articulate minority who supported the Cause. What of the inarticulate majority? The sad answer is, of course, that we do not know. We know in general very little about the lives of ordinary men and women in the seventeenth century. Demobilized New Model Army men in 1660 went back to their former occupations, or found new ones if they were lucky. Some would no doubt re-enlist in the army, the navy or the mercantile marine. Others emigrated—to Europe, to North America, to the West Indies. Two historians drew a thought-provoking picture of Henry Morgan's pirate band closing in for the brutal sack of Panama in 1671 'in

---

[1] See pp. 113, 256–7, 271–2 above.
[2] In Irène Simon, *Three Restoration Divines*, II, p. 60. It was not long since South had been writing poems celebrating Oliver Cromwell, in the company of John Locke (*Musarum Oxoniensium*, 1654, pp. 40, 45, 94–5).
[3] Cf. pp. 204, 256 above, and B. Bailyn, *Ideological Origins of the American Revolution* (Harvard UP, 1967), pp. 35–54. Nayler's later thinking also stressed sin.

the faded red coats of the New Model Army'.[1] By 1660, as we have seen, few of the rank and file of this Army were likely to be ideologically motivated. Those for whom the Cause had once seemed to offer help to simple people against the rich and powerful no doubt relapsed into sullenly passive hostility to the restored government: historians are just becoming aware of the massive evidence for this hostility recorded in State Papers and local archives.[2]

It is difficult to generalize about the effects of the great persecution of 1660–88.[3] Dissenting clergymen lost their livings after the restoration, without compensation. A few, like Ralph Josselin, managed to hold on to their livings without abandoning too many principles too quickly.[4] Others were maintained precariously by voluntary contributions from their former congregations, or by the patronage of a wealthy individual. Laymen who would not conform to the national church were purged from the government of corporations—and this purge was effective because it was entrusted to local gentry, who had none of the loyalty to urban independence which had often protected royalists in the 1640s and 1650s. Old scores were settled at the expense of urban supporters of Parliament. A series of penal statutes was passed against dissenters, though the rigour with which they were enforced depended on local circumstances. There is much heartening evidence of town officials and other neighbours protecting dissenters by warning them of raids, by refusing to buy distrained goods, etc. But these were exceptions to the sufferings many dissenters—especially Quakers—had to endure during the great persecution. Perhaps the arbitrariness and irrationality of the incidence of persecution was one of its main hardships. Some dissenters

---

[1] P. K. Kemp and C. Lloyd, *The Brethren of the Coast* (1960), p. 17.

[2] Some evidence for this statement will be found in *WTUD*, pp. 354–5, and references there cited; my 'Republicanism After the Restoration', *New Left Review*, May 1960, pp. 46–8; Roger L'Estrange, *Considerations and Proposals in Order to the Regulation of the Press* (1663), esp. pp. 1–7, 24–31; *Calendar of Clarendon State Papers*, V, pp. 255, 266, 618; Ludlow, *A Voyce from the Watchtower*, pp. 285, 302, 315–16; Capp, op. cit., pp. 205–6, 209–11, 220; C. E. Whiting, *Studies in English Puritanism from the Restoration to the Revolution, 1660–1688* (1931), pp. 556–8; H. A. Kaufman, *Conscientious Cavalier* (1962), pp. 193–4; T. Curtis, 'Quarter Sessions Appearances and their Background: A Seventeenth-Century Regional Study', in *Crime in England, 1550–1800*, ed. J. S. Cockburn (1977), pp. 143–5; D. Dymond, *Portsmouth and the Fall of the Puritan Republic* (Portsmouth Papers, 11, 1971), p. 14; K. Lindley, *Fenland Riots and the English Revolution* (1982), p. 234; Howard Hudson, *Cheshire, 1660–1780* (Chester, 1978), p. 2. A forthcoming book by John Walter will produce and analyse a great deal more evidence.

[3] G. R. Cragg, *Puritanism in the Period of the Great Persecution, 1660–1688* (Cambridge UP, 1957), *passim*.

[4] See p. 209 above.

managed to prosper with the support of co-religionists and sympathizers: these are the decades in which the argument came to be accepted that dissenters are economically too valuable to be persecuted out of the country. But others might happen to be ruined. Here too God's justice was sometimes difficult for human understandings to appreciate.

It was more difficult to get round the exclusion of non-Anglicans from the universities. Dissenting academies gave in many ways a better education than Oxford or Cambridge, but they lacked social cachet. Scottish or Dutch universities were the other resort for those who could afford them.

The period after 1660, we may suspect, was for many ordinary people one of unheroic passive opting out from the church they nominally adhered to: Lollards and Familists had practised it long before the defeated of the English Revolution. Durant Hotham in 1652 distinguished between Quakers, who refused to compromise, and Ranters who 'would have said and done as we commanded, and yet have kept their own principle still'.[1] The Muggletonians perfected the Ranter technique for avoiding trouble, and 'raised flight to a moral principle'.[2] But for the rest we just do not know. This section is intended as a reminder of this huge area of ignorance.

---

[1] Fox, *Journal*, I, p. 95; cf. *WTUD*; p. 257.
[2] *The World of the Muggletonians*, p. 142; cf. pp. 43–6, 99–100, 137.

Chapter 10

Conclusion: Milton and the Experience of Defeat

> It seemeth marvellous to me that many mechanics (few able to read, and fewer to write their names), turning soldiers and captains in our wars, should be so soon and so much improved.... I profess, without flouting or flattering, I have much admired with what facility and fluentness, how pertinently and properly they have expressed themselves, in language which they were never born nor bred to, but have industriously acquired by conversing with their betters.... I am so far from thinking ill of them for being bred in so poor trades that I should think better of them for returning unto them again.
>
> Fuller, *Mixt Contemplations on these Times* (1660), pp. 319–21.

1 The Apostasy and the Wilderness

A second conclusion which was borne in on me whilst writing this book was the importance to radicals of the linked concepts of the apostasy, the wilderness and the anointing. Such ideas had no doubt had a long history in the pre-1640 religious underground. Wyclif and the Lollards, followed by nonconformists of the late sixteenth and early seventeenth centuries, attributed the apostasy to the age of Constantine, to the establishment of an endowed state church.[1] This was an argument against the established Church of England and its lord bishops; but it accepted a state church if reformed. Jewell, Foxe and the ecclesiastical establishment, on the other hand, saw Constantine's reign as the age in which true Christianity triumphed.[2] Significant in this respect is the adulation of Charles II as a new Constantine after 1660.[3]

---

[1] *Selections from English Wycliffite Writings*, ed. A. Hudson (Cambridge UP, 1978), p. 184.
[2] *MER*, pp. 84–6.
[3] Carew Reynel, *The Fortunate Change* (1661), pp. 7–8 (unnumbered). I owe this point and this reference to Nicholas Jose of the Australian National University.

Elizabethan Presbyterians and moderate Puritans looked back to the primitive church for their models. But some agreed that purity had not continued long. William Whitaker thought that Antichrist 'began to work in the Apostles' age and so continued still forward in the Fathers' days'.[1] The radical Walter Jones, who refused to conform after 1604, believed that from about AD 110 'the generation of the Apostles being worn out, then the church began to be defiled.'[2] William Bradshaw, another radical, added that there was 'no one Father that wrote since the Apostles' time but have erred in some matters of doctrine.' 'The best Christians that are or ever have been since the Apostles' times may be infected with some parts of antichristianism.'[3]

The freedom of the press in the revolutionary decades allowed such ideas to surface again, and to be pressed further. It was one thing to say that apostasy had *started* in the days of the Apostles: the evidence of the New Testament made that difficult to refute. But it was quite another to say, as Roger Williams was alleged to do, that there had been 'no church, no sacraments, no pastors, no church-officers or ordinance in the world since a few years after the Apostles'.[4] To put apostasy of the whole church back to the time of the Apostles was by implication to reject any form of visible church. It cut across discussions of whether bishops or elders had ruled the primitive church. It had consequences for politics as well as for religion.

The Traskite tailor Hamlet Jackson was said to have believed in the 1620s that 'the light of the law was more fully discovered to him than to any since the Apostles'.[5] Erbery, as we saw, held that there had been apostasy since the Apostles' time: it was only confirmed by Constantine. 'In the apostasy we now are,' Erbery wrote, 'we cannot company with men, no not with saints, in spiritual worship, but we shall commit

[1] Whitaker, *An Answere to a certaine booke written by M. William Reynolds* (Cambridge UP, 1585), pp. 96–7, 140–1, quoted by P. Lake, *Moderate Puritans and the Elizabethan Church* (Cambridge UP, 1982), p. 96.

[2] Quoted by Lake, op. cit., p. 250. The conformist William Chaderton preferred to emphasize the purity of the church *before* AD 110, leaving its later state an open question.

[3] Bradshaw, *A treatise of divine worship* (Amsterdam, 1604), p. 40, quoted by Lake, op. cit., p. 267; Bradshaw, *The unreasonablenesse of the separation* (Dort, 1614), Sig. C–Cv, quoted by Lake, op. cit., p. 273. John Knox perhaps had similar thoughts (P. Collinson, *Godly People: Essays in English Protestantism and Puritanism* (1983), p. 280.

[4] R. Baillie, *Letters and Journals, 1637–1662* (Edinburgh, 1775), II, p. 43. Samuel Butler attributed this view to all 'fanatics', *Prose Observations*, p. 31.

[5] [Anon.], *The History of King-Killers* (1719), pp. 37, 39, quoted by D. S. Katz, *Philo-Semitism and the Readmission of the Jews to England, 1603–1655* (Oxford UP, 1982), p. 21. This pamphlet is not perhaps a very reliable source.

spiritual whoredom with them.' The church was in the wilderness.[1]
Clarkson learnt from Erbery and Sedgwick that there had been no true
church since the Apostles' time: preaching and praying were to cease, a
doctrine shared by John Saltmarsh and which Walwyn, Coppe and the
Muggletonians took over.[2] Penington held that the true church had been
driven into the wilderness from the time of the Apostles: persecution was
for him a sign of apostasy.[3] Burrough, Samuel Fisher, Fox and other
Quakers agreed,[4] and so did Bishop; but he also said that the discipline
which Fox began to impose in the 1660s 'leads into the apostasy'.[5]
Thomas Goodwin, who thought England had become better than any
nation since the Apostles' time, Carew, who believed that the
Parliamentarian Cause was 'the noblest since the apostles' time',[6] and
Wither, for whom Cromwell had made more progress towards God's
kingdom on earth than any 'since Christ ascended',[7]—all of these must be
drawing on a common assumption that the apostasy had started early.
Owen thought it began in the days of the Apostles;[8] so, rather
unexpectedly, did Neville.[9] Finally, Stubbe is as devious and complicated
on this subject as on most others. In public he praised Charles II's
Declaration of Indulgence for following 'the primitive policy of
Constantine'. Privately he wrote that Christianity had been corrupted by
Constantine, and implied that apostasy dated from St. Paul.[10] Stubbe was,
I believe, unique in associating the apostasy with the rise of Islam, which
incorporated early Christian heresies similar to many seventeenth-
century English heresies.[11]

---

[1] Erbery, *Testimony*, p. 100; see pp. 89–95, 99–100, 122–4, 153 above and pp. 297–301 below.
[2] See pp. 89, 99–100 above; Clarkson, *Look about You*, p. 1; Saltmarsh, *Sparkles of Glory*, p. 79; I. F., *John the Divines Divinity* (1649), pp. 14–15. Despite the attribution, this tract is probably by Coppe. It said there was no need of ordinances such as preaching, baptism, supper, church-fellowship, etc. For Muggletonians see pp. 46, 49–50 above.
[3] See pp. 122–3 above. Marvell thought there had been persecution from the time of the Apostles, not by the secular power but by priests (*A Short Historical Essay touching General Councils, Creeds and Impositions in Religion*, in *Complete Works*, ed. A. B. Grosart, 1872–4, I, pp. 94–8).
[4] See pp. 153 above; Fox, *The Lambs Officer*, p. 14; J. Gwynn Williams, 'The Quakers of Merioneth during the Seventeenth Century, Part I', *Journal of the Merioneth Historical and Record Soc.*, VIII (1978), p. 134; S. Fisher, *Baby Baptism meer Babism* (1653), p. 573.
[5] Bishop, *An Epistle of Love*, p. 7.
[6] See pp. 181, 71 above.
[7] Wither, *A Suddain Flash* (1657), p. 16, in *Miscellaneous Works*, II.
[8] Owen, *Works*, XIV, p. 534.
[9] See p. 204 above.
[10] See pp. 260, 263–4, 272–3 above.
[11] The point about Islamic origins is made in N. O. Brown's intriguing 'The Prophetic Tradition' in *Studies in Romanticism*, 21 (1982), pp. 367–86. Brown does not refer to Stubbe.

This idea of the apostasy implies that there is no legitimate church on earth. There are only individual souls, who may help one another but should not combine organizationally. Roger Williams, Walwyn, Winstanley, many Ranters and Seekers, Erbery, Reeve, Colonel Hutchinson, Wither and Milton held some such view.[1] In the wilderness Christianity has nothing to do with the church or churches: all we can do in the apostasy is to wait. The claim to a special apostolic commission in 1642 split the Seeker church of Samuel Blacklock and Richard Blunt.[2] Ten years later God gave such a commission to John Reeve, and so for the Muggletonians the apostasy came to an end.[3]

What was Milton's attitude towards the apostasy? In *Milton and the English Revolution* I perhaps too easily assumed that he believed it dated from Constantine's reign.[4] But it is not as simple as that: this seems to be one of the points on which Milton swayed between Puritan and radical theology, inclining to the latter. He never said in so many words that the apostasy had started in or just after the Apostles' time. But he often seems to suggest it. In *Of Reformation* 'the most virgin times' were 'between Christ and Constantine'.[5] But in *The Reason of Church Government* (1642) he spoke of 'the general apostasy ... the perverse iniquity of 1,600 years'.[6] That gets us back to a decade after the death of Christ, though perhaps we should not press Milton's round figure too hard. In *Areopagitica*, however, 'a wicked race of deceivers' arose 'straight after' the Ascension 'and his Apostles after him were laid asleep'.[7] In *Tetrachordon* (1645) Milton spoke of the age of Constantine as 'cried up still for the most flourishing in knowledge and pious government since the Apostles'—where 'cried up still' leaves his own belief uncertain.[8] On other occasions he was less precise. Episcopacy did not prevail 'till many years after the Apostles were deceased', he wrote in *Eikonoklastes* (1649).[9] Similarly 'for the first three hundred years', Milton found no

---

[1] See pp. 89–92 above; *MER*, pp. 112–13; Haller and Davies, op. cit., p. 337; Wither, *Three Private Meditations* (1666), pp. 46–8, in *Miscellaneous Works*, IV.
[2] *Biographical Dictionary of English Radicals*, I, pp. 68, 78.
[3] *The World of the Muggletonians*, p. 73; cf. p. 126.
[4] *MER*, pp. 84–6.
[5] *CPW*, I, p. 551.
[6] Ibid., I, p. 827. In the *De Doctrina Christiana* there was more than 1,300 years' apostasy, perhaps to AD 1500 (*CPW*, VI, p. 117).
[7] Ibid., II, p. 549.
[8] Ibid., II, p. 701. Earlier in this pamphlet Milton had spoken of Justin Martyr as writing 'within fifty years after St. John died', in 'those pure and next to the Apostles' times'. But then Milton was using Justin Martyr as an authority in his argument for divorce.
[9] *CPW*, III, p. 493.

trace of tithes, 'though error by that time had ... in many other points of religion miserably judaized the church'.[1] But the Waldensians continued without bishops and without tithes 'since the Apostles'.[2] In the *De Doctrina Christiana* Milton uses Acts, 20:29–30, 2 Corinthians, 11: 13 and 1 John, 2:18[3] to lay the basis for *Paradise Lost*, XII. 507–51:

> In their [the Apostles'] room, as they forewarn,
> Wolves shall succeed for teachers, grievous wolves,
> Who all the sacred mysteries of heaven
> To their own vile advantages shall turn
> Of lucre and ambition, and the truth
> With superstitions and traditions taint...[4]

This leads on, without a break, to

> So shall the world go on,
> To good malignant, to bad men benign,
> Under her own weight groaning till the day
> Appear of respiration to the just,
> And vengeance to the wicked.

So for Milton, the apostasy, which started soon after the Apostles' time, was to continue till the Second Coming.

To say that the church has long been in the wilderness, like the Israelites between Egypt and Canaan, is of course an old idea: it goes back at least to the Waldensians.[5] The Familist Niclaes picked it up. Erbery thought the church had been there since the Apostles' time. The saints will continue 'be-wildernessed' until the outpouring of the spirit in the Third Dispensation, in the latter days.[6] But the phrase had been anticipated by William Sedgwick, who told MPs in June 1642 that 'in this wilderness ... you are our watchers.' The saints 'are in a wilderness, in a desolate barren estate', he said in 1648.[7] The phrase was used by the very

---

[1] Ibid., VII, p. 290. Vavasor Powell dated the prevailing of Antichrist two or three hundred years after Christ (*Christ Exalted above all Creatures*, pp. 73–4: a sermon preached to Parliament on 28 February 1650).

[2] *CPW*, III, p. 514; VII, pp. 291–2; cf. *MER*, pp. 84–6.

[3] *CPW*, VI, pp. 595, 604.

[4] Note 'lucre and ambition' = 'avarice and ambition'.

[5] See G. H. Williams, *Wilderness and Paradise in Christian Thought* (New York, 1962), pp. 62–3, 74–5, 80–4, and *passim*.

[6] H. N., *Terra Pacis* (1575), pp. 11, 21–2, repr. 1649. See p. 89 above for Erbery.

[7] See pp. 98–100, 105 above.

heretical Mrs Attaway, who like Erbery 'was in the wilderness, waiting for the pouring out of the spirit',[1] and by Roger Williams (who in America was literally as well as spiritually surrounded by a wilderness), by Edward Sexby (who told the Army Council at Putney in 1647 'You are in a wilderness condition'), by John Saltmarsh, Winstanley, Sir Henry Vane and Isaac Penington.[2] Fox saw the world as 'a briary thorny wilderness', in contrast to the fertile Quaker ploughed fields.[3] Owen and Ludlow also spoke of the wilderness.[4] Clarkson was travelling through the wilderness in the late 1650s.[5] Muggleton thought there were only three estates—Egypt, the Wilderness and Canaan.[6]

The wilderness is a continuing presence in *Paradise Lost* and *Paradise Regained*. 'A steep wilderness' denied access to Paradise (*PL*, IV. 35); Adam and Eve descend into the wilderness at the end of the poem. They knew by then that ultimately Christ will

> bring back
> Through the world's wilderness long wandered man
> Safe to eternal Paradise of rest.
>
> (XII. 313–5)

The Israelites founded their government and laws whilst 'in the wide wilderness' (XII. 224–35). Milton emphasizes that Satan would set 'Our second Adam in the wilderness' to tempt him (XI. 382–3): *Paradise Regained* sings 'Eden raised in the waste wilderness' (*PR*, I.7). The fact that the Son of God was 'wandering in the wilderness' is repeatedly emphasized (I.156, 290–302; II.232, 307, 383–4; III.23; IV.372, 375, 416, 543, 606).

The church, Milton said in 1642, had taken 'flight into the wilderness' because of 'the perverse iniquity of 1600 years'.[7] This long sojourn in the wilderness explains the lack of emphasis on the sixteenth-century reformation by Milton and others. The magisterial reformation had perpetuated a different kind of state church—doctrinally better, perhaps, but still suffering from the defects of the old hierarchical church. The

---

[1] *Gangraena*, I, p. 87. For Milton's admirer, Mrs Attaway, see p. 90 above, and *The World of the Muggletonians*, p. 67.
[2] Woodhouse, op. cit., p. 102; Saltmarsh, *Sparkles of Glory* (1647), pp. 294–5; Winstanley, *The Mysterie of God* (1648), p. 39; Vane, *Two Treatises*; pp. 72–3, 122–3 above.
[3] Fox, *Journal*, I, p. 35.
[4] Owen, *Works*, VIII, p. 6; see p. 77 above.
[5] See p. 47 above.
[6] Muggleton, *The Neck of the Quakers Broken* (1663), p. 27.
[7] *CPW*, I, p. 827.

radical reformation of the sixteenth century had by definition been an opposition movement. Seventeenth-century religious radicals looked back to Wyclif and Hus rather than to Luther and Calvin, the persecuted, not the successful. Some thought that the Waldensians, 'who kept thy faith so pure of old', were the woman in the wilderness of Revelation XII, the only religious group to preserve the purity of the Apostles' time since the universal apostasy. Milton and many others preferred to look back to them as predecessors rather than to the protestant reformers or even the Lollards.[1] The Gospel was everlasting, not the church.

A. L. Morton has dealt definitively with the Everlasting Gospel. Belief in it fits in with belief in an apostasy since the Apostles and in the anointing. Since the reign of Elizabeth a line had been drawn between those who wanted to reform and those who rejected the national church. Familists were said to preach the Everlasting Gospel. John Foxe attacked it.[2] Winstanley, Coppe, Clarkson, Erbery, Harrison, Carew, Ludlow, Penington, Burrough, Fox, Venner, all preached the Everlasting Gospel.[3] Owen referred to it, perhaps perfunctorily.[4] To them we may add the ex-Leveller and Baptist preacher Henry Denne,[5] the radical legal reformer John Warr,[6] Tobias Crisp, John Saltmarsh, Thomas Collier, William Dell,[7] Reeve and Muggleton,[8] Wither,[9] and Mrs Lead, the Philadelphian friend of John Pordage.[10] The Rev. Sampson Bond, who in 1678 became unpopular in Bermuda for wishing to educate the children of slaves and to liberate Christian slaves, described himself as a 'preacher of the Everlasting Gospel'.[11] Eighteenth-century Shakers carried the Everlasting Gospel to North America.[12]

---

[1] Morton, *The World of the Ranters*, pp. 115–42.

[2] Foxe, *Acts and Monuments of the Christian Church*, ed. J. Pratt, (n.d.) II, pp. 520–1.

[3] See pp. 64, 145, 156 above; Sabine, op. cit., pp. 122, 169; Coppe, *A Fiery Flying Roll*; Penington, *Works*, III, pp. 494–7, IV, pp. 81, 102, 297–9, 543; Ludlow, *A Voyce from the Watchtower*, p. 228; cf. W. Sewel, *The History of the ... Quakers* (1722), esp. pp. 620–2; W. Deusbury, in Barbour and Roberts, op. cit., pp. 191, 203.

[4] Owen, *Works*, VIII, p. 41.   [5] *Gangraena*, II, p. 77.

[6] Warr, *Administrations Civil and Spiritual ... in Two Treatises* (1648), pp. 23, 42.

[7] *WTUD*, p. 148.

[8] Reeve, *A Remonstrance from the Eternal God* (1653), p. 10, reprinted with *A Divine Looking-Glasse* (1719); Muggleton, *A True Interpretation of ... the Revelation* (1665), p. 141.

[9] Wither, *A Memorandum to London* (1665), p. 52, in *Miscellaneous Works*, IV; *Ecchoes from the Sixth Trumpet* (1666), pp. 89, 96, in *Miscellaneous Works*, VI; *The Prisoners Plea* (1661), p. 26, in *Miscellaneous Works*, IV; *Parallelogrammaton* (1662), p. 6.

[10] D. P. Walker, *The Decline of Hell: Seventeenth-Century Discussions of Eternal Torment* (Chicago UP, 1964), pp. 226, 230; cf. pp. 121, 235–6, 247, 261. For Mrs Lead see p. 222 above.

[11] A. Day Bradley, 'Friends in Bermuda in the 17th Century', *JFHS*, 54 (1976), pp. 9–10.

[12] E. D. Andrews, *The People called Shakers* (New York, 1953), p. 68.

2 The Anointing

No state church, no established ministry: and great scepticism about any
organized church at all. This meant rejection of ordination by laying on
of hands or election by a congregation. A ministry was justified only by
'the anointing' poured out on the regenerate by God. Edwards in 1646
did not fail to denounce this heresy. He attributed it to Paul Hobson, but
it is also to be found in Roger Williams.[1] Carew, Erbery and Sedgwick all
emphasized the anointing.[2] Coppe in 1649 told the saints, 'you have the
anointing which showeth you all things.'[3] Edward Reeve, preaching to
the Society of Astrologers in 1651, said that if any of them had received
the anointing from God 'ye need not that any man teach you.'[4] John
Rogers resisted Cromwell to his face 'in the strength of the anointing'.[5]
George Whitehead and Edward Burrough in 1661 spoke of 'the anointing
within to teach all that do believe'.[6] Disruptive of a state church, the idea
fitted in perfectly with the existence of 'mechanick preachers', whose
congregations were held together by the charisma of an individual and his
preaching, not by organization or even by beliefs.

The fullest use of the concept was made by Winstanley. The anointing
'is Christ in you'. Kings and generals are not the Lord's anointed,
Winstanley declared: the elect are[7]—a point on which Dell, Milton and
Wither agreed with him.[8] In the early 1640s Feake thought 'the better
part of the House of Commons, with some few in the House of Lords',
had 'an anointing upon them from the Lord'.[9] If the King's political
authority related to belief that he was God's anointed, it was logical that
his successor should be the anointed saints. Others claimed that the
people are the Lord's anointed referred to in Psalms 105 and 115. This
'conceit' had been 'buzzed into the people's brains' everywhere,

---

[1] *Gangraena*, I, pp. 44, 91; Roger Williams, *The Bloudy Tenent of Persecution* (Hanserd
Knollys Soc., 1848), p. 210. First published 1644.
[2] For Carew see *A Complete Collection* (of the regicides' speeches), pp. 16, 18, 20; for Erbery
and Sedgwick see pp. 22, 110–12 above.
[3] *Some Sweet Sips, of some spirituall Wine*, p. 43.
[4] E. Reeve, *The new Jerusalem* (1652), p. 11.
[5] E. Rogers, op. cit., p. 193.
[6] Whitehead and Burrough, *The Son of Perdition Revealed* (1661), p. 33; cf. I. Penington, *Some
Directions to the Panting Soul* (1661), p. 8, and Fox, p. 163 above.
[7] *The Law of Freedom*, p. 143.
[8] *CPW*, III, pp. 586–7; VII, pp. 475–6; Wither, *Fides-Anglicana* (1660), pp. 20–2, in
Miscellaneous Works, V; Dell, *Several Sermons*, p. 160. Cf. R. G., quoted on p. 193n above.
[9] Feake, *A Beam of Light*, p. 6.

exploded an indignant royalist in 1642.[1] A lecturer in Chelmsford at the beginning of the war prayed for Parliament as the Lord's anointed.[2] Samuel Chidley in 1652 thought that the Lord of Lords had anointed the General Council of the Army.[3] 'All yokes upon the inward and outward man', A Standard Set Up proclaimed in 1657, will be 'destroyed because of the anointing'.[4] Stubbe's defence of Valentine Greatrakes's healing gift called in question the special power of the Lord's anointed King: he was accused of 'levelling'.[5]

Winstanley believed that when 'the whole bulk of mankind' lives 'in the light and strength of pure Reason', then all mankind will become 'a man anointed', perfect and free from the curse.[6] 'Christ ... the anointing within ... teacheth us all things, and leads us into all truth.'[7] Every man is 'a Son of the Father': anointing makes Christ and the saints 'but one mystical body', 'but one Son of God'. This composite Christ 'shall break the Serpent's head'.[8]

Tobias Crisp, who died in 1643, had preached that 'Christ is to be considered collectively.'[9] Erbery, who praised Crisp, said much the same: so did Milton.[10] Coppe, like Winstanley, believed that the saints were filled with God, and that they and Christ made up but one body, one perfect man.[11] Fox claimed to be the Son of God, in 'unity with the Son and with the Father'.[12] Howgil believed that Christ 'is all in his saints'.[13] Samuel Fisher in his Baptist days accused Ranters of holding that the resurrection meant the rising of Christ in believers.[14] The regicides

---

[1] [Anon], The Soveraignty of Kings: Or An absolute Answer and Confutation (1642), Sig. A iv, A 3.
[2] [Bruno Ryves], Angliae Ruina (1643), p. 31.
[3] Chidley, A Cry against a Crying Sin, in Harleian Miscellany (1744–6), VIII, p. 462.
[4] A Standard Set Up, p. 6.
[5] See pp. 266–7 above.
[6] Sabine, op. cit., pp. 120–1; cf. pp. 166, 169.
[7] The Law of Freedom, p. 232.
[8] Winstanley, The Breaking of the Day of God (1649), pp. 10–11; cf. p. 6; The Mysterie of God (1649), p. 6; both first published 1648. See The Religion of Gerrard Winstanley, pp. 5–6, 8, 13–14, 28–9, 32–3, 48; and pp. 38–9 above.
[9] Crisp, Christ Alone Exalted, III (1648), pp. 346–7.
[10] Erbery, Testimony, p. 68; cf. pp. 85, 87–8, 93, 96 above; CPW, VI, pp. 499–500; MER, pp. 303–5; PL, V. 609–13. It was Satan who in PR echoed Winstanley in saying 'all men are Sons of God' rather than the elect only (PR, IV. 520).
[11] See pp. 43–4, 46–7 above. The doctrine is Familist.
[12] See p. 163 above.
[13] Howgil, The Inheritance of Jacob Discovered (1656), p. 14.
[14] Fisher, Baby Baptism meer Babism, pp. 511–13. Winstanley held that belief as well.

Carew and Harrison both believed that they had become Sons of God.[1] Thomas Goodwin, earlier, had also looked forward to the time when the world would belong to the Sons of God.[2] Venner believed that in consequence of the reforms advocated in *A Standard Set Up* the effects of the Fall would be 'in a great measure done away with', and that all saints 'may be delivered into the glorious liberties of the Sons of God'.[3] This was one of the senses in which men could get back behind the Fall on earth, as Winstanley, Coppin and Wither as well as Milton believed.[4] The doctrine leads Milton on to what Empson perspicaciously called 'the abdication of God'. At the end of time, when (in the Son's words) 'all my redeemed' are 'made one with thee as I with them', then Christ will lay his 'regal sceptre' by, and 'God shall be all in all.'[5] For Winstanley God becomes all in all by means of a communist society on earth: 'as one spirit of righteousness is common to all, so the earth and the blessing of the earth shall be common to all; for now all is but the Lord, and the Lord is all in all.'[6]

The anointing is a doctrine of religious anarchy. To question the need for an ordained priesthood was to call in doubt the livelihood of 9,000 ministers. Theological differences between Calvinist and Arminian, high and low, were insignificant by comparison with what united the clergy as a profession. And it linked them with the gentry, who owned impropriated tithes and who in the long run were going to control any state in which there was no army to enforce toleration of those who attacked tithes. State church or Army: tithes or none? Those were always linked questions.[7]

---

[1] See p. 7 above; cf. Joshua Sprigge, *Certain Weighty Considerations* (1648–9), pp. 7–8 (I owe this reference to Mr Laydon); Cradock (1648) quoted by Nuttall, *The Holy Spirit in Puritan Faith and Experience* (Oxford, 1946), p. 107; Dell, *Several Sermons*, pp. 351–5; John Sadler, *Christ Under the Law: with the Times of the Gospel and Fullness Thereof* (1664), pp. 3–4; G. Bishop, *A Vindication of the Principles and Practice of the People Called Quakers* (1665), p. 27.

[2] See pp. 181–2 above.

[3] See p. 65 above.

[4] See pp. 38–9, 43–4 above; Wither, *The Psalms of David* (1632) (Spenser Soc., 1881), p. 246; *Juvenilia* (Spenser Soc., 1870–1), I, pp. 263–4; *Vaticinia Poetica*, p. 27, in *Miscellaneous Works*, IV.

[5] W. Empson, *Milton's God* (1961), pp. 130–46; L. Martz, *The Paradise Within* (Yale UP, 1964), p. 181; *MER*, Chapter 23 *passim*, esp. pp. 303–4. The Rosicrucian John Heydon still proclaimed in 1663 that man could 'ascend to so great a perfection that he is made the Son of God ... and is united with him' (Heydon, *Theomagia*, Book III, p. 101, quoted by J. R. Jacob, *Robert Boyle*, pp. 161–2). Heydon had some connection with the Duke of Buckingham, Wildman's patron. Boyle of course had no use for such ideas.

[6] Sabine, op. cit., p. 184.

[7] See pp. 218–19 above.

3   God on Trial

Men later recalled the 'tenderness', the 'simplicity', 'seriousness' and 'sincerity' which in the blissful early days of the Revolution had united God's people.[1] A climax of elation was reached in 1649, only to be followed by the slow betrayal of the 1650s. How could the God who willed 1649 also will 1660? And how could he sacrifice his servants then even if others had let down his Cause?

Men had believed that their Cause was invincible because it was God's. The defeat therefore called in question either God's goodness or his omnipotence, or their understanding of God's will. All three reactions could be subversive of traditional ideas of God. Many experienced spiritual crisis in the 1640s or 1650s—Fox, Burrough, William Deusbury, John Crook, Johnston of Wariston, Bunyan, Mrs Baxter, Anne Bradstreet, Thomas Traherne.[2] The successive apostasies, Bishop said, had led sincere Christians to doubt whether there was such a thing as truth, and to question everything.[3] As early as 1650 Penington was stressing the omnipotence of God who 'impartially destroyed the perfect and the wicked'.[4] Clarkson in 1659 had heard men say that God was a devil and a tyrant; 'he hath done that he cannot make good.' They openly preferred a 'money-God'.[5] Thomas Goodwin's *Discourse of the Punishment of Sin in Hell* started from the assumption that God is 'an enraged enemy'.[6]

'The Lord had blasted them and spit in their faces,' wailed Major-General Fleetwood.[7] Regicides could not avoid the question of God's apparent desertion of his servants. When a man told Harrison that he could not understand God's behaviour, Harrison could only urge him to wait and trust.[8] 'Have you not hard thoughts of God', Colonel Okey was asked, 'for this his strange providence towards you?'[9] George Rust,

---

[1] See pp. 123–6, 137, 140, 150–1, 158 above.
[2] *WTUD*, pp. 171–2; Ann Stanford, 'Anne Bradstreet, Dogmatist and Rebel', in *Puritan New England: Essays on Religion, Society and Culture*, ed. A. T. Vaughan and F. J. Bremer (New York, 1977), pp. 293, 296.
[3] *An Epistle of Love* (1661), pp. 3–4.
[4] See pp. 118–19 above.
[5] Clarkson, *Look about you*, pp. 29–30.
[6] See p. 183 above.
[7] *Clarke Papers*, IV, p. 220; *Clarendon State Papers*, III, p. 633.
[8] But cf. p. 71 above.
[9] H. G. Tibbutt, *Colonel John Okey, 1606–1662* (Bedfordshire Historical Record Soc., XXXV, 1955), p. 154.

former member of Milton's college, Christ's, Cambridge, noted in 1661 that men emphasized the justice of God to the exclusion of his mercy.[1] For where was God's mercy in 1660? 'Shorten the days of trouble', the Baptist John Whitehead prayed in 1662, lest 'thy little ones ... faint and their adversaries triumph and say "Where is now the God in whom they trusted?"'[2] Robert Boyle in the 1650s and 1660s was concerned with the problem of evil and the need to exonerate God.[3] So was George Wither in 1660.[4] Henry Newcome was tempted to atheism.[5]

Johnston of Wariston's intimate friend Andrew Hay found Job the most suitable reading in January 1660;[6] and Bulstrode Whitelocke composed many lectures on the same book of the Bible in the years that followed.[7] Vavasor Powell put *The Lamentations of Jeremiah* into verse.[8] 'God did seem to be more cruel than men,' Muggleton admitted. Nevertheless, God was omnipotent: 'a prerogative power and will of God is not to be contended with.'[9] Reeve in *A Divine Looking Glasse* (1656) had criticized 'doleful expressions' of a God 'of injustice or senseless cruelty' which some of his contemporaries uttered, though he equally rejected belief in 'God's pretended universal love to the whole creation' which he had held in his Ranter days. When Muggleton reissued this tract in 1661 he deleted Reeve's remarks about a cruel or unjust God. He presumably had his doubts about God's benevolence and justice—at least by human standards.[10]

In 1660 John Sadler, former member of the Council of State and friend of Milton, published a political romance called *Olbia: The New Island lately discovered*. It starts with the hero caught in a storm and wrecked with the loss of all his shipmates, 'their hopes and ship broken together, splitting on a scraggy rock.... He lay gasping on the top of a scrag.' Ultimately 'a grave aged person' approaches, whose 'many years' experience of much affliction and sorrow' had taught him to 'sympathize

---

[1] Quoted by C. A. Patrides, *Milton and the Christian Tradition* (Oxford UP, 1966), pp. 140–1.

[2] J. Whitehead, *The Written Gospel-Labours* (1704), quoted by C. Holmes, *Seventeenth-Century Lincolnshire*, p. 231.

[3] J. R. Jacob, *Robert Boyle*, pp. 160–1.

[4] Wither, *Speculum Speculativum* (1660), pp. 142–4, in *Miscellaneous Works*, V.

[5] See p. 211 above.

[6] *The Diary of Andrew Hay of Craignethan, 1659–1660*, ed. A. G. Reid (Scottish Hist. Soc., Edinburgh, 1901), p. 248.

[7] R. H. Whitelocke, *Memoirs, Biographical and Historical, of Bulstrode Whitelocke* (1860), p. 450.

[8] In *The Bird in the Cage*.

[9] Muggleton, *The Acts of the Witnesses of the Spirit*, pp. 23, 27–31.

[10] *The World of the Muggletonians*, pp. 93, 119; *MER*, pp. 347–52.

with all dejected spirits'. God startles us, this wise man suggested, by 'his thunders or his earthquakes or his fire in the bush' until we learn to 'turn aside from the noise and dust and crowd of the world'. Then we shall overcome 'all our fears and frowardness ... till we come to hope'.[1] Four years later Sadler foretold that Jesus Christ would come again before 1680, or at latest around 1690. 'Wait on the Lord,' he concluded, 'and he shall exalt thee to inherit the earth. And when the wicked are cut off thou shalt see it. So that a man shall say, Verily there is a reward for the righteous; Verily there is a God that judgeth the earth.'[2] Clearly these last two propositions no longer seemed self-evident.

Samuel Pordage's epic of 1661 started from the triumph of evil in the world: scoffers argue that there is no God, others worry about the flourishing of the wicked.[3] Milton was writing *Paradise Lost* in exactly these years, to assert eternal Providence and justify the ways of God to men. Unless the freedom of man's will could be established, he believed, there would be 'an outcry against divine justice'.[4] 'Impatience towards God', he admitted in the *De Doctrina Christiana*, is 'a sin which even saints are sometimes tempted to commit'.[5] 'Shalt thou give law to God?' Abdiel asked Satan.[6] In what sounds like an autobiographical passage, Milton recognized that 'even the faithful are sometimes insufficiently aware of all these methods of divine Providence, until they examine the subject more deeply and become better informed about the Word of God.'[7] Lady Radzinowicz suggests that throughout *Samson Agonistes* God is on trial: his justice and/or his benevolence are continually questioned.[8] Traherne, Dryden and Bunyan all thought God's justice was on trial.[9]

---

[1] Sadler, *Olbia*, pp. 1–3, 323. See Woolrych, *Commonwealth to Protectorate*, pp. 203–9.

[2] Sadler, *Christ under the Law: with the Times of the Gospel and Fullness thereof* (1664), p. 74.

[3] See pp. 278–9 above; cf. p. 109.

[4] *CPW*, VI, pp. 397–8.

[5] Ibid., VI, p. 663.

[6] *PL*, V. 822.

[7] *CPW*, VI, p. 339.

[8] M. A. Radzinowicz, *Towards Samson Agonistes: the Growth of Milton's Mind* (Princeton UP, 1978), pp. 19, 31–2, 35–6, 85–6, 95, 291–2; cf. A. Milner, *John Milton and the English Revolution: a Study in the Sociology of Literature* (1981), p. 139.

[9] Traherne, *Christian Ethicks*, esp. pp. 19–20, 43; *MER*, p. 360; Bunyan, *Works*, II, p. 344. Cf. p. 120 above.

4 Samson Agonistes

In *Milton and the English Revolution* and in the present book I have tried to show that Milton was not isolated in his reaction to the Revolution's defeat. His last three great poems deal with intensely topical problems set by the defeat of God's Cause.

The Fall of Man was central to everybody's thinking about politics: it was crucial to the question of human freedom. Emphasis on the fall of the rebel angels, from Boehme onwards, was a way of exonerating God. Evil originated with Satan, who took advantage of the freedom which God had given to man. Keith Thomas demonstrated an apparent increase in the power of the devil in sixteenth- and early seventeenth-century England.[1] At the reformation men were told not to believe in ecclesiastical magic—the mediating saints, holy water, exorcism, relics, pilgrimages, etc., etc. But misfortunes and tragedies continued to occur. God could not be blamed: only the very toughest-minded could accept full human responsibility; evil spirits remained. Yet protestantism had started ideas which could not be checked. The abolition of priestly and heavenly mediators had established a direct relationship between man and God which led to a new self-respect. If all believers were priests, all had liberties and rights. Human sinfulness was long given as a reason for refusing to recognize the rights of the saints or the natural rights of man: but during the Revolution demands for both were made. After its defeat the sinfulness of fallen man became an explanation of failure to establish them.

There are analogies in the 'subjects' of Milton's last three poems. *Paradise Lost* deals with a man and woman who were tempted and fell; *Paradise Regained* with a perfect man who withstood temptation; *Samson Agonistes* with a fallen man who recovered by overcoming temptation. Lady Radzinowicz has beautifully established the political context of *Samson Agonistes*—the sense of national failure,[2] which makes Samson—like Milton—an alien in his own country, accepting the rule of his enemies only so long as he must.[3] He was a representative, elected not born into leadership. He 'prophesied a potent political movement through the educative power of the tragedy itself'. The diagnosis of

---

[1] Thomas, *Religion and the Decline of Magic*, pp. 256, 469–77.
[2] Radzinowicz, *Towards Samson Agonistes*, Parts II–IV.
[3] Ibid., p. 175; *SA*, lines 1365–7; cf. *CPW*, VIII, p. 4.

national failure leads to the prophecy of the conditions necessary for a successful republic.[1] I am not quite so sure about Lady Radzinowicz's conclusion, that Milton's ultimate aim is the establishment of consensus for a chastened, quieted, tolerant people. I think Milton's aim is more positive and indeed more pugnacious than that.[2]

Here I believe that some points which have emerged in this book may be relevant. Those who read *Samson Agonistes* as a quietist play, despite its manifest political content, stress the fact that the slaughter of the Philistines by the biblical Samson did not lead to the liberation of Israel. Consequently they see Samson's death as, politically, a vain sacrifice; and the final words of the Chorus as an ironically misleading comment. Some see Samson as a fundamentally flawed character, comparable to the Philistine Harapha. They do not believe that he has been changed, even by the end of the play; or, if he has changed, it is a matter of personal regeneration only.[3] The slaughter of the Philistines did not offer his people an opportunity for liberating themselves, but was just one more senseless atrocity.

There are several points to make here. First, Milton, like everybody else in his time, saw Samson as a type of Christ. He applied the phrase 'the great deliverer' to the Son of God in *Paradise Lost* (XII. 149) as well as to Samson (*SA*, lines 40, 274, 1214). This makes it impossible to equate him with Harapha, a swashbuckling Cavalier, a restoration bully.[4] Secondly, Samson was often used as a symbol for the New Model Army and/or the Good Old Cause, by no means only by Milton.[5] The evidence which I have given of continuing radical faith in the Army as a potential revolutionary force right down to 1660 is relevant here. Thirdly, if Milton shared the radical belief that the apostasy dated from the time of the Apostles, as I have tried to show, then the Son of God failed in his

---

[1] Radzinowicz, op. cit., pp. 70, 81, 167, 178.

[2] Ibid., pp. 108, 406. I prefer the analysis of Isabel Rivers, *The Poetry of Conservatism, 1600–1745* (Cambridge, 1973), pp. 97–102.

[3] W. R. Parker, *Milton's Debt to Greek Tragedy in Samson Agonistes* (Baltimore, 1937); *Milton: A Biography* (Oxford UP, 1968); Irene Samuel, 'Samson Agonistes as Tragedy', in *Calm of Mind: Tercentenary Essays on Paradise Regained and Samson Agonistes*, ed. J. A. Wittreich (Case Western Reserve UP, 1971); Wittreich, *Visionary Poetics: Milton's Tradition and his Legacy* (Huntington Library, 1979).

[4] Cf. Jackie DiSalvo, '"The Lord's Battles": *Samson Agonistes* and the Puritan Revolution', *Milton Studies*, IV (1972), p. 52. The Argument to the poem does not suggest that Milton thought the scenes with Dalilah and Harapha important for the evolution of the plot.

[5] *MER*, pp. 435–8. For an interesting additional example, see the document quoted by M. A. Kishlansky in *The Rise of the New Model Army* (Cambridge UP, 1979), p. 252; cf. *Walwyns Wiles* (1649) in Haller and Davies, op. cit., p. 287.

liberating role no less than Samson. His kingdom has not yet come.

Milton, I think, no more intended his readers to write off Samson than he intended them to write off Jesus Christ. If he had so intended, it was such a sensational breach with convention that it is very remiss of him not to have made his intentions clearer. To take only characters mentioned in this book, Thomas Goodwin thought Samson a type of Christ: both were victorious in death.[1] 'Samson's strength did Jesus' typify' sang Samuel Pordage.[2] Wither said that Samson executed 'God's vengeance upon the enemies of his country'.[3] Milton makes clear in the Argument to *Samson Agonistes* that the Chorus is composed of Samson's friends and *equals*. They as well as Samson were to be re-educated; and through them the audience.[4] Milton faced a collapse of morale among God's servants in England. In *Paradise Lost* it was 'the conquered also and enslaved by war' who, 'cooled in zeal, ... shall practice how to live secure'.[5] In *The Defence of the People of England* Milton had said it was Samson's duty to slay tyrants even though a majority of his fellow citizens 'did not balk at slavery'.[6]

In his Preface to *Prometheus Unbound* Shelley observed that Greek writers had not scrupled to adapt mythology to their own purposes; he now 'presumed to employ a similar license'.[7] That good classicist Milton could have drawn Shelley's conclusion for himself, and he would not have been unique in applying it to a biblical story. Dryden's *Absalom and Achitophel* ignores the fate which befell Absalom in the Bible. Naturally: for Dryden too was writing not history but a tract for the times. He was advising the Duke of Monmouth on action to be taken in England at the time of writing, just as—I suggest—Milton in *Samson Agonistes* was offering advice to God's servants in England.[8] Milton's and Dryden's readers would have been well aware of the liberties taken with biblical history in each case. The *Commentary on Judges* of Milton's favourite Martin Bucer treats Samson as a type of Christ, the Saviour of the people, first in oppressing the enemies of God, then 'in his beginning rather than completing the liberation of God's people from the

---

[1] Goodwin, *Works*, V, pp. 149–53.
[2] Pordage, *Mundorum Explicatio*, p. 233.
[3] Wither, *Epistolium-Vagum-Prosa-Metricum* (1659), p. 27, in *Miscellaneous Works*, I.
[4] Cf. Radzinowicz, op. cit., pp. 55, 62, 98–9, 179; *MER*, p. 430.
[5] *PL*, XI. 797–802.
[6] *CPW*, IV, p. 402.
[7] I owe this reference to the brilliant book by Richard Jenkyns, *The Victorians and Ancient Greece* (Harvard UP, 1980), p. 101.
[8] I owe this point to Mr John Purkis of the Open University

power of the enemy'. This last point was developed more than the others.[1]

I do not think either *Paradise Regained* or *Samson Agonistes* is to be read as a tragedy of defeat, despite our historical hindsight. 'That their liberation will ... be short-lived', Joan Bennett wisely comments of the Israelites, 'does not invalidate the justice of Samson's cause or the justice of the Philistines' punishment, or the basis for the Israelites' dimly understood hope.'[2] History indeed looks different when you know the end of the story: the defeat of Israel, the apostasy of the early Christians. But both of Milton's poems are allegories for his own time rather than histories. In history the end is closed: we know what it is and can only be. In art it is open: it is what we make of it. We cannot be certain what God's purposes are until history has unveiled them. Samson's destruction of the Philistine aristocracy and clergy, the Son of God's triumph over Satan, opened up possibilities which in the past were not acted upon; but the people of England for whom Milton was writing might one day do better, 'let but them/Find courage to lay hold on this occasion'.[3] Milton stressed in the *De Doctrina Christiana* 'that God made no absolute decrees about anything which he left in the power of men, for men have freedom of action'. God's decrees are frequently contingent.[4] Human history as revealed to Adam in Books XI and XII of *Paradise Lost* looks like an unending series of defeats. Rather it is a series of examples which challenge us in the present. Some time we must break out of the cycle of failure and defeat. Why not now? Both Samson and the Son of God faced temptations to which political leaders are likely to be exposed, temptations to which the English revolutionary leaders of the 1650s had succumbed. The fact that both successfully withstood temptation links the two poems, notwithstanding the relative failure of both leaders in their own time. Both poems offer hope.

In *Paradise Lost* Milton had rejected 'Wars, hitherto the argument/ Heroic deemed'.[5] After the war in heaven reached stalemate, Stella Revard persuasively argues, the angels realized that they could not win without

---

[1] W. B. Stephens, *The Holy Spirit in the Theology of Martin Bucer* (Cambridge UP, 1970), pp. 151–2.

[2] Joan Bennett, 'Liberty under the Law: the Chorus and the Meaning of *Samson Agonistes*', *Milton Studies*, XII (1978), p. 161; cf. pp. 146–8, 151.

[3] *SA*, lines 1715–16. The words are Manoa's. They are hard to pronounce without a heavy emphasis on 'them'.

[4] *CPW*, VI, pp. 155–6.

[5] PL, IX. 27–81; cf. *PR*, III. 71–83.

God.[1] In the last two poems it is the use of force for worldly ends, or its *untimely* use by God's servants, that is condemned. Neither the Son nor Samson rules it out altogether. Milton criticized the avarice and ambition of the Parliamentary leaders and generals: like Marvell, he never condemned the Good Old Cause itself, nor indeed Oliver Cromwell.[2] It was the leadership that had gone wrong, betraying the Cause: not, as Sedgwick argued, the Cause itself. Samson's ability to purge himself of pride, anger, ambition, lust, qualifies him to play the same role as the Son of God whose type he was: the Saviour of his people.

I believe that Milton printed *Paradise Regained* and *Samson Agonistes* in chronological order.[3] Lady Radzinowicz argued convincingly that Milton arranged his shorter poems in the 1673 edition in the most politically effective order:[4] certainly, to follow *Paradise Regained* by *Samson Agonistes* is politically effective. The Son of God's fierce denunciation of 'the people' in the former poem suggests that Milton despaired of the people of England. But Stella Revard concludes that 'Jesus in *Paradise Regained* clearly places the responsibility on the Roman people; it is not for him to save those who would not save themselves.... Political liberty must spring from a free people's support of its liberators, if ultimately it is to work.'[5] In *Samson Agonistes* the remarkable line, 'the vulgar only 'scaped who stood without' seems to suggest a more optimistic attitude. Milton indeed went out of his way to save the people from destruction. In the Hebrew, Septuagint, Vulgate and Authorized Version texts of Judges 16:27 the people—3,000 of them—stood on the roof of the building Samson destroyed. Milton is unique in putting the common people outside, safe from Samson's vengeance. He also innovated when he made a priest urge Dalilah to betray Samson, which leads up to his other departure from the Bible in insisting that only the Philistine aristocracy and clergy perished.[6]

I can see no reason for these innovations of Milton's except to condemn the clergy and aristocracy whom he regarded as the principal

---

[1] Revard, 'The Warring Saints and the Dragon: A Commentary upon Rev. 12: 7–9 and Milton's War in Heaven', *Philological Quarterly*, 53 (1974), p. 193.

[2] See pp. 249–50, 281–3 above.

[3] Parker's eccentric attempt to date *Samson Agonistes* early is now, I think, generally rejected.

[4] Radzinowicz, op. cit., pp. 129, 142.

[5] Revard, 'Milton and Classical Rome: the Political Context of *Paradise Regained*', in *Rome in the Renaissance: the City and the Myth*, ed. P. A. Ramsay (New York, 1982). Henry Stubbe arrived at the same conclusion (see pp. 254, 257–8, 272 above).

[6] I owe these points to the editorial commentary on lines 857–61 and 1605 of *SA* in Milton's *Complete Poems* (Everyman new edn., 1980).

enemies of God in restoration England: and perhaps to show that he now had more hope of 'the vulgar' responding to a purged and purified leadership than when he wrote *Paradise Regained*.[1] What indeed could be achieved in England after 1660 without some participation of 'the people'? The rule of the saints seemed even less likely than it had been in the 1650s. When Milton felt able to resume pamphleteering two years after the publication of *Samson Agonistes* he addressed himself not to the elect but to the English people, including Anglicans.[2]

There is no evidence that Milton ever adopted the post-1661 Quaker position of pacifism and abstention from politics. He did not shift God's kingdom to another world. In 1660 he refused to compromise with the victors. He repeatedly insists in the *De Doctrina Christiana* that 'some hatred ... is a religious duty, as when we hate the enemies of God and of the church.'[3] 'We are not forbidden to take or to wish to take vengeance upon the enemies of the church,' Milton wrote. 'We are even commanded to curse them.'[4] The ultimate object of Christ's kingdom is indeed 'to conquer and crush his enemies'.[5] Milton had written in his *Defence of the People of England* 'it was not ... permissible and good to put a tyrant to death because God commanded it, but rather God commanded it because it was permissible and good.' Milton cited 'the heroic Samson' as one who 'thought it not impious, but pious to kill those masters who were tyrants over his country'.[6] In *Paradise Lost* we have the authority of the Son for hating the Father's enemies, and for executing 'fierce vengeance on his foes'.[7] Adam did not lament 'for the whole world of wicked men destroyed' by the Flood, but rather rejoiced at Noah's survival.[8]

Nor is this just a personal whim of Milton's. No scholar ransacking the Bible as the best guide to Christian conduct could fail to notice passages in the Old Testament justifying hatred of God's enemies. In the *De Doctrina Christiana* Milton cited Psalm 18 to demonstrate that a cruel

---

[1] In *Samson Agonistes* Milton suggested that the patience of the saints made 'each his own deliverer', rather as Luther taught the priesthood of all believers, Lilburne that every man should be his own lawyer and Culpeper every man his own physician. Cf. Radzinowicz, op. cit., pp. 94, 107 and my *Change and Continuity in Seventeenth-Century England*, pp. 164–5.

[2] *Of True Religion, Heresy, Schism, Toleration: and What Means may be used against the Growth of Popery* (1673), in *CPW*, VIII; cf. *MER*, p. 219.

[3] *CPW*, VI, p. 743.

[4] Ibid., VI, pp. 675, 755; cf. p. 762.

[5] Ibid., VI, pp. 435–7.

[6] *CPW*, IV, pp. 407, 402.

[7] *PL*, VI. 734–5; III, 393–9.

[8] Ibid., XI. 874–8.

enemy should not be spared.[1] There was good protestant authority for
Milton's position. 'To steal, rob and murder,' William Tyndale had
written, 'are holy when God commandeth them.'[2] Four years after the
publication of *Samson Agonistes* the mild Thomas Traherne, in his
treatise of *Christian Ethicks*, emphasized the duty of hating those 'to
whom hatred is due'.[3] Bunyan, whose experience had been as bitter as
Milton's, described with some satisfaction in his *The Holy War* the
slaughter of the Diabolians; he leaves us in little doubt that the
Diabolians corresponded to the royalist aristocracy and gentry in
restoration England.[4]

The onus of proof is surely on those who argue that in *Samson
Agonistes* Milton had abandoned a conviction which he had expressed
both publicly and privately, and which was widely held among his
protestant contemporaries. Milton had shown in his divorce pamphlets
that he was capable of evading the clear implications of biblical texts; and
in this case he could have made use of Christ's adjuration to love one's
enemies. His careful distinction between 'our enemies' and 'God's
enemies' shows that he knew exactly what he was doing. If the poem is
'about' Samson's regeneration, it is incompetent to leave his last action
ambiguous. It is, of course, possible for the regenerate to mistake a
'rousing motion' from the devil for one from God. In *Paradise Regained*
the Son's 'rousing motion' clearly came from God. If Samson's hardly-
won regeneration through suffering, blindness and degradation leads
only to another let-down, surely Milton should have made the point
more clearly? If there is positive evidence that Milton thought Samson's
rousing motion was not from God, that Samson was not heroic, that he
was wrong to think it pious to kill those who tyrannized over his
country, that he 'dies in vain'[5] and that his fellow citizens who 'did not
balk at slavery' were right—then this evidence has still to be produced.

Modern critics naturally start with an unexpressed assumption that
Milton cannot in *Samson Agonistes* have meant what he wrote in the *First
Defence* and in the *De Doctrina Christiana*.[6] If we look only at the words

---

[1] *CPW*, VI, pp. 490–1.
[2] Tyndale, *Doctrinal Treatises* (Parker Soc., 1848), p. 407.
[3] Traherne, *Christian Ethicks*, ed. M. Bottrall (1962), p. 108.
[4] Bunyan, *Works*, III, pp. 311, 322, 348–9; this point was made by Jack Lindsay in his pioneer-ing study, *John Bunyan, Maker of Myths* (1937), pp. 221–2. Feake and several Quakers praised the Army for its victories in Ireland, which included mass slaughter (pp. 62, 133 above.).
[5] Parker, *Milton: a Biography*, p. 937.
[6] Or, like Professor Patrides, they try to wish the *De Doctrina Christiana* out of existence ('*Paradise Lost* and the Language of Theology', in *Bright Essence: Studies in Milton's Theology*, by W. B. Hunter, C. A. Patrides and J. H. Adamson, Utah UP, 1971, pp. 168–9)

on the page, isolated from their historical context, this is a possible
reading of the poem. But there is no need to suppose Milton had changed
his views. He continued to work on 'his dearest and best possession', the
De Doctrina Christiana, until his death. Professor Low insists on the
'close compatibility between *Samson Agonistes* and the *Christian
Doctrine*'.[1] And if Milton did believe it a Christian duty to hate God's
enemies, who could be more clearly God's enemies than the Philistine
aristocracy and priests, or their counterparts in restoration England?

Refusal to accept the plain evidence that this remained Milton's
position has prevented some good scholars taking *Samson Agonistes* at its
face value. It is a credit to their hearts, but not to their knowledge of the
world in which Milton lived. We would find it difficult to justify hating,
conquering and crushing God's enemies quite as cold-bloodedly as
Milton and Bunyan did because we have not been through what they
went through. For Milton the wrestle to justify God's ways to men had
involved rethinking history from the creation to the end of the world,[2]
through the falls of angels and men, through the life and death of Christ,
on to the English Revolution whose 'most heroic and exemplary
achievements since the foundation of the world' had resulted from
following God's 'manifest guidance'.[3] Only one thing could possibly be
more 'heroic and exemplary' than the life and death of Christ: ending the
apostasy which had frustrated the achievements of the Son of God.
Milton and his like believed this had happened during the Revolution.
The restoration of Charles II and bishops brought back the apostasy, as
Samson had been imprisoned and degraded after his first victories. But
what had once been overthrown could be overthrown again. Or so one
must hope. It is only hell to which hope never comes.[4] Samson's name
was believed in the seventeenth century to mean 'here the second time',
the words used in Milton's Argument to describe the entry of the public
officer who came to call Samson to the temple of Dagon where he took
his second chance.

Whilst others adapted to the experience of defeat, Milton, I suspect,
knew there must be a way forward again. 'It is intolerable and incredible

---

[1] A. Low, *The Blaze of Noon: A Reading of Samson Agonistes* (Columbia UP, 1974), p. 222;
CPW, VI, p. 121.
[2] Cf. Mr Danielson's argument that freedom is built into Milton's chaos and so is with us from
the beginning (D. R. Danielson, *Milton's Good God: A Study in Literary Theodicy*,
Cambridge UP, 1982, Chapter 2).
[3] *CPW*, IV, p. 549.
[4] *PL*, I. 65–6.

that evil should be stronger than good,' he declared in the *De Doctrina Christiana*. That was how he knew that God existed.[1] It was not something to be proved: eternal Providence was asserted. Anything else would be like 'inventing a long argument to prove that God is not the devil'.[2] If Samson had died in vain, the doubts about God's justice expressed at the beginning of the play would have been justified. Good must triumph: that is an uncontrovertible article of faith. Abdiel—the angel with the human name—had the courage to tell evil itself that it could not win. The 'better fortitude/Of patience and heroic martyrdom' was Milton's epic theme.[3] Satan puts up a show of fortitude in Book I of *Paradise Lost*: the difference between him and Abdiel was that the latter knew he was right, as Milton knew he was right. Charles I and Charles II would, no doubt, have been 'racked with deep despair' if they had been as intelligent as Satan.[4]

Unlike some of his radical contemporaries after 1660 Milton did not emphasize the consolations of the after life. The happier Paradise within was still to be regained on earth. Samson perhaps regained it for himself at the moment of exultation when the roof of Dagon's temple came crashing down. But a part of his exultation must have derived from the fact that the great deliverer had in fact given his people the chance to liberate themselves. Parker's 'tragic' view of the conclusion of the play seems to me equivalent to saying that Milton had lost faith in the ultimate triumph of good over evil, had ceased to assert eternal Providence, could no longer justify the ways of God to men.

Milton's thinking thus in a sense represents a dead end, with its blind assertion that good will triumph. Harrington and Stubbe in their different ways opened up a more flexible path from defeat towards deism, to a rational God, capable of moving with the times. The Latitudinarians whose sermons Pepys and Evelyn appreciated announced God's approval of the capitalist system.[5] Nonconformists like Baxter and Henry longed for a 'face of godliness' in the land. Even Milton had to place the reign of Christ on earth through his saints in a more distant future than in the ebullient 1640s, though it still remained a

---

[1] *CPW*, VI, pp. 131–2.
[2] Ibid., VI, p. 166. For this reason I am not quite happy about Mr Milner's argument that God was no longer needed in Milton's philosophy (Andrew Milner, *John Milton and the English Revolution*, pp. 113–18, 156–61).
[3] *PL*, V. 877–907; IX. 31–3.
[4] Ibid., I. 126
[5] E.g., Pepys, *Diary*, 23 August 1668; Evelyn, *Diary*, 27 December 1671, 19 August 1675, 23 May, 1688.

necessary phase in which tyranny and superstition would be overcome, before God could abdicate because all men had become his Sons.

5 Harrington and Milton

The material in this book will, I hope, confirm some of the points I perhaps too easily assumed in *Milton and the English Revolution*. First, it brings out the significance of the Revolution for at least radical contemporaries of Milton. Mr Fletcher's excellent analysis of petitions to Parliament in 1640–1 illustrates the sense, even at that date, of Parliament's 'appointed role in bringing to an end a period of arbitrary government by a "full and complete reformation"'.[1] These were the petitions of laymen of the propertied class, not of the godly. Chapter Six, section 2 above showed how in the late 1630s Thomas Goodwin had forebodings of great changes to come. Mr Fletcher shows the formation, for perhaps the first time in English history, of what we may begin to call public opinion—not a united opinion, but a zone of discussion within the political nation on what the nature of the English state and church should be.[2] Civil war was the discussion carried on by other means, and by wider social groups: there was no going back to a state of affairs in which political discussion was abnormal.

> God's shaking nations, trying men,
>   And changing times and customs.

So Winstanley expressed a general radical conviction.[3] The contrast between the 1630s and 1640s had been no less astonishing than the reversal after 1660. 'The Lord hath appeared in our days to do great things,' declared Ludlow.[4] Harrison saw 'the finger of God' in England's deliverances, and Carew agreed.[5] 'The Lord rent the heavens and rent the earth,' wrote Penington.[6] 'God hath gone with you,' Owen told the House of Commons, 'the God of the Parliament'.[7] 'Was there in any man's memory such changes in government, and marvellous transactions

---

[1] A. Fletcher, *The Outbreak of the English Civil War* (1981), p. 99.
[2] Ibid., pp. xxv–vii, 75, 77–9, 117, and *passim*.
[3] Winstanley, *The Law of Freedom and Other Writings*, p. 390; cf. pp. 23–4 above.
[4] Ludlow, *A Voyce from the Watchtower*, p. 305; cf. p. 78 above.
[5] See p. 71 above.
[6] See pp. 125–6 above.
[7] See p. 173 above.

in them, as in these our days?' asked Reeve. 'The mighty God of Jacob hath brought it to pass.'[1] Cromwell never tired of expatiating on the theme.[2] Stubbe saw 'the actings of our God' in the miraculous overturning of monarchy, church and nobility.[3] The Ranter Joshua Garment likewise thought that the 'strange overturnings' of the 1640s were miraculous.[4] 'God hath done great and honourable things' by the agency of the Long Parliament, Burrough declared. He 'overthrew that oppressing power of kings, lords and bishops'.[5] The Bristol Baptist Robert Purnell rejoiced over 'the best times in England that ever we had', when the Lord takes 'princes and lords which were so high' and brings 'their heads so low as the block'.[6] 'No history can parallel such shakings,' Tillinghast agreed.[7] Bishop thought the Parliamentarian Cause 'the highest on which men were ever engaged in the field',[8] Carew 'the noblest since the Apostles' time';[9] 'the greatest outward alterations that were in any age', wrote Goodwin.[10] 'The just God' had appeared 'visibly and miraculously for this Cause of freedom', said R. G.[11] Philip Henry, no enthusiast, nevertheless believed that Parliament's Cause was 'in general the Cause of God'.[12] Erbery and Venner thought that the Lord had raised up the Army.[13] John Cook said its achievements were 'God's own handiwork'; its 'new mouldng' was 'visibly from heaven'.[14]

Marvell anticipated Harrington in his sense of impersonal destiny at work in the execution of Charles I and the establishment of the Commonwealth: Sedgwick had something of the same feeling. England, Marvell recognized, was being pushed out of one epoch into another. He realized, as did the rulers of France and Spain, that an English Commonwealth would be far more powerful, far more effective 'for increase' (in Harringtonian terms) than the traditional monarchy could

---

[1] *The World of the Muggletonians*, pp. 25, 132.
[2] See pp. 184–7 above.
[3] See p. 254 above.
[4] Garment, *The Hebrews Deliverance at Hand* (1651), quoted by Katz, *Philo-Semitism and the Readmission of the Jews to England*, p. 113.
[5] See pp. 150–1 above.
[6] Purnell, *Good Tydings* (1649), p. 33; cf. *No Power but of God* (1651): the Lord's 'blessed presence in the head of our armies' (pp. 164–8; cf. pp. 224–5).
[7] *Mr Tillinghasts Eight Last Sermons*, p. 42.
[8] See p. 133 above.
[9] See p. 71 above.
[10] See pp. 181–2 above. Milton thus had much support for his version, quoted on p. 317 above.
[11] See p. 193 above; cf. Thomas Horne in 1656, quoted by Lamont, *Richard Baxter and the Millennium*, p. 179.
[12] See p. 211 above.
[13] See pp. 85–6, 63–4 above.
[14] Cook, *Redintegratio Amoris*, p. 68.

ever have been. And a commonwealth, Harrington added piously, 'is not made by man but by God'.[1]

The radicals, then, were conscious of God at work in England, bringing about great revolutions. The first was the landslide of 1640–1, when suddenly the apparently all-powerful government of Charles and Laud found itself unable any longer to persecute the saints; and when by overwhelming majorities in Parliament the repressive machinery of the prerogative courts was swept away so as to establish civil liberties for 'the people'. When the King tried to resist, God raised up an army against him; when stalemate seemed likely to occur, God and Oliver Cromwell created the New Model Army, 'wherein there is not one lord'.[2] When a deal with the King seemed on the cards, the Army prevented it, in the summer of 1647 and the winter of 1648–9.

The second great revolution was that of 1648–9. The King was brought to trial and execution, the House of Lords was abolished and the Commonwealth proclaimed. God continued his favour by permitting the conquest of Ireland and of Scotland, the Navigation Act and the consequent aggressive imperialist foreign policy—the Dutch War, the Spanish War, Dunkirk seized, piracy brought under control. This revolution, according to the point of view, was either extremely wicked but unfortunately completely successful; or it was 'God's own handiwork'. For Erbery and Feake as well as for Sedgwick it was the enormity of what the Army did in 1649, its outrageous break with custom and tradition, which carried conviction of God's presence. Previously Sedgwick had been reconciling himself to the idea that monarchy and the power of the natural rulers were after all divinely ordained.

This helps to explain the success after 1649 of theories insisting that any power which rules *de facto* must be obeyed because it is ordained of God. Acceptance of such theories, and of Hobbism, was not merely a rationalization of recognition of defeat; it was also a recognition of the social necessity of the Commonwealth. Good men agonized over the attempt to ascertain what God was up to. 1660[3] and 1688 had to be accepted for the same reason.

---

[1] See pp. 197–201, 204–5 above. The revolution in political thinking is described by R. Eccleshall, *Order and Reason in Politics: Theories of Absolute and Limited Monarchy in Early Modern England* (Oxford UP, 1978), Chapters 5 and 6.

[2] [Walwyn?], *A Pearle in a Dounghill: or, Lieu. Col. John Lilburne in New-gate* (1646), in *Freedom in Arms*, ed. A. L. Morton (1975), p. 85. See also pp. 86–7, 107 above.

[3] Cf. pp. 115–16 above.

For the radicals the Army was God's instrument because it deliberately cut across what the unthinking social consensus had always assumed. In so doing it united most radicals in its support. But this was a once-for-all moment. The radicals, themselves a minority, were soon to be totally disunited. Those Independents and Baptists who had hitherto supported the Levellers chose the Army in 1649 in preference to ideologues who seemed disruptive of the godly interest, and themselves had no alternative power base. Saints and republicans held together against Levellers, Diggers and Ranters. When Fifth Monarchists tried to revive extremist policies, they too were rejected by propertied saints, by yeomen, parish élites, those who were doing well out of the Revolution. The radical groupings had diverse aspirations, different timetables; the natural rulers remained monolithic. In face of this disunity the increasingly isolated, increasingly arbitrary Army came rapidly to look less like God's instrument, more like an ordinary military dictatorship.

So the third revolution came about. The landslide of 1660 must have struck contemporaries as much more like the landslide of 1640 than it does us. We look at ideologies and see Arminian bishops overthrown in the one case, sectaries suppressed in the other; we look at institutions and see monarchy gravely weakened in the one case, restored in the other. But to 'the people' the rule of the Army must have seemed in its effects very like the rule of Laud. The central government in each case rode roughshod over the wishes of natural rulers and parish élites; taxes were collected which had not been voted by 'a free parliament' (Cony's Case exactly paralleled Hampden's); prerogative courts and Major-Generals alike short-circuited due common-law process. Only the rule of the Army was worse because it was more effective. The landslide of 1660, like that of 1640, was for a restoration of 'free Parliaments' and of the law at least as much as of the King: Harrington had grasped that point.[1] Prudently, Charles I had on his last stage proclaimed his adhesion to and indeed personification of the law. If they can execute *me* without law, Charles argued, who is safe?

This picked up the idea of the Answer to Parliament's Nineteen Propositions of 1642, that the King was not supreme but one of the three estates of Parliament. The King is no longer—as he had been in the 1630s—above and therefore contra-posed to the law: he is its symbol and guarantee. The King's conversion came rather late in January 1649, perhaps; but as we saw when discussing the regicides, especial

---

[1] See p. 202 above.

significance attached to the words of a dying man, even more to those of a dying king. And in 1660 the law really was what in 1640 the Parliamentarians claimed it ought to be: the legislation of 1641 was automatically confirmed in 1660; the abolition of feudal tenures (plus confirmation of copyhold) was re-enacted in 1660; so was the Navigation Act, and with it the new commercial foreign policy. The latter was an achievement of the years of military rule which was not to be abandoned. Nor was the new system of taxation which financed the grandiose foreign policy. The call for stability in 1660 was an appeal to the propertied classes, and especially to commercial groups.

It was no use Milton denouncing 'the vain and groundless apprehension that nothing but kingship can restore trade':[1] in the exceptional circumstances of 1660 it was neither vain nor groundless. Charles II, shrewd man, took up the cue: the Bible was the book he loved above all others, but trade was ever first in his thoughts. That is why conservative Parliamentarians were able so easily to adapt to the new regime. The restoration was a closing of the ranks of the propertied, divided in 1642 and 1649, against the radicals whose existence had been revealed in the 1640s. The restoration was brought about by men who had supported the Protectorate; the royalists stood by and watched. The regicides' judges included many former Oliverians: all the non-regicides who suffered severe penalties—Vane, Lambert, Haslerig, Harrington— had been opponents of kingship for Oliver.

In retrospect 1660 came to seem as providential as 1640–1 and 1648–9.

> Neither man's power nor policy had place...
> The astonished world saw 'twas the mighty work of heaven.[2]

But with a difference. In 1649 the Army had acted positively as God's instrument, had brutally but effectively shattered the image hitherto worshipped as divine; in 1660 it was the return of the traditional rulers that seemed providential. God was now as overwhelmingly on the side of the old order as he had previously been on the side of shocking innovation. The Army's behaviour in 1659–60 looks like historical tragedy repeating itself as farce. From Sedgwick's perspective those who had been instruments of the omnipotent God in 1648–9 were now

---

[1] *CPW*, VII, p. 461.
[2] Sir Francis Fane, quoted by J. Sutherland, *English Literature of the Later Seventeenth Century* (Oxford UP, 1969), p. 3.

revealed as impotent men, for whom the God of history had no more use. The militia, the army of liberty and property, replaced the Army of the Lord of Hosts. Ham was subordinated to Shem and Japhet.[1]

Many saints must have taken the point. The Army crumbled, as they had forewarned, because it had deserted and betrayed God's Cause. The gentry, revived, swept like a flood back over the land. Their displacement had been an exceptional act of God, executed by his Army. But God had now withdrawn his hand, in natural resentment of the avarice and ambition of the Army leaders, their tyranny and financial oppression. God had deserted those who had thought they were his peculiar servants. Their embattled defence of what had become indefensible left them without fresh resources now that retribution had come. But had God deserted England? The people of England had not been good enough to sustain a republic, Milton and Stubbe thought: not an *equal* commonwealth. It remained to be seen what could be salvaged.

Unrepentant radicals like Milton could only hope for a new divine intervention, through the educative force of regenerate individuals like Samson. For the Harringtonians it was easier. For of course Providence had not merely restored the old order. The revolutions of Christ in the 1640s and 1650s had not been in vain. The Harringtonian concept of the balance was not evolved to justify the pre-1640 state of affairs but its overthrow: transfer of power from King and church to the natural rulers represented in Parliament was a reassertion of the balance, and would lead to a commonwealth even if headed by a prince. The Providential swing of 1660, which seemed like a great natural force, had been impelled by the City of London no less than by the gentry. As Sedgwick pointed out, it came in spite of rather than because of the royalists.[2]

Millenarian theories then converged with economics. Radicals in the 1640s and 1650s had seen the English Revolution as exportable to all states not free. Soon this narrowed to an ideology of English colonial expansion, expressed in general approbation of the brutal conquest of Ireland, in Fifth Monarchist support for the Dutch War, in Marvell's millenarian praise of Cromwell, in Goodwin's vision of England as 'the top of nations',[3] in Dryden's *Annus Mirabilis*, in Pepys's naval reforms. Harrington picked up this millenarianism and argued that only a

---

[1] See p. 110 above.
[2] See pp. 110–11 above. Cf. Fuller on the 'strength' of 'this great City', in *Mixt Contemplations in Better Times*, p. 336.
[3] See pp. 246–7, 181.

commonwealth (in his sense) would be capable of financing it. In the hands of R. G., Stubbe, Warren and Neville, Harringtonianism was revised so as to accommodate the City of London at the centre of power. Neville had been a commercial imperialist before Harrington wrote. ''Tis London which stands in the way' of the papists, Warren claimed.[1] As in Oliver's days, toleration for protestant dissenters was essential if the trading community was to be carried along to finance colonial wars. Charles II recognized this social point: the Declaration of Indulgence of 1673 was part of a package which included the Third Dutch War; Stubbe defended it on those grounds.[2] But the policy broke down because the Stuart kings, unlike Oliver, wanted toleration (and more) for Catholics.

So the three providences of 1640, 1649 and 1660, millenarian and Harringtonian, combined to produce eighteenth-century Whiggery, a sense of England's destiny to rule the world. William's landing on Guy Fawkes Day, 1688, seemed indeed a fourth providential revolution, a landslide like 1640 and 1660, a reassertion of the predestined social order, not only against popery and absolutism but also against revolt from below. De facto theories of political obligation did duty after 1688 no less than after 1649.

In one sense the eighteenth-century natural rulers were the lineal descendants of those who took over government once the artificial constraints of Charles I's personal rule had been abolished. But they had undergone an oceanic change, and were now shareholders in a world empire. This empire itself seemed to its beneficiaries to fall unsought into England's lap; and the Industrial Revolution was another unplanned gift from heaven. The secular millenarian interpretation of England's historical destiny was validated by these providential revolutionary transformations. Newtonianism, formulated by the Boyle lecturers, gave theoretical underpinning to the alliance of Latitudinarians and the Royal Society whose significance Stubbe had spotted.[3]

Looked at with historical hindsight the New Model Army was indeed the instrument which made possible this series of historical changes; but Sedgwick, Marvell, Stubbe and the Harringtonians were equally right to see 1660 as the restoration of a more stable balance of forces which could

---

[1] Warren, op. cit., pp. 119–20.
[2] The economic argument for toleration was used by Burrough and Owen as well as by Stubbe and Warren (see pp. 152, 177–8, 272 above and Warren, op. cit., pp. 89–90).
[3] M. C. Jacob, *The Newtonians and the English Revolution, passim.*

now subsume and take for granted the revolutionary transformations of the preceding decades: though a further adjustment was needed in 1688.

In this light, Marvell's remarks about the Good Old Cause deserve another glance. The Cause was too good to have been fought for, as Charles I should have realized (the Providence of 1640–1); and it compares with 'his present Majesty's happy restoration', another landslide which happened without men's officiousness. By implication the 'officiousness' of the second revolution was repudiated, direct intervention by those who claimed to be God's instruments. In the 'Horatian Ode' Marvell had seen Cromwell as the personification of God's Providence, carrying out a revolution which was also the product of pent-up historical forces. God's Providences of 1640–1 and 1660 come to look in retrospect more like the work of Harringtonian forces working through individuals but regardless of them. The Harringtonians incorporated some of the second revolution into their account of the first. For once the prerogative courts and feudal tenures had gone, and the Navigation Act had come, capitalism itself became a historical force affecting the balance, and affecting the state. Merchants were no longer excluded from political decision-taking.[1]

So the answer to the question, how the God of 1649 could have willed 1660, turns out to be 'because he had already willed 1640–1'. The oscillations of 1649 and 1660 temporarily prevented the balance operating freely, but in 1688 society stabilized on the new and true balance. Professor Trevor-Roper once said that there were no problems in 1641 which could not have been solved by sensible men sitting round a table. This suggests that historians are more intelligent than those who lived through the events which historians contemplate in the tranquillity brought by several centuries of hindsight. But the God of Harrington must have known all along that 1688 was the school solution: something very like it could have been attained in 1641, 1646 or 1648 under the House of Stuart, in 1657 under the House of Cromwell. But the passions of unsensible men delayed the outcome until 1688. To some this way of putting it may seem a little Whiggish. If so, we have to admit that Dr Johnson was wrong in hailing the devil as the first Whig. The God of Harrington has a better claim.

When I started writing this book I had not thought that Harrington

---

[1] Cf. Stubbe's appeal to them in 1673 (pp. 270–3 above).

and the Harringtonians would become so central: I had expected to end with Milton. We have seen that there was a wide variety of reactions to the experience of defeat. But two variants emerge. Once we get beyond the immediate agony of the restoration, Harringtonianism appears to take over. Defeat further fragmented and depoliticized the saints: their answer could only be either rewards in the after life, or Milton's blank assertion that good must win in the end. The Harringtonians' Cause had always been firmly rooted in the world as it actually existed, in social transformations which appeared stronger than ideology. It could shrug off apparent defeat with confidence in the future. Its millenarianism was this-worldly too, infinitely adaptable as history unrolled in surprising ways. It was a long time before men thought again of 'an equal commonwealth'. But meanwhile they got a very effective commonwealth for increase.

Yet in the still longer run the experience of defeat left more than Harringtonianism. Milton's confidence in the ultimate victory of good over evil was not peculiar to him. Something similar underlay the dogged refusal of Quakers to surrender under persecution, or to compromise. Such obstinacy among ordinary people had not been seen in England since the days of the Marian martyrs, earlier survivors who had retained hope even in defeat. From *Comus* to *Samson Agonistes* Milton depicted characters capable of standing alone in discouraging circumstances against the power of evil. We later refer to this ancient phenomenon as the nonconformist conscience, though it antedates the emergence of dissent. But in the relative religious toleration of the revolutionary decades men and women became aware that others shared their convictions. Milton's great poems, and Bunyan's *The Pilgrim's Progress* and *The Holy War*, by giving literary expression to these convictions, helped to fortify those of the defeated who were to be second-class citizens for nearly two centuries after 1660. The nonconformist conscience was a wholly individualist force, more allied to 'the dissidence of dissent' than to the embattled chapels which disappointed Erbery. But it remained a power in British politics down to our own generation.

Moses Wall may have the last word. In his prophetic letter to Milton he said that before liberty could be won 'there should be an improving of our native commodities, as our manufactures, our fishing, our fens, forests and commons, and our trade at sea, etc.', as well as the abolition of tithes and copyhold, 'which would give the body of the nation a comfortable subsistence'. Until then 'the people are not free but straitened in accommodations for life'. Consequently 'their spirits will be dejected and servile'.[1] Harrington's commonwealth for increase solved these economic problems, for men as men. But what of the saints? After two decades of prophecy whose message still survives for us, they were defeated and silenced. Milton was almost alone in continuing to exercise his talent as poet and prophet. The experience of defeat led him to take this role not less but more seriously. And when programmes for liberty did revive in England, when the French Revolution made men think—wrongly—that good might after all prevail, then Blake called on Milton as an ally against Newtonianism; he, Wordsworth and Shelley turned back to Milton the libertarian, the republican, the poet who believed in inspiration, the prophet. The title of David Erdman's book, *Blake: Prophet against Empire*,[2] makes the distinction between the inheritance of Harringtonianism and the vision of the poet-prophet. Now that England's historical destiny has whimpered to its end we may perhaps see that the defeated had points to make which got forgotten in the two-and-a-half centuries of imperial success. We would no doubt define an equal commonwealth differently; but it might seem a more attractive ideal than being the top of nations. In 1644 Milton saw England as 'a nation of prophets'. Where are they now?

---

[1] Masson, *Life of Milton*, V, pp. 602–3.
[2] Princeton UP, 1954.

Index

Since there are references to John Milton and the New Model Army on nearly every other page, I have not indexed the latter, and of Milton I have indexed only works referred to in the text.

Jerry Bauer

CHRISTOPHER HILL was born in York in 1912 and now
lives in Oxford. A Fellow of All Souls College,
Oxford, from 1934 to 1938 and a Fellow and Tutor of
Balliol College from 1938 to 1965, he recently retired as
Master of Balliol. He is the author of eleven other
books on English history.